Histories of Canadian Children and Youth

Nancy Janovicek & Joy Parr

OXFORD
UNIVERSITY PRESS

OXFORD
UNIVERSITY PRESS

70 Wynford Drive, Don Mills, Ontario M3C 1J9
www.oup.com/ca

Oxford University Press is a department of the University of Oxford.
It furthers the University's objective of excellence in research, scholarship,
and education by publishing worldwide in

Oxford New York
Auckland Bangkok Buenos Aires Cape Town Chennai
Dar es Salaam Delhi Hong Kong Istanbul Karachi Kolkata
Kuala Lumpur Madrid Melbourne Mexico City Mumbai Nairobi
São Paulo Shanghai Taipei Tokyo Toronto

Oxford is a trade mark of Oxford University Press
in the UK and in certain other countries

Published in Canada
by Oxford University Press

National Library of Canada Cataloguing in Publication

Histories of Canadian children and youth / edited by
Nancy Janovicek and Joy Parr.

Includes bibliographical references.
ISBN 0-19-541792-5

1. Children—Canada—History. 2. Youth—Canada—History.
3. Family—Canada—History. 4. Education—Canada—History.
I. Janovicek, Nancy, 1968– II. Parr, Joy, 1949–

HQ792.C3H58 2003   305.23'0971   C2002-906141-5

1 2 3 4 - 06 05 04 03
This book is printed on permanent (acid-free) paper ∞ .
Printed in Canada

This book is dedicated to the memory of
Kʷiɫpic'e (Kristine Angeline Mike),
1991–2000

Contents

Acknowledgements

We are grateful to Harold Averill, Paul Axelrod, Rebecca Coulter, John-Henry Harter, Yasmin Jiwani, Francois Lachance, Don McLeod, Janice Matsumura, Sean Matvenko, Neil Sutherland, and the members of the Simon Fraser University History of Childhood Seminar of 2001–2 for their advice and encouragement.

Introduction

The eighty thousand British child apprentices, the youngest three or four years old, who came to Canada between Confederation and the interwar years were the first 'kids with a past' I got to know as a would-be historian. By the time I went looking for them in 1973, most were dead, but their lives had left traces. In the store-rooms of the agencies that sent and brought them to Canada were their photographs, as they had come in from the streets or their own homes, and as they were posed in sailing parties, about to depart for new lives overseas. For many there were case records in which their charitable and state guardians wrote down what they understood about these young peoples' pasts, their case histories. For some there were letters, in their own hand, describing their new lives and their hopes for their futures. For almost all there were some reports by Canadian inspectors, from either the Department of Immigration or British agencies, on how they seemed to be faring in the households they had joined in the Dominion. Later in the 1970s I found some of them and listened to their stories. Since then, many of their children in turn have found and befriended me. But mostly, like all the historians whose writing about children and youth you will find between these covers, I became acquainted with these young people by looking at paper: photographs on paper, the paper files of schools, government, and voluntary organizations about them, and personal collections of drawings, diaries, and letters these children had made to hold on to their pasts and to pass on their stories to others.

No one who met them doubted that the Home Children, as these young British immigrants were called, had pasts. The whole immigration project was to separate them from past lives on the streets and with their families. Canadians identified, mocked, feared, and loved them for, and despite, their childhood origins and the indelible marks they believed those beginnings would leave on the youths and adulthoods they would make for themselves as workers, neighbours, and kin in Canada. Some of these marks were visible on their bodies. The Home Children were usually smaller than Canadian boys and girls of the same age. Many bore the physical traces of youthful illnesses and accidents and the legacies of what we would now call 'low birth weight'. Some of the marks were cultural, for they had *learned* to be children in industrial and commercial cities far distant, in more than geographical distance alone, from the farm and village households they joined here in Canada. In the turbulence of their early years, of which immigration was a part, the Home boys and girls learned to be self-sufficient and stoical, agile, and responsible. They had learned to work, but not at the kinds of the domestic work that would be required of them in Canadian homes, or with the animals and tools of the wide and scantily peopled spaces of Canadian farms. Canadian adults, comparing them with their own girls and boys, often thought the Home Children dull and inept, so unresponsive as to seem sneaky, so guarded as to seem unloving, and, as a result, to be unlovable. These distinctions were developed in pasts with which their Canadian masters and mistresses had little experience, and in presents that the girls and boys found daunting and unfamiliar. Those who met the Home Children in Canada summed up these distinctions into the category of essential difference that, in the late nineteenth and early twentieth centuries, was often named 'race'.

And so these kids had several kinds of pasts, as all of us do. They had the personal pasts they had lived, which they combined with the resources around them and used to make sense of the times and places in which they lived. Those who encountered the British child immigrants read the bodies, characters, and origins they seemed to display, and made for them the social pasts that would determine their place within the Canadian social world. And then, after some time, and always at some illusory remove, their lives were analyzed in books and articles, with footnotes and interpretive controversies, and thus written into the formal fabric of Canadian history. In August 2001, a National Historic Sites plaque was erected in Stratford, Ontario, at one of the reception centres through which the Home Children had passed. This plaque set down for posterity, in bronze letters, some part of what we know from their own telling and from the paper traces their lives had left behind.

Turning personal and social pasts into histories is, and should be, a careful and caring art. As writers and readers of history we have a responsibility to try to get the story right. But, as I learned from my search for the Home Children, the task is not easy. The gaps in the record and the memory are many. The assumptions about human nature and society with which we approach the study of history are quite different from the assumptions that organized the world we seek to understand. And so, here at the start I offer you three cautions that I think are especially important to consider as you begin to analyze these histories of Canadian children and youth.

The first is that childhood is made by *both* culture and biology. Even though children are physically different from adults, and through time the processes by which children's bodies become adult bodies have changed only a little; even though children are biologically more similar to their families than to persons with whom they share no blood ties, and these similarities endure through generations; still it is misleading to think of childhood as founded in nature. Childhoods are shaped by historical processes and transformed by their economic and cultural contexts. Humans know the world through their sensing bodies, and carry their knowledge of the world through their bodily habits, but these perceptions and physically tuned reflexes too are inflected by the particularities of time and place. And so, even when studying life-cycle stages such as childhood and youth, it is best to begin not with the body, but with the 'when' and 'where', with economic needs, social priorities, and exercises of power, for these are environments in which childhood and youth crucially are embedded, and within which they most scrutably persist and change.

The second caution follows from the first. *The* history of childhood and youth does not exist. The histories we study, like the lives we lead, are made of many convergent and discordant strands. They are difficult to convey definitively through straight-line chronologies or homogeneous categories. To begin to make sense of the past we fashion helpful tools for ourselves. These are saving fictions of our own devising with which we select out what seems more similar from what seems different. The only way to do this is to set aside the discordant bits, the parts of the past living space that our categories will not hold, the elements of the chronological progression that are moving along at a different pace, and in a different direction. We *make* historical meaning by sorting things out in this way. How else could we still the tumult we find in the documentary record? Yet to work well, we need to work reflexively, always to be checking back to be sure that the history we are making is not too still, too settled, to be sure we keep attending to the differences that do not fit into the samenesses we have made.

This book had a predecessor, *Childhood and Family in Canadian History*, published twenty years ago. That book was arranged in a fairly linear chronological order. It began in seventeenth-century New France and moved in the solemn progress we contributors made for it, following a theory about the stages of economic development, from mercantile trade in furs, timber, and grain, through subsistence to commercial agriculture, to commercial and industrial cities, to the beginnings of post-industrial life in the emerging welfare state. This book is more ragged, and we think the better for it, for the regions of the territory that became Canada were not parts of a single economic system. The people who lived here turned at different times to different cultural, religious, and political systems of thought to give their lives meaning. How they knew themselves by age, gender, and ethnic origins changed over time, in ways that could, and often did, bear no simple relationship to the economy about them.

This caution, to be wary of chronologies that are too certain and categories that are too smooth, to be watchful for differences that these necessary but fictional clarifying tools set to the side, is especially important, for this book, unlike its predecessor, focuses particularly on children and youth. Young people lived daily lives. They formed habits, practices, and preferences within their circumstances. But, by and large, they were less party than adults to the clarifying fictions that made meaning of their own times and after.

Which brings us to the third caution. Cynthia Comacchio has pointed out that family historians have a clearer grasp of ideologies about family in the past than about the practices of daily life within families. We historians of childhood face similar paradoxical asymmetries between what it is easiest to find out and what we most urgently want to know. For example, the Canadian advice literature addressed to parents about their children is prodigious. From the earliest days of European settlement, religious leaders passed on these injunctions to their congregations in sermons. In the century just past, this advice was more often from secular sources, some of the first and most widely disseminated being the *Little Blue Books*, published by the federal division of Maternal and Child Welfare. Later, newspapers and magazines carried columns by psychologists and physicians. These prescriptions for parenting surely had some influence on some children's lives. In an extreme case, the Dionne quintuplets could scarcely evade expert influences, for through their early years the foremost Canadian source of pediatric advice, Dr William Blatz, led a team with extraordinary, almost carceral, control over all their waking and sleeping hours. But in most cases, the relationship between the advice their parents might have read, and the daily lives the children led was less certain than the advice-givers surely would have wished. So, while the advice literature will tell us something about the circumstances, the social pasts, of some children, but to get to their subjectivities, their personal pasts, to come closer to seeing their worlds through their eyes, we will need other sources and other methods. Thus, in this book we have included more sections in which young people, among them war orphans, First Nations students in residential schools, and late twentieth-century refugee children, tell their own stories through their own drawings and words.

The history of childhood and youth, like all history, is never finished. Our history writing is always an interim report on what sense we can make from where we are *here*, in the present, of girls and boys *there*, in the past. As the philosopher and historian Walter Benjamin observed from the turmoil of interwar Germany, we are able to interpret only the parts of the past we can recognize. What we in the present can make recognizable about the past, what we can make into histories, changes as our tools and circumstances change.

Demographers and cliometricians were the pioneer historians of Canadian children and youth. Using nominal records alone, the names of children on census, tax, and parish records, on lists from ships, schools, orphanages, hospitals, missions, and fur-trade posts, first linked slowly by hand in the 1920s and 1930s and later from the 1960s more quickly using computers, these scholars found some similarities in the circumstances of some young people. From this work we now know the *filles du roi* by where they came from in France and by the choices these girls and young women made amongst their suitors in New France. The nominal records of New France and Quebec are so exceptional that we can know the children of the St Lawrence Valley over three centuries by their birth order, their number of siblings, and their progress toward adulthood through work, the religious sacraments, and marriage. By similar methods, based on the manuscript censuses from 1841 to 1901, we know at decade intervals the children of the countryside, villages, towns, and cities in certain important respects: the composition of their households, the patterns in their school attendance, their participation in paid work, and the probable ages at which they left their parents' homes.

The other early work on the histories of children and youth came to us from the curators in museums and at historic sites across the country. These scholars used the durable material culture of textiles, metal, ceramics, and wood to tell us about the clothes some young people wore, the toys with which they may have played, and the tools they may have used in their work. From archaeological evidence and building plans, these students of material culture have told us about the physical spaces where some young people spent their days and how the physical partitioning of these spaces may have organized children's contact with their kin, their employers, and the social world beyond.

From the mid-1950s we've had another way to get to know kids with a past, through the public and private organizations with which they came in contact. The adults who ran child welfare and educational institutions kept records as they conducted their daily work and these documents often have been deposited in archives. As historians began to work with these collections, we came to know more about the philosophies and the practical concerns that drove the institution-builders. Many British North American orphanages began in the plague years that accompanied the European immigrations of the 1830s and 1840s. The origins of mass schooling can be located in the changing philosophies about child development and the changing demands of workplaces in the mid-nineteenth century. Urban feeding stations and daycare centres developed in the late nineteenth century to meet the needs of the increasing numbers of children whose mothers now worked from home. Some of this work explored the history of sentiments and the ways in which changing religious and secular thinking, and the shifting incidence of morbidity and morality amongst the young, remade the fabric of affective ties between the generations.

Historians of children and youth shared the changing emphases and practices of the 1960s, as many students of the past began to focus less exclusively on politicians and the institutions of governance and attended more to the governed and to the politics of everyday life. The interpretive tools developed by historians of the working class to understand cultures of work and resistance in the past were also resources for historians of childhood and youth seeking to understand how power relationships functioned within families, households, schools, and charitable organizations. This work of the 1960s and 1970s was particularly helpful in understanding how the lives and life chances of young people differed depending upon the class into which they were born or to which social circumstances assigned them.

Young people were consistently recorded by their sex in the census and parish records. Early historians of childhood and youth incorporated this information into their demographic portraits of the households and communities to which girls and boys belonged. From the late 1970s historians of women began to revisit these questions by exploring the social, cultural, and political meanings attached to sexual difference. To hold these meanings, and distinguish them from the differences which some biologists and psychologists theorized as rooted in the material body, social scientists and historians developed a new analytical category: gender. These scholars used gender first to sort out those attributes and capabilities, some bestowed and some claimed, by which females were known historically, in their time and place, as women and girls. Within a decade this work became the model for studies in the social construction of masculinity. Through the 1980s, historians began to use gender, class, ethnicity, and region as mutually informing conceptual tools with which to interpret the social and personal pasts of girls and boys, at home, school, and work, and especially in their encounters with the regulating social welfare and juvenile justice regimes of the twentieth century. These explorations of how differences were formed historically made recognizable other features in the pasts of children and youth.

At this stage historians turned for conceptual guidance to literary scholars, particularly those who, in their studies of comparative literature contrasted the cultural works of colonizing and colonized writers. These scholars focused upon 'race', how it was confected from visible and hypothetical distinctions, articulated in time, and particularly how 'raced'-thinking arrayed the elusive and unequal privileges of citizenship. This thinking, they argued, was the glue that held nineteenth-century empires together and that left the often toxic residue of colonization in its wake. In histories of empire, Canada had been classified as a 'white settler Dominion'. This label, once unquestioned, now gave scholars pause. Who had this category sorted in, who had it sorted out, and with what effect?

Historians of children and youth came to recognize the institutions they studied as parts of this racially inflected nation-building process. In the 1980s and 1990s, Canadian scholars began to see how the curricula and work programs of federally sponsored residential schools for First Nations children were linked to broader national goals of cultural and 'racial' assimilation. And they noticed how these policies became patterns for similar projects to efface difference in other colonial settings. Students of the eugenics movements of the 1930s and twentieth-century public health initiatives noted how visible distinctions had been used to appraise children's physical fitness and how these distinctions were systematically summed into differences in their life chances as adult citizens. In social pasts when colour mattered a good deal, white too was a colour. Scholars observe now that generations of Canadian children were learning to be 'white' as they sat at their classroom desks before maps of the far-flung rose-coloured reaches of the Empire, their perimeters decorated with the product labels of British chocolate manufacturers. Consider as you read the last sections of this book how the refugee children who tried to make themselves at home in the Canadian classrooms of the 1940s and 1970s encountered the legacies of these lessons.

In writing the histories of children and youth, the most recent turn in recognition has been back toward the body, to part of the past that was set to the side in the 1970s as scholars sought a stark distinction between physical sex and social gender. But if bodies could learn to play hockey and the violin—and some bodies readily mastered these skilled physical arts while others, no matter how hard they tried, kept missing the puck and playing off key—then the physical self had a hand in the making of the social self and the social past of that self. The body became recognizable as more than an inert mannequin on which the vestments of the social circumstance were hung. Bodies had dispositions that influenced the way the humans who were those bodies wove themselves and were woven into the social pasts on which they lived. By the 1990s the circuitry between the physical and the cultural had become observably multiple and multi-directional. Bodies had orientations, among them sexual orientations, which were part of how girls and boys might know themselves and how, in time and place, they might be known. These were personal and social identities linked to pleasures and practices, some socially authorized and some, socially, even criminally, denied. Youths of the past entered on an unequal footing these sensual spaces where some bodily urges were celebrated and consecrated and others were repressed and reviled. Some easily found a warm if regulating welcome for the dawning yearnings of adolescence and others found only a socially enforced silence edged with threat. This difference remains into our own day and surely accounts in part for historians' late and comparatively recent recognition of these contours in the social pasts of children and youth.

And so, in this non-linear chronology made of homogeneous categories sequentially recognizable as heterogeneous, what clues should you, the novice historian of children and youth, be watching for? As someone no longer a novice, trailing a long record of paths taken and then with retuned curiosity retraced, I offer these pointers. Ask whether the child you meet in the following pages was likely to live long enough to make the investment of adult energy in her worthwhile. Consider what she was contributing to her household and the conventions governing the contributions she could and was obliged to make. Wonder what influence his birth order and the size of his family had on the timing of his departure from home, and what resources he would carry with him when he left. Think about the power relations that ordered her life, the matriarchal and patriarchal authority of her family, the laws about attending school and being part of the labour force, about being in public places alone and in company, about seeking and bestowing pleasure. Don't overlook the possibility that these power relations could be subverted even by, or perhaps especially by, the young. Pay attention to how the labelling systems of religion, class, race, gender, and sex were constituted and deployed in the times and places in which these young people lived, and notice how these systems persisted or altered with the passage of time. Examine critically the content of clerical, pedagogical, medical, and psychological advice for what it says about the advisors and their times. And don't fail to appraise as best you can who was listening and who, by accident or intention, was out of earshot. Notice which of the many parts of a young person's identity took precedence over others, and how these changed chronologically and spatially. Savour the ragged, distrust the smooth. Practise care and respect as you form your historical judgements. May you share our pleasures in this work, and as you learn be both unsettled and replenished.

Joy Parr

PART 1

How Do We Know the Histories of Children and Youth?

Historians of children and youth rely primarily on the words and deeds of politicians, educators, and social reformers, whose changing anxieties as adults influenced how they conceptualized childhood. The agendas of the child-saving movement, educational reform, child-labour legislation, and sex education disclose as much about national anxieties as about how children lived and came of age. Class, gender, and race hierarchies were embedded in these national anxieties.

Historical writers, too, had political agendas. André Turmel's historiographical essay argues that the different images of the country in English Canada and French Canada influenced the writing of the history of children. Turmel's connection between perceptions of nation and the histories of children interrogates how social, economic, and cultural politics inform historical analysis. These social relations have also influenced how adults remembered their childhood. Neil Sutherland explores the potential and limitations of oral history. Oral histories add to the historical record the life stories of individuals who did not think that their lives were significant enough to record. Sutherland advises historians to be aware of the unique methodological problems raised by oral histories about childhood. The paradox is that it is only as adults can we find the words to describe complex feelings of childhood.

Nancy Janovicek

Historiography of Children in Canada

André Turmel

Like the country itself, the historiography of children in Canada is characterized by its duality. English and French Canada each have their own histories of children, which differ significantly in topics, scope, and trends. Is it possible to find a common ground where the histories of children from both parts of the country can meet?[1] I am still not sure of the answer to this question.

In this respect, it is interesting to note that Rooke and Schnell's entry 'Canada' in the international handbook edited by R. Hiner and J. Hawes, *Children in Historical and Comparative Perspective*, is silent on the main trends in research on childhood in Quebec.[2] I found only two references to such research: Peter Moogk's "'Les Petits Sauvages", The Children of the Eighteenth Century New France', and Bettina Bradbury's 'The Fragmented Family: Family Strategies in the Face of Death, Illness, Poverty, Montreal, 1860–1885', both published in Joy Parr's *Childhood and Family in Canadian History*.[3] This may be a matter of oversight, or the traditional language barrier; but I would blame a structural impediment whose main consequence is the profound ignorance that separates the two solitudes from one another.

At first glance, the differences in the two histories of childhood are thematic: for instance, child immigration is an important object of investigation in Canada, no such immigration took place in Quebec;[4] juvenile delinquency was a persistent concern among English-Canadian historians, but appears to be of only peripheral interest in Quebec—which does not mean that the problem did not exist. Another important difference lies in the fact that in English Canada, research into the history of childhood has been done by historians, among them historians of education, while in Quebec the work has been done as much by demographers, sociologists, and anthropologists as by historians. Furthermore, I must mention that English Canada's historiography of childhood was rather British-oriented, while Quebec's was somewhat French-oriented, and that both have been influenced, though in different ways and degrees, by the most salient American orientations and trends.[5] There are also important conceptual differences between the two traditions, and even more important differences in scope and perspective.

Let us start with what appears to be the most striking difference between the two traditions. It seems important to distinguish between the empirical, actual lives that Canadian children led and the ways that historians interpret those facts and trends. Although these histories were more or less the same in terms of the historical sequences of development, there were slight differences in the rhythm and scope of change from one society to the other.[6]

The most important difference concerns the status and position of the child study movement in the two traditions. This movement was less important as an object of research among Quebec scholars, at least in general works offering an overview of a specific historical period. It was so, I would suggest, because the history of children (and child protection) did not take the form of such a movement; child protection was monitored and organized differently. By contrast, in English Canada one can find many important large-scale syntheses in areas typical of the history of child studies, such as care of neglected and dependent children or child welfare; child health, hygiene, and labour; child development; thus child-protection institutions; delinquency, compulsory universal schooling, etc. In both cases, the empirical social problems were much the same, but the societies responded to them in quite different ways.

The period under study here is the turn of the century (the nineteenth century, especially the pre-Confederation period,[7] has not attracted as much attention from academics in Canada as it has in the United States). In both cases, there is a debate about the nature of the data and their reliability, which affects the way historians and other scholars interpret the events and the period. The interpretations are organized around three major axes: a consensus perspective, a gender perspective, and a social class perspective that includes economic structure and the role of poverty. There is also an implicit debate among scholars around the concepts of social control and regulation with regard to the shift in the provision of services for children, from philanthropy to the state: was the child study movement instrumental in imposing a new type of social control on children and families?

I shall begin with the seminal work of Neil Sutherland, *Children in English-Canadian Society*. This book constituted an event in itself because it was the first scholarly work focused on a systematic study of childhood, and opened a whole new field of research. Many of Sutherland's colleagues and former students later carried forward the various research hypotheses that he so brilliantly set up.[8] Sutherland organized his book around three themes—the public health movement, juvenile delinquency, and school reform—from the perspective of changing attitudes toward children in English-Canadian society at the turn of the century. In so doing, he marked out the great historical themes of childhood in Canada found in most of the other works with a few additions.[9] I want to stress that a very original aspect of Sutherland's work is the methodological point of view that he adopts: he is much more interested in hearing children themselves than adults talking about children, with all the problems raised by oral history and the reconstitution of memory.

Sutherland convincingly shows how the concept of the child was changing; how the health of children and their families was seen as a prerequisite to the health of the society; how proper childrearing was necessary to mould the rising generation of citizens; the formative aspect of hard work, etc. In this context, three different metaphors are indicative of the changes in the concept of the child. First is the medical metaphor, in which the fear of social disintegration constructed the link between the health of the child, the family, and the society. Second is the metaphor of children as 'a resistive, refractory, but nonetheless basically plastic raw material. Out of this tough matter, parents and other adults could, if they were persistent enough, fashion moral, hard-working, productive adults'.[10] This metaphor illustrates the Lockean notion of the *tabula rasa*. Finally there is the metaphor of the child as a growing plant, based on J.J. Rousseau: 'both parents and teachers had to be sure that his physical, spiritual, and educational setting were well suited to growth.'[11] These metaphors illustrate the changing social treatment of children at the turn of the century.[12]

Two aspects of Sutherland's work were debated by his critics: the question of the consensus on child-saving and the question of social control. Some authors maintain not only that the consensus on child-saving was fragile and constantly needed to be reconstructed, but that the debates were sharp and vigorous, the disagreements were numerous, and the movement's direction was not clearly established. The more conceptual question of social control, on the other hand, refers to the transition from the philanthropy and charity that characterized the movement at the beginning to the rational, generalized intervention of the state, etc. Did this represent simple progress, or a gradual imposition of control with the spread of modernization? Or was it an attempt by public authorities to bring the social regulation of (children's) behaviour within bounds acceptable to the larger society?

In *Discarding the Asylum*, Rooke and Schnell go even further, stating that a national consensus on the policies and practices did not exist in the 1920s, as child welfare advocates such as C. Whitton testified. Their book examines the social transformation of sporadic, voluntaristic, and charity-oriented child-rescue into more systematic methods. 'By correlating the rescue motive to the asylum-building generally, it demonstrates how ideas on institutionalization were projected into patterns of social organization.'[13] Their primary focus is not health and training for citizenship but the relations between institution-building and social organization.

One should not be surprised that important works on childhood emerge from studies in the area of gender. Veronica Strong-Boag's *The New Day Recalled*[14] is a gender-focused work that looks at the intrusion of the experts into both the nursery and the infant-mother relationship.[15] She is interested in the way the new experts on childhood developed their influence and consequently dispossessed the mother of her traditional skills and qualifications. These various experts put the issue of scientific childrearing and motherhood on the national agenda, emphasizing the dichotomy between maternal 'ignorance' and expert knowledge. The advice literature exemplified the thinking of the professionals in child study in the 1920s, who almost always placed the responsibility for failure in childrearing on the parent, particularly the mother, who as a result had to upgrade her qualifications.

Cynthia Comacchio's perspective, in *Nations are Built of Babies*, is gender-based, but more focused on issues of social class. Whereas Strong-Boag looked at experts in general, Comacchio looks at the impact of one particular group among those who became predominant in the field of childhood: medical doctors. She suggests that what mattered most where infants and mothers was concerned was that, to protect their own position, doctors constructed the infant-mother relationship in terms of health, illness, and the delivery of health care, whereas the mothers and babies most in need of health care were looking for affordable services, not just free advice and expensive medical attention. Doctors consistently downplayed the role of poverty in both health itself and access to health care. By insisting that material circumstances counted less than attitude and receptivity to expert instruction, doctors were able ignore the role played by socio-economic inequality.

I want to stress that all these different authors agree at least on one thing: the advice literature reflected a decidedly urban and middle-class culture. As Sutherland acknowledges, 'those doing most of the talking were speaking from and for the middle class.'[16] Both middle-class women's associations and middle-class child welfare advocates joined medical professionals in upholding motherhood as the source of national regeneration and in educating the working-class family according to their own exacting hygienic standards.[17]

The situation in Quebec was quite different in most respects. The most important difference, in my opinion, is that Quebec has produced no general study to compare with the English-Canadian studies noted above. Neither the movement nor the golden period of child-saving has been the subject of a large-scale publication. This is not to say that Quebec had no equivalent of the child-saving movement, but rather that the study of childhood developed along different paths.

First of all, I must mention the academic work in historical demography that has outlined the issue of Quebecers' so-called overfertility in earlier generations as well as specific problems such as infant mortality, public hygiene. or general sanitary conditions affecting infants' lives,[18] and changes in the shape of population pyramids as well as age-based life course diagrams. The title of one article summarizes the spirit of this approach: 'The children that we don't have anymore'.[19]

It is important to realize that Quebec's academics and historians came to examine childhood mostly through general research on the family, especially the rural family. I want to emphasize the importance of G. Bouchard's book *Quelques arpents d'Amérique*,[20] which summarizes 25 years of research on the patterns of rural family reproduction. 'Reproduction of the rural family includes all of the plans and arrangements—sometimes taking the form of true strategies—made by rural couples in each generation to apportion their assets (both land and personal property) among their immediate descendants while serving a variety of sometimes divergent interests. Those assets included all the forms of exchange that children could benefit from, such as schooling, or work performed by other members of the family. . . .'[21] Among the objectives of family reproduction Bouchard includes the survival of the name or the lineage; the establishment of as many children as possible on the land; the possibility of making a career, and achieving the best possible standard of living for those children who had to leave the farm.

This pattern resulted in different social practices on the level of work as well the level of schooling. The dominant pattern of family reproduction aimed to establish a maximum of children on the land and to provide comparative advantages for the others. The distinct family-reproduction social practices of Quebecers were an indirect result of the continuing importance of child labour in the family economy. They continued to seek economic security and material stability by combining the labour of different family members. The relatively weak attachment to schooling among francophones appears understandable in this perspective. Children were part of a larger unit that needed their work and labour in order to reproduce itself.[22]

Another important work in the same area of thought is Dominique Marshall's *The Social Origins of the Welfare State: Quebec families, compulsory schooling and family allowances, 1940–1955*. Interested in the emergence of the universal welfare state, she tries to find how it transformed both families and children through the introduction of family allowances, child labour laws, and compulsory schooling. She outlines the framework of an institutional apparatus with an extensive capacity to monitor the practices of families and children as well. This apparatus opens up original perspectives; indeed, she sees in it a new era of well-being as well as the beginning of contemporary individualism. In the long term, the welfare state contributed to the weakening of the solidarity of family unit, its sense of responsibility, and the common pattern of family reproduction.[23]

Much of our knowledge of yesterday's children comes from village monographs. Thus Miner, Moreux, and Verdon[24] described childhood in traditional villages: reliance on communal responsibility, the extended family, and kinship ties, socialization through imitation of adults, early integration into the labour force, disciplinary models characterized by the religious culture and formal hierarchical relationship, and gender separation in play. Anne-Marie Desdouits in *Le monde de l'enfance* compares Québécois traditions with customs in Normandy (France) concerning the stages of child development, rites of passage, play and games, integration into the job market, etc. Two studies on childhood material culture must be mentioned here: one by Louise Gagnon about fashions in children's clothes as nineteenth-century bourgeois iconography; the other by Michel Lessard about photography as a technology for the reconstruction of the image of the child in the twentieth century, particularly as an obligatory support for the rituals of childhood.[25]

Denyse Lemieux deserves special mention. On the basis of the *Jesuit Relations* she tries to understand how European representations of childhood came together with Aboriginal representations, producing a new concept of childhood that finds echoes in the words of comfort offered to parents afflicted with a death of a child. Then she studies autobiographies of people who were children at the turn of the century, trying to catch how the feeling of childhood was expressed then and those who lived in that period remembered it. Those childhood memories show in a narrative way the side of reality that statistics cannot capture.[26]

Those large-scale works are complemented by general books about the family and childhood. Bettina Bradbury's *Working Families in Montreal* and Terry Copp's *Working Class and Poverty* look at the problems of working-class poverty and the social and sanitary conditions affecting children and child labour, the first for the nineteenth century, the second for the turn of the century. Michael Bliss's *Plague*[27] can be placed in the same category; it examines the terrible devastation that the smallpox epidemic of 1885 caused in Montreal, where 80 per cent of the 5,000 victims were children under ten years old.

Education is an important topic in any historiography of childhood and a crucial one in Canada. Rooke and Schnell maintain that the advent of mass compulsory schooling is fundamental in the history of children. 'Indeed, we are convinced that a history of children with their families is, in large part, a history of their lives in schools'.[28] C. Gaffield's work appears central in this respect. His basic postulate is that the main thread in the history of Canadian childhood is the emergence of schooling as a dominant aspect of the experience of growing up. The school promoters were convinced that mass schooling was needed for the modern state and would be an effective instrument for instilling appropriate behaviour and ways of thinking in children. The primary purpose of school systems was not the acquisition of academic knowledge. Consequently, school attendance varied regionally and seasonally, and school leaving was not linked to the formal acquisition of a diploma. One of the key findings in Gaffield's research is his critical assessment of the inverse correlation between labouring and learning. He questions the generally accepted correlation, over time, of work and learning.[29] In his view, these processes are tremendously complex, and by no means mechanical; thus less work does not automatically mean more schooling.

By contrast, Quebec historians of education have focused almost entirely on the question of compulsory education. Thérèse Hamel analyzes the different factors that delayed the passage of legislation making school attendance compulsory: the persistence of child's labour; the survival of self-subsistence family farming; the strength of the Church's opposition; and the late development of industrial capitalism. She shows how the labour movement, while fighting against the exploitation of child labour, was divided on compulsory schooling, and consequently could not fight for it. Dominique Jean, on the other hand, looks at this problem from the opposite perspective: how the decline of child labour came about.[30]

I will close with a word about my own work. In more or less the same way that Comacchio and Strong-Boag look at the intrusion of the experts into the family, I am analyzing the social construction of the normal child at the turn of the century in the medical (as opposed to the advice) literature and, later, in the psychological literature, in order to compare those two models of normalcy. It seems to me of utmost importance to stress that if the physicians were, along with the hygienists, the first 'experts' on childhood, they were not the last. The psychologists came along shortly after, and the normalizing effect of their expertise has had an enduring effect.[31]

Notes

1. In this respect, the two conferences on Socio-Historical Research on Childhood in Canada, held in Calgary (1994) and Montreal (1995), were designed to be a first step to bridge that gap. The participants believe that this effort must be carried on.
2. Even if Rooke and Schnell's text 'Canada', ignores totally the research on childhood in Quebec, it talks about the 'history of Canadian child studies', etc. as if their perspective

was global and their point of view was that of Canadian society as a whole. The least that one can say is that this history is incomplete. See P.T. Rooke and M.R. Schnell, 'Canada', in J.M. Hawes and N.R. Hiner (eds), *Children in Historical and Comparative Perspective* (New York: Greenwood, 1990), pp. 179–215.

3.   Joy Parr, *Childhood and Family in Canadian History* (Toronto: McClelland and Stewart, 1982); Peter Moogk, '"Les Petits Sauvages", The Children of Eighteenth Century New France' (pp. 17–43) and Bettina Bradbury, 'The Fragmented Family: Family Strategies in the Face of Death, Illness, Poverty, Montreal, 1860–1885' (pp. 110–32).

4.   Between 1869 and 1930, 80,000 children, unaccompanied by their parents, emigrated from Britain to Canada. The Juvenile Migration Movement has been a major theme in Canadian child studies history. See Neil Sutherland, *Children in English-Canadian Society: Framing the Twentieth-Century Consensus* (Toronto: University of Toronto Press, 1976); Joy Parr, *Childhood and Family in Canadian History* (Toronto: McClelland & Stewart, 1982); P.T. Rooke and M.R. Schnell (eds), *Studies in Childhood History: A Canadian Perspective* (Calgary: Detselig Enterprises, 1982); R. Smandych, G. Dodds, and A. Esau (eds), *Dimensions of Childhood, Essays on the History of Children and Youth in Canada* (Winnipeg: Legal Research Institute of University of Manitoba, 1991).

5.   For example the Rockefeller Foundation was instrumental for the mental hygiene movement as T. Richardson has already suggested. Physicians were the other major source of influence, especially those who studied in American universities; most of the specialists did studies in these universities. See Theresa Richardson, *The Century of the Child, The Mental Hygiene Movement and Social Policy in United States and Canada* (New York: State University of New York Press, 1989).

6.   The fight against infant mortality is probably the best example to illustrate these differences in rhythms of changes, Quebec trailing behind English Canada in the adoption of different hygienic and sanitary measures, although the *Gouttes de lait* movement was first implemented there. See Terry Copp, *Classe ouvrière et pauvreté. Les conditions de vie des travailleurs montréalais, 1897–1929* (Montreal: Boréal Express, 1978); Patricia Thornton, Sherry Olson, and Quoc Thuy Thach, 'Dimensions socials de la mortalité infantile au milieu du XIXe siècle', *Annales de Démographie historique* (1988), pp. 299–325; Patricia Thornton and Sherry Olson, 'Family contexts of fertility and infant survival in nineteenth-century Montreal', *Journal of Family History*, XVI, 4 (1991), pp. 401–17; André Turmel and Louise Hamelin, 'La grande faucheuse d'enfants: la mortalité infantile depuis le tournant du siècle', *Revue canadienne de Sociologie et d'Anthropologie*, XXXII, 4 (1995), pp. 438–63. It is also interesting to note that the IQ testing prevailed on the west coast much earlier than it did in central Canada. See Neil Sutherland, *Children in English-Canadian Society* (Toronto: University of Toronto Press, 1976).

7.   The pre-confederation period has not drawn as much attention from historians as the turn of the century in both traditions. But things are starting to change and new interest is rising for the study of this period. The history of childhood in the seventeenth and eighteenth centuries is in an even weaker position. See Charlotte Neff, 'Pauper Apprenticeship in Pre-Confederation Ontario', *Journal of Family History*, XXI, 2 (1996), pp. 144–71; Bettina Bradbury, *Familles ouvrières à Montréal. Age, genre et survie pendant la phase d'industrialisation* (Montreal: Boréal, 1995).

8.   Among them, I must mention that Theresa Richardson, Brian Low, Norah Lewis, Juliet Pollard, Michael Marker, Tony Aruda, Jean Barman, Veronica Strong-Boag, and J. Donald Wilson are among Sutherland's collaborators.

9.   I want to draw the reader's attention to Sutherland's book title: *Children in English-Canadian Society* (1976), and the three themes organizing this study. They are prevalent

in the English-Canadian society, but the first two are not as relevant for a history of childhood in Quebec.

10. Sutherland, *Children in English-Canadian Society*, p. 11.

11. Ibid., p. 18.

12. It is interesting to note that the historians of education identify the metaphor of the family as relevant for schooling rather than one of the three that I have just mentioned above. Why has this metaphor been chosen for schooling and not the other three? See Alison Prentice, 'Education and the Metaphor of the Family: The Upper Canadian Example', in Michael B. Katz and Paul Mattingly (eds), *Education and Social Change: Themes for Ontario's Past* (New York: New York University Press, 1975), pp. 110–32; Chad Gaffield, 'Children's Lives and Academic Achievement in Canada and the United States', *Comparative Education Review*, XXXVIII, 1 (1994), pp. 36–64.

13. P.T. Rooke and M.R. Schnell, *Discarding the Asylum: From Child Rescue to the Welfare State in English Canada, 1800–1950* (Landham, MD: University Press of America, 1983), quoted in P.T. Rooke and M.R. Schnell, 'Canada', p. 186.

14. Veronica Strong-Boag, *The New Day Recalled: Lives of Girls and Women in English Canada, 1919–1939* (Toronto: Markham, 1988)

15. See also Katherine Arnup, *Education for Motherhood* (Toronto: University of Toronto Press, 1994); Cynthia Comacchio, *Nations are Built of Babies. Saving Ontario's Mothers and Children* (Montreal: McGill-Queen's University Press, 1993).

16. Sutherland, *Children in English-Canadian Society*, p. 14.

17. The question has two distinct dimensions: one concerns the middle-class orientation for the child-saving movement; the other is about the role of poverty and economic inequalities in the access to and delivery of health care. This latter dimension is directly related to the question of the so-called mother's ignorance, the physicians leaning toward such views rather than an analysis in terms of poverty. See Sutherland, *Children in English-Canadian Society*; Comacchio, *Nations are Built of Babies*.

18. There was and still is a huge debate about the relationship among the so-called overfertility, infant mortality, and sanitary conditions. This debate concerns the cultural differences in infant feeding practices such as early weaning among French Canadian infants, the question of birth spacing, the role of poverty, density, and inequalities of income; their impact on feeding habits, hygiene, and quality of habitat; the variations of such practices among linguistic and religious groups; the problem of seasonality in IM rates; the relations between literacy and infant feeding practices; the differences between rural and urban areas, etc. See Thornton, Olson, and Thach, 'Dimensions sociales'; Turmel and Hamelin, 'La grande faucheuse d'enfants'.

19. André Lux, 'Les enfants qu'on n'a plus au Québec', *Recherches Sociographiques*, XXII, 3 (1981), pp. 391–2; Jacques Henripin, *Naître ou ne pas être* (Québec: IQRC, 1989).

20. Gérard Bouchard, *Quelques arpents d'Amérique* (Montréal: Boréal, 1995).

21. Ibid, p. 162.

22. There is still a huge and important debate among Quebec scholars about these questions that is summarized in a single question: why was schooling not overwhelmingly seen as instrumental for social mobility in this particular society?

23. The Bouchard model of rural family reproduction and the Bradbury model of working-class family reproduction concerns the pattern of the nineteenth century and beginning of the twentieth century family reproduction. D. Marshall's model is quite different because she is working on the emergence of the welfare state in the second half of the twentieth century and the way it affected family reproduction. Thus it remains to see how to bridge the first two models and the latter one. See Bouchard, *Quelques arpents*

d'Amérique; Bradbury, *Familles ouvrières*; Dominique Marshall, 'The Role of the Universal Welfare State and the History of Childhood: Quebec, 1940–1955', *Canadian Historical Review* (1997); Dominique Marshall, *The Social Origins of the Welfare State: Quebec families, compulsory schooling and family allowances, 1940–1955* (Montreal: Presses de l'Université de Montréal, 1997).

24. See Horace Miner, *St-Denis, a French-Canadian Parish* (Chicago: Chicago University Press, 1963); Colette Moreux, *Douceville en Québec. La modernization d'une tradition* (Montréal: Les Presses de l'Université de Montréal, 1982); Michel Verdon, *Anthropologie de la colonisation au Québec. Le dilemme d'un village du Lac St-Jean* (Montréal: Les Presses de l'Université de Montréal, 1973).

25. See Anne-Marie Desdouits, *Le monde de l'enfance. Traditions du pays de Caux et du Québec* (Québec-Paris: PUL-CNRS, 1990); Louise Gagnon, *L'apparition des modes enfantines au Québec* (Québec: IQRC, 1992); Michel Lessard, 'Le petit oiseau va sortir . . . Le photographie et l'enfant', *Cap-aux-Diamants. Regards sur l'enfance*, XXXII (hiver 1993), pp. 22–7.

26. Lemieux's research is essential in the sense that, working within a Weberian framework, she can argue convincingly against any fatalistic interpretations of the high infant mortality rates among Quebec children and the way that parents, and especially mothers, were emotionally involved with their children. See Denyse Lemieux, *Une culture de la nostalgie* (Montreal: Boréal Express, 1984); Ibid., *Les petits innocents. L'enfance en Nouvelle-France* (Quebec: IQRC, 1985); Ibid., 'Enfants et familles du passé: une histoire entre mythes et réalités', in Ibid. (ed.), *Familles d'aujourd'hui* (Québec: IQRC, 1990), pp. 55–72.

27. Michael Bliss, *Plague. A Story of Smallpox in Montréal* (Toronto: Harper & Collins, 1991).

28. They even argue that English Canadian historians came to study childhood through their interests in schooling and compulsory schooling. Rooke and Schnell, 'Canada', p. 180.

29. This is to say that lesser work, either at the family farm or at the factory, didn't automatically mean a higher amount of time for learning. Taking children out of work was a necessary first step to send them to school, but that step was not enough in itself; it had to be completed with other steps, among them laws on compulsory schooling. See Chad Gaffield, 'Children's Lives'.

30. Thérèse Hamel, 'Obligation scolaire et travail des enfants', *Revue d'Histoire de l'Amérique Française*, XXXVIII, 1 (1984), pp. 39–58; Dominique Jean, 'Le recul du travail des enfants au Québec entre 1940 et 1960: une explication des confits entre les familles pauvres et l'Etat providence', *Labour/Le Travail*, XXIV (1989), pp. 91–129.

31. André Turmel, 'Absence d'amour et presence des microbes: sur les modèles culturels de l'enfant', *Recherches Sociographiques*, XXXVIII, 1 (1977), pp. 89–115; André Turmel, 'Science and Normalcy: Science's Construction of the Normal Child' (1997).

When You Listen to the Winds of Childhood, How Much Can You Believe?

Neil Sutherland

The place to which you go back to listen to the wind you heard in your childhood—that is your homeland, which is also the place where you have a grave to tend. Though I chose to live in Quebec partly because of the love for it which my mother passed on to me, now it is my turn to come back to Manitoba to tend her grave. And also to listen to the wind of my childhood.

Gabrielle Roy, *The Fragile Lights of Earth*

In a recent interview a woman born in Vancouver in 1941 recalled that her merchant seaman father died during the Second World War, that a year and a half later her grandfather died, and that she remembered 'as a child going to school and sometimes I would worry . . . not sometimes but a lot, that something would happen to my grandmother. Everybody seemed to be . . . leaving.' Since her widowed mother had to work, the woman's grandmother lived with them and looked after the house, staying on even after her mother remarried. 'If I wanted to talk to anybody I would go to my grandmother and talk with her. . . . She was always easy to approach.' If either the girl or her brother 'came into the room and sat next to her—there could be a big room with a lot of chairs—but I always came and sat right beside her on the chesterfield to watch TV . . . and she would always . . . put her hand on my hand . . . or just on my knee, or hold onto my arm, there was always a lot of physical contact . . . it wasn't rushing and hugging and kissing but just very subtle. . . . It was the same thing with my brother.'

Why would anyone want to tape-record and transcribe this homely little glimpse into the workings of one Vancouver family as it was in the late 1940s and early 1950s? In the view of one critic, what readers often gain from what he describes as 'exotic forays into remote lives' is 'not historical actuality; it is voyeuristic empathy'. Such 'vivid intimacies promote historical sympathy but attenuate historical understanding' because they underscore 'universal constants of human feelings' as they ignore 'the particular social and cultural trends that both link the past with, and dif-

ferentiate it from the present.'[1] Much social history, particularly although not exclusively that of the popular sort, does indeed employ 'vivid intimacies' in the way
described. Although this recollection might also lend itself to an example of
'voyeuristic empathy', I am in fact employing it, together with companion pieces
drawn from other interviews, as evidence for a discussion of the complex roles that,
until recently, grandmothers played in the economic and social dimensions of the
lives of many Canadian families.

Whether they collect memories for voyeuristic purposes or as evidence for serious historical or social scientific investigations, researchers must confront certain
questions about the nature of this data. What is memory? How reliable a guide to
the past is it? These are, of course, not new questions. Psychologists have studied
the question for a century or more, in recent years quite intensively.[2] Historians are
now also probing more deeply into the nature of what has always been a central element in their stock-in-trade.[3] My own interest in questions relating to memory
grew out of my research into the history of childhood. For the past decade I have
examined how Anglophone children grew up in the years between about 1920 and
1960. I approached this task through case studies drawn from the childhoods of
those who were born between about 1910 and 1950.

In reporting my findings I am laying out the structures of children's lives, and
how children experienced their own lives in such settings as the home, the congre-
gation, the classroom, their place of work, and on streets and in playgrounds; in
short, in the 'communities' of their childhoods.[4] To actually 'get inside' childhood,
I decided that I had to ask adults to describe their youthful experiences for me. But
how much confidence could I or anyone else place in such memories? One can perhaps believe that the recollected words for a playground rhyme, once upon a time
chanted over and over again, may be reasonably accurate, but what of events that
were less discrete but of more moment? Since memories are in fact my most important primary source, they give rise to what is my most difficult historiographic problem: can one use the recollections of adults to recreate the internal worlds of
childhood? If so, then how? In the remainder of this paper I will outline what I
believe to be reasonably satisfactory answers to these questions. Because I have come
to an integration of theory and practice in the context of my own research, I shall
draw most of my examples from it.

Recollections of childhood are of two sorts and each sort is produced in two different ways. Adults tell us about how they or others reared their children. Adults
also recall incidents, feelings, and experiences and the like about their own childhood. Recollections are either self-created, such as those that appear in informal
family histories, in autobiographies or novels dealing with childhood or adolescence, or are generated deliberately and systematically by social investigators, social
scientists, and historians through case reports and records, hearings, questionnaires, and interviews. Since memories of adults about how they reared their children do not raise methodological questions about memories of childhood per se,
I shall not consider them here.

Before examining any one kind of recollection in detail, let me summarize the
historiographic problems posed by recollections, and especially those of childhood,

and the ways that historians have developed to cope, at least partially, with them. The first problem is, of course, that memory is fallible; events may be forgotten or transformed with the passage of time. Memoires provide the most obvious example of these failings, perhaps prompting one to agree with A.J.P. Taylor's remark that 'written memoires are a form of oral history set down to mislead historians'.[5] Taylor's comments, however, were directed as such memoirists as politicians, generals, and the like whose activities have traditionally attracted the attention and judgments of historians. When ordinary people set down their life stories, they may err in all sorts of ways, but few set out deliberately to deceive their readers or listeners. What is essential to note is that people's memories are fallible even in circumstances in which they have no need, no intention to deceive, indeed in which the whole thrust of their effort is to be as accurate as possible. In an extremely revealing experiment, for example, psychologist Richard T. White carefully recorded one event each day for a year. Six months later he had no recollection of 40 per cent of them.[6] Thirty years after the 'Blitz' of 1940, Tom Harrisson asked some of the original Mass Observation participants to rewrite from memory experiences they had originally written about right after they had happened. Time had so transformed their accounts that Harrisson concluded that 'the only valid information for this sort of social history . . . is that recorded at the time on the spot.'[7] Of the million-odd words she wrote for Mass Observation between 1939 and 1945, novelist and poet Naomi Mitchison commented, in 1984, that 'some of this comes new to me. . . . It is odd that events or sights that I remember vividly don't seem to have made it to the diary . . . was I as I appear in the diary? I rather hope not as I don't like myself much. . . .'[8]

Adults seem unable to remember anything of events before they were three or four years old. Psychologists explain this phenomena by arguing that forming a memory depends on an initial capacity to interpret what is going on. Since the very young lack this capacity, 'early autobiographical memory is [not] lost in infantile amnesia but . . . never existed as such.'[9] While most of us would probably concur with the commonsense notion that memories of childhood from about four years of age onward tend to be more vivid than adult ones, and that we can recollect some of them more easily than we can those of events in our adult lives, we have, despite claims to the contrary, no evidence that these memories are any less fallible.[10] We must, therefore, be at least as skeptical of childhood memories as we are of any others.

Memory is not only fallible, but it is also shaped by the circumstances that prompt it. Autobiographers quite naturally write briefs in advocacy of their subjects; each is an *apologia pro vita sua*. And, as with its prototype, each life story is told or written from the point of view of the present and is designed to convey a message to the present. In autobiographical accounts written years apart, for example, Leslie Thomas has given two very different accounts of his life as a Barnardo boy. In his author's note in *In My Wildest Dreams*, published in 1984, Thomas remarks that his first book 'about my days in Barnardo's, and called *This Time Next Week* was written twenty-one years ago. It was a fragment of autobiography but I have not reread it. . . . After all an autobiography is how you remember things *now*.'[11] And indeed, the stance of the successful novelist in his fifties produced a very different book than that written by an ambitious journalist in his early thirties. As exemplified in his different versions of how he learned the shocking news that he and his brother were bound for Barnardo's, the older Thomas gives a more professional polish to events that both books recount.[12] The difference between the two books, however, is deeper than a matter of style. Despite the fact that *In My Wildest Dreams* is the better-written book, *This Time Next Week* will remain as Thomas's lasting testament to orphanhood and life in an institution for boys. Of the boys' home, the younger Thomas wrote, 'There grew from this ugly old place, with its dripping rooms, its hollow dormitories, its riotous boys, a sense of warmth, of familiarity, of fun, of fellowship, that was strong and real . . . a dramatic unceasing stream of life flowing. . . .'[13] The younger Thomas captured this quality of life in the home more effectively than did the older.

David Vincent, who used autobiographies as his sole source to create a rich and convincing portrait of aspects of working-class childhood in the nineteenth century, argues that, for historians, what a good autobiography requires 'above all is energy of insight, an ability to comprehend fully the significance and coherence of past experiences, together with the literary skill to transmit an account in such a way as to make the widest connection with the experience and the imagination of the readership'.[14] Here, however, Vincent asks that autobiographies display an overall coherence and sense of unity that does not characterize life itself. As prisoners of the chaos of living, of circumstances they did not make and over which they have little or no control (what Aleksandr Solzhenitsyn calls 'the pitiless crowbar of events'), most people live lives that are an agglomeration of choices, chance, contradictions, false starts, accidents, lucky and unlucky breaks. After each major change in personal circumstances—perhaps triggered by such events as moving from one town to another, being promoted from elementary to high school, joining the work force, leaving home, getting married, undergoing an intense religious experience, losing a job, suffering a serious illness, the death of a child, a parent, or a spouse—people quickly establish new priorities and personal continuities. Each time life 'happens' to them, they adopt a new structure (or what Craig Barclay calls a 'self-schema') that will contextualize the new phase of their lives.[15] Thus although at each stage people perhaps see the accumulation of their experiences as adding up to a unified and coherent whole, this unity is accomplished by a generally unconscious reordering and editing of the past. Further, while men and women tend to tell or write their stories chronologically, they approach them from very different socially conditioned stances. Both my own experience and that of others who conduct oral histories indicate that men's stories tend to revolve around their systematic activities, their games, their work, their sequence of occupations, displaying their narrator as the central subject. Women's stories usually focus on their relationships to such significant others as parents, spouses, children, fellow workers, and friends.[16] Recollections or novels that deal extensively with childhood are often written by those whose early lives were unhappy ones.[17]

Taken together, then, these characteristics of life stories indicate that whether we think that earlier events, scripts, or schemata are significant, or whether we even remark on them at all, depends on how we *currently* structure our lives and how we describe, explain, and justify ourselves and our relationships with others at these different points in our lives. The skills, therefore, that will produce a more coherent life story or more readable autobiography, and one that will perhaps provide historians with sharper insights into events that took place when the autobiographer was an adult, may actually take us away from the realities of childhood. Alternatively, a series of basically unconnected but vividly recalled vignettes suggests a childhood on which the interviewee has not yet reflected or taken a final stance, and which may come fairly close to the actualities of the childhood from which the anecdotes were drawn. Support for this latter position is provided by certain psychologists. We have already noted that for an event to impinge on our consciousness, we must have some capacity to interpret or understand it. From this position psychologists go on to explain that the shape that a memory takes is as much the product of the process of remembering as it is of the actual characteristics of whatever it is that is being recalled. Thus they argue that a memory is really a *reconstruction* of what is being recalled rather than a *reproduction* of it and, further, that a succession of reconstructions of the same event form themselves into a chain that tends to diverge more and more from the original.[18] Consider an oversimplified example. When she is four, a girl is joined in her family by a baby brother. Since she is old enough to understand this event, she will also have the capacity to recall it. When prompted by some event in her adult life—say the birth of a child of her own—she will reconstruct it in light of her present circumstances. When she reconstructs it another time—say when her brother also becomes a father—she will then reconstruct it in the light of both the original event itself and of her previous reconstruction of it, and so on.

The fact that people tend to write their autobiographies or tell their life stories during or after that stage that psychologists call the 'life review' strengthens reservations about life stories and autobiographies. At this point in their lives many people feel the necessity to look back over their whole existence in order to justify themselves to themselves, to make the self-edited sum of their lives to have been worth living. At this stage, Paul Thompson notes, people are more willing to remember and are less concerned than younger people are about fitting their stories to social norms.[19] On the other hand, as Robert Roberts explains, at this stage of their lives at least some people tend to look 'through a golden haze' at events they once looked on objectively.[20] Both of these circumstances may contribute to a coherent life story or autobiography that satisfies the teller's or writer's need for a life that he or she can look back upon as being worthwhile. Unhappy, embarrassing, shameful, or unpleasant events can be transformed or omitted as the narrator moves towards his or her 'happy ending'. They may, as well, be a product of the cumulative effects of the extending chain of reconstructions of the past that accompany a life review.[21]

Social scientists and historians have tried in a number of ways to reduce or even eliminate the subjectivity of unstructured recollections. They give questionnaires to their subjects, or in their interviews ask a series of narrowly focused questions. Nonetheless, interviews and even the collection of questionnaires take place in a social relationship, however fleeting it may be. Referring to recollections collected by oral historians, Thompson explains that the form that they take varies because of differences in style among interviewers; the sex, race, and 'social presence' of the interviewer; whether the interview is conducted anonymously, privately, or in a group setting; and whether the interviews take place in an office, home, or tavern.[22] Those whose recollections are deliberately solicited may set out to make a strong, positive impression of themselves on the interviewer. Further, even if they do not consciously or unconsciously tailor their recollections to what they think the interviewer wants to hear, or what they want to hear about themselves, those who had unhappy childhoods or unhappy lives may suppress details, or refuse to be interviewed at all because their memories may be too painful to summon up. When some of those I have interviewed come to talk about their schooling, they make their first negative remark either assertively or tentatively, as if they are expecting someone from the educational establishment to take issue with criticisms of schools or teachers. Other reticences are more deeply rooted. When I asked one middle-aged woman, 'Would you mind talking to me about your childhood?' she replied, 'My childhood was so awful I don't even want to think about it. Even your asking the question has upset me.' Until recently, those who were sexually or otherwise abused as children have been particularly silent on the topic.[23]

If the fallibility and subjectivity of recollections pose such major problems, then why use them at all? My response is twofold. On the one hand I will draw on two conditions rooted in historiography, on the other I will argue from the point of view of necessity. First, and most generally, then, one must note that memories are more similar to other historical sources than may at first appear to be the case. Many written sources begin in an oral form—a police officer interrogates the mother of the assaulted child; a census taker asks the 'head of the household' for details regarding its children; a newspaper reporter talks to children lined up to see Santa Claus; the diarist overhears the conversation of her youngsters; the letter writer proudly tells relatives of the clever sayings of his sons and daughters. As Thompson notes, with most individual and even aggregated data, 'what we receive is *social meaning*'.[24] Further, reports of oral situations that involved different social classes are usually transformed into their written version by the class that possesses hegemony over the others.[25] Nonetheless, the historiographic problems posed by oral evidence are mostly the problems posed by recollections themselves rather than by any particular mode of collecting them. Thus, although misnamed as an 'oral history', the text of an interview is really no more a history than is the text of the Treaty of Utrecht. From the very beginnings of their discipline, historians have applied the canons of their craft in ways that have enabled them to use recollections (and all other sources) to good effect.[26] As Thucydides wrote in the preface to his *History of the Peloponnesian War*:

> As regards the material facts of the war, I have not been content to follow casual informants, or my own imagination. Where I have not been an eyewitness myself, I have investigated with utmost accuracy attainable every detail that I have taken at second hand. The task has been laborious, for witnesses of the same particular events have given versions that have varied according to their sympathies or retentive powers.[27]

There is no reason to believe that historians cannot also employ their traditional procedures in their investigations of childhood.

As they utilize memories, historians receive considerable help from the fact that certain types of recollections are more reliable than others. We have learned that people can remember with reasonable accuracy what some psychologists have described as 'schemata' and as 'scripts'. Schema theorists argue that we develop mental representations of the general characteristics of events, activities, and even places to which we are repeatedly exposed. Thus, for example, we all develop a sense of the age-old structure that stories assume.[28] Scripts (what Thompson calls 'recurrent events') are a particular kind of schema. They are the way in which our memories organize those events in our lives that are very similar to each other. Roger C. Schank and Robert P. Abelson argue that memory is 'episodic'; that is, 'memory is organized around personal experiences or episodes'. Since many 'episodes' in life are very similar to each other, people remember them 'in terms of a standardized generalized episode', or 'script'.[29] Indeed, recent research suggests that from their very earliest years, children employ scripts as the framework around which they organize most of their experience and perhaps develop a sense that they are gaining some control over what they do.[30] Our schemata of house, yard, school, and neighbourhood, for example, provide the stages on which we recall the enactment of the scripts of our childhood.

There are two sorts of 'scripts'—situational and personal. The daily routine of family life in the 1920s and 1930s, for example, was made up of numerous situational scripts. Members arose in the same sequence each weekday morning, and certain people were charged with such regular tasks as lighting fires, preparing breakfast, feeding siblings, clearing the table, washing the dishes, filling the woodbox or sawdust hopper, and so on. Thus, although people cannot recall any particular morning, they find it relatively easy to remember the breakfast routines and other family scripts of their childhood. They can describe in what ways Saturday and Sunday scripts differed from weekday ones. Personal scripts take place within the situational ones. For example, each and every day they went to school, and in all the classrooms they entered, certain children always behaved in such a way as to draw as little attention to themselves as possible. They dropped their eyes if the teacher scanned the room, they held back when teachers or pupil leaders were picking members of teams, they stayed away from noisy or extroverted children. They had a whole series of personal, self-effacing scripts that they acted out in the context of the many situational scripts that existed in their schooling.

The same script may be played out in different families cheerfully or in an atmosphere of hostility and tension. Mothers and daughters doing the daily dishes together used to be one of the most common scripts of family life. In some families following it, the 'dishes' script was generally a pleasant occasion. Daughters told mothers about the day's events at school and gossip about their friends and their friends' families. At this time, mothers often passed on the oral traditions of the family, and this is perhaps why women tend to know these traditions better than men, and why they know more about their mother's family than they do about their father's. In later years, the dishes were sometimes done with the radio on, and mother and daughter shared in an aspect of the popular culture of the day. In other families, the same script took place in an atmosphere of hostility and resentment.

Mothers used the opportunity to criticize the behaviour of their youngsters, and the quality of their work, and to make other critical or derogatory remarks. Thus while both versions of this script have the same job as its core, done in almost the same way, and is thus recollected similarly, they also had very different emotional dimensions that are also well remembered.

Two characteristics of recurrent events, or scripts, are especially important here. First, like the rest of us, children spend most of their time in situations that are highly structured. Thus the components of the life of a primary grade child—the time before school each morning, the trip to school, the time in the classroom, recesses, and so on—embed themselves in a complex of everyday routines. In turn, personal and situational scripts comprise the central elements in the complex of daily, weekly, and seasonal routines that, when added together, form the structures of children's lives. Further, each stage of a child's life possesses structural unity; those of preschoolers possess a different unity from those of primary grade children, and so on. This unity varies from family to family—children in large families have different structures than those in small ones; those with one parent from those with two; those from working-class backgrounds from those in the middle class; those of Chinese origin from those of Scottish; and so on. While each aspect or stage of childhood must be understood as much as possible in its own enclosed context, it is also part of a chronological sequence. Second, while each human life is unique, containing both events and scripts that are unique to it, each person also shares with others scripts that are, in many of their features, virtually the same. Those whose lives share many similar scripts had enough structure in common to enable us to generalize about them. Thus older children in all but the most well-off of large families grew up in similar routines of chores and duties involving the care of their younger brothers and sisters. Youthful child minders shared with each other not only the scripts of infant and child care, but also the same ambivalent feelings about their siblings. ('Nursie really knows how to hate. She has brothers and sisters.'[31]) Interviews showed that the classroom scripts of Halifax children were virtually identical to those described by their Vancouver counterparts.[32] My collection of about 200 interviews shows that while childhoods differed considerably along class, gender, religious, and ethnic lines, adults from these different backgrounds are all able to recall the scripts of their childhoods for us, and that I can find common patterns in them.

The second dimension of the argument for using recollections in writing history is a practical one. Oral and other life histories collected by historians and social scientists are the principal source that can take us across those barriers, of which class is but one, that separate the few who might write down their memories from the vast majority who do not. More important, if we are ever to get 'inside' childhood experiences, then we must ask adults to recall how they thought, felt, and experienced their growing up. Childhood is suffused by periods of sadness, embarrassment, shame, fear, and intense hatred. Children have a different relationship than adults with their physical selves, with animals, with aspects of the physical world. They learn only over a long period of time the difference between the real world and imaginary ones, between figurative and literal meanings in the discourse of adults, and the difference between appropriate and inappropriate behaviour (which varies, of course, along gender, class, religious, and ethnic lines).

[. . .]

For the years before the memories of those still living, autobiography, fiction, and responses made to earlier investigators are the only form of recollection available to historians. Those dealing with the fairly recent past are more fortunate in that they are also able to select their own subjects. In my own work, I have collected and am using the memories of certain people born between 1910 and 1950. [. . .] What I have done was to conduct (with the help of research assistants) extensive interviews that produce segments of life histories, detailed looks at one part of the life courses of my subjects.[33] I then tie in what I have found in more traditional sources. [. . .] My research assistants and I have now conducted over 200 interviews. I stopped at this point for two reasons. First, time and resources had run out. Second, and for this I was very thankful, most of the content of the more recent interviews enriched what earlier interviews had already told me rather than adding major new insights.

[. . .]

[. . .] I chose Vancouver as a case study for urban anglophone Canada and a small community in the Bulkley Valley area of north central British Columbia as a case study for those areas of rural Canada that, in the years following the First World War, were still in the pioneering stage of development.

I think it is important at this point that I underline a central effect of this practice. Given the realities of research costs, the practicality of time, and so on, to decide to investigate those whose experiences overlap with each other is also to decide *not* to employ quota samples. As I indicate below, I have taken steps to take into account those variables such as gender, class, ethnicity, religious denomination, and geographic region that have the most important effect on the structure of children's lives. I must emphasize, however, that while I believe that my sampling proved to be both practical to carry out and satisfactory for my purposes, it was more rough-and-ready than the means usually employed by sociologists, political scientists, and, indeed, by some other historians. And only time, and the research of others, will tell whether my case studies are representative of anything more than themselves, or merely maps of one or two of what Cole Harris calls the 'archipelagoes of Canada'.[34]

I selected my pioneer interviewees from among the 59 pupils who attended one rural school between its opening in 1920 and its closing in 1946. I also interviewed some of those from the area who later attended the 'consolidated' school that replaced the one-room one. Most of my Vancouver interviewees came from cohorts who grew up in one east side and one west side neighbourhood. Although both neighbourhoods displayed the mix of classes characteristic of much of Vancouver at the time, middle-class families predominated in west side Kerrisdale and 'respectable', working-class ones predominated in east side Cedar Cottage. ('Maybe the area was even poor but it was respectable with lots of families and churches.') In each neighbourhood, children played together in the street and in playgrounds, belonged to various organizations for girls and boys, and attended local churches and schools. For practical reasons I used a local elementary school as a focal point for each of my neighbourhoods and, in effect, defined the cohorts that I sampled as being those who entered grade one in a particular year. Once I selected a neighbourhood and a cohort in it, I moved from one interviewee to another along a 'chain of acquaintanceship'. In some instances this merely meant that people were in a school classroom or neighbourhood group at the same time and identified as such from class photographs or other documentary evidence. In others we talked to people with closer ties, such as siblings and those who were best friends.

My goal has been to explore common schema, events, scripts, and structures through more than a single memory. Overlapping memories also help overcome another factor that psychologists have noted—namely, that we tend to remember the good things about ourselves and forget the bad. More important, they enable one to compensate for what one psychologist calls a 'superiority complex', which manifests itself in overestimating our own contribution to tasks or events, and seeing ourselves in a better light than we see others.[35] As one man explained, 'Because that is the way I remember myself, being helpful.'

For each of my communities or neighbourhoods, therefore, I have put together an informal sample that has a great deal of overlap in the lives of the interviewees built into it. My research assistants and I have interviewed working-class and middle-class men and women. I organized the interviews in such a way that about half were conducted by members of the same sex as the interviewee. We tried to interview those who, at least by external standards, may not have led successful or happy lives. Such people are difficult to locate. They lead harder lives than most, physically and emotionally, and many die far short of a full life span. Many are naturally reluctant to talk about their lives. Others have so creatively employed their life histories in order to make a case to a truant officer or parole board that their narratives, however plausible, must be treated with more than usual caution. We have therefore collected fewer such life stories than I would like, but this lack is perhaps partly compensated for by the fact that some appear in the case records and life histories collected by child care institutions, sociological studies, and the like. Some Vancouver childhoods, for example, are vividly described in a series of University of British Columbia Master of Social Work theses written in the 1950s and 1960s.[36] [. . .]

How one actually conducts interviews about childhood is the second methodological question I wish to discuss. Considerable experience in other investigations that involved interviewing suggested two characteristics that I have framed in this research.[37] First, only long interviews build in the interviewee a commitment to its outcome, and create a sense of intimacy and trust that brings people to talk about things they have rarely if ever shared before. Second, open-ended, relatively unstructured interviews often lead people, eventually, to talk about those things that really mattered to them.[38] We began each interview with a brief discussion of the project, answering any questions interviewees have about it. We supported this phase with a two-page summary of the work that we usually mailed out beforehand. These preliminaries usually took very little time because interviewees had primed themselves to talk about themselves and not about the research or the researchers. For each interview my research assistants and I have an informal list of topics that we hoped to cover in it and our initial questions grow directly out of this list. ('What is your earliest memory?' 'What happened in your house before you went to school in the morning?' 'What do you remember about your early days in school?')

In confirmation of research that shows that people's memories range across the senses, we found that people recollect childhood scripts through all of their senses, and we therefore asked about them.[39] Thus adults recalled the smells and sounds of their classrooms, the taste of iodine pills, and the pain of the pinched ear. ('As I begin to think about it two dominant things stand out; the smells of the room—plasticine, the smell of rubber erasers . . . the sour paste—and the sounds—crackling of radiators'; '. . . it never really twigged until you asked about what kind of furnace, and then it brought back the smell of sawdust and the hopper and you know . . . you need a little trigger to bring those remembrances back'; 'Do you remember the sound of a bike on a street that has been watered? I can just hear the flicker of water coming off the wheels.') Although we were unable to provide people with their own versions of a madeleine and tea, or their 'Rosebud', we did find that we could trigger memory with such artefacts as class photographs, staff lists, or copies of prescribed textbooks, or from asking for comments on words—'conkers', 'sinkers', 'alery'—that were once part of the vocabulary of children. Novelist Wallace Stegner describes what seems to take place.

> One touch, and his skin remembered. Magic. He sat drenched in another of those showers of sensations. . . . What a Rube Goldberg wiring job man was! How enduring were the circuits stamped into a boy when he was dizzy with hormones and vulnerable to experience as dry blotting paper to water! Push the right button and you floodlighted him like a temple. Push another and you got into the whole *son et lumiere*.[40]

Pressing the right buttons, as Stegner puts it, is more complex than one might imagine. In many ways ideal interviewees are those who claim not to remember much about their childhood. In such cases, memories flow slowly, and initially need a lot of prompting through questions or the further display of artifacts (but *not* through hypnosis or drugs).[41] In many ways such a beginning is more reassuring than an initial outpouring of recollections. One senses in the former case that one is getting the past 'fresh' as it were; that the items have not been drawn out and refurbished, or honed into a good story or anecdote. One must be particularly wary of the well-used anecdote about childhood or a well-crafted school story. One begins to recognize those items that have become part of an interviewee's regular lore, told to amuse, or to make a point about the 'good old days', or to emphasize, to today's youngsters, 'did I ever have it tough as a kid.' Each has been told many times to his or her family and friends. These stories are perhaps true in essence, but the fine honing that comes from constant reconstructing, telling, and polishing also removes them further and further away from the reality that they are supposedly portraying.

At this point I must emphasize that we only employed questions, artifacts, or other 'buttons' at the *beginning* of an interview. Since it is *their* lives as *they* saw them that we were interested in we shifted, as soon as we could, responsibility for the agenda over to our interviewees. We wanted to have a minimal effect on their reconstruction of the past. Thus we worked hard to get people into the right mood, one in which their memories were stimulated. Mostly this meant letting silences go on until the interviewee felt the need to fill them. As a good interview proceeds, people get more and more involved in their own life story. One memory triggers another, which in turn uncovers other scenes, other events, other feelings, all of which begin to crowd in on each other.[42] People shift from describing events themselves to their feeling about them. They become more articulate, less diffident about revealing themselves. At first they are polite, holding back, waiting for comments or questions; they seem at the beginning almost to view the interview as a conversation in which the interviewer has a right to a certain say as well as the interviewee. The longer a good interview goes on, the less tolerant interviewees become of any intervention; they show impatience at distractions such as questions, the asking for a name again, or how something is spelled, or anything that breaks into the flow of their narrative, and especially so when they are in the midst of a recollection that has a strong emotional dimension. They glance with ill-concealed impatience if the interviewer gets behind in his or her note taking.

People pause occasionally, gaze into the distance, not seeing the interviewer but perhaps events or people that the questions or narrative have triggered in their memories. At this point, the wise interviewer greets this silence with silence and not a question. After they have finished describing certain—often intimate—events, some people give out signals that they do not want to go back to it again; that one is lucky that they opened up on the particular point and should be grateful for it in whatever form they chose to give it to one. If anyone is responsible for potential errors then it is the fault of the interviewer for not taking his or her notes down correctly. In such circumstances, I find it wiser to go ahead rather than back. To ask too many questions, to follow a schedule, leads to a series of discrete responses that may or may not tell us very much about what the interviewee feels is the reality of his or her childhood. I cannot overstress the importance of this point. Open-ended interviews may be quite disconnected, may contain items that are not closely related one to another, nor fit into a temporal sequence, but they also produce material that is very intimate and personal; material that people are sometimes surprised that they recall and even more surprised that they would tell to someone else ('I've never even told that to my husband!').

[. . .]

I want to close by returning to the story with which I opened this paper, that of the woman in her forties talking about her grandmother. Let us suppose that someone had studied her family when she was about ten years old, someone who possessed the full panoply of modern psychological devices and observational or participant-observational techniques. Undoubtedly that person could then have described the family's scripts more fully and accurately than I or any other historian could reconstruct them from oral evidence collected a generation later. The researcher would have learned how the grandmother felt about her grandchildren and would have learned some and inferred more about the granddaughter's feelings about her grandmother. Nonetheless, there would have come a point beyond which the investigator would have been unable to go. Only as an adult did the woman have the vocabulary and, indeed, the conceptual and contextual structure that enabled her to put her childhood feelings into words. What is clear, too, from what we know about memory is that if the child has been pushed too hard, too persistently to describe her feelings at the time, that pushing would have made any later effort at accurate recreation even more difficult to accomplish. The more thoroughly she had been probed by my notional social scientist in her childhood, the more likely it would be that that discussion, rather than the inchoate but complex underlying feelings, would frame any later reconstructions. Indeed the paradox is that the closer in time you try to probe the feelings of childhood, the further away they may go. In this regard Gabrielle Roy, who provided the epigraph and title for this paper, also posed its concluding question. 'Is it possible', she asks, 'to record in a book the spellbinding powers of childhood, which can put the whole world inside the tiniest locket of happiness?'[43] My answer is, of course, yes, but only if a pensive adult looks back on and tries to capture his or her 'lockets of happiness'.

[1992]

Notes

I have tried out versions of this paper on a number of audiences and readers, all of whom have helped me clarify my ideas on the topic. I would especially like to acknowledge, among the many to whom I am deeply in debt, Marion Amies, Jean Barman, Roderick Barman, Rebecca Coulter, Jane Gaskell, Theresa Richardson, R.J.W. Selleck, Rita Watson, Richard T. White, Alan Wieder, J.D. Wilson, and a reader for this journal. I must also express my gratitude to those who have generously shared recollections of their childhoods with me. The words of some of them appear in unacknowledged quotations in this paper. Lily Kuhn typed its many drafts. The current phase of this and other aspects of the Canadian Childhood History Project have received generous support from the Social Sciences and Humanities Research Council of Canada and the University of British Columbia. This is a much revised version of a paper that appeared in the Canadian History of Education Association, *Bulletin* V (Feb. 1988), 5–29, in abstract form in *Resources in Education*, and available on microfiche and hard copy, ERIC, 1989.

The quotation by Gabrielle Roy appears in *The Fragile Lights of Earth: Articles and Memoires 1942–1970*, trans. Alan Brown (Toronto: McClelland and Stewart, 1982), 147.

1. David Lowenthal, 'The Timeless Past: Some Anglo-American Historical Preconceptions', in *Memory and American History*, ed. David Thelan (Bloomington and Indianapolis: Indiana University Press, 1990), 149.
2. I have explored psychological research in memory through Elizabeth Loftus, *Memory* (Reading, MA: Addison-Wesley, 1980); David C. Rubin, ed., *Autobiographical Memory* (Cambridge: Cambridge University Press, 1986); Ulric Neisser and Eugene Winograd, eds, *Remembering Reconsidered: Ecological and Traditional Approaches to the Study of Memory* (Cambridge: Cambridge University Press, 1988); and Edmund Blair Bolles, *Remembering and Forgetting: An Inquiry into the Nature of Memory* (New York: Walker, 1988). The field is currently an extremely active one and the literature appears to be growing exponentially.
3. Until recently, the most influential work was Paul Thompson, *The Voice of the Past: Oral History* (Oxford: Oxford University Press, 1978). The essays and notes in Thelan, *Memory and American History*, are an excellent introduction to current historical approaches to the topic.
4. As a metaphor from architecture, the term 'structure' perhaps suggests a greater degree of rigidity than I really mean to convey. It is, however, a useful metaphor in many ways or I would not employ it. There is a framework—another architectural metaphor—within

which youngsters live most of their lives. Families followed a pattern of days—Monday, washday; Tuesday, ironing day; and so on—that laid out what parents, and especially mothers, had to do. Children fitted into this pattern in a variety of ways. When they were small, their task was to keep under the eye but out of the way of their mothers. As they got older they may have begun to take a certain share in the chores. On washdays, older children kept younger siblings out of the way; in another part of the room, in another part of the house, out in the yard, and so on. When children started school, they entered another world, one that was tightly structured by the clock, and in which they played a central role, but had no part in determining its structure. See Neil Sutherland, 'The Triumph of "Formalism": Elementary Schooling in Vancouver from the 1920s to the 1960s', *BC Studies* 69–70 (Spring-Summer 1986): 175–210, published simultaneously in R.A.J. McDonald and Jean Barman, eds, *Vancouver Past: Essays in Social History* (Vancouver: University of British Columbia Press, 1986); Neil Sutherland, '"Everyone Seemed Happy in Those Days": The Culture of Childhood in Vancouver between the 1920's and the 1960's', *The History of Education Review* 15 (1986): 37–51; Neil Sutherland, '"We Always Had Things To Do": The Paid and Unpaid Work of Anglophone Children between the 1920s and 1960s', *Labour/Le Travail* 25 (Spring 1990): 105–41; Neil Sutherland, '"I Can't Recall When I Didn't Help": The Working Lives of the Children of Modern Pioneers', *Histoire sociale/Social History* 24 (Nov. 1991): 263–88; Neil Sutherland, 'Anglophone Children in Their Family Settings, 1918–1960', a working paper of the Canadian Childhood History Project, 1991.

5. Quoted in Thompson, *The Voice of the Past*, 94.
6. Richard T. White, 'Memory for Personal Events', *Human Learning* 1 (1982): 171–83.
7. Tom Harrisson, *Living through the Blitz* (London: Collins, 1976), 330.
8. Dorothy Sheridan, ed., *Among You Taking Notes . . . The Wartime Diary of Naomi Mitchison 1934–1945* (London: Gollancz, 1985), 12.
9. Katherine Nelson, 'The Ontogeny of Memory for Real Events', in *Remembering Reconsidered*, ed. U. Neisser and E. Winograd, 268.
10. See Paul Thompson, 'Introduction', in *Our Common Heritage: The Transformation of Europe*, ed. Paul Thompson with Natasha Burchart (London: Pluto Press, 1982), esp. 15–16; for the psychological perspective see Loftus, *Memory*, chaps. 6 and 7, and Bolles, *Remembering and Forgetting, passim*.
11. Leslie Thomas, *In My Wildest Dreams* (London: Arlington, 1984), 11.
12. Thomas, *In My Wildest Dreams*, 95; Leslie Thomas, *This Time Next Week* (London: Constable, 1984), 27–8.
13. Thomas, *This Time Next Week*, 49.
14. David Vincent, *Bread, Knowledge and Freedom: A Study of 19th-Century Working Class Autobiography* (London: Methuen, 1982), 6.
15. Craig R. Barclay, 'Schematization of Autobiographical Memory', in *Autobiographical Memory*, ed. D. Rubin, chap. 6.
16. See Isabelle Bertaux-Wiame's comments on this point in 'The Life History Approach to the Study of Internal Migration', in *Our Common Heritage*, ed. P. Thompson with N. Burchart, 195.
17. See, for example, William Kurelek, *Someone With Me: An Autobiography* (Toronto: McClelland and Stewart, 1980), and Charlotte Vale Allen, *Daddy's Girl: A Very Personal Memoir* (Toronto: McClelland and Stewart, 1980).
18. Barclay, 'Schematization'.
19. Thompson, *The Voice of the Past*, 113.
20. Robert Roberts, *The Classic Slum: Salford Life in the First Quarter of the Century* (Harmondsworth: Penguin Books, 1973), 25.

21. Lawrence W. Barsalou, 'The Content and Organization of Autobiographical Memories', in *Remembering Reconsidered*, 236.

22. Thompson, *The Voice of the Past*, 119.

23. See, for example, Sylvia Fraser, *My Father's House: A Memoir of Incest and Healing* (Toronto: Doubleday Canada, 1987), and Women's Research Centre, *Recollecting Our Lives: Women's Experience of Childhood Sexual Abuse* (Vancouver: Press Gang, 1989).

24. Thompson, *Voice of the Past*, 96; see also his 'Introduction' in *Our Common Heritage*, ed. P. Thompson with N. Burchart, 9–20.

25. Alessandro Portelli, 'The Peculiarities of Oral History', *History Workshop* 12 (Autumn 1981): 96–107.

26. I do not mean to suggest that this or any other historical task is an easy one to do. For a fine analysis of two of the major historiographic problems facing the historian of childhood see Jean Barman, 'Accounting for Gender and Class in Retrieving the History of Canadian Childhood, CHEA *Bulletin* V (May 1988): 527. Also of interest is Michael H. Frisch, 'The Memory of History', *Radical History Review* 25 (1981): 9–23, as are the many items cited in Barman's notes.

27. *Greek Historical Thought from Homer to the Age of Heraclius*, intro. and trans. by Arnold J. Toynbee (New York: Mentor, 1952), 40–1.

28. Barclay, 'Schematization'; Ulrich Neisser, 'What Is Ordinary Memory the Memory Of?' in *Remembering Reconsidered*, ed. D. Rubin, chap. 14.

29. Roger C. Schank and Robert P. Abelson, *Scripts, Plans, Goals and Understanding: An Inquiry into Human Knowledge Structures* (Hillsdale, NJ: Erlbaum, 1977), 17–19.

30. Katherine Nelson, Robyn Fivush, Judith Hudson, and Joan Lucariello, 'Scripts and the Development of Memory', in *Trends in Memory Development Research*, vol. 9, ed. Michelene T.H. Chi, *Contributions to Human Development* (Basel: Karger, 1983), 108–15. It may be that history based at least in part on the analysis of shared scripts may help bridge the gap between 'people's' history and 'social science' history. See Louise A. Tilly, 'People's History and Social Science History', *International Journal of Oral History* 6 (Feb. 1985): 5–18; 'Between Social Scientists: Responses to Louise A. Tilly', *ibid.*, 19–46.

31. William Kinsella, 'Nursie', in *Thrill of the Grass* (Toronto: Penguin, 1984), 80.

32. See Sutherland, 'The Triumph of "Formalism"'.

33. Glen Elder, 'History and the Life Course', in *Biography and Society: The Life History Approach in the Social Sciences*, ed. Daniel Bertaux (Beverly Hills: Sage Publications, 1981), 77–115.

34. R. Cole Harris, 'Regionalism and the Canadian Archipelago', in *Heartland and Hinterland*, ed. L.D. McCann (Scarborough: Prentice-Hall, 1982), 459–84.

35. Loftus, *Memory*, 134–7.

36. For a convenient introduction to this work see The University of British Columbia, School of Social Work, *Social Work Research at the University of British Columbia, 1947–1956* (Vancouver: The School, n.d.). See also Joy Parr, 'Case Records as Sources for Social History', *Archivaria* 1, 4 (1977): 122–36.

37. The methodology for the first large-scale project in which I took part and in which interviews comprised a major component is described in Eleanor Duckworth, 'Assessing the Canada Studies Foundation, Phase 1: An Approach to a National Evaluation', *Canadian Journal of Education* 2, 1 (1977): 27–34.

38. On the merits of unstructured interviews, see also Dagfinn Slettan, 'Farm Wives, Farm Hands and the Changing Rural Community in Trongelag, Norway', in *Our Common History*, ed. P. Thompson with N. Burchart, 153.

39. Loftus, *Memory*, 16–17; since psychological research suggests that 'high visualizers' recall

early events more readily and more accurately than 'low visualizers', I would like to include as many such people in my sample as possible. Unfortunately, there is no practical way of sorting out 'high visualizers' from the rest of the population! See Demetrios Karis, 'Individual Differences in Autobiographical Memory', paper presented to the American Psychological Association, New York, Sept. 1979.

40. Wallace Stegner, *Recapitulation* (New York: Doubleday, 1979), 26–7.
41. For a skeptical view of the notion that memory can be stimulated by either hypnosis or drugs, see Loftus, *Memory*, 54–62.
42. On this point see the eminent autobiographer Ved Mehta, *Vedi* (New York, Oxford, 1982), *i*.
43. *The Fragile Lights of Earth*, trans. A. Brown, 149.

Suggestions for Further Reading

Comacchio, Cynthia, '"The History of Us": Social Science, History, and the Relations of Family in Canada,' *Labour/Le Travail* 46 (Fall 2000): 167–220.

Curtis, Bruce, *The Politics of Population: State Formation, Statistics, and the Census of Canada, 1840–1875*. Toronto: University of Toronto Press, 2001.

Gleason, Mona, 'Embodied Negotiations: Childrens' Bodies and Historical Change in Canada, 1930 to 1960,' *Journal of Canadian Studies* 34, 1 (Spring 1999): 112–138.

Lewis, Norah L., ed., *"I Want to Join Your Club": Letters from Rural Children, 1900–1920*. Waterloo: Wilfrid Laurier University Press, 1996.

Sutherland, Neil and Jean Barman, 'Out of the Shadows: Retrieving the History of Urban Education and Urban Childhood in Canada,' in Ronal Goodenow and W.E. Marsden, eds, *The City and Education in Four Nations*. Cambridge: Cambridge University Press, 1992.

Thompson, Paul, *The Voice of the Past: Oral History*, 3rd edn. New York: Oxford University Press, 2000.

PART 2

Colonial Childhood, 1700–1880

European migration to the colony changed familial obligations and relations both in indigenous societies and the European settlements of New France and British North America. The articles in this section are snapshots of childhood and family life in the early and the late periods of the fur trade. The political economy, the minimal influence of the state and church, and the mixed origins of the European settlers inhibited the entrenchment of old customs and community bonds. Survival in the colony depended on the family more than it had in Old France because there were few employment opportunities and no other institutions to care for individuals during difficult times. Peter Moogk demonstrates that *Canadiens'* dependence on the family contradicted the predictions of contemporary French observers. Children's behaviour did not accord to the manners and customs of Old France, but the observers' assumptions that children were unhindered by familial bonds were overstated. French Canadian families did not abandon Old World practices, but adapted them to suit social and economic patterns of colonial life.

Mixed-race families upset French officials. France's official policy was based on the ideology of pure blood. Unions between fur traders and Aboriginal women seemed to threaten the purity of the European race. Still, the Company of New France encouraged these relationships because they facilitated the fur trade. The children of mixed-race unions possessed skills that gave them particular advantages in the fur-trade economy. Juliet Pollard explores the rhythm of Métis family life in the Pacific Northwest. There was a racial hierarchy in nineteenth-century British Columbian society, but 'mixed-blood' and 'half-breed' were not pejorative terms. British immigrants were distressed by the disruption of the racial order and over the course of the nineteenth century encouraged fur traders to abandon their indigenous wives and children to establish a 'white' society in British Columbia. Daniel Harmon's commitment to his family demonstrates that some fur traders did not agree with British prohibitions against mixed-race families.

Nancy Janovicek

Les Petits Sauvages: The Children of Eighteenth-Century New France

Peter N. Moogk

In French Canada today little children are sometimes called *les petits sauvages*. This characterization of Canadian children as little Indians or savages would have been accepted by the administrators of New France. In their correspondence French officials described the youth of the North American colony in the blackest terms. Young *Canadiens* were rarely mentioned and then only with adjectives that expressed censure and disapproval. The boys of the colony were reproached with being lawless and disobedient; the girls were portrayed as vain and lazy. Even Father Charlevoix, a Jesuit teacher who knew the *Canadiens* well and excused many of their faults, ventured his own criticism of their children. The healthful climate and fertility of New France ought to have retained the native Canadians, he wrote, 'but inconstancy, aversion to assiduous and regular work, and a spirit of independence have always caused a large number of young people to leave the colony'.[1]

In the late seventeenth century the governors and intendants of Canada blamed involvement in the fur trade, wandering in the woods, and association with the Amerindians for the insubordination of the young males. In 1685 Governor Brisay de Denonville wrote that 'the great liberty of long standing which the parents and Governors have given to the youth, permitting them to dally in the woods under the pretext of hunting or trading . . . has reached such an excess that from the time children are able to carry a gun, fathers are not able to restrain them and dare not anger them'.[2]

In the eighteenth century, when the fur trade involved only a small minority of male *Canadiens*, French observers shifted the blame for the rebelliousness of the colony's youth to the Canadian home. Charlevoix mentioned the *dissipation* in which young colonials were brought up. In 1707 Intendant Jacques Raudot was more specific: 'the residents of this country have never had a proper education because of the over-indulgence (*la foiblesse*) resulting from a foolish tenderness shown to them by their mothers and fathers during their infancy. In this they imitate the Amerindians. It prevents them from disciplining the children and forming their character'. According to the Intendant, the children of the colony developed 'a hard and ferocious character' and they showed no respect for their parents 'as well as toward their superiors and parish priests'.[3] Another writer claimed that the children would abandon their mothers and fathers whenever it suited them.[4] Even Father Charlevoix chided the young *Canadiens* for 'the small amount of kindness many show to their parents who, for their part, have an ungoverned fondness for their children'.

[. . .]

As we trace the sequence of life in Canada before the end of French rule in 1760, we shall see that child-rearing was not so permissive nor were the children so unruly as these writers claimed. Conditions in early Canada encouraged self-reliance and assertiveness while reducing the social distance between ranks. French observers exaggerated, rather than falsified, the facts. Their conception of a good and orderly society required the clear subordination of children to their parents, even after the child had reached adulthood. By our standards, the life of the young might even appear hard and circumscribed. The following narrative explores the reality that underlay the characterization of the children of eighteenth-century New France as *les petits sauvages.*

Defining Childhood

The French word *enfant* refers more to a social relationship than to a stage of life. The 1728 edition of Antoine Furetière's *Dictionnaire Universel* defined *enfant* as 'a son or daughter who owes his or her birth to someone, in relationship to a father or mother'. Thus, an adult might properly be described as the *enfant* of a certain person, although the terms *fils de* (son of) or *fille de* (daughter of) were preferred. Secondarily, according to Furetière, '*Enfant* is used for a boy or girl when they were under 12 or 15 years of age, without reference to the father and the mother'. A 1787 edition of the French Academy's dictionary repeated Furetière's primary definition. In the secondary sense, however, it stated that '*Enfant* is still used for a very young boy or girl, and until the age of ten or twelve years'. These definitions were an extension of the older legal definition of *enfance* as a stage ending at the age of seven. The older explanation was retained by Claude-Joseph de Ferrière in his *Dictionnaire de Droit et de Pratique*, first published in 1734. De Ferrière used *impuberes* (pre-pubescents) for both infants and sexually immature children above the age of seven. Canonical and Roman law placed the age of puberty at twelve for girls and fourteen for boys. *Impuberes* could be guilty of, but not physically punished for, a crime. Since both of the literary dictionaries placed the end of *enfance* or early childhood at the age of twelve or, possibly, fifteen, that word seems to have acquired a more extensive, secular meaning in the eighteenth century.

Despite the tendency to identify *enfance* with the period of life before puberty, sexual maturity rarely brought an end to the dependence of childhood. In theory, a person who had reached puberty could be married and marriage was an attribute of grownups. Contemporary summaries of population censuses in the French regime separated married or widowed persons from another group made up of children and unmarried persons. Marriage emancipated one from the legal disabilities of being a minor, yet the social and legal benefits of matrimony did not encourage early marriages in eighteenth-century New France. The demographer Jacques Henripin has noted that 'for the marriages celebrated in Canada during the period 1700–30, the mean age was 22.4 for spinsters and 26.9 for bachelors'.[5] Legal emancipation was automatic at the age of majority and, under the civil laws of the colony, majority was attained at the age of twenty-five. This was the standard age throughout most of France.

It seems clear that a person was still not an adult at puberty. It was also apparent that, socially, one could assume adult responsibilities before the legal age of majority, twenty-five. Between these two poles, where did the transformation from child to adult occur? The fifteenth or sixteenth year of life seems to have been a critical point. After 1688 population censuses classified single males and females as being under fifteen or as being fifteen and older. By the late seventeenth century New France was a society dominated by youth: just over 70 per cent of the colonists were under the age of thirty-one.[. . .]In Acadia in 1698 just over half of the population of 789 persons was under the age of sixteen. In New France boys were enrolled in the militia at sixteen and, on average, craft apprentices were indentured between the ages of sixteen and seventeen. The apprentices were expected to be masters of their trade within three years.[6] Preparation for manhood began in earnest at the age of fifteen or sixteen. Even at this age, farm children would be already well-versed in agriculture and the care of livestock. Yet, the link with childhood was not severed.

The fact that, after the age of fifteen, one could still be considered a child is evident from censuses that divided the population into the married, the widowed, and 'enfants'. The percentage of 'children' always exceeded the 42 per cent to 44 per cent who were under the age of fifteen. In peninsular Acadia in 1714 the 'enfants' accounted for 66.5 per cent of the population. In 1733 they were 64 per cent of the people on the St John River. In the St Lawrence settlement 'boys' and 'girls' were 68.5 per cent of the population in 1714 and 64.5 per cent in 1737. In the last census of this region before the British conquest, the enumeration of 1754, the category of 'children of all ages and servants' comprised 70 per cent of the population of 55,009. It therefore appears that the use of 'enfant' was not confined by the contemporary definitions of enfance; people above the age of fifteen and as old as twenty could be classified as children. The word adolescent, though known to the educated, was not used. It is likely that, for all practical purposes and the civil law notwithstanding, one became an adult at around twenty. Most craft apprentices would be ready to earn their living at nineteen or twenty, and orphans, paupers, and foundlings were indentured to foster parents until their eighteenth or twentieth year. In practice, then, the people of New France recognized a 'functional' adulthood that was attained by the age of twenty.

The Patriarchal Family

Birth brought the young person into a network of legally reinforced family relationships. In rural New France the nuclear family was strengthened by the dispersal of private dwellings and the confined living conditions of each family. A farmhouse was customarily a one-storey structure measuring, in English feet, about twenty-three by nineteen. Inside there was a common area for cooking and eating, and this also served as a living room. Bedrooms were separated from this area by wooden partitions, and an overflow of children would sleep in the attic. The young, however, had the advantage of numbers. Adult *Canadiens*, with an average of six living children per family and plenty of work to do, would be hard pressed to give their progeny the strict and continuous supervision recommended by French observers.

For the legislators and magistrates of New France, the patriarchal family was the ideal social unit. The *Coutume de Paris* subjected the wife and children to the fatherly authority or *puissance paternelle* of the adult male. He was the overlord or *seigneur* of the couple's joint property and his consent was required for all property transactions and legal acts by his dependents. Remember that an unmarried child was legally dependent until the age of twenty-five. The corollary of subordination was that the law protected the material interests of the wife from an imprudent or unjust husband and father. Children were equal as heirs and the immovable properties that they were to inherit from a dead parent could not be disposed of by the surviving spouse. Disinheritance out of pure malice was also frowned upon. At the age of seventeen, Marie-Jeanne Renaud Desmeloizes was betrothed by her grandfather and guardian to a man that she did not wish to marry. When she resisted the marriage, her infuriated grandfather gave a large portion of her estate to the intended groom. In 1716 Marie-Jeanne's brother-in-law protested this action and the Crown Attorney of Quebec's lower court agreed that she had been unjustly disinherited.[7] These safeguards protected only the rights of legitimate children; illegitimate children had no claim on the estate of their natural parents.

After the British conquest of New France in 1760, the *Canadiens* in what became the Province of Quebec opposed changes in the civil laws inherited from the French regime. Those laws maintained French Canada's identity and they perpetuated the *Canadiens'* distinctive social values. When the civil usages of the Province of Quebec were modernized and codified in 1866, they retained that compassion for the weak and the submission demanded from inferiors which characterized institutions in New France. On the subject of children, the articles of the Civil Code of Quebec stated:

166.   Children are bound to maintain their father, mother and other ascendants [e.g., grandparents] who are in want . . .

242.   A child, whatever may be his age, owes honor and respect to his father and mother.

243.   He remains subject to their authority until his majority or his emancipation, but the father alone exercises this authority during marriage, . . .

244.   An unemancipated minor cannot leave his father's house without his permission.

245.   The father and, in his default, the mother of an unemancipated minor have over him a right of reasonable and moderate correction, which may be delegated to . . . those to whom his education has been entrusted.

In the terms of the Civil Code, 'reasonable and moderate correction' meant physical punishment without injury or danger to life. Society in New France was tolerant of the male who occasionally did beat his wife and children. Since the courts were reluctant to intervene in family disputes, the violence used by a man against his dependents had to be extreme and notorious before it received judicial attention. Without grievous injury or death, domestic violence was a civil matter that required a private complaint. A wife could ask for legal separation from a brutal, insane, or profligate husband; he might even be deprived of his paternal authority by interdiction. An abused child, however, could not make a legal complaint by himself. Like Marie-Jeanne Renaud Desmeloizes, he needed the assistance of a grownup kinsman.

The continuing subordination of an unmarried child to his parents, even after the attainment of majority, is evident from legal documents called *summations respectueuses* or respectful requisitions. Because marriage entitled one to the aid and support of in-laws, parents had the right to approve the choice of their child's marriage partner. During the child's minority this was an absolute right; after the age of twenty-five for women and thirty for men, it was a social, but not a legal, right. Parental disapproval might entail the withholding of a dowry or a contribution to the newlyweds' estate. It was also believed that a parent could disinherit a child of any age who married against his or her elders' wishes. To avert this possibility, adults who had been refused parental approval registered three respectful requisitions begging their father and mother for their consent. Once this was done, the future couple could obtain the opinion of a magistrate or of other relatives that there was no lawful impediment to the marriage and then proceed with the wedding. In the 1730s, when twenty-one-year-old Jean-Claude Louet *fils* vowed to marry an English shoemaker's daughter, whom he had made pregnant, his father, who was a royal notary, opposed the match. 'Could it be possible,' asked Jean-Claude in his second respectful summons, 'that the great tenderness that you formerly showed to your child might be changed into perpetual disgrace? I beg you most humbly, my dear father, to once again look upon me as your own child'.[8]

Infancy

In Antoine Furetière's words, *enfance* was 'the first and most tender age of man, until he has attained the use of reason'. Life began in the mother's bed at home. The birth was assisted by a *sage femme* whose knowledge of midwifery was acquired by experience. In the first months of life, infants were tightly bound in swaddling clothes which, it was believed, would help to straighten the legs and back of the newborn child. A swaddled baby also tended to be more tranquil than an unbound infant. There was no awareness of the need for hygiene. For example, in the absence of mother's milk or a wet nurse, infants were given raw cow's milk diluted with river or well water. As a result of this and other unsanitary measures, many children died in infancy. Jacques Henripin's demographic studies of the early eighteenth century show that one child in four died in the first year of life. 'We may also assume—on the basis of less reliable information—', wrote Henripin, 'that almost 45 per cent died before the age of ten years, and 50 per cent before the age of twenty'.[9] This mortality rate, which was close to that in France, was countered by a phenomenal birth rate. After the birth of the first child and until the age of thirty-five, a married *Canadienne* bore one child every two years. Such fecundity amazed European visitors, who noted the prodigies of reproductive valour. Jacques Henripin's figures are less astounding. When both partners survived to the age of fifty, they would have, on average, 5.65 living children.

In early French Canada chronological age was a vague thing that became less certain as a person grew older. In documents it is common to find adolescents described as being of so many years of age '*ou environ*' (or thereabout), or as being of one age or another. An exact figure in years and months is exceptional. The anniversary of the birthdate does not seem to have been remembered or celebrated. A person's *fête* was the feast day of that individual's patron saint, and the saint's day did not have to be related to the person's date of birth.

Birthday or no birthday, the *Canadiens* favoured certain saints in the choice of names. The child's namesake was usually his or her patron saint. The favourites in New France were the Virgin Mary, Mary Magdelene, Joan of Arc (*Jeanne*), and the male saints Joseph, John, Peter, and Francis (*François*). Many parents shrewdly laid claim to the favour of two saints by giving their children such 'double-barrelled' names as *Joseph-Marie* or *Marie-Anne*. *Marie*, alone or in combination, was the most popular name in Canada.

Christian names are given at baptism and, in New France, baptism was required within three or four days of birth. The clergy preferred to administer this sacrament themselves and they were annoyed by some *Canadiens* who used the distance and difficulty of travel in winter to justify lay baptism at home. The approved procedure was to have the parents present the newborn infant to the nearest priest for baptism. The parents were accompanied by the child's godfather and godmother who gave surety for the young person's religious education. The spiritual relationship between a godparent and child was almost as binding as blood kinship. A godparent would be expected to favour the child in later life with influence or assistance. In the eighteenth century godparents were customarily drawn from the parents' own social and occupational group.

[...]

In the first year or two of life, the infant slept in a wooden cradle. The cradles of early French Canada were open pine troughs on rockers. They were also fitted with turned birchwood posts that could be grasped to rock the child. At night a cord could be attached to one of these posts to enable the mother to rock a fretful infant without leaving her bed. The incidence of births suggests that children were weaned at around fourteen months of age. The infant who had learned to use its hands was given a rattle to play with. The rattles that appear in inventories of the French regime were made of wood, bone, and silver. Surviving examples in France and Canada consist of a short staff girdled with bells, with either a ring or teething bar at one end.

Guardianship and Foster Parentage

Death was familiar to the people of New France. The population was ravaged by smallpox epidemics, by war, and, in the seaports, by shipborne infections. Nearly half of the adolescents in the colony had lost one parent. When the father died, there was a well-established procedure to ensure continuity in the maintenance and upbringing of the minor children. A council of seven or more relatives and friends was convened to determine the future of the orphans. Contributions for their upkeep might be apportioned among the kin who elected a tutor and 'subrogate tutor' to record and then manage each child's inheritance as well as oversee the child's upbringing. The widow was eligible to be one of the tutors, but she was not considered to be competent enough to be her children's sole guardian. She would be given the assistance of an adult male, usually an uncle of the children and sometimes her own grownup son. When she remarried, which was very likely, her role as tutor passed to her new husband.

Without kin in the colony, which would be the case with poor immigrants, food and shelter were obtained for orphaned and destitute children on hard terms. A single mother had no bargaining power. In 1736 an abandoned wife at Quebec described herself as 'incapable of feeding and maintaining' her eight-year-old son. She was forced to bind him to a merchant as 'a domestic servant until . . . the full age of twenty years'. A Louisbourg widow likewise indentured her son to someone who could provide his upkeep, 'not being in a situation to do it (herself) without help'.[10] Children under the age of twelve were disdained as apprentices by craftsmen; they were only acceptable as servants. Thus the children of the poor and other young unfortunates without family support were customarily hired out to work without pay until the age of eighteen or even twenty-one. These paupers and orphans were typically indentured at five or six years of age and they were destined for a dozen or more years of servitude for the sake of food, clothing, and shelter.[11] Mature and able-bodied *Canadiens* scorned the servant's life and it appears that indentured children provided nearly two-thirds of the household servants in New France. This explains why the 1754 census treated 'children of all ages and servants' as one category; most of the servants were children!

Far from regretting this private system for settling young paupers and orphans, the colonial administration enforced children's indentures and copied them in dealing with foundlings and bastard children. Illegitimate births were an increasing problem in eighteenth-century New France and the royal officials were slow to react. Pregnancies out of wedlock were indicative of the breakdown of communal social restraints in the rural parishes where, according to Intendant Michel Bégon, 'this disorder is becoming extremely common'.[12] From 1701 to 1760 the church registers in what is now the Province of Quebec recorded the baptism of 1,112 illegitimate children. At the beginning of this period bastards accounted for two out of every thousand births; in the last decades of the French regime they represented 12.2 out of every thousand.[13] Because the rate fell after the conquest, wartime conditions and the presence of thousands of French regular troops must have contributed to the growing number of illegitimate births in the 1740s and 1750s. These figures are incomplete because, in spite of laws requiring the disclosure of illicit pregnancies, illegitimate children born to *Canadiennes* were frequently given to the Amerindians in preference to letting the infants die of exposure. Infanticide was a capital crime. In the villages of the Christian Amerindians, Louis Franquet observed numerous illegitimate children of the French colonists as well as white children abducted from the English colonies. The youngsters were adopted by the native peoples and they fully accepted the aborigines' way of life.

For most of the French regime the settlement of foundlings depended on private sponsors and religious institutions. Foster parents expected some payment for accepting an infant who was not yet capable of earning his keep and there was no regular source of funds for these payments. In the late seventeenth century the short-lived Poor Boards of Quebec and Montreal placed foundlings with families or delivered the children to the Quebec *Hôpital-Général* and the Montreal hospice of the Charon Brethren. Craft apprenticeship was not used, as it was in the English colonies, for the settlement of paupers; very few foster parents promised to teach the child a trade or skill.

In France royal court officials were made responsible for the care of foundlings by an edict in November, 1706. The first Canadian *enfant du Roi*, as the foundlings were called, was placed at Montreal in 1709. The local King's Attorney paid the receiving couple eighty *livres* and they promised to raise the boy until the age of eighteen. When the putative father of a bastard could be found, he was charged with the full cost of the child's upbringing. The Crown was still reluctant to bear all of the expenses of settlement. An Intendant's ordinance issued in February, 1722, authorized payments from the revenues of the tax farm and other sources to wet nurses caring for the *enfants du Roi*. The same ordinance set severe penalties for concealed pregnancies and for giving illegitimate children to the Amerindians. An ordinance of June, 1736, complained about the cost of maintaining the growing number of foundlings; it therefore reduced the amounts paid to wet nurses and called upon the King's Attorneys 'to indenture the said children as soon as they are four years old, and sooner if possible'.[14]

In 1748 Intendant Gilles Hocquart sanctioned an increase in the forty-five *livres* 'ordinarily agreed to and paid' to foster parents in order to dispose of the foundlings still being supported by the Crown. In the Montreal region there were twenty *enfants du Roi* above the age of three for whom no homes had been found.[15] At Quebec the King's Attorney paid as much as 240 *livres* to the foster parent of an abandoned boy.[16]

The evident reluctance of the *Canadiens* to accept the *enfants du Roi* when they would receive young paupers or orphans as unpaid servants might be explained by two things. The first is the extreme youth of the foundlings. They were unable to perform profitable labour for a few more years. Moreover, as sponsors, the royal officials were in a stronger position than any widowed or single parent to compel the foster parents to live up to their obligations. The King's Attorneys were able to obtain favourable terms for their wards. Witness this foundling's contract concluded in the house of the King's Attorney at Quebec in November, 1729:

Before the Royal Notaries in the Prévôté of Quebec here resident and undersigned were present Joseph Demers, habitant of Saint-Nicolas, Côte de Lauzon, who has acknowledged and stated that, with the approval and consent of Monseigneur the King's Attorney, he has taken by contract a child born of an unknown father, named Jean-Baptiste and aged five years, two months or thereabout. The boy is to serve him in all that will be commanded of him, provided it be licit and decent and proportionate to his strength as he grows older ..., until the full age of eighteen years. The said Demers binds himself to raise him (Jean-Baptiste) in the Catholic, Apostolic and Roman religion, to feed and maintain him, and to take care of him as one of his own children. At the end of the said term he will give the boy four shirts of Meslis cloth, a hooded coat, vest, and breeches of Mazamet cloth, a pair of Saint-Maixent stockings, a pair of French shoes, and a hat—all new and in addition to the other clothes that Jean-Baptiste will have received by then. Moreover, he will give the boy (at the end of service) twenty-five *livres* in the currency of this land, for thus has been agreed . . . [17]

The King's Attorneys were empowered in 1748 to bind the foundlings out until the age of eighteen or twenty; Jean-Baptiste's term was the shorter of the two. The gift outfit of new clothing was not unusual; the bonus payment was, however, exceptional. Both served to encourage the boy to serve out his full term and not to run away.

Tender Youth

Tendre jeunesse was an expression used to describe that stage of life that took a young person from the end of infancy to the beginning of puberty. Though clothing did not signal the transformation from child to adult, it did mark the passage from infancy to youth. Swaddling was characteristic of the first months of life; afterward the infant was wrapped naked in a cloth. Once the child was able to crawl or walk, it was dressed in a shift or long shirt. The shift may have been longer for girls, but both sexes wore the same costume. We see the infant's attire in a painting of the Guardian Angel executed in about 1707 and now in the Quebec hospital. The

Votive painting of Madame Riverin and her four children. Courtesy Ste-Anne de Beaupré Shrine.

little girl sheltered by the angel wears a lined cap tied under the chin, and a long, loose gown with a sash at the waist.

Seven had been the conventional age for the end of infancy. In New France the costume of infancy was abandoned at the age of four or earlier. This is apparent from the votive painting of Angélique Gaulthier, Madame Riverin, and her four children. She was the wife of a French-born magistrate, landowner, and company director. This work was painted in 1703 to testify to their survival from a shipwreck through the intercession of St Anne, to whom the Riverins had addressed their prayers. At the time the children were aged three, four, five, and six. They were all infants and yet they are all dressed as miniature adults. Five-year-old Denis-François wears a flared *justaucorps* with a ruff, just like a man. The girls' clothing copies that of their mother: a high headdress of lace and ribbons *à la Fontanges*, a pearl necklace, and a velvet or silk gown trimmed with lace. Soon after his arrival in the colony, Bishop Saint-Vallier had deplored the fact that in New France 'at an early age . . . little girls, even those of lowly birth, are dressed and adorned like dolls and appear with bare shoulders and necks'.[18] The only distinction between little Marie-Clémence and Marie-Madeleine Riverin and their mother and older sister is that the youngest girls have round collars rather than a low-cut front. It would not be surprising if there were also ribbons or leading strings attached to the back of the three-year-old's dress. Leading strings, familiarly called *tatas*, were used to assist a toddler who was still learning how to walk. The Riverin portrait was ostensibly a religious painting; it was also an opportunity for a family of the colony's ruling class to parade its wealth and rank. The clothing portrayed is not representative of the everyday attire of lower-class colonists.

It has been suggested that because West Europeans of the seventeenth and early eighteenth centuries dressed their children as miniature adults, they did not have a conception of childhood and adolescence as stages of life that were separate from adulthood. Ross W. Beales has shown that this is a false assumption, when applied to colonial New England.[19] In New France, though young and old shared many activities, there was that period of 'tender youth' between the ages of four and twelve and an adolescence in which the young gradually assumed the duties and prerogatives of adulthood. The characteristics of *tendre jeunesse* were expressed in the adjectives applied to children of this age: small, weak, innocent, foolish, and unreasonable. French writers, such as Bossuet and Molière, used the child as a metaphor for someone who believed in fantasies, prattled about trivial things, or lived only for the present.

The journals kept by Marie-Elisabeth Rocbert, Madame Bégon, from 1748 to 1750 are a rare, perhaps unique, chronicle of childhood in early French Canada. Her world was that of the privileged elite. Widow Bégon raised her late daughter's two children at Montreal. She left an affectionate and indulgent portrait of her granddaughter, Marie-Catherine-Elisabeth, in words. Marie-Catherine was nine in 1748. The girl is called *notre chère petite, chère innocente*, and *chère mignonne*. The grandmother delighted in the girl's childish traits. Like most *Canadiennes*, Marie-Catherine loved to have her hair curled and to be dressed up for formal occasions. She would hop for joy when invited out to a grownups' supper or when she was told that the governor of the colony would be visiting them. Marie-Catherine recited fables and verses for the governor and, at the dinner table, her chirpy conversation delighted the adults. According to Madame Bégon, Marie-Catherine 'is devoted to mischievousness; she believes in phantoms, but never in tranquility'.[20] Marie-Catherine played April Fool's jokes and could be short-tempered and disobedient. Her grandmother did not punish her and accepted the promise of future good conduct. Madame Bégon frequently referred to the girl's 'mutinous' temper. She described this humour as a family trait and looked upon it as unalterable.

While Madame Bégon took pleasure in Marie-Catherine's childish behaviour, she was also proud of her granddaughter's precocity. Although the girl disliked confession, she was very solemn about religious matters. The two recited prayers and went to Mass together. When Marie-Catherine bowed her head in prayer at mealtime, the governor teasingly called her 'madame l'abbesse'. Most Canadians simply crossed themselves before eating. Marie-Catherine was truly Canadian in not letting her religious scruples extend into submission to the moral dictates of the clergy. When a priest said that he would permit her to read *Don Quixote*, the nine-year-old replied, 'I need only the permission of *maman* (grandmother) who, I believe, is capable of judging if I might read a book or not'.[21] Madame Bégon was inwardly pleased by her granddaughter's bold assertions and by the girl's ability to uphold her own views in discussions with adults. On the anniversary of Monsieur Bégon's death, she proudly wrote that Marie-Catherine had consoled her 'like a twenty-year-old girl'.

The world of play is inseparable from childhood. Marie-Catherine once received a doll, played with other little girls, and amused herself in the garden. Her grandmother did not mention other toys nor did she describe the games that must have been a part of Marie-Catherine's life. Documents surviving from the French regime do not provide much information on the amusements of youth. The notarized estate inventories that facilitate the reconstruction of material life in New France were made for adults with heirs. Toys, however, belonged to children and, because they were often homemade, they were of little value. On those rare occasions when the things of infancy and childhood appear in the inventories, the description is a cursory phrase such as 'four new napkins for children'. Robert-Lionel Séguin, a folklorist who has mined the notarial records of the Montreal region, found only a dozen references to babies' rattles, toy carts, dolls and their clothing, marbles, sleighs, and skates.[22] The skates and sleighs could have belonged to grownups. The estate inventories made at Louisbourg mention furniture especially made for the young.

The most extensive collection of children's toys from the French regime is to be found in the archaeological finds from the site of the fortified port of Louisbourg on Cape Breton Island. The playthings confirm the existence of childhood as a recognized stage in life while revealing where the world of children overlapped with adult life. Things that unquestionably belong to the young are the stone and clay marbles, a jack, and a miniature plate and bowl suitable for a girl. For boys there is a wooden sailboat that was found in a pond, a lead anchor for another toy boat, a small bronze cannon, and a six-inch wooden sword. This rough-hewn weapon is probably not the 'little child's sword' mentioned in a merchant's inventory of 1756.[23] Other Louisbourg toys were homemade: there were round counters chipped from

Assorted playthings used at Louisbourg (by row from top to bottom): 1. whistles; 2. a jack and marbles; 3. miniature crockery; 4. whizzers; 5. circular counters; 6. game tally sticks; 7. a chequer piece, a pawn, dice, and rolling ball; 8. jew's harps and toy flute. Courtesy Fortress Louisbourg National Historic Park.

pottery fragments and whizzers fashioned from broken roof slates or salvaged lead. A looped string would be passed through the two holes in the centre of the circular whizzer and, by alternating the tension on the string, a child could make the disk spin and produce a whirring sound with its rough or serrated edge.

As parents well know, children enjoy making noise. The collection from Louisbourg contains bone and metal whistles, a small flute, and several jew's harps. Were the modern reader able to visit eighteenth-century New France, he might also see children pounding drums and playing with tops and cup-and-ball—a mania for all ages in seventeenth-century France. The absence of these things among archaeological finds does not mean that they never existed; paper, leather, and wood are simply more perishable than bone, glass, pottery, and metal.

Jacques Stella's illustrated book, *Les jeux et plaisirs de l'enfance* (Paris, 1657), provides the context for the toys of New France. This book shows children rolling dice for money, using toy swords in duels and mock wars, firing cannons improvised from hollow keys, and rolling marbles at holes in a game called *fossette*. Marbles were also thrown at pyramids or 'castles' of an opponent's marbles in an attempt to knock them down. Widespread children's games that would leave no material evidence of their existence were blind man's buff, king of the castle, and 'hot cockles', in which a child with face hidden and a bared hand behind tried to guess who had slapped his palm.

It was the games of the naughtiest of the *petits sauvages* that received the attention of legislators in New France. At Quebec children bowled over water barrels and threw stones from the battery overlooking Sault-au-Matelot in the Lower Town.[24] In 1741 and 1753, with very little evidence of success, a pompous French magistrate in Montreal called Guiton de Monrepos tried to outlaw the throwing of snowballs in the town's streets.[25] In winter grownups and the young slid down the streets of Quebec on skates, sleighs, or whatever came to hand. Intendant François Bigot described the sliders as a menace to passers-by because of 'the speed with which they fall upon them, not giving them the time to move aside to avoid the sliders'. As in the case of stone-throwers, the fine against violators was ten *livres*, and Bigot threatened to hold the delinquent children in prison until their parents had paid the fine.[26]

The recognition of childhood as a distinct phase of life did not mean that childhood was divorced from adult life; children, without ceasing to be juveniles, probably had more in common with their elders than children today. In *Centuries of Childhood* (1962), Philippe Ariès observed that among the lower classes of France, children and adults continued to dress alike and to find diversion in the same pastimes during the eighteenth century. In New France the blending of age groups was evident on the icy streets of Quebec and from the fact that the jew's harps, bowling ball, ivory dice, and gaming counters found at Louisbourg could have been used by people of all ages. Gambling was a passion among the colonists which was countenanced among the young. Even the toy sailing boat, the miniature crockery, the cannon, and the sword uncovered at Louisbourg reflected the activities of grownups in that fortified seaport. In a way, these toys prepared children for adult life.

At home, and especially on the farms, children were introduced to productive labour before adolescence. Beyond the age of infancy, youngsters became valued contributors to the family's welfare. In the countryside the littlest boys and girls helped by scaring birds away from the ripening crops and by herding cows. They could assist their mother by amusing the baby and, with a firm grip on the leading strings, taking toddlers for a walk. Service indentures reveal that children in New France dug in the vegetable gardens, sifted flour, helped in sowing seeds, and gathered firewood. Adolescents were strong enough to cut cordwood and to thresh and winnow grain. At harvest-time every member of the family was expected to lend a hand: the boys at mowing and cutting and the girls at raking hay and stooking wheat. With the exception of Louisbourg and Quebec, there was no sharp division between rural and urban life. Within their palisades or walls, most towns were open villages with large gardens and paddocks separating the houses. There were stables to be cleaned, livestock and gardens to be tended. Whether in town or in country, the young of families without servants were up at dawn to bring in firewood and to light the hearth fire. During the day, they would be employed in scraping dirty boots, emptying chamber pots into the outside privy, and sweeping floors. Running errands and fetching water from the river for cooking and washing were commonplace duties of the young. At Quebec in 1749 the Swedish-speaking botanist Peter Kalm watched boys take barrel-laden carts drawn by dogs down to the river to fill the water barrel. The young ladies of Quebec, he noted, left the household work to their mothers. By contrast, the girls of Montreal—a town more influenced by the North American frontier-were 'not quite so flighty, and more industrious': working in the kitchen with the servants, doing needlework, and going to the market to buy food.[27] Kalm's picture of feminine activities was likely drawn from observations in the homes of the educated and prosperous colonists; the life of most young *Canadiennes* would have been less genteel.

Adolescence and Formal Education

The lack of education among Canadian children that was noted by French writers needs to be precisely defined. For these observers, education meant training in self-discipline as well as formal schooling. On the first point there was unanimity: young *Canadiens* were undisciplined and their parents were to blame. 'You will be surprised', wrote Antoine-Denis Raudot in 1709, 'to learn that fathers keep their children busy only when they are able to do so (by persuasion), . . . they love their children too much to compel them to do something against their will'.[28] On the matter of schooling, we must distinguish between religious instruction, occupational training, and academic education. In each area there was a great variation in the level of instruction.

Father Charlevoix, who was a trustworthy witness, praised the Canadians for their knowledge of the Christian faith. 'What, above all, ought to make our colonials respected is their great capacity for piety and devotion, and there is no deficiency in their religious education'.[29] Instruction in catechism was one form of institutional education that was provided to all children in the colony. Catechism prepared the young for the first communion, which itself was a major step toward adulthood. A catechumen who had been examined and confirmed became, theo-retically, a full member of the church. As intended, catechism conveyed the creed and moral standards of the Roman Catholic Church. In the absence of a compet-ing ideology, the church defined community standards of behaviour. These stan-dards were often violated, but they were not supplanted.

In his *Catéchisme du Diocèse de Québec* (1702), Bishop Saint-Vallier did not spec-ify the age at which one should receive formal religious instruction. There is sec-ondary evidence that children attended catechism classes soon after puberty. The evidence comes from servants' and apprentices' indentures made in the 1730s and after. For children under the age of sixteen, a clause was inserted that gave the ward leave to attend catechism until he had made his first communion. Farm families hes-itated to surrender their children for prolonged instruction and the religious train-ing of rural children was, perforce, cursory. In the 1720s one country parish scheduled instruction for one Sunday of each month.[30] During Bishop Dosquet's episcopate (1729–1739), such classes were to be held, at the very least, in the three weeks preceding confirmation ceremonies and the children's first communion.[31] Bishop Saint-Vallier foresaw the limitations of time available and of a child's com-prehension, because his large catechism contains an abridged *Petit Catéchisme* of twenty-five pages for 'very young children or coarse persons (*personnes grossières*)'.

Catechism classes involved the memorization of set answers and prayers; they intro-duced the child to abstract ideas without demanding independent inquiry. Here are a few of the preliminary questions and responses from Saint-Vallier's large catechism:

What is Catechism?
It is simple instruction at which one learns Christian truths, how to serve God, and to save oneself . . . .

Are all sorts of persons obliged to attend Catechism?
Yes, if they are ignorant of things concerning their salvation, as are ordinarily children, craftsmen, male and female servants.

Who must see that children and servants attend Catechism?
Fathers and Mothers, Masters and Mistresses will answer for it before God, unless they instruct them (these dependents) themselves at home . . . .

How many parts are there to this Catechism?
There are three parts.

What are they?
Sacred History (the Bible story), the Christian Doctrine, the explanation of the holy days, of the sacred rituals and ceremonies of the church.

The idea that children should also receive free education in reading, writing, arithmetic and, perhaps, Latin did have currency in New France. The reality fell short of the ideal. Writers blamed the colonists for their lack of an elementary and academic education. As early as 1664 Pierre Boucher claimed that the children of the colony were 'a bit dissolute, that is to say, it is difficult to captivate them with studies'.[32] Over fifty years later Charlevoix noted that 'many people are persuaded that they (the *Canadiens*) are unsuited for the sciences that require great application and methodical study. I am unable to say if this prejudice is well founded but, we have not yet seen a Canadian who has attempted to disprove it. It is due, perhaps, to the carelessness (*la dissipation*) of their upbringing.[33] The truth is that, apart from catechism, poor boys without a religious vocation had little chance of obtaining a free elementary or secondary education in New France.

Boys and girls were educated separately and there was a shortage of schoolmasters for the boys. The French Crown upheld the prerogatives of the Roman Catholic Church as the principal educator: an Intendant's ordinance in 1727 decreed that lay schoolteachers would have to be licensed by the Bishop of Quebec. In the early eighteenth century the Charon Brethren of Montreal sponsored teachers of proven virtue in the countryside. Virtue was not a sufficient qualification because, in 1730, the Crown ended its subsidy of the brothers' schools after receiving reports of their financial mismanagement and ineffectiveness.

The main burden of providing boys with a free elementary education fell on the overworked parish and missionary priests of the colony. The clergy were not only responsible for their customary ecclesiastical duties, but they also kept parish records and acted as notaries and scribes. In 1740 there were seventy-six diocesan priests as well as sixty-nine Franciscans and Sulpicians capable of acting as diocesan priests for a scattered population of 43,400 in the St Lawrence Valley. Some of the resident clerics were able to establish *petites écoles* in which they instructed boys in catechism and other subjects. At St Joachim, Peter Kalm found 'two priests, and a number of young boys, whom they instruct in reading, writing and Latin. Most of these boys are designed (destined) for the priesthood'.[34] It is not surprising that rural illiteracy, always widespread, increased in the eighteenth century. Even in the towns, which were well-endowed with schools, illiteracy was common. Of 506 Montreal householders surveyed in 1741, nearly 60 per cent declared that they did not know how to write their names.[35]

Sexual segregation in the schools of New France benefited lower-class girls, especially those in the countryside, because the problems that beset the elementary education of boys had less effect on the instruction of girls. Female education belonged to nuns and sisters as well as to priests and schoolmasters. Unlike the Charon Brethren, the female religious orders were vigorous and well-organized. This was particularly true of the Sisters of the *Congrégation de Notre-Dame*, whose community had been founded in seventeenth-century Canada. The sisters took simple vows, were not cloistered, and were devoted to education. In the 1750s, with about eighty members, theirs was the largest female religious community in the colony. Their schools spread throughout the towns and countryside. 'In many places in the country', wrote Kalm, 'there are two or more of them (sisters).' He added, 'their business is to instruct young girls in the Christian religion, to teach them reading, writing, needlework and other feminine accomplishments.'[36] Most of the girls attended these schools for one or two years as day-students. Thanks to the Sisters of Notre-Dame, country girls were sometimes better educated than their brothers.

[. . .]

The administrative, judicial, and military elite of New France was concentrated in the towns and had access to lucrative offices; it had no trouble obtaining elementary and secondary education for its children. Secondary education, however, was reserved for boys. Elementary education in reading and writing seems to have coincided with catechetical instruction and for most children it took no more than one year. The *Petit Séminaire* of Quebec trained boys in Latin, rhetoric, philosophy, and theology; in the late seventeenth century, youths between the ages of nine and fifteen and with some knowledge of reading and writing were admitted to this school.[37] At Quebec older boys and seminarians attended the Jesuit College, which followed the *ratio studiorum* of classical studies. There was a seminary at Montreal that was comparable to the Quebec *Grand Séminaire*. The French Crown also sponsored occasional courses for young men in hydrography, pilotage, surveying, and the law.

Education does not require an institutional framework and in early French Canada parents, tutors, and master craftsmen taught more children than were instructed in schools. From the 1670s there are contracts in which private tutors promised to teach their employers' children at home how to read and write within one year.[38] Notaries of the colony sometimes acted as schoolmasters and as tutors. In the mid-eighteenth century a Montreal notary taught a child of the Panet family how to write; the boy's writing exercises have survived because they were written on the blank pages and empty spaces in the notary's index of documents. The boy was told how to hold his pen and, after the notary had written a model text, the child copied it ten or more times underneath. Young Antoine Méru Panet reproduced legal phrases, commercial bills and receipts, and such philosophic reflections as 'God consoles the afflicted in their afflictions; he is with us in our persecution, he bears us up in moments of weakness.'[39]

Manual trades and the professions of notary, surgeon, and merchant were usually learned in adolescence by association with a skilled practitioner. In most cases the practitioner was the pupil's father or another close relative. When the instructor was not kin, a formal apprenticeship was in order. Some agreements were verbal, some were by unregistered contract, and others were made before a notary who filed the indenture. Considering that the last category represented a fraction of all the apprenticeships made, and that a sixth of the notarial files have been lost, it is remarkable that there are still in existence some 1,200 notarized apprenticeships from this underpopulated French colony. This flourishing and widespread form of instruction reveals the importance of non-institutional education in New France. As a means of learning a manual trade, private apprenticeship, whether formal or casual, had no rival; not from the short-lived hospice of the Charon Brethren in Montreal, where orphans learned joinery, metalwork, and the manufacture of stockings; nor from the Quebec Seminary and its farms, where unsuccessful students and peasant children learned farming and handicrafts.

The conventional formula of contracts summed up the apprentice's motives by describing him as 'desiring to make his fortune and establishment and to earn his living'. Personal inclinations and the economic prospects of a trade determined the choice of most apprentices. The absence of craft guilds and the near disappearance of the master's fee in New France gave apprentices access to a wide range of occupations. Though the Canadian apprentices might have selected any skill, from wig-making to saddlery, they preferred blacksmithing, shoemaking, cooperage, and joinery—crafts whose products were in demand.

The boys of the colony benefited most from craft apprenticeship. Scarcely one apprentice in a hundred was a female and the girls were all destined to become seamstresses. If a young woman did not intend to join a religious community, she was expected to make marriage her career. The *Canadiennes,* 'especially the girls', whom Peter Kalm characterized as vain and flirtatious, 'commonly sing songs in which the words *amour* and *Coeur* are very frequent' while working indoors. Much has been made of a few female entrepreneurs in New France, but unless a woman had evaded marriage until the age of twenty-five or became a widow while still wealthy and energetic, she had little hope of being self-employed.

For one Quebec seamstress, apprenticeship in a trade was a last resort and it had failed her. At the age of twenty-four, she stated that 'in her childhood (*enfance*), having no family estate to allow her to live (independently), she had been obliged to learn the craft of seamstress. Since that time she had worked for the public and had great difficulty in feeding herself, having received no help from her parents, who were incapable of assisting her', nor from her godfather, a notary. A farmer had offered to marry her, yet her parents disapproved of the match. She therefore petitioned a magistrate for permission to issue a respectful summons to her parents. For the seamstress, marriage was an escape from her 'sorry situation'.[40]

∗   ∗   ∗   ∗   ∗

The characterization of Canadian children as unruly savages has been overdrawn. It is true that the youth of New France had little formal schooling. By the standards of the mother country, they were shockingly presumptuous and precocious. Among 'the common people', Peter Kalm saw 'boys of ten or twelve years of age' who 'run about with a pipe in their mouth'.[41] Young *Canadiens* drank brandy, refused to doff their hats in the presence of ladies while indoors, and rode about on their own horses of which they were inordinately proud. The fact that in New France young peasants rode horses and country girls dressed in the finery of gentlewomen did not accord with the outsiders' sense of propriety.

The official culture of France glorified submission to authority, both secular and clerical. The family, the church, and the state were organized as hierarchies in which authority descended from the top. An orderly society was one in which people accepted their hereditary social rank and obeyed their superiors without question. Small wonder, then, that the ambitious, wilful, and proud *Canadiens* offended senior administrators from France.

Were the children of early French Canada any worse than their parents? The weakening of communal restraints in New France had opened the door to anti-social behaviour by children. Institutions such as municipal corporations had disappeared from the colony. Thanks to dispersed settlement in the countryside, villages, which had provided the framework for French rural life, were slow to develop in Canada. Only nine communities in the St Lawrence Valley were worthy of being called towns or villages. The increase in births out of wedlock was evidence of the relaxation of social restraints. According to Louis Franquet, rural children stole produce from their parents in order to buy trifles from country merchants. In the Intendants' ordinances compelling the heirs and in-laws of aged and destitute people to provide assistance, we see evidence of a callousness that would not have been acceptable in a closely knit society.

In the rural areas of New France, where over three-quarters of the population resided, the enforcement of social discipline belonged, initially, to the family. Colonial society had fragmented into autonomous family groups. Within the nuclear family there was a conflict between the customary obligation to maintain paternal authority and the need to win the consent of the subordinates. The large number of children also undermined parental authority. Children under fifteen constituted at least 42 per cent of the population. Like a mild but persistent acid, little children can eat away at their elders' rigid standards for youthful behaviour. It was also difficult to maintain social differences while living together in close proximity.

Lower-class *Canadiens* were dependent on their children and this dependence was a good reason for considering the opinions of the young. Parents did protect themselves from the caprice of their children by giving one adult son or heir the family farm or workshop in return for providing their needs until death. Yet all of the children were morally bound to support their aged and infirm parents. Sons and daughters were not only necessary for a secure retirement; they also contributed to the success of the family as an economic unit in their youth. The proverb 'children are the riches of the poor' rang true because a family was required to run a farm or manage a shop. In New France hired labour was scarce and costly and, as we have seen, the young could be usefully employed. Colonial children were economic partners as well as social subordinates. Just as the dependence of the French colonists on the Amerindians as trading partners and military allies made the *Canadiens* more respectful toward the native peoples, so the dependence of adults on their children forced grownups to consider the wishes of the young. Thus the expression '*les petits sauvages*' provides an insight into the changing relationship of parents and children in early French Canada.

A good reason for regarding this characterization of children in New France as more indicative of French attitudes rather than of Canadian reality is the fact that British travellers who visited the United States from 1845 to 1935 described American children in similar terms. The travellers agreed that children in the United States were detestable, hard, and precocious. 'Precocity', wrote Richard L. Rapson, 'politely expressed the British feeling that American children were pert, impertinent, disrespectful, arrogant brats'.[42] Like the French visitors to New France, the British writers attributed the deficiencies of the children to indulgent and negligent parents. In a favourable interpretation of these observations, Richard Rapson presented the independence and self-reliance of the young as the products of an egalitarian and companionate family structure that was suited to republican and democratic values. The parallels with monarchical and undemocratic New France, however, suggests that existence of a more widespread phenomenon: a North American departure from the European perception of the ideal child from the Old World standards for raising the young. In Canada the levelling process did not reach the extremes observed in the United States. The limited sources from the French regime only permit an impressionistic picture of the world of youth. This picture reveals that, if young *Canadiens* were not *petits sauvages*, they were truly children of the New World.

[1982]

Notes

The author thanks Jean Barman, and Neil Sutherland for their helpful comments on early drafts of this article. The emphasis on little girls is due, in part, to my daughter, Anna.

1. Pierre François-Xavier de Charlevoix, *Histoire et description générale de la Nouvelle-France*, 6 vols. (Paris: Nyon fils, 1744), III, 253.
2. Governor de Denonville to M. de Seignelay, 12 November 1685, quoted in J.H. Stewart Reid et al., eds, *A Source-Book of Canadian History* (Toronto: Longman Canada, 1976), 34.
3. Public Archives of Canada (hereafter PAC), C11A Series transcript, Vol. 26, pp. 28–30, Intendant Raudot to the Minister of the Navy, 10 November 1707.
4. Antoine Silvy [actually Antoine-Denis Paudot], *Relation par Lettres de l'Amérique Septentrionale* (Paris: Letouzey & Ane, 1904), 4.
5. Jacques Henripin, 'From Acceptance of Nature to Control: The Demography of the French Canadians,' in Michiel Horn and Ronald Sabourin, eds, *Studies in Canadian Social History* (Toronto: McClelland and Stewart, 1974), 76; see also Henripin's *La Population canadienne au début de xviie siècle* (Paris: Presses universitaires de France, 1954), which served as a source of data.
6. Peter N. Moogk, 'Manual Education and Economic Life in New France', *Studies on Voltaire and the Eighteenth Century*, Vol. 167 (Oxford: Voltaire Foundation, 1977), 125–68.
7. Archives de Québec (hereafter AQ), Collection de Pièces judiciares et notariales, No. 551 3/4, 23 juillet 1716.
8. AQ, Pièces detachées de la Prévôté de Québec, No. 929, 3 janvier 1733. This document is transcribed in Pierre-Georges Roy, 'Les "sommations respectueuses" autrefois', *Rapport de l'Archiviste de la Province de Québec* (hereafter RAPQ), 1921–2, 59–78.
9. Henripin, 'From Acceptance of Nature', 75.
10. AQ, GNRF, Jacques Barbel, 30 mars 1736; ANF, AC, Outremer, G3 Series, Vol. 2058, pièce 22, 11 avril 1725. This last reference comes from Kenneth Donovan, 'Rearing Children in Louisbourg—A Colonial Seaport and Garrison Town 1713–1758', paper presented at the Atlantic Society for Eighteenth Century Studies meeting, April 1979.
11. Edouard-Zotique Massicotte, 'Le travial des enfants à Montréal, au XVIIe siècle', *Bulletin des Recherches historiques* (hereafter BRH), 22 (1916), 57; 'Comment on disposait des Enfants du Roi', BRH, 37 (1931), 49–54. Volumes 18 (1956) and 19 (1960) of the *Inventaires des Greffes des Notaires* series published by the Quebec Provincial Archives provide synopses of private paupers' and orphans' indentures passed by the notary Louis Chambalon.
12. Quoted in Fortier De la Broquerie, 'Les "Enfants Trouvés" sous le régime français', *Trois Siécles de Médecine québécoise* (Québec: Société historique de Québec, 1973), 113–26.
13. Cyprien Tanguay, *Dictionnaire généalogique des familles canadiennes*, 7 vols. (Montreal: Eusèbe Sénécal, 1871–90), Vol. 4, 607–8.
14. Yves-François Zoltvany, ed., *The French Tradition in North America* (New York: Harper & Row, 1969), 75.

15. *Arrêts de Réglements du Conseil supérieur de Québec et Ordonnances et Jugements des Intendants du Canada* (Québec: E.R. Fréchette, 1855), 395–6. Synopses of indentures of *enfants du Roi* from the files of Joseph-Charles Raimbault can be found in Volume 21 (1964) of the *Inventaires des Greffes des Notaires* series noted above. Unpublished indentures from the Quebec region are to be found in AQ, GNRF, Jean-Etienne Dubreuil, and Henri Hiché, *passim.*

16. AQ, GNRF, Henri Hiché, 20 septembre 1735.

17. AQ, GNRF, Henri Hiché, 28 novembre 1729.

18. Zoltvany, *The French Tradition*, 83.

19. Ross W. Beales, 'In Search of the Historical Child: Miniature Adulthood and Youth in Colonial New England', *American Quarterly*, XXVII, 4 (October 1975), 379–98.

20. 'La Correspondance de madame Bégon, 1748–1753,' RAPQ, 1934–35, 51,

21. 'La Correspondance de madame Bégon', 22.

22. Robert-Lionel Séguin, *Les Jouets anciens du Québec* (Ottawa: Editions Lemeac, 1976), 117.

23. ANF, AC, Séries G2, Vol. 203, dossier 380, pièce 3—Estate inventory of Jean Castaing, 6 June 1756, and noted in Donovan, 'Rearing Children in Louisbourg'.

24. PAC, C11A transcript, Vol. XXV, p. 32—de Louvigny to the Minister, 21 October 1706; Pierre-Georges Roy, ed., *Inventaire des Ordonnances des Intendants de la Nouvelle-France*, 4 vols. (Beaucefille: L'Eclaireur, 1919), Vol. I, 218.

25. Edouard-Zotique Massicotte, *Répertoire des Arrêts, Edits, Mandements, Ordonnances et Réglements conservés dans les archives du Palais de justice de Montréal, 1640–1760* (Montréal: G. Ducharme, 1919), 120; BRH, 24 (1928), 526.

26. *Arrêts et Réglements*, 398.

27. Adolph B. Benson, ed., *Peter Kalm's Travels in North America*, 2 vols. (New York: Dover Publications, 1966), Vol. II, 526.

28. Silvy, *Relation par Lettres*, 4.

29. Charlevoix, *Histoire et description générale*, Vol. III, 257.

30. Roy, *Inventaire des ordonnances*, Vol. I, 237.

31. Cornelius Jaenen, *The Role of the Church in New France* (Toronto: McGraw Hill-Ryerson, 1976), 27.

32. Pierre Boucher, *Histoire Véritable et Naturelle des moeurs et productions du pays de La Nouvelle France* (Parris: Florentin Lambert, 1664), 139.

33. Charlevoix, *Historie et description générale*, Vol. III, 255.

34. Benson, *Peter Kalm's Travels*, Vol. II, 481.

35. Edouard-Zotique Massicotte, 'Un recensement inédit de Montréal, en 1741,' *Mémoires de la Société Royale du Canada*, Serie III, Vol. XV (mai 1921), 6.

36. Benson, *Peter Kalm's Travels*, Vol. II, 538.

37. Archives du Séminaire de Québec, Manuscript 2, Annales du Petit Séminaire de Québec, 1668–c. 1780; Manuscript 6, a variant of the Annales.

38. AQ, GNRF, Gilles Rageot, 18 avril 1674; AQ (Montréal), GNRF, Bénigne Basset, 18 août 1677.

39. AQ (Montréal), GNRF, François Le Pallieur, index for 1733–1739. The internal evidence suggests that these writing exercises were done in 1771.

40. Petition of Catherine Frontigny to the *lieutenant-général* at Quebec, 9 September 1745, in RAPQ, 1921–2, 66–7. She falsely claimed she was twenty-seven in the petition.

41. Benson, *Peter Kalm's Travels*, Vol. II, 510.

42. Richard L. Rapson, 'The American Child as Seen by British Travelers, 1845–1935', *American Quarterly*, XVII, 3 (Fall 1965), 520–34.

A Most Remarkable Phenomenon: Growing Up Métis: Fur Traders' Children in the Pacific Northwest

Juliet Pollard

Throughout the nineteenth century fur trade children were 'guinea pigs' for scientific theories and speculations about species and races.[1] By the late 1870s 'scientists' working in the new field of anthropology travelled the Northwest under the auspices of such agencies as the Smithsonian Institution studying native and Indian-white mixed blood populations.[2] One member of this new school of 'science', Dr Victor Harvard, reported in 1879 that there were 32,921 mixed-bloods sprinkled in communities on both sides of the border stretching from the Great Lakes to the Pacific Ocean and he determined that the best name that could be applied to the French, and non-French mixed-bloods who associated with them, was the old French term, Métis.[3] He was aware that this word was traceable from the Spanish, 'mestizo', meaning mongrel, but like many of his colleagues whose views were heavily imbued with Darwinian concepts of race, this was not a racist slur, but a recognition of the mixed-bloods' position in the evolutionary scheme of mankind.[4]

The 'scientific' recognition of the Métis identified not only a new people, but also a new culture. While some attempts were made to describe the culture, more concern was given to the effects of inter-racial breeding. The British Association for the Advancement of Science instructed its investigative committee:

> Especial importance attaches to the examination of mixed races. . . the resemblances and differences between the offspring and the parent stock, the number of generations during which inherited race characteristics are distinguishable, and the tendency to revert to one or other of the ancestral types.[5]

It was generally held that hybrids approximated the lifestyle of one or other of their progenitors. Nevertheless, it was noted that between these two extremes of half-breeds who lived as whites, and those who lived as Indians, there was a large middle group of intermarried mixed-bloods who as 'the true representative of race' were especially noticeable in the territory of the Hudson's Bay Company where they assumed the status of independent tribes of farming-hunters, distinct in 'manner, habit and allegiance' from Indians and whites.[6] This 'most remarkable phenomena', [sic] as ethnologist Daniel Wilson termed it, might also be regarded as a huge educational process whereby fur trade youngsters acquired a value system and lifestyle uniquely their own.[7]

One Hudson's Bay Company area where Métis culture flourished in the first half of the nineteenth century was the Pacific Northwest. Close to present day Portland, Oregon, stood Fort Vancouver, headquarters for the region and gateway to the Willamette River Valley where retired company servants and American mountain men farmed and supplemented their incomes as free trappers and traders. By the time the fort was established in 1824, mixed-blood children, fathered by men of John Jacob Astor's abortive fur enterprise in the region, and later, Nor-Westers, many of whom were themselves mixed-blood, had rooted Métis families in the region.[8] The uniqueness of this culture arose from the intermarriage of traders with women whose native cultures were considerably different from Indian wives east of the Rocky Mountains, and in the politics of joint occupation with its mingling of American and British traders, and its mixture of paternalism, as practised by the Hudson's Bay Company, and individualism, as characteristic of the American fur trade.[9]

School began at Fort Vancouver in November 1832. During that month the first five students—David McLoughlin, Billy McKay, Ranald MacDonald, Louis Labonte, and Andrew Dominique Pambrun—were gathered in the cramped chambers of a New Hampshire schoolmaster for their first taste of formal education.[10] By 1838, the school had its own building and an enrolment of 60 pupils between the ages of five and fourteen.[11] Education was no longer restricted to employees' sons but embraced all the girls and boys of school age living in the vicinity of the fort, as well as some pupils that boarded. The school was free, non-denominational, and appears to have been compulsory. The children's lessons were drawn from texts current in English and American classrooms of the time.[12]

With the exception of Louis Labonte, the son of a Hudson's Bay Company servant, the boys in the first class went on to more advanced education in eastern United States, Great Britain, or Red River. All returned home to what had become Oregon Territory. David McLoughlin was general manager of his father's milling operations in Oregon City.[13] Billy McKay, by then Doctor McKay, clerked and practised medicine.[14] Ranald MacDonald settled at old Fort Colville after teaching English in Japan before US relations were established with that country.[15] Louis Labonte worked for the Hudson's Bay Company, farmed and trapped.[16] Andrew Pambrun was variously a schoolmaster, businessman, and farmer.[17]

Judged by the 'white values' which came to dominate the region, these boys achieved varying degrees of success, but if that is the only criterion used then the more important values in these boys' lives are lost. For these first schoolboys in the Pacific Northwest were all designated 'half-breed' by the incoming white society, even though Pambrun and McLoughlin were more white than native, McKay more native than white, and only MacDonald and Labonte could claim equal heritage from Indian and white parentage.[18] While their histories reveal an ability to make their way in white society, these boys increasingly rejected the opportunity to be identified as 'white' as they reached middle and old age. Although they would be closely associated with native peoples at various times, two of them living out their lives on Indian reservations, they did not consider themselves Indian.[19] The bonds which tied these boys and many other fur trade children together went far beyond being collectively labelled 'half-breeds'. Their identities were rooted in their childhood nurturing in the Métis culture which developed in the region. They shared in youth, as they would in old age, a Métis consciousness that transcended the class structure of the Hudson's Bay Company and the ethnic heritage of their parents—a sense of self that was neither white nor Indian.[20]

Children in the fur trade culture might struggle for existence from the time of their conception to their birth. Some were unwanted. Wives were an asset, children were a liability.[21] Wives provided sexual satisfaction and companionship, performed a wide range of domestic tasks, and furthered trade ties with native peoples.[22] In the wider Euro-American society where pregnancies were often also unwanted, children could be a source of labour on farms or of income in factories.[23] In the all-encompassing organization of the Hudson's Bay Company, however, where there was full employment and job security, where food, shelter, and clothing were largely provided, children had little economic value. According to Company policy, traders who fathered children had to 'make such provision for the same as circumstances called for and their means permit'.[24]

To the 200 native wives living at Fort Vancouver by the late 1830s, pregnancy could have more immediate concerns. The great variety of natural childbirth methods which served well among the thirty-eight different cultures they represented were not always as successful when the father was white or part-white.[25] The mixed-blood baby could be larger, labour could be prolonged, and the possibility of death of mother and/or child could be greater. When increased massage, the use of a girdle, and other external remedies did not work, the labouring woman was left to her fate.[26] One doctor wrote:

> We find abortion quite frequent; some tribes have a reason for it, on account of the difficult labour which endangers the life of the woman bearing a half-breed child, which is usually so large as to make its passage through the pelvis of the Indian mother almost an impossibility.[27]

During childbirth, fur trade wives were sometimes assisted by their husbands as was customary among some native people, women on the American frontier, and in rural areas in Great Britain.[28] When difficulties arose, however, fort doctors might attend and use their crude forceps as best they could.[29] At that time, caesarian sections were not yet performed, but a craniotomy, whereby a crochet hook was inserted, the skull perforated, the brain drained, and the dead fetus removed, may have been performed when the baby was regarded as too large for the mother to deliver.[30]

Compounding economic and childbirth considerations, the genetic inheritance of the child was not without meaning to expectant fur trade parents. Some wives came from tribes which held strong beliefs about racial purity and disapproved of or disowned women who engaged in interracial unions.[31] Such views equated with those of the traders who generally concurred in the widely held notion that character and culture were quite literally carried in the blood. The educated gentlemen of the Company were also familiar with the arguments of polygenists who contended half-breeds were 'faulty stock', and the pre-Darwinian evolutionary concepts of phrenologists who postulated, among other ideas, that inter-marriage with inferior people would lead to long-term effects on character and hinder mental progress.[32]

When a child was born, however, maternal and paternal feelings appear to have superseded other considerations. Infanticide, the result of cultural confrontation between Chinook mothers who wished to flatten their child's skull, rather than have an 'ugly baby' ranked as a slave, and trade fathers who refused to allow their wives this liberty, had largely ended with the ascendancy of the Hudson's Bay Company in the region.[33] Parental views about race, however, were never fully eradicated. The child, more indulged than abused, was treated differently than the wholly Indian or white child.

In contrast to attitudes in both Euro-American and native cultures, girls appear to have been the preferred sex. In the absence of white women, mixed-blood daughters were the most desirable marriage partners. Females became a strategic resource, symbolizing property and status being joined together. They were the pride of their gentlemen fathers, who, in a kind of 'Eliza Dolittle' fashion, attempted to mold them into what they thought a lady should be. Through carefully arranged marriages with incoming gentlemen traders, these daughters assured continuation of family wealth and power in the region. The fort, if not quite a female prison, secluded officers' daughters from inter-class entanglements with seekers of status and power and from possible liaisons with Indian males. Increasingly, the virtues of modesty and chastity were stressed.[34] Eloise McLoughlin, daughter of the Chief Factor, noted in her recollections of girlhood at the fort:

> We lived separate and private entirely. Gentlemen who came to trade never saw the family. The first Americans we saw were a very strange sight . . . When the missionaries [sic] ladies came . . . we mingled more.[35]

Since every daughter represented a possible marital alliance, daughters of company servants could gain upward social mobility by marrying a gentleman or his son thus breaking the rigid rank and class structure of the company and linking fur trade families in tighter and tighter familial relationships over time.[36] As the 'trappings of civilization' expanded with the coming of missionaries and white settlers, the 'tutored' daughter could, and often did, replace the 'untutored' mother in 'white' social settings. While native mothers were respected and retained a large measure of their native lifestyles, daughters who were Christianized and educated were accepted as white women with Indian blood.[37]

Such thinking was seldom extended to their brothers who were generally regarded as Indians with white blood. With sons, gentlemen traders were less able to reconcile their racial biases with their paternal feelings. They might view their sons as heirs, but usually provided for all their children in equal proportions in their wills.[38] They loved their sons as they did their daughters, but the nub of their mental dilemma was their inability to see their sons as their 'second chance' as they might have done in their native lands.[39] Since they were 'white' and therefore, 'inherently superior', their sons as part-Indian were 'inherently inferior' and would be unable to surpass them in intellect or vocation. They held out little chance that they would be able to enter the 'white world' through marriage as their sisters were able to do. At best, they hoped their sons could receive a good education, preferably abroad, marry fur trade daughters of equal social standing and that positions could be secured for them with the company or through friends and relatives. Ranald MacDonald's father reflected this view about sons when he wrote a fellow parent:

> Much better to dream of less for them . . . and to endeavour to bring them up in habits of industry, economy and morality, than to aspire to all this visionary greatness for them. All the wealth of Rupert's Land will not make a half-breed either a good person, a shining lawyer, or an able physician, if left to his own discretion while young.[40]

Fathers cultivated 'macho' masculinity in their sons, but feared they would 'go Indian'. They did not want their boys stirring up Indian troubles or disrupting the fur trade. To avert such possibilities, David McLoughlin's father, Chief Factor Dr John McLoughlin opposed the company policy and established the retired servants' settlement in the Willamette. He wrote: 'As half-breeds are in general leaders among Indians, and they would be a thorn in the side of whites, I insisted they should go to the Willamette, where their children could be brought up as whites and Christians.'[41]

Both mixed-blood servants, who identified themselves as French or Canadians, and white gentlemen traders oriented their sons in varying degrees towards a 'white world'. The gentlemen strove the hardest to retain their Euro-American cultural heritage and pass it on to their mixed-blood youngsters by attempting to raise them as white. The servants, who were no less concerned with the preservation of their Quebec traditions, were more flexible in adopting native customs and allowing their children freer association with native peoples. Both classes sought to eradicate or curb their sons' 'Indian dispositions' through education. Religion was given a prominent place in the process. 'The Canadians', wrote Father Blanchet, 'had not forgotten their religion.' They petitioned the Bishop of Montreal for a priest each year from 1834 to 1836. 'Our children', they wrote in their 1836 petition, 'are learning very fast which makes us very eager for your assistance.'[42]

By the time Catholic clergy arrived one year later, American Methodists were established in the Willamette, American Presbyterians were in the Walla Walla–Spokane area, and a lone English Anglican priest was about to disembark to minister at Fort Vancouver. Teachers at the fort school were drawn from the missionaries and it followed that classes were generously steeped in religion. Here the students were not only encouraged to digest an education befitting 'white' Euro-American youths, but they were also required to absorb agricultural training of the type used in mission schools to 'civilize and Christianize' native peoples. The mission school approach covered all possibilities. If sons showed promise they could be sent abroad for further education, but if they weren't capable of educational advancement, as judged by teacher and father, then digging in the fort garden every afternoon, it was believed, would serve them best in later life.[43]

Even in households where 'race' was never mentioned, Métis children soon learned they were regarded as inferior people. American missionaries who taught the children were the first to write Home Boards encouraging white immigration as a means of keeping the half-breed 'descendants of the Hudson's Bay Company' from achieving ascendancy in Oregon.[44] Textbooks like William Mavor's *The Elements of Natural History* first published in 1808, but still used in the fort classrooms in the 1840s, claimed that native peoples were 'diminutive and ill shaped, their aspects as forbidding as their manners are barbarous. . .'[45] In short, concepts of white superiority based on so-called scientific evidence were strengthened with each passing decade as the children grew. The immigrants had come in search of upward social mobility, but when they reached Oregon the established Métis population were the 'haves'—they were the 'have nots'. The newcomers had much to say about equality, but recognized a 'natural superiority' among men.

Against this backdrop, children acquired much of their value systems in the larger classroom of the fur trade itself. Contrary to popular belief that fur trade families were large, population figures for the servants' village outside Fort Vancouver indicate that the majority of families had only one child and few had more than two.[46] Even though families appear to have been small, there was also a chronic shortage of housing and extended households and multi-family living arrangements were the norm. Under such circumstances the only child was seldom the only child in the household. In addition, many Chinook-speaking wives who made up the largest proportion of women in the village retained their slaves after marriage and their numbers swelled the ranks of the household.[47] Single male boarders and visiting relatives of the wives were also common in fur trade homes. Although the practice was dying out, a child might be raised in a household where his father had more than one wife. A visitor to the Willamette settlement recalls:

> I boarded the first three months at J.B. Desportes, a halfbreed, whose family consisted of two wives, besides one absent, by all, seven children, four or five slaves and two or three hired Indians, besides cats and dogs without number. All inhabited one room in common.[48]

As the children grew, they increasingly came under the care of others. Accidents shortened the lives of fathers and many mothers died before they were forty. Remarriage made common child rearing with step-parents, half-brothers, and -sisters. Orphans were assigned to families for care.[49] Under such conditions the Euro-American middle-class concept of personal privacy had little meaning. The lifestyle tended to be co-operative, rather than competitive. Communal living which required the acquisition of tolerance and compromise at an early age, became, in modified form, the preferred way of living for many of the children in adult life.[50]

Families were transient moving in and out of cramped quarters and from fort to fort or on fur trade brigades depending on the work assignment of the father. Children born at Fort Vancouver could expect to be living in a new environment by the time they reached their fourth birthday.[51] Gentlemen continued to teach their children wherever they were stationed, whereas servants' children, if they received any formal education, did so in haphazard fashion.[52] Their world, like

that of their parents who were mainly illiterate, relied heavily on memory retention and oral presentation.[53]

On any given day the children at Fort Vancouver could expect to hear thirty or
forty distinct languages being spoken. French was the lingua franca of the fort, but
English was used for business. There were at least thirty native languages including
that spoken by the Kanakas, Hawaiian Islanders who laboured for the Company, as
well as Gaelic, the tongue of some fathers. Such diversity promoted the development
of Chinook Jargon, a composite of languages which permitted communications
between the fur trade population and their Indian trading partners. The jargon
bridged national, ethnic, and racial differences of parents and gave their offspring
a new language unique to the Métis culture in the Pacific Northwest.[54]

The fort school was taught in English. In the classroom, 'the scholars came in
talking in their respective languages . . . Cree, Nez Perces, Chinook, etc., etc.,' —
language indicative of the bonding between mother and child during infancy.[55]
Children were breast fed on demand and were therefore the constant companions
of their mothers who carried them in cradle boards on the horn of their saddles or
in baskets slung on the side of their horses while travelling.[56] When weaned at age
two or three, they would be securely tied to their own horses or ponies and would
begin to acquire the equestrian skills Pacific Métis were famous for.[57] About this
time fathers appear to have played an increasing role in their children's lives. From
their mothers they learned to be consumers of the natural environment; from their
fathers they learned the economics and technology of the fur trade, agriculture, and
other Company enterprises. The school moved the child from the mother's culture
where discipline was by shaming and learning by imitating, to their father's where
'spare the rod and spoil the child' was a concept applied to both discipline and
learning.[58] The children grew up aware of both Indian and white values and were
able to harmonize both systems in their own lifestyle.

In this culturation process, Fort Vancouver, the major institution of social organization and industry, was important. Within were the school, church, hospital,
tradesmen's shops, and retail outlet; without, the dairy, ranch, and 1,000 acres under
cultivation. The latter furnished a diet superior to other working class peoples, while
the former provided care for the population from the cradle to the grave.[59] A bell,
used like a factory whistle, punctuated the day into blocks of time for specific tasks.
The workday began when the bell rang at 5 a.m. At 8 o'clock the bell signalled breakfast. Two one-half hour breaks for smoking clay pipes and an hour for mid-day dinner, noted by the bell, broke the remaining 9 to 6 p.m. day, five days a week. On
Sunday the bell announced Sunday school and church services. Evenings were regulated by curfew.[60] The rhythm of the fort and the school, which stressed punctu-
ality and regularity, taught the children time-thrift habits. The beating of furs,
helping in the gardens, and other chores led the youngsters into the work-cycle. Full
initiation into the routine of their parents took place around puberty when lads
apprenticed in company labour and girls prepared for marriage which usually took
place before their eighteenth birthday.[61]

*   *   *   *   *

Although social scientists have been debating theories of culture for the past hundred years, they have yet to arrive at a precise definition of the term. There seems to be some consensus, however, that whatever culture is, it is not as simple as 'one culture per society', nor it would seem, is there any restriction on individuals or groups operating in one or more cultures concurrently or at different periods of their lives.[62] The education of fur trade youngsters equipped them with what has been described as 'response-abilities'. These abilities allowed them to successfully adapt to the changing environment in the Pacific Northwest after the demise of the fur trade and function so well in both white and Indian cultures that their apparent disappearance led past historians to be 'culturally blind' and conclude they were 'victims of higher civilizations'.[63] The individual genealogies of the children reveal the development of a bi-cultural pattern which continues to exist among descendants who have some family members living on reservations, while others live within the mainstream of white society. What the genealogies fail to note is that most of the fur trade children carried their Métis traditions into their new social environments and although they modified these traditions to some extent, they continued to adhere to them and organize their lives along traditional patterns. In the second half of the nineteenth century the children were able to retain a Métis consciousness through a complicated network of kinship relationships which stretched through the entire region. Such patterns refute the myth that fur trade children were forced to 'go Indian' in later life because of racial prejudice in the dominant society. They also belittle the underlying assumptions in this myth—namely, that native people readily accepted mixed-bloods, that racial prejudice was the prime factor in determining the children's lives, and that Métis had no free will in making decisions on their own behalf.

In the 1850 Census of Oregon fur trade children were classified as foreigners, Canadians, French (meaning French-Canadian), or Scottish. As such they were a privileged group within the mixed-blood group which had developed after the settling of the territory. Classification as whites entitled them to US citizenship and 320 acres under the Donation Land Act of the same year—rights denied other half-breed children because of Indian blood.[64]

Most of the children in this study settled in family groups on the fringes of the new society—here they founded new communities in British Columbia, Washington, Oregon, and Montana. Some of these settlements granted under the Donation Land Act squatted on Indian lands and fell within reservation boundaries established in later years. In such cases, Métis, by virtue of their prior settlement, were awarded special status on the reservations. Native people, however, could be hostile towards 'frenchies' joining them.[65] The development of French Prairie, St Paul, and other Métis communities in the Willamette which remained a nucleus for the culture was curtailed by incoming settlers who bought Métis farms and the California gold rush where more than 200 French-speaking Métis in the valley died of fever in the mining regions.[66] Attempts by retired Chief Factor McLoughlin and Métis leaders to establish half-breed reservations failed.[67] Those that lived with native tribes, did so in cultures which were so altered by white technology and foreign ideologies that they resembled the fur trade culture of decades before.

While racism in the society cannot be denied, the degree of racial bigotry, largely propagated by the elite, must be measured against racial tolerance evident in the reminiscences of ordinary citizens. It must be equated with the fact that immigrants were largely single white males, who like their predecessors in the fur trade, united with native and mixed-blood women and had a vested interest in the welfare of the children they fathered. It must be balanced against the lives of these children who were found not just at the lower rungs of the new social structure, but on every rung from the highest political offices on down.[68] The most important point, however, is neither the amount of Indian blood nor the biological reality, but that the children themselves understood the outside world's view of them and fought the image of themselves as inferior people where and how they could.[69] Racial prejudice threw them back upon themselves, reinforcing their culture, and strengthening their identities as Métis people.

One aspect of survival is to take on the protective coloration of the invading culture. Métis adaptation did not mean capitulation of mixed-blood identities. Rather than victims, the Métis offspring of the traders challenged the dominant culture and often consciously chose to reject white society in favour of perpetuating a cultural identity which they retain to this day. In the twilight of Métis culture, consciousness remains. But in the late 1870s when two fur trade daughters, Christina MacDonald and Amelia Douglas, wife of Sir James Douglas, first governor of British Columbia, met for the first time, Christina noted: 'We talked in our excitement in French, in Indian and in mixed English and Lady Douglas remarked how she liked to hear the old language again.'[70]

[1984]

Notes

1. Nineteenth-century scientific interest in Indian-white mixed-blood populations stemmed from a larger interest in the origin and nature of species and races. From the debates over Comte de Buffon's 'definition of Species', *Histoire Naturelle* (1749), to those which arose over Charles Darwin's *Origin of Species* (1858), 'half-breeds' were cited as 'evidence' to prove or disprove various ideas about species. See: Bentley Glass, Owsei Temkin, William L. Strauss, Jr, eds, *Forerunners of Darwin: 1745–1859* (Baltimore: Johns Hopkins Press, 1968); Robert Bieder, 'Scientific Attitudes toward Indian Mixed-Bloods in Early Nineteenth Century America', *Journal of Ethnic Studies*, 8, 2 (Summer 1980); Juliet Pollard, 'Fur Trade Children: The Making of the Métis in the Pacific Northwest' (PhD thesis, UBC).

2. Although the word 'anthropology' was much employed, few of the men who published under the title were 'professional' anthropologists. Although the main focus of Lewis Morgan's work, for example, was the study of native peoples, as a kind of 'spin-off' were discussions about Métis and 'half-breeds'. For example, after a visit to Red River, Morgan wrote: 'As far as my personal observation has extended among the American Indian nations, the half-breed is inferior both physically and mentally, to the pure Indian...' Lewis H. Morgan, *Systems of Consanguinity and Affinity of the Human Family* (Smithsonian Contributions of Knowledge, Vol. XVII, 1871, reprinted 1970) Fn. p. 207.

3. Victor Harvard's paper was first delivered to the Anthropological Society of Washington, DC, 20 May 1879. It was later published as 'The French Half-Breeds of the Northwest',

Annual Report of the Board of Regents of the Smithsonian Institution, 1879 (Washington, DC, 1880), pp. 309–27. Noting that 'Métis' referred to French mixed-bloods, while English mixed-bloods were known as 'half-breeds', Harvard found that classification via paternal ancestry (blood line) did not fit the culture he examined. See also John Reade, 'The Half Breed', *Proceedings and Transactions of the Royal Society of Canada*, Vol. 3, 1885, p. 11.

4.   Research into the origin and meaning of the term Métis conducted by Jose Hatier, President of the Métis Indian Alliance of North America, indicates that the word has been applied to French-native mixed-blood populations throughout the world. For those engaged in 'scientific' studies in the latter part of the nineteenth century it seems clear that they intended it as a pejorative term meaning 'mongrel'—a term consistently used along with 'hybrid' in species debates throughout the century. For example, see 'Review of "Darwin on the Origin of the Species by Means of Natural Selection"', *Canadian Naturalist and Geologist*, Vol. V, Reade, 'The Half Breed', p. 11; Jennifer Brown, *Strangers in Blood: Fur Trade Company Families in Indian Country* (Vancouver: UBC Press, 1980), pp. 172–3; correspondence and discussions between Jose Hatier, President, Métis Indian Alliance of North America and author, May 1983–January 1984.

5.   The committee members were: Dr E.B. Taylor, Dr G.M. Dawson, Gen. Sir J.H. LeFroy, Dr D. Wilson, H. Hale, R.G. Haliburton, and G.W. Bloxam, *British Association for the Advancement of Science: Committee on North Western Tribes of The Dominion of Canada Report, 1887*, (London, 1887), p. 2.

6.   Harvard, 'The French Half-Breeds of the Northwest', p. 314; Daniel Wilson, 'Pre-Aryan American Man', *Proceedings and Transactions of the Royal Society of Canada*, Vol. I, 1882–1883, p. 43; Reade, p. 11.

7.   Ibid.

8.   The term most frequently applied to the people under study was 'French', while individuals were known as 'half-breeds' or 'half-bloods'. Since the first term would be confusing, and the latter two derogatory, the term Métis (somewhat less derogatory and increasingly being applied to mixed-blood populations in North America by academics) is used throughout the paper. Nearly all histories of Oregon discuss the fur trade era in the region. In particular, see J.A. Hussey, *Champoeg: Place of Transition* (Portland, Oregon Historical Society, 1967).

9.   A discussion on how these forces shaped the culture is given in Pollard, 'Fur Trade Children'.

10. Debbie Bond, 'How Public School Started', *Clark County History*, 1975, p. 56.

11. John Ball, *Autobiography of John Ball* (Grand Rapids: Dean Hicks Co., 1925), p. 93; Thomas Jessett (ed.), *Reports and Letters of Herbert Beaver* (Portland: Champoeg Press, 1959), p. 30.

12. John Hussey, *Fort Vancouver: Historic Structure Report*, Vol. II (Denver Service Center, National Park Service, US Department of the Interior, 1976), pp. 291–315.

13. William R. Sampson, (ed.), *John McLoughlin's Business Correspondence, 1847–48* (Seattle, University of Washington Press, 1973), pp. 139–42; H.K. Smith, *John McLoughlin and His Family* (Lake Oswego: Smith, Smith and Smith Publishing Co., 1976), pp. 8–9.

14. William Cameron McKay, 'Additional Light on the Whitman Matter', *Oregon Pioneer Association Transactions*, 1887, pp. 91–3; William C. McKay Papers, Ms. 413, Oregon Historical Society, Portland; 'Reminiscences of Leila McKay', *Oregon Journal*, October 1927; Keith and Donna Clark, 'William McKay's Journal, 1866–67; Indian Scouts, Part I and II', *Oregon Historical Quarterly* (hereafter, OHQ) (Summer, Fall 1978).

15. William S. Lewis and Naojiro Murakami, eds, *Ranald MacDonald* (Spokane: Inland-American Printing Co., 1923), pp. 152–233; Maria Leona Nichols, *Ranald MacDonald*,

Adventurer (Caldwell, Idaho: Caxton Printers, 1940), pp. 100–39; Ranald MacDonald to E.E. Dye, Ms. 1089, Oregon Historical Society, Portland.

16. H.S. Lyman, 'Reminiscences of Louis Labonte', *Oregon Historical Quarterly*, Vol. 1, 1900, pp. 169–87.

17. Andrew Dominique Pambrun, *Sixty Years on the Frontier in the Pacific Northwest* (Fairfield: Ye Galleon Press, 1978).

18. See footnotes 13–17; Harriet Duncan Munnick, 'Annotations', *Catholic Church Records of the Pacific Northwest: St. Paul, Oregon, 1839–1898*, Vols. I, II, and III (Portland: Binford and Mort, 1979).

19. See footnotes 13–18 for biographical sketches.

20. For a fuller discussion of Métis culture and consciousness, see Pollard, 'Fur Trade Children'.

21. Ross Cox, *The Columbia River* (Norman: University of Oklahoma Press, 1955), p. 362.

22. For information on fur trade wives in general, see: Brown, *Strangers in Blood*; Sylvia Van Kirk, *'Many Tender Ties': Women in Fur Trade Society in Western Canada, 1670–1870* (Winnipeg: Watson and Dwyer, 1980).

23. For examples, see: William L. Langer, 'Infanticide: A Historical Survey', *History of Childhood Quarterly*, Vol. I (1973–1974), pp. 353–65; Neil McKendrick, 'Home Demand and Economic Growth: A New View of the Role of Women and Children in the Industrial Revolution' in McKendrick, ed., *Historical Perspectives: Studies in English Thought and Society* (London: Europa Publications, 1974); Ivy Pinchbeck and Margaret Hewitt, *Children in English Society*, Vol. II (Toronto: University of Toronto Press, 1973).

24. E.E. Rich, *The History of the Hudson's Bay Company, 1670–1870*, Vol. II (London: The Hudson's Bay Record Society, 1959), p. 453.

25. Female population figures and tribal affiliations at Fort Vancouver are drawn from the figures compiled by Susan Kardas in 'The People Brought This and the Clatsop Became Rich: A View of Nineteenth Century Relations on the Lower Columbia Between Chinookian Speakers, Whites and Kanakas' (Ph.D. thesis, Bryn Mawr College, 1971), pp. 208–10.

26. George J. Engelmann, *Labor Among Primitive Peoples Showing the Development of the Obstetric Science of To-day from the Natural and Instinctive Customs of All Races, Civilized and Savage, Past and Present* (St Louis: J.H. Chambers and Co., 1883), pp. 2, 9–10, 196. Dr George Engelmann rationalized that since peasant and native women had shorter labours than their more 'refined' sisters (or so it was believed), there could be a connection between shorter labour and the positions they assumed during labour. Engelmann sent out letters to doctors asking for information, the information about difficult labour due to larger babies born to Indian-white parents came from their responses. In the early twentieth century biologists who had rediscovered Gregor Mendel's neglected laws of inheritance began applying them to human heredity and the phenomenon of 'increased size', known as F1 (first hybrid generation) was used as proof that inter-racial breeding produced inferior offspring—the larger baby being regarded as 'abnormal' and therefore inferior. Others argued that 'increased size' meant superiority. See W.E. Castle, 'Biological and Social Consequences of Race-Crossing', *American Journal of Physical Anthropology*, IX, 2 (April–June 1926, pp. 145–56). Such factors as birth rank, age of mother, maternal diet, and physical size of parents, known to be significant factors in 'overweight' births today were not observed in the period under study. See: Pollard, 'Fur Trade Children'.

27. Englemann, *Labor Among Primitive People*, p. 2. See also Nellie B. Pipes, 'Indian Conditions in 1836–38', *OHQ*, Vol. 32 (1931), p. 335.

28. Records of husband-assisted births are found throughout *Labor Among Primitive People*.

29. O. Larsell, 'An Outline of the History of Medicine in the Pacific Northwest', *Northwest Medicine*, Vol. 31 (1932), p. 484.

30. Jane B. Donegan, *Women and Men Midwives: Medicine, Morality, and Misogyny in Early America* (Westport: Greenwood Press, 1978), pp. 42–3.
31. For example, see 'Nancy Winecoop', *Told by the Pioneers, Reminiscences of Pioneer Life in Washington*, Vol. I (1937), p. 114.
32. For the extent of phrenologist influence, see George B. Roberts, 'Letters to Mrs F.F. Victor, 1878–83', *OHQ*, Vol. 63 (June-Sept. 1962), pp. 202–34; William Fraser Tolmie, *Physician and Fur Trader* (Vancouver: Mitchell Press, 1963), pp. 333, 363; Bieder, 'Scientific Attitudes towards Indian Mixed-Bloods in Early Nineteenth Century America', p. 24; David De Giustino, *Conquest of Mind: Phrenology and Victorian Thought* (London: Croom Helm, 1975), pp. 139–40.
33. Frederick Merk, ed., *Fur Trade and Empire: George Simpson's Journal* (Cambridge: Harvard University Press, 1968), p. 101.
34. By educating their daughters at home, fur-trade fathers were following a pattern of female education in Euro-American society. Chinook Indians also attempted to keep daughters chaste in order to further trade ties through advantageous marriages with white traders. See Merk, *Fur Trade and Empire*, p. 99; Jessett, *Reports and Letters of Herbert Beaver*, pp. 67–8.
35. Mrs Daniel Harvey (nee Eloise McLoughlin), 'Life of John McLoughlin, Governor of the Hudson's Bay Company's Possessions on the Pacific Slope at Fort Vancouver', Portland, Oregon, June 20, 1878 (handwritten manuscript, Bancroft Library, Berkeley, California), p. 13.
36. Kin relationships which transcended rank and class in the company are evident in Harriet Duncan Munnick, ed., *Catholic Church Records of the Pacific Northwest: Vancouver*, Vol. I and II, and *St. Paul*, Vol. I, II, and III (Portland: Thomas Binford Publisher, 1979, 1980).
37. For example, see Angus MacDonald to Christina MacDonald, E.E. Dye Papers, Ms. 1089, Oregon Historical Society, Portland. MacDonald writes to his daughter: 'You see now the value of education and money, the ignorant is always kept down. I hope you will be rich enough to take me to Edinburgh and Paris before I be much grayer ... Your mother made her trip to Nez Perce (her people) all right. She spent two months on the trip and lost a valuable colt ...'
38. Hudson's Bay Company Wills, A36, Hudson's Bay Company Archives, Winnipeg, Manitoba; Annie Laurie Bird, 'The Will of Thomas McKay', *OHQ*, Vol. 40 (1938), pp. 15–18.
39. Examples of fatherly love for sons are sprinkled throughout fur trade sources. For example, F.N. Ainnoine to James Murray Yale, Oct. 17, 1832, Yale Family Papers, Vol. II, BC Provincial Archives, Victoria. For the growing view of sons as a 'second chance' see Daniel Beekman, *The Mechanical Baby: A Popular History of Theory and Practice of Child Raising* (New York: Meridian, New American Library, 1977), p. 104.
40. Lois Halliday McDonald, *Fur Trade Letters of Francis Ermatinger written to his brother Edward during his service with the Hudson's Bay Company: 1818–1853* (Glendale: Arthur H. Clark Company, 1980), p. 254.
41. 'Copy of a Document found among the Private Papers of the late Dr John McLoughlin', *Oregon Pioneer Association Transactions*, 1880, p. 49.
42. Archbishop F.N. Blanchet, *The Catholic Missionaries of Oregon* (Portland, 1878), p. 3.
43. Ibid., Cyrus Shepard of the Methodist Mission of Oregon to the *Zion's Herald*, Boston, October 28, 1835; 'Mrs Whitman—The Diary', in C.M. Drury, ed., *First White Women over the Rockies: Diaries, Letters, and Biographical Sketches of the Six Women of the Oregon Mission who made the Overland Journey in 1836 and 1838* (Glendale: Arthur H. Clark Company, 1963), pp. 99–114; Jessett, *Reports and Letters of Herbert Beaver*; McDonald, *Fur Trade Lettters of Francis Ermatinger*, pp.185–204. Ermatinger instructed his brother

in Upper Canada to 'make a farmer' of his son since he was considered 'dull' at the Fort Vancouver school.

44. Rev. Myron Eells, *Marcus Whitman Pathfinder and Patriot* (Seattle: Alice Harriman Company, 1909), pp. 136, 148.
45. William Mavor, *The Elements of Natural History, Chiefly Intended for the Use of Schools and Young Persons* (London: Richard Phillips, 1808), p. 13; Hussey, *Fort Vancouver*, p. 315.
46. Kardas, 'The People Brought This and Clatsop Became Rich', p. 209. While Kardas's figures may be questioned, they fall within the pattern of 'small family size' in the Euro-American community. See, for example, Michael Katz, 'Household, Family, and Social Structure', *The Canadian Social History Project*, Report No. 5, 1973–74 (Toronto: The Ontario Institute for Studies in Education, 1974). Indian families have traditionally been regarded as 'small'.
47. Elsie Francis Dennis, 'Indian Slavery in Pacific Northwest', *OHQ*, Vol. 31 (1930), pp. 194–5; Pipes, 'Indian Conditions in 1836–38', pp. 336–7.
48. John Ball, 'Across the Continent Seventy Years Ago', *OHQ*, Vol. 3 (1903), p. 103.
49. Munnick, *Catholic Church Records*.
50. For example, see Ranald MacDonald to E.E. Dye, Aug. 8, 1892, Ms. 1089, Oregon Historical Society.
51. Kardas, p. 170. See also Fn. 46.
52. In the latter days of the fur trade some chief traders engaged teachers and opened their kitchen classrooms to other pupils besides their own children. See *Told by the Pioneers*, pp. 87, 113, 114, 118.
53. Munnick, *Catholic Church Records*, Henry Buxton to E.E. Dye, Sept. 28, 1892, Ms. 1089, Oregon Historical Society.
54. Chinook jargon was in use prior to the arrival of the Hudson's Bay Company, but during their rule it developed more fully. One of the most interesting accounts of the jargon is given in *Notices and Voyages of the Famed Quebec Mission to the Pacific Northwest being the Correspondence, Notices, etc., of Fathers Blanchet and Demers together with those of Fathers Bolduc and Langlois* (Oregon Historical Society, Portland: Champoeg Press, 1956), pp. 12, 14, 18–19, 21, 80, 87, 90, 150, 169.
55. Hussey, *Fort Vancouver*, p. 291. Similarly, Lewis Morgan noted that Cree was the 'mother tongue' of many of the English speaking 'half-bloods' at Red River. Morgan, *Systems of Consanguinity and Affinity of the Human Family*, p. 206.
56. Ranald MacDonald to E.E. Dye, March 21, 1892, Ms. 1089, Oregon Historical Society, MacDonald discusses travelling in a basket in early childhood. Information on swaddling via the native cradleboard is given in C. Hudson and H. Phillips, 'Rousseau and the Disappearance of Swaddling among Western Europeans', *Essays on Medical Anthropology* (Athens: University of Georgia Press, 1968), p. 14.
57. 'John Work Journal', Aug. 27, 1824 (BC Provincial Archives).
58. Examples of childhood disciplining are given in Hussey, p. 291; Pambrun, *Sixty Years on the Frontier*, pp. 27–37.
59. Information on the diet of the working class in England is contained in Charles Francatelli, *A Plain Cookery Book for the Working Class* (London: Scholar Press, 1977; copyright 1852). Pinchbeck and Hewitt, *Children in English Society*, pp. 407, 420, 428; E.P. Thompson, *The Making of the English Working Class* (New York: Penguin Books, 1979), pp. 220, 316, 319–20. For the diet of the Fort Vancouver worker, see Lester A. Ross, 'Early Nineteenth Century Euroamerican Technology within the Columbia River Drainage System' (Fort Vancouver National Historic Site Report, n.d.); Douglas Leechman, 'I sowed Garden Seeds', *The Beaver*, Winter 1970, p. 32.

60. Harvey, 'Life of John McLoughlin', pp. 6, 9; Thomas Roulstone, 'A Social History of Fort Vancouver: 1829–1849' (MA Thesis, Utah State University, 1975), pp. 99, 134–5.

61. Some ages of marriage are given in Munnick, *Catholic Church Records*; others can be calculated from *Early Marriage Records: Clackamus County, Wasco County, Oregon* (Tualatin Chapter Daughters of the American Revolution, Oswego, Oregon, 1960).

62. Sidney W. Mintz, 'Culture: An Anthropological View', *The Yale Review*, 71, 4 (1982), pp. 499–527.

63. Duke Redbird, *We Are Métis* (Toronto: Ontario Métis and Non-Status Indian Association, 1980), pp. 6–7.

64. *United States Census of Oregon, 1850*. Oregon Historical Society; *Genealogical Material in Oregon Provisional Land Claims*, Vols. I–VIII, 1845–1849 (Genealogical Forum of Portland, Oregon, 1982); *Oregon Donation Land Claims*, Vols. I–IV (Genealogical Forum of Portland, Oregon, 1967).

65. John P. Gaines, Alonzo A. Skinner, Beverly S. Allen to Hon. Luke Lea, Commissioner Indian Affairs, May 14, 1851, *Message From the President, 1850–1851*, pp. 468–72; Thomas Jessett, *Chief Spokan Garry: 1811–1892* (Minneapolis: T.S. Denison and Company, 1960), pp. 96–8, 108, 113, 119–20.

66. Willard Rees to Hubert Bancroft, Sept. 18, 1879 (Bancroft Papers, Bancroft Library, Berkeley). There were 48 Métis land claimants in 1842 in the Willamette Valley. See J.N. Barry, *The French Canadian Pioneers* (Portland, 1936).

67. Pambrun, pp. 134–8; Sampson, *John McLoughlin's Business Correspondence*, p. 69.

68. By 'elite' I mean scientists, academics, politicians, clergy—people who had access to media coverage. The reminiscences given here contain many examples of life in communities where white men and native women were the norm, and indicate a high degree of racial tolerance. See *Told By the Pioneers*; Fred Lockley, *Conversations with Pioneer Women; Conversations with All Sorts and Conditions of Men; Visionaries, Mountain Men and Empire Builders* (Eugene: Rainy Day Press, 1981, 1982). Many people who would later be well known in public life emerge from fur trade childhoods. Take as an example, Dr S.F. Tolmie, premier of British Columbia (1928–33), who was the seventh son of trader Dr W.F. Tolmie and his Métis wife Jane Work, daughter of Chief Trader John Work. See S.R. Tolmie, 'My Father William Fraser Tolmie', in Tolmie, *Physician and Fur Trader*, pp. 385–95.

69. By 'biological reality' I mean the present biological evidence which suggests there is no such thing as races. See: Richard H. Osborne, ed., *The Biological and Social Meaning of Race* (San Francisco: W.H. Freeman and Company, 1971), pp. 3–13; Stephen Jay Gould, *Ever Since Darwin* (New York: W.W. Norton and Company, 1977), pp. 231–7. In their writings, fur trade children seemed compelled to prove that they were as good as white men. See McKay to E.E. Dye; Lewis and Murakami, *Ranald MacDonald*; Pambrun, *Sixty Years on the Frontier*; Robert Birnie, 'Life and Adventures of Robert Birnie born at Astoria, Oregon, Feb. 7, 1824', San Francisco, 1972, Ms. 65-33, Bancroft Library.

70. Christina MacDonald McKenzie Williams, 'The Daughter of Angus MacDonald', *Washington Historical Quarterly*, 13 (1922), p. 116.

From *A Journal of voyages and travels in the interiour of North America*

Daniel Williams Harmon

1811

April 21, Sunday. A few Days ago I sent the most of our People to McLeods Lake to prepare for the voyage to Rainy Lake—and tomorrow I shall accompanied by Mr. Quesnel &c. set off for the above mentioned place and take along with me my Son George, in order to send him to my friends who are in the United States, that he may be in time instructed in the Christian Religion. From this to Montreal Mr. J. M. Quesnel will have the care of him.

[. . .]

May 8, Wednesday. People arrived from Stuarts Lake and inform me that my Woman on the 25th Ult. was brought to bed of a Daughter—whom I name Polly Harmon. As the Ice in the River begins to be bad, it is expected that a few Days hence the navigation will be open, when Messrs. Stuart & Quesnel &c. will embark with the Returns for the Rainy Lake. Dallaire remains here and tomorrow I shall set off for Stuarts Lake where God willing I shall pass the ensuing Summer—but all my most serious thoughts are taken up on reflecting on the separation which is so soon to take place with me and my beloved Son—who a few months hence will be at such an immense distance from his affectionate Father! And it is very probable I shall never see him again in this World! What can be more trying to the feelings of an affectionate Parent than thus to be separated from so young and so tender a Darling Child? There is no consideration that could induce me to send him down (especially while so young) but the thoughts that he will soon be in the arms of my kind Relations who will have it more in their power to bring him up in the paths of virtue in the civilized part of the World, than it could be possible for me to do in this Savage Country—and as I do what I flatter myself will in the end be to his advantage, so I also earnestly pray our Gracious God to protect him while in this world of trouble and sin & bless him in the next. Amen.

[. . .]

1813

December 14 [12], Sunday. On the 1st Inst. I sat off for McLeods Lake [Fort McLeod], where I found several Letters from my Brothers, which announced the most grievous and truly heart-rending tidings—that my beloved Son George was no more to be numbered among the living! He who was enjoying good health the second of March was on the 18th of the same Month a lifeless Corpse! For some time I could not bring myself to credit what I read, yet I had no reason to doubt of the sad news being but too true! This stroke of Providence was so sudden and so great that I could hardly bear up under it with a becoming resignation to the dispensations of an ever just God! All my love and affections were placed on my darling Boy! and I had flattered myself with the pleasing hope and expectations that he would be the solace and comfort of my latter Days! But alas! delusive hope! he is no more! On what a weak foundation do we build our happyness in this World of disappointments and sorrow! Yesterday I thought myself one of the happyest of Men living; but now am the most miserable! What is there now this side the Grave worth placing my affections upon? My promising Son is no more! for whom alone I wished to live or should have been willing to die! Perhaps I placed too much of my love and affections on my departed Child, which was due only to my Creator—then I hope with Gods assistance I shall learn and become sensible of this all-important truth, that there is nothing in this changeable and fleeting World worth placing our affections upon, but ought to know that our hearts and souls belong wholly to our Gracious Maker, as well as believe that whenever we are chastised it is not without a sufficient cause—and should the dear object of our love be taken from us we may rest assured that all ultimately must be for the best, however grievous it may now be to us to bear up under. May the change my darling Son has so early made, be a happy one to *him*, and a seasonable warning to *me* to prepare myself with Gods aid (without which I am conscious I can do nothing) to meet that awful event which according to the course of nature must soon take place. Amen.

On my return from McLeods Lake I was accompanied by Mr. McDougall & Family, who are come over to mourn with me & my departed Son's Mother the loss of our Darling Child!

[. . .]

1819

February 28, Sunday. Mr. George McDougall has arrived here from Frazer's Lake, to remain, as I am going to McLeod's Lake, to prepare for a departure for Head Quarters; and my intention is, during the next summer, to visit my native land. I design, also, to take my family with me, and leave them there, that they may be educated in a civilized and christian manner. The mother of my children will accompany me; and, if she shall be satisfied to remain in that part of the world, I design to make her regularly my wife by a formal marriage. It will be seen by this remark, that my intentions have materially changed, since the time that I first took her to live with me; and as my conduct in this respect is different from that which has generally been pursued by the gentlemen of the North West Company, it will be proper to state some of the reasons which have governed my decision, in regard to this weighty affair. It has been made with the most serious deliberation; and I hope, under a solemn sense of my accountability to God.

Having lived with this woman as my wife, though we were never formally contracted to each other, during life, and having children by her, I consider that I am under a moral obligation not to dissolve the connexion, if she is willing to continue it. The union which has been formed between us, in the providence of God, has not only been cemented by a long and mutual performance of kind offices, but, also, by a more sacred consideration. Ever since my own mind has turned effectually to the subject of religion, I have taken pains to instruct her in the great doctrines and duties of christianity. My exertions have not been in vain. Through the merciful agency of the Holy Spirit, I trust that she has become a partaker with me, in the consolations and hopes of the gospel. I consider it to be my duty to take her to a christian land, where she may enjoy Divine ordinances, grow in grace, and ripen for glory. —We have wept together over the early departure of several children, and especially, over the death of a beloved son. We have children still living, who are equally dear to us both. How could I spend my days in the civilized world, and leave my beloved children in the wilderness? The thought has in it the bitterness of death. How could I tear them from a mother's love, and leave her to mourn over their absence, to the day of her death? Possessing only the common feelings of humanity, how could I think of her, in such circumstances, without anguish? On the whole, I consider the course which I design to pursue, as the only one which religion and humanity would justify.

[. . .]

[From W. Kaye Lambe, ed., *Sixteen Years in the Indian Country: The Journals of Daniel Williams Harmon 1800–1816* (Toronto: Macmillan 1957). Originally published as *A journal of voyages and travels in the interior of North America: between the 47th and 58th degrees of north latitude, extending from Montreal nearly to the Pacific Ocean, a distance of about 5,000 miles, including an account of the principal occurrences during a residence of nineteen years in different parts of the country; to which are added a concise description of the face of the country, its inhabitants, their manners, customs, laws, religion, etc., a considerable specimens of the two languages most extensively spoken, together with an account of the principal animals to be found in the forest and praires of this extensive region* by Daniel Williams Harmon (Andover, Mass., 1820).]

Suggestions for Further Reading

Brown, Jennifer S.H., 'Children of the Early Fur Trades,' in Joy Parr, ed., *Childhood and Family in Canadian History*. Toronto: Oxford University Press, 1982.

Hubert, Denis and Bertrand Desjardins, 'Effect of Family Rupture and Recomposition on the Children of New France.' *History of the Family* 2, 3 (1997): 277–93.

Landry, Yves, 'Gender Imbalance, Les Filles du Roi and Choice of Spouse in New France' in Bettina Bradbury, ed., *Canadian Family History*. Toronto: Irwin, 1992: 14–32.

Magnuson, Roger, *Education in New France*. Montreal & Kingston: McGill-Queen's University Press, 1992.

Peterson, Jacqueline and Jennifer S. Brown, eds, *The New Peoples: Being and Becoming Métis in North America*. Winnipeg: The University of Manitoba Press, 1985.

PART 3

Youthful Workers in Resource and Manufacturing Industries, 1841–1923

Many children raised in working-class families in the late nineteenth and early twentieth centuries worked for wages. The Industrial Revolution altered family economies. In agricultural communities, children provided valuable labour. Clothing and food was produced domestically. Children worked alongside their parents to build the family farm and might inherit a share of the family enterprise. In cities, families bought most of their food and clothing and the precarious labour market destabilized the family economy. Working-class families relied on waged labour, the unpaid domestic work of mothers, homework, and diverse money-saving strategies to survive. Children's paid and unpaid work was crucial to the family economy. Young workers were extremely vulnerable because, before the 1880s, there were no laws to regulate factory safety, wages, or the minimum age at which they could enter the factory. Campaigns for minimum standards in work conditions gave children legal protection from employers. However, as the testimonials of Miss Georgiana Loiselle and J.M. Fortier before the 1889 Royal Commission on the Relations of Labor and Capital demonstrate, manufacturers flouted minimum-age requirements and often treated young factory workers poorly.

Capitalists, eager for profit, hired women and children at lower wages, thus undercutting men's wages. These patterns were not uniform. In his study of young mine workers in Nova Scotia, Robert McIntosh argues that older and more experienced colliers protected their status in the pits by labelling the work of boys 'unskilled'. Yet a boy's early participation in the mines often secured him a better-paid job when he matured into manhood, thus enhancing his status in the family. Girls could not expect similar advancement or independence. Rebecca Priegert Coulter shows how one young woman negotiated poverty, racism, violence, and moral supervision to gain some control over her life. Ethel T.'s circumstances were unique, but her limited economic opportunities and the unsympathetic judgments against her character have parallels elsewhere. Because girls lived away from their families' supervision, social reformers worried more about their leisure time than their wages or work conditions. Young working men earned respect and a relative degree of autonomy; young working women posed a moral dilemma.

Nancy Janovicek

The Boys in the Nova Scotian Coal Mines: 1873-1923

Robert McIntosh

A correspondent of the *Scottish American Journal*, who visited the Albion Mines in Pictou County in 1880, could not help but be struck by a sharp division in the mine labour force: 'The boys seem(ed) happy enough, and were bright little fellows from 11 to 15 years of age; the men were respectful and small in stature, but they appeared dull and phlegmatic by contrast with the younger generation.' Unfortunately, colliery boys have not caught historians' attention as they did this Victorian correspondent's. While the relatively 'dull and phlegmatic' older Nova Scotian miners have been the subject of an extensive amount of recent historical research, the boys have been virtually ignored.[1]

The boys were by no means a homogeneous group. In the provincial Mines Act, the term 'boy' was taken to refer to anyone under 18; within the mining community, it was often applied to anyone not yet meriting the use of the handpick—in other words, one who had yet to attain the position of coal cutter, or miner proper. 'Boy' described individuals aged from eight to 21, engaged in a variety of occupations within the mine. From 1880 to 1890 the proportion of boys in the provincial colliery workforce rose from 17.1 to 21.5 per cent but they failed to participate fully in the large expansion in the mine workforce after the turn of the century. Their relative strength in the mine workforce fell steadily during the early twentieth century as their average age increased and by 1910 they comprised only 8.8 per cent of the mine workers. In 1923, legislation virtually excluded boys from the province's coal mines.[2]

Boys were in the mines for a number of reasons. The state of technology in the late nineteenth century required that individuals under a certain size be employed for particular tasks. Wage levels have also to be stressed: the labour of boys was cheaper than that of their fathers and older brothers. The presence of young workers in the mine had further advantages for older workers: by equating 'boys' with low-skill, poorly paid work, the status of the 'skilled' collier was safeguarded. At the same time, the boys' employment was welcomed within mining families, since they could then contribute to the family income and since their early initiation into the Victorian coal mine was expected to lead eventually to the most highly skilled positions.

One important factor determining the number of boys employed was the method of late nineteenth- and early twentieth-century coal mining. The technique used over this period, labelled 'room and pillar', had been introduced into Nova Scotia by the General Mining Association in the middle third of the nineteenth century.[3] A variety of levels were driven outward from the core shaft in the mine; balances were cut up into coal seam from these levels. In each balance, 'rooms' from which coal was mined in an initial cutting alternated with the 'pillars' of coal left to buttress the mine ceiling. This technique of extraction gave the mine a characteristic 'honeycomb' appearance. Popular with the miners—the disparate workplaces within the mine allowed them a good deal of autonomy—it persisted in the province against the inroads of more modern mining techniques. Notwithstanding minor nineteenth-century experiments, the more regimented 'longwall' system of mining did not first appear in a major Springhill pit until 1924; 'room and pillar' endured into the 1920s and beyond on Cape Breton and not until 1930 did longwall begin to replace 'room and pillar' in Pictou County.[4] Loading continued to be undertaken by hand at least as long.[5] Although improvements in haulage continued to be introduced over this period, horses had yet to be displaced by 1923. While the introduction of mechanical cutters transformed facework between 1873 and 1923, boys' work was substantially unchanged.

Two early nineteenth-century innovations in mining greatly increased the demand for child labour. Pioneered in Great Britain, these and other state-of-the-art mining techniques were subsequently introduced into Nova Scotia by the General Mining Association. In Great Britain, the introduction of horses and some wheeled vehicles underground had gradually displaced women, the traditional 'beasts of burden.' As the burden of work became lighter, women were replaced by the less expensive labour of boys. By mid-century the task of hauling coal generally fell to 14- to 17-year-old boys, called drivers, and the horses they led. Where seams were too narrow to permit the passage of horses (or adults), coal continued to be moved manually by boys on all fours dragging sledges. A second technological innovation early in the nineteenth century encouraged the employment of even younger children. As mines extended deeper underground, problems of ventilation became more pressing. Under the compound system of mine ventilation developed by John Buddle, doors known as 'traps' were introduced into mines. Generally closed so as to channel air throughout the mine, these doors had to be frequently opened to allow the passage of drivers, their horses and material. 'Trappers', often less than 10 years old, were employed to perform this task. These boys worked long days relative even to the miners, since they were the first down the shaft and the last to leave the mine at the end of the shift. At Victorian mines where 'expansion and technical progress' were most pronounced, child labour was most extensive.[6]

The child's experience of work in the mine, shaped by the technology of the day, changed as he grew older. The boy, introduced to the mine by his father, would likely be employed in various odd jobs on the surface, if he were not immediately placed by a trap. Surface employment might include running errands, cleaning lamps or distributing picks. Far less pleasant work involved the sorting of coal; perched above a belt carrying the recently-mined coal, it was the boys' responsibility to remove any stone inadvertently brought up with the coal. The work of trapper boys was no more appealing. Labouring 'under conditions which were very like solitary confinement in darkness', these boys almost welcomed the bullying of passing drivers as a relief from tedium.[7] [...]

The variety of tasks a boy might perform in the course of his education in 'practical mining', as the miners called it, was described to the 1888 Labor Commission by a number of Springhill mine workers. William Terrace, a veteran of the mine at 15, had first worked at the age of ten turning a fan and had recently started driving. Murdoch McLeod, a 29-year-old miner, had entered the pit at nine as a trapper; he had 'worked [him]self up', spending many years as a driver before becoming a miner. Elisha Paul's path to coal cutter was even more varied. Employed first as a trapper, Paul graduated to the position of driver within a few months. His next occupation was on a balance, supervising the movement of empty boxes up to the miners' workplaces and the passage of boxes full of coal down to the levels. By 16 he was a cage runner; he removed full boxes from the balance and replaced them with empty ones for the return trip back to the miners. Later he was employed as a loader; he filled the boxes with the coal freshly cut by the miner. At 19, Paul became a cutter.[8] The experience of these boys was not untypical of the late nineteenth-century Nova Scotian colliery; the hierarchy of tasks was not rigid and boys who aspired to the handpick could follow a variety of routes to the position of cutter.

[...]

A boy's experience of the mine might end yet another way: in death or disability. The youngest workers, less attentive and knowledgeable, nonetheless shared the dangers of the mine with older miners. Like them, the boys fell victim to the great mine disasters. The explosion in the number one mine at Springhill in 1891 killed 125—17 of them boys 16 years of age and younger.[9] Although far less striking, the daily small accidents in the colliery were in fact the greater killers. Death or disability could occur in a variety of ways. A roof fall, a common accident, killed a boy at Little Glace Bay in 1882. George Jones, approximately 14 years old, died in an explosion in 1889 while hauling timber on the nightshift; his brother James was badly burned at the same time. That same decade a boy lost his arm in an accident in the blacksmith shop at the Drummond colliery in Westville.[10] Only the fortunate survived to enjoy what PWA leader John Moffatt described as the goal of the respectable miner: 'a good, comfortable home, education, music, good literature, [and] insurance with sufficient wages to lay by to help out in old age.'[11]

The circumstances of boys' work in the mine changed little over the turn of the century. Boys continued to occupy the same kinds of positions and to receive the same levels of pay relative to adult mine workers. C.O. Macdonald estimated that in 1880 the average pay of a boy employed in a Nova Scotian colliery was 65 cents per day. An adult labourer received 50 per cent more than a boy; a cutter, nearly $2^1/_2$ times as much.[12] These different wage rates remained intact as long as boys were employed in the mines. At Sydney Mines, boys had closed the wage differential somewhat by 1920, likely because the youngest children had been excluded from the Nova Scotia mines by then, but a mine worker classified as a boy could still expect to receive approximately 60 to 70 per cent of a man's pay. Boys, limited to tasks designated for them, continued to be paid at a discriminatory rate.[13]

From these observations, it should be clear that neither changes in the technique of mining nor a substantial narrowing of differential wage rates can fully explain the boys' gradual exclusion from the mine. In fact, a change in social attitudes was the most important single cause of the boys' dwindling place in the colliery workforce. This crisis of legitimacy, as it will be labelled here, was expressed in a series of amendments to the provincial Mines Act, which raised the minimum age required for work in the mine from 10 in 1873, to 12 in 1891, and to 16 in 1923.[14]

[...]

In the 1880s [...] Nova Scotian mine workers could congratulate themselves that neither women nor girls had ever been employed in provincial collieries.[15] The burden of supporting the family therefore fell to the principal male breadwinner and as many of his sons as were employed. In the provincial coalfields, miners took steps to safeguard their employment by attempting to control the market for mine workers. In 1879, when they formed the Provincial Workmen's Association, miners sought to establish a system of 'apprenticeship' to protect the integrity of coal mining as skilled labour. [...]

The struggle over employment in the coalfields, whereby the miners attempted to restrict and management fought to broaden access to the picks, was closely tied to the question of child labour. Because they were 'apprenticed' to the craft of mining, the boys would have been given priority over newcomers to the mine by the PWA. It was never able to accomplish this objective. At a meeting of the PWA Grand Council in 1884, a delegate announced indignantly that 'at one of the mines lads verging on manhood and who had been brought up in the mine and were capable of mining were denied the picks, while those about whom the officials knew nothing were given them.'[16] [...]

In the clash between workers and mine management the participation of boys was also evident. Indeed, the boys' response to mine work was noteworthy for its vigour: the small, frightened trapper boy matured rapidly and mine boys consistently demonstrated resilience and self-reliance. An early editorial in the *Trades Journal*, the official PWA newspaper, remarked on the boys' general lack of respect for their elders and on their readiness to abuse verbally mine officials—in the expression of the day, their 'saucing'.[17] In Springhill in 1887 a boy was ordered, and refused, to travel through a section of the mine he considered dangerous. 'Harsh words passed between them', reported the *Trades Journal*, 'the boy using the harshest it is said.'[18] Their brazenness was more than merely verbal: boys' strikes over the turn of the century were a continual irritant to mine management—and, occasionally, to older mine workers.

Boys demonstrated repeatedly their willingness to quit the mine; in fact, they may have struck more often than older mine workers. Former PWA Grand Secretary and *Trades Journal* editor Robert Drummond remarked that for two years after the Dominion Steel Company gained control of Dominion Coal in 1910 there was 'not even a boy strike.'[19] In 1925 A.S. MacNeil, General Superintendent of the British Empire Steel Company mines, testified to the Duncan Royal Commission that 'a boy if he was disciplined in any way, or did anything wrong, he was liable to go home and would cause a strike in that part of the mine, or the whole of the mine, or two or three mines.'[20] A variety of motives prompted the boys to strike. Even verbal clashes with mine officials could lead to a general walkout of boys.[21] Recreational strikes— the lure of a circus or a game of baseball—also occurred periodically.[22] As well, boys struck in defence of traditional patterns of work. Dominion Coal drivers walked out to resist the replacement of contract pay by a daily rate in 1904.[23] More importantly, boys and officials consistently disputed what constituted a fair day's work and a just level of pay. Boys struck a pit at New Waterford in 1921, for instance, over hours of work—whether horses were to be stabled on the company's or the boys' time.[24] One of the earliest strikes recorded by the *Trades Journal* stemmed from a dispute over pay at Stellarton.[25] The boys' frustration at the restrictions placed on their access to promotion also gave rise to strikes. The boys at the Drummond colliery in Westville walked out for a day in June 1887 in protest against their obligation to perform boys' work—at a maximum of 75 cents per day—until the age of 18. Although mine boys were unable to graduate to the position of loader, mine neophytes—'greenhorns'— were taken on for this task. Although the *Trades Journal* believed the boys to have 'acted a little rashly', it acknowledged their 'just cause of complaint'.[26]

The qualification in this editorial reflects the ambivalence of adult miners regarding independent action on the part of boys, and suggests that tension existed between boys and older mine workers. Although employment enhanced the boy's status within the family and may have been welcomed by the boy for that reason, the boy whose father carried him to the put, 'the little fellow being unable [to manage] the long journey', probably entered the workforce unwillingly.[27]

At the Reserve Mines (Cape Breton), one observer reported in the 1880s, the 'parents generally ask for the work.'[28] At the same time, adult miners, while condoning their boys' entry into the workforce, balked at their assumption of adult roles. Reports of drunken colliery boys on mine pay days were not uncommon: a couple of 'drunk and disorderly' Stellarton boys, aged 12 and 14, found themselves jailed in the course of a particularly boisterous evening in 1888. Adult miners found intoxicated boys, in the expression of the day, 'a hard-looking sight.'[29]

[. . .]

Certainly miners' unions in Nova Scotia sanctioned discrimination against those labelled 'boys' in terms of tasks and pay. [. . .] Although trapper boys and coal sorters were generally on the company payroll, at times, particularly in the nineteenth century, drivers and loaders were paid directly by the miners. The failure of the PWA to implement satisfactorily its system of apprenticeship—as a result of the access of 'greenhorns' to the mine—and thus protect the job market led to discontent among the boys who were subject to discriminatory wage levels, especially since boyhood apprenticeship did not directly involve the acquisition of the skills of the handpick miner. Nonetheless, the pattern of initiation into mining which the PWA sought to safeguard had relative advantages. Many of the occupations available to children at this time were barred to them when they reached maturity.[30] By entering the mine, in contrast, a boy could expect to acquire the handpick eventually, and to remain a miner throughout his working life.

One of the consequences of this practise was a low level of formal education among miners. In the late nineteenth century the mining community made 'practical mining' the focus of a boy's education; although schooling could be combined with work in the mine, this made school attendance irregular and to some extent seasonal. In Cape Breton in the 1880s, attendance was relatively good over the winter when mines were closed. At other times of the year, colliery boys attended school on the days when the pit was idle.[31] Commitment within the mining community to this customary, casual approach to children's education was eroded over the turn of the century, due partly to pressure from the province, which continually raised the minimum acceptable level of formal education and established the means to enforce this minimum. The impact on the colliery boy of this evolving provincial position on education was profound.

By virtue of successive provincial school acts over the turn of the century an increasingly greater proportion of Nova Scotian children attended school to a greater age for a greater portion of the year.[32] Contemporary changes in the way childhood was defined, aspects of which emerged as early as the mid-nineteenth century, reinforced ideas about the need for universal and compulsory children's education. When the child became defined as dependent on adults and at the same time in need of protection from adults, the door was opened to extensive interference with the manner in which parents raised their children.[33] In tandem with the emergence of this modern notion of childhood appeared the outlines of a universal system of schools.

In Nova Scotia, the 'Free Schools Act' of 1864 established the framework for a common school system and an 1865 act guaranteed this system's viability by providing for compulsory assessment of property owners for the upkeep of schools. A child's formal education was not necessarily ensured by the mere existence of a school system and no provision was made in the 1860s for compulsory attendance. In 1883, however, local school boards were permitted to oblige children between 7 and 12 to attend school for at least 80 days per year and to fine parents who did not send their children to school. In 1895 the 'Towns' Compulsory Attendance Act' was passed by the province; at local option, school boards could compel every child aged between 6 and 16, resident in an incorporated town, to attend school at least 120 days per year. At the same time provision was made for truancy officers who were empowered to arrest children absent from school. Their parents were subject to fines; the child, in certain circumstances, to imprisonment. Exemptions from school were, however, granted to children over 12 with at least a grade seven common school education and any child over 13 whose income was indispensable. Because many mining communities remained unincorporated until well into the twentieth century their school boards were subject to the provisions of the Education Act pertaining to rural areas; the stipulations of 1883, which compelled children from 7 to 12 to attend school at least 80 days per year, remained in force. In 1915 the urban upper age limit was raised to 16; the House of Assembly did not inaugurate province-wide compulsory school attendance (for those 7 to 14) in rural areas until 1921. In 1923 rural school boards were given the discretion to require 6 to 16 year olds to attend school and the framework of a modern primary system of education was established in Nova Scotia.[34]

Concern for children's education was reflected not only in school legislation, but also in mines legislation. Although age restrictions on Nova Scotian mine workers had been in place since the first provincial Mines Act of 1873, which had prohibited the employment of boys under ten in or about the mines, amendments in 1891 were the first in Nova Scotia to place educational restrictions on boys entering the mines. Legislation passed in 1908 prohibited from the mine any boy between 12 and 16 who had not completed grade seven.[35] A general concern for the child's welfare and concern specifically for his education began to push the boy from the workforce.

The role of the Nova Scotian mining community regarding legislation restricting the employment of its boys was ambivalent. Robert Drummond, in his submission before the Royal Commission on the Relations between Labor and Capital in 1888, pressed for a minimum age of 12 for work underground in the mines. Other witnesses stressed to the commissioners the need within the mining community for the boys' income.[36] Even with Drummond, the question of child labour held a low priority. In 1882 the *Trades Journal* had reported that an eight-year-old labourer, 'a very precocious little chap', was employed at the Halifax Company colliery in Pictou County. The newspaper did not note that his employment brazenly contravened existing provincial statutes, but stressed that the child was foregoing 'a fair chance of education.'[37] Drummond was very reluctant to sanction interference with parental control of children in areas apart from education. When disturbing reports of child abuse at J.M. Fortier's Montreal tobacco factory arrived in Nova Scotia in 1888, Drummond maintained that it was more important to protect the worker than his child. Although he acknowledged that some protection in law was desirable for both parent and child, he insisted that 'the parent, or the guardian of the child has surely certain rights which should not be interfered with.'[38] Although the question of child labour was of limited importance to Drummond, he was concerned that a child receive a minimum level of schooling.[39] This concern, as an examination of PWA activity shows, was also limited.

PWA efforts on behalf of formal schooling focused on protecting the integrity of the miners' trade. At a meeting of the PWA Grand Council in October 1890, Drummond stressed the desirability of keeping uneducated boys out of the mine, because they were a threat to safety within the mine and they demeaned the status of the mining community generally. The Council, acknowledging the importance of schooling for miner certification, instructed the PWA legislative committee to propose to the province a minimum age of 12 for colliery workers; in addition, a boy was not to be permitted to work 'unless he was able to read, write and count as far as fractions.' The Fielding government acquiesced and the desired amendment to the Mines Act passed without debate in 1891. Although the PWA Grand Council continued to discuss child labour intermittently, the initiative for delayed entry into the collieries in order to acquire an extended formal education passed from the miners' unions in Nova Scotia to a larger community.[40]

PWA interest in children's schooling was limited to the youngest and confined to the rudiments. Even so, it appears to have been more concerned than the mining community as a whole. The *Trades Journal* reported regularly on school activities, and just as regularly berated parents for their lack of interest.[41] As late as 1908, the provincial director of technical education, F.H. Sexton, singled out the mining community for criticism, charging that boys remained ill-educated in mining towns owing to their early entry into the mine.[42] School attendance improved steadily over the turn of the century, bolstered not only by heightened provincial requirements for education but also by improved wage levels which reduced the mining family's dependence on boys' pay.[43] Nonetheless, given the entrenched sanction within the mining community for child labour, the income it brought the family, and the promises held out by formal education, the decision to send a boy into the mine or to school—or to continue school—must often have been anguished.[44]

In 1923, when the Mines Act was amended to exclude from colliery work everyone under 16, the employment of individuals who would be unhesitatingly labelled children came to a close. A variety of factors prompted the 1923 amendment. Following World War One a crisis occurred in the coal industry and there was a general rise in unemployment. Adult miners could no longer afford the luxury of apprenticed boys. By excluding boys from the mines, jobs were created for family heads. Nova Scotia also lagged seriously behind the rest of Canada with respect to legislation restricting child employment within the mine; Ontario, for instance, had prohibited the employment of boys under 15 in 1890 and in 1912 set the minimum age at 17.[45] Finally, in 1923 Nova Scotian rural school boards also received approval to raise the school-leaving age to 16. Provincial sanction had been won for a new status for children, who were universally now defined as school children. This particular amendment simply capped a lengthy process whereby the traditional sanctions for the employment of children collapsed. Social attitudes changed slowly, childhood was redefined, and new means of educating children were instituted. By this process, traditional notions of apprenticeship and collective contributions to the family budget were succeeded by state-enforced provisions for a universal, minimum level of formal education. The colliery boy gave way to the school child.

[1987]

Notes

1. *Trades Journal*, 15 September 1880. Recent theses on the miners include David Frank, 'Coal Masters and Coal Miners: the 1922 Strike and the Roots of Class Conflict in the Cape Breton Coal Industry', MA thesis, Dalhousie University, 1974; 'The Cape Breton Coal Miners (1919–1925)', MA thesis, Dalhousie University, 1979; Don Macgillivray, 'Industrial Unrest in Cape Breton 1919–1925', MA thesis, University of New Brunswick, 1971; Ian McKay, 'Industry, work and community in the Cumberland coalfields, 1848–1927', Ph.D. thesis, Dalhousie University, 1983; Robert McIntosh, 'A Community Transformed: The Nova Scotian Coal Miners 1879–1925', MA thesis, Carleton University, 1985; Sharon Reilly, 'The Provincial Workmen's Association of Nova Scotia 1879–1898', MA thesis, Dalhousie University, 1979. A recent exception to general inattention to mine boys is Ian McKay's article 'The Realm of Uncertainty: The Experience of Work in the Cumberland Coal Mines, 1873–1927', *Acadiensis* XVI, 1 (Fall 1986), pp. 3–57.
2. Nova Scotia, Department of Mines Reports, in *Journals and Proceedings of the House of Assembly*, for 1880, 1890, and 1910; Nova Scotia *Statutes*, 1923, 13 Geo. V, c. 54, sect. 1.
3. Donald MacLeod, 'Miners, mining men and mining reform: the changing technology of

Nova Scotian gold mines and collieries, 1858–1910', Ph.D. thesis, University of Toronto, 1982, p. 308.

4. McKay, 'Industry, work and community', p. 243; Frank, 'Coal Masters and Coal Miners', p. 220; James M. Cameron, *The Pictonian Colliers* (Halifax, 1973), p. 120.

5. At the more technologically advanced US bituminous mines, the first successful mechanical loader was not introduced until 1922. See Alexander Mackenzie Thompson, 'Technology, Labour and Industrial Structure of the United States Coal Industry: A Historical Perspective', Ph.D. thesis, Stanford University, 1979, p. 61.

6. See J.S. Martell, 'Early Coal-Mining in Nova Scotia', *Dalhousie Review*, XXV, 2 (July 1945), pp. 156–72; D.A. Muise, 'The GMA and the Nova Scotia Coal Industry', *Bulletin of Canadian Studies*, VI,2/VII,1 (Autumn 1983), pp. 70–87; Neil K. Buxton, *The Economic Development of The British Coal Industry* (London, 1978), pp. 27, 131; Angela V. John, *By the Sweat of Their Brow: Women Workers at Victorian Coal Mines* (London, 1980), pp. 23, 33.

7. Sir Llewellyn Woodward, *The Age of Reform* (Oxford, 1962), p. 153; John Benson, *British Coalminers in the Nineteenth Century: A Social History* (Dublin, 1980), p. 49.

8. Royal Commission on the Relations of Capital and Labor, *Nova Scotia Evidence* (Ottawa, 1889), pp. 302, 288; Greg Kealey, ed., *Canada Investigates Industrialism (The Royal Commission on the Relations of Labor and Capital, 1889)* (Toronto, 1973), pp. 402–3.

9. Roger David Brown, *Blood on the Coal: The Story of the Springhill Mining Disasters* (Windsor, NS, 1976), p. 13.

10. *Trades Journal*, 11 October 1882, 26 June 1889, 10 June 1885.

11. Quoted in Robert Drummond, *Recollections and Reflections of a Former Trades Union Leader* (n.p., c.1926), pp. 184–5.

12. C. Ochiltree Macdonald, *The Coal and Iron Industries of Nova Scotia* (Halifax, 1909), p. 45.

13. See the schedule of wages recommended by the Board of Arbitration under Judge G. Patterson for the Nova Scotia Steel and Coal Corporation, in the *Labour Gazette* (April 1920), p. 394.

14. In 1947 the minimum age for underground employment became 17; in 1954, 18. Nova Scotia *Revised Statutes*, 1873, c. 10, sect. 4; *Laws* of Nova Scotia, 1891, 54 Vic., c. 9, sect. 3, 1923, 13 Geo. V, c. 54, sect. 1; 1947, 11 Geo. VI, c. 39, sect. 7; 1954, 3 Eliz. II, c. 56, sect. 14.

15. *Trades Journal*, 18 March 1885.

16. (Semi-) Annual Meeting of (PWA) Grand Council, *Minutes* (April 1884), p. 59, Labour Canada Library, Hull.

17. *Trades Journal*, 11 August 1880. See as well the *Trades Journal*, 15 February 1888 for miners' complaints regarding a pick boy 'having a tendency to be a boss.'

18. *Trades Journal*, 17 August 1887.

19. Robert Drummond, *Minerals and Mining Nova Scotia* (Stellarton, 1918), p. 243.

20. Duncan Commission, *Minutes*, p. 2555.

21. This occurred, for example, after the altercation in Springhill mentioned above. The boy was sent home, at which time the rest of the boys in the slope struck, closing it down. *Trades Journal*, 17 August 1887.

22. Ian McKay refers to instances of boys at the Joggins mines foregoing work in favour of baseball in 'Industry, work and community', p. 608; *Halifax Herald*, 15 August 1905, 7 June 1906.

23. *Halifax Herald*, 30 January, 2 February 1904; *Maritime Mining Record*, 10 February 1904. My thanks to one of the anonymous readers for this reference.

24. 'Strikes and lockouts' file, RG 27, vol. 327, no. 171, Public Archives of Canada (PAC).

25. *Trades Journal*, 2 June 1880.

26. *Trades Journal*, 8 June 1887.

27. See McKay, 'Industry, work and community', p. 598; Annual Meeting of Grand Council, *Minutes*, 1890, p. 221.
28. Macdonald, *Coal and Iron Industry*, p. 57.
29. *Trades Journal*, 21 November 1888, 2 January 1889.
30. Gareth Stedman Jones, *Outcast London: A Study in the Relationship between Classes in Victorian Society* (Harmondsworth, 1971), pp. 68–70.
31. Macdonald, *Coal and Iron Industry*, p. 48.
32. Measured as the percentage of those enrolled in daily attendance in the winter term, attendance figures rose slightly over the late nineteenth century, from 53.2 in 1878 to 55.8 ten years later. Attendance in the second quarter (November through January) stood at 63.7 in 1900, 70.2 in 1910, and 74.4 in 1922. These figures are taken from the 'Annual Report on Schools' for the relevant year, found in Nova Scotia, *Journals and Proceedings of the House of Assembly*. Averages in mining counties such as Cumberland or Cape Breton do not differ significantly from the provincial average, but county-level figures will obscure to some extent those from mining communities.
33. A useful introduction to the extensive literature on education is Chad Gaffield, 'Back to School: Towards a New Agenda for the History of Education', *Acadiensis*, XV, 2 (Spring 1986), pp. 169–90. Early research on childhood dated the emergence of modern ideas on childhood at the turn of the century. See Neil Sutherland, *Children in English-Canada: Framing the Twentieth Century Consensus* (Toronto, 1976). Subsequently, a case has been made for an earlier, mid-nineteenth-century change in public attitudes towards children. See Patricia T. Rooke and R.L. Schnell, 'Childhood and Charity in Nineteenth-Century British North America', *Histoire sociale/Social History*, XV, 29 (May 1982), pp. 157–79. In neither instance is consideration given to the changing role of children in the workplace in shaping our notion of childhood.
34. P.L. McCreath, 'Charles Tupper and the Politics of Education in Nova Scotia', *Nova Scotia Historical Quarterly*, 1, 3 (September 1971), pp. 203–24; William B. Hamilton, 'Society and Schools in Nova Scotia' in J. Donald Wilson et al., eds, *Canadian Education: A History* (Scarborough, 1970), pp. 86–105. 46 Vic., c. 17, 'An Act to Secure Better Attendance at Public Schools'; 58 Vic., c. 1, sect. 4; 5 Geo. V, c.4, 'The Cities' and Towns' Compulsory Attendance Act'; 11–12 Geo. V., c. 59, sect.7; 13 Geo. V., c. 52, sect. 11. A synopsis of much of this legislation is found in Department of Labour, *The Employment of Children and Young Persons in Canada* (Ottawa, 1930), p. 98.
35. *Revised Statutes of Nova Scotia*, 1873, c. 10, part I, Nova Scotia, *Laws*, 1891, 54 Vic. c. 9, sect. 3; 1908, 7 Edward c. 8, sect. 19. The principle requiring a minimum level of formal education before children were permitted to work was adopted in British collieries in 1860, when legislation was enacted stipulating that 10- and 11-year-old boys could only be employed if they had earned an educational certificate or if they attended school at least two days a week for at least three hours per day. See Frederic Keeling, *Child Labour in the United Kingdom* (London, 1914), p. xiv.
36. Kealey, ed., *Canada Investigates*, p. 440; Labor Commission, *Evidence*, pp. 294, 301, 303, 351, 414.
37. *Trades Journal*, 6 December 1882.
38. *Trades Journal*, 14 March 1888.
39. The minimum age Drummond recommended, 12, was well below that recommended by the royal commissioners, 14. See also the *Trades Journal*, 24 April 1889.
40. Annual Meeting of Grand Council, *Minutes*, 1890, pp. 221–2; Nova Scotia, House of Assembly, *Proceedings and Debates*, 1891; see the Annual Meeting of Grand Council, *Minutes*, 1906, p. 532, for a debate on child labour in the context of the night shift. One

delegate argued with passion that 'it is unfair and almost inhuman to have a boy of ten-der years go into the coal mine to be stunted in physical growth and in intellect, or else be injured, possibly fatally as sometimes occurs.' The PWA showed much greater interest in adult education. See Donald MacLeod, 'Practicality Ascendant: The Origins and Establishment of Technical Education in Nova Scotia', *Acadiensis*, XV, 2 (Spring 1986), pp. 68–9.

41. See, for instance, *Trades Journal*, 4 November 1885, for Drummond's complaints about poor parental attendance at school examinations.

42. See the 'Annual Report For the Public Schools, 1907–08', in Nova Scotia, *Journals and Proceedings of the House of Assembly*, 1908, p. 81.

43. Wages in the provincial collieries improved significantly after the turn of the century. See Ian McKay, 'The Provincial Workmen's Association', in W.J.C. Cherwinski and G.S. Kealey, eds, *Lectures in Canadian Labour and Working-Class History* (St John's, 1985), p. 130.

44. McKay, 'Industry, work, and community', p. 598, discusses this in reference to the Cumberland County mines.

45. Quebec had set the age for male underground employment at 15 in 1892; Ontario had raised the age to 18 by 1919; Saskatchewan to 14 in 1917; Alberta to 16 in 1908; and British Columbia to 15 in 1911. See Department of Labour, *Employment of Children and Young Persons in Canada* (Ottawa, 1930), Table C.

Between School and Marriage: A Case Study Approach to Young Women's Work in Early Twentieth-Century Canada

Rebecca Priegert Coulter

Some may know how hard it is to get work of any kind in the winter, so when one has tramped the streets for three weeks in summer shoes, and only one meal a day to save the [baby one is carrying]. . . . You who have . . . everything to make life worthwhile do not often think of the things many of us have to go through . . . We have not the talent, nor the education that some of your children have, and I am one of those who do not have that opportunity.[1]

So spoke a destitute and pregnant young Edmonton woman in 1925. Her poignant words well illustrate the conjunction of class, gender and age as it was experienced by many female youths in English Canada between the wars. Poverty and unemployment were common for young, working-class women after they left school and, indeed, it was often similar circumstances within their families of origin which led to the 'things many of us have to go through' of which she speaks. The words of this young woman both reveal an elementary consciousness of class differences ('You who have everything') and the self-blaming, hidden injuries of class ('We have not the talent').[2] Revealed, too, is the belief that an opportunity to attain higher educational levels would have made a difference in her life chances.

This young woman, although she speaks of hunger and the lack of work and money, is less explicit about those other circumstances, directly related to her femaleness, that she had 'to go through' and which resulted in an unwanted pregnancy. As a 1915 social survey of Toronto showed, and as evidence from other regions illustrates,[3] many young women were forced to turn to prostitution during lay-offs or periods when other work could not be found or when meagre earnings from other occupations were insufficient to maintain life. Indeed, some girls were forced into situations where they exchanged sex for nothing more than food and lodging. And, as Strong-Boag notes, many women also had to engage in sexual activity with male employers or customers simply to keep their jobs. As one nineteen-year-old waitress put it, 'getting screwed' by a 'most objectionable little creep' who owned the restaurant where she worked was 'part of the job'. She never told anyone because her mother 'would have died' and her family desperately needed the money she earned.[4] For this woman, too, her sex and her class had implications for the ways in which she experienced her life.

With the resurgence of the women's movement in the last two decades and the growth of feminist scholarship supported by that resurgence, a sizeable literature on women's work has appeared. Feminists have engaged in lengthy and involved theoretical debates about how we should understand the significance of domestic labour, the relationship of reproductive and productive work and their links to the sexual division of labour, and the relative importance of class and sex/gender relations in women's lives.[5] It is not our purpose here to rehearse all the arguments; that 'society has to be understood as constituted through the *articulation* [emphasis in original] of both sex/gender and class antagonisms'[6] is clear when we examine the actual labour market experiences of young women in Canada in the first half of the twentieth century. This 'doubled vision of feminist theory', as Joan Kelly called it, enables us to look at '*the simultaneous operation* [emphasis in original] of relations of work and sex, relations that are systematically bound to each other—and always have been so bound'.[7]

[. . .]

It is also true that feminism draws our attention to the importance of individual experience and understanding and to the collective experiences of women in the past. It compels us to listen to the voices of women as they speak of their lives and their struggles and how they understood and worked to control or change their situations. As Geraldine Jonçich Clifford has said:

> The meanings people attach to their experiences; their sense of what drives or limits their actions; the victories and defeats of their lives; what builds them up and what tears or wears them down; the struggle within as well as the struggle without—these are also the data of history.[8]

On this basis, it is appropriate to look at the more generalized experiences of young women entering the labour market through the prism of those specific lives the sources enable us to uncover. It is this approach which offers one way to examine how young women attempted to shape and control their own lives within the structures or 'circumstances not of their own choosing'.

Ethel T. was born in 4 May 1900 of black, Baptist parents in San Bernadino, California.[9] In infancy she lost her biological mother, whether through death, divorce or desertion we do not know. In any event, when Ethel was three she acquired a step-mother named Alice. In 1913 the family moved to Canada and though they originally settled in Edmonton, Alberta, they also appeared to have filed for a homestead about one hundred miles north of the city, in a region where a substantial community of black settlers already lived. In 1914 Ethel's father died and in October of that year Ethel and her step-mother moved out to the homestead, presumably with the intention of fulfilling the legal obligations to live on and clear the land in order to obtain title to it and, perhaps, with some desire to join the existing black community located in the vicinity.

Fourteen-year-old Ethel and her step-mother worked side-by-side to survive the rigours of homesteading and a northern Alberta winter and managed to plant a crop in the spring. Their situation was extremely difficult. In the words of Ethel's step-mother, Alice, Ethel

> stayed there [on the homestead] with me until I got hard of means and I didn't know what to do. I had the crop in and no money. Then she said 'Mama, you get me some work and I'll go and work for you'.

Thus Ethel, like generations of dutiful daughters before and since, contributed free labour in the home and on the farm as part of a family strategy for survival and then went out into the world to earn money which would also be used to support the family. [. . .] In Alberta, however, the evidence for the early twentieth century suggests that while women's wages were so low as to make life very difficult, many young women from farms nonetheless managed to scrimp and save enough to send money to their families of origin.[10] Furthermore, even when daughters did not send money home, their families may have felt direct reductions in the household budgets since the girls would not be consumers of food, clothing and other items within the family economy. [. . .] The under-valuing of women's domestic work and the relative invisibility of much of it would thus encourage the view that farm daughters were expendable and mothers could do without their help, whereas sons were essential and fathers needed their labour power.

In urban families, however, daughters living at home and engaged in wage labour could make important contributions to family budgets as well as contribute their unpaid labour to the management of the household. Unlike their rural sisters who would be seen as making their most important contribution to the family by moving away, urban girls were encouraged by fathers, some employers and the state to live at home under the protection and control of their fathers until marriage when they would move to dependency on other men, their husbands. In the same context, domestic service was seen by the patriarchal state as the most desirable occupation for rural girls seeking paid employment since it provided an acceptable surrogate for the families they had left behind.[11]

Returning to Ethel's story we find that she did indeed repeat the traditional pattern of entering domestic service. She was able to secure employment as a live-in servant in a town located twenty-five miles from the homestead at a wage of $14.00 per month, a fortuitous circumstance in some respects since job opportunities for young women in rural areas were scarce. Illustrating the very insecure and tenuous nature of domestic service employment in general, Ethel found that shortly after commencing work, her job simply disappeared when her employer travelled to California for an operation. Ethel returned to the homestead but was re-engaged a few months later. Within weeks, Ethel's step-mother, having completed the harvest, moved to Edmonton to secure paid employment of her own. Ethel was left behind and in the care of her employer. It is likely that at this point Ethel believed that she was out in the world on her own, that she had to make her own way. Cut off from the only family she had in Canada, she almost certainly would have felt a sense of loneliness and isolation and may even have thought that she had been deserted by her step-mother.

In many respects Ethel was in a strange situation. On the one hand, she had left her family and was earning a wage of her own, an arrangement that might be thought to afford adult status. On the other hand, because she was in domestic service, her employer felt that Ethel should be treated as a young daughter, as a dependent, and, as a consequence, that she should be subjected to close supervision in all aspects of her life. There is obviously a tension here between the potential for independence and the reality of dependence. In fact, of all of the aspects of domestic service criticized by young employees—low wages, long hours, unbearable sleeping arrangements in damp basements or with the toddlers of the household, uncaring bossiness from employers, sexual harassment from the men in the family—it is the fact of close supervision about which young women most often were bitter. While perceiving themselves as independent wage earners, they were subjected to the worst aspects of being young and female, namely the drudgery, isolation and boredom of housework, without necessarily experiencing any of the potentially offsetting factors such as family affection and warmth. Their lives were closely monitored, they had little opportunity for social interaction with peers and few days or even evenings off during which they might take up outside interests. In important respects, domestic service for young women simply extended the period of dependency they had known as children.[12]

Ethel chose to rebel against this dependency, for shortly after her step-mother left for the city, Ethel's employer reported that the girl had begun to 'run wild'. As evidence of this, it was reported that Ethel had once stayed out all night and had, on two other occasions, stayed out until midnight. Ethel was threatened with termination of employment but, taking matters into her own hands, she ran away to the city. As a result of this, she was reported to the police. Flight from domestic service in this, and many other instances, was seen as a 'crime' with moral dimensions rather than as a decision to resign with one's feet from an unsatisfactory employment position.[13]

This attitude can be partly explained by examining what was considered appropriate behaviour for young females in English Canada in the first part of this century. While Canadians began increasingly to speak of 'adolescence' as that period of life confined to the teenage years and marked by the struggle for independence and self-knowledge, it is clear that this period of growth and exploration, of restlessness and searching, of storm and stress was to be reserved for young males only. In fact, as Barbara Hudson[14] convincingly argues, the youth/adolescence construct significantly contradicts the 'femininity' construct which is based on a discourse of passivity and dependence. Girls, therefore, cannot be 'youths/adolescents' without challenging society's perceptions of them as 'feminine' and the very signs of independence and self-discovery that would be lauded in a teenage boy's behaviour are thoroughly condemned in a girl's behaviour. That was why a boy could 'sow his wild oats' with relative impunity for this was seen as fulfilling his need to explore, struggle with and control his world, this was how he became a man while at the same time confirming the pattern of male dominance and female subordination. Girls, on the other hand, had to meet a very different set of behavioural expectations and 'saucy', self-reliant girls were the cause of much alarm for adults. Independent, aggressive, self-directed girls were seen as aberrant as, in a positive sense they were, for they threatened the concept of ideal womanhood cultivated by a patriarchal and capitalist society, an ideal which reinforced women's subordination. It might be expected, too, that challenges to the prevailing structures and dominant ideology by women would be dealt with in one form or another by elements of the state apparatus or even by individuals, especially, but not necessarily, men. Such a fate awaited Ethel.

After she left her rural placement, Ethel made her way to the city of Edmonton where she once again secured work as a domestic. It was in this situation that child welfare authorities, following up on the police report of her 'running away', found her. On discovering that she was gainfully employed as a domestic servant and living in with the family, they noted that she seemed to be 'doing alright' and dropped the case.

However, Ethel did not stay long in domestic service for another girl told her she could make more money going out to do washing. She soon found being a washerwoman too hard on her back and she again changed jobs, this time taking on a position as a waitress. The café at which she worked went out of business soon after Ethel started and she moved on to a job in a meat packing plant. This rapid progression of jobs, four in less than a year, was typical of the experiences of many young women who moved from one work site to another in pursuit of marginally better money or somewhat improved working conditions or because the employment situations they found rarely guaranteed job security. Seasonal work and lay-offs were common.

All young women experienced difficulties of various kinds as they participated in the paid labour market. The organization of gender relations structured the kinds of work they would be allowed to do or would consider doing, the levels of pay they could expect to achieve and the treatment they would receive from male employers. The commonly accepted notion and the reality that paid work was, for young women, a temporary experience sandwiched in between childhood and their *real* adult work of housewifery and motherhood, made it easier to exploit their labour. The organization of class relations meant that some young women, like Ethel, would find themselves at the bottom of the hierarchy of women's jobs, precisely because, as the destitute Edmonton girl quoted at the beginning stated, they lacked education and opportunities.

Throughout the first decades of the twentieth century, clerical work became the most sought after employment for substantial numbers of young women partly because it provided the best pay and often the most dependable and continuous employment. Sometimes there were even opportunities for promotion. However, as Hunter and Rotella point out, certain specific skills such as typewriting and a facility in reading, writing and arithmetic were required and the place to acquire them most easily was the formal setting of the school, especially in commercial courses or in private business colleges.[15] Girls who left school early either because their families could not afford to support their attendance or saw no use in girls getting an education, failed to acquire the necessary skills to enter clerical work or, for that matter, teaching or nursing. In fact, as Graham Lowe has observed, the clerical labour market was itself internally stratified and dependent on levels of education, skill and experience. Even during years of serious labour shortages such as 1916, when Ethel entered the Edmonton labour market, '[p]oorly trained and inexperienced young women still had trouble finding work.'[16]

Because Ethel's life circumstances forced her out of school and into the work force at age fourteen, she was condemned to work in less lucrative areas such as domestic service and waitressing. When her stint of work in the meat packing plant was cut short by illness, not surprising given the harsh working conditions usually found in that industry, she lived with a female friend while recuperating and continued to live there even after taking up another position as a domestic servant, again for $14.00 a month. As has been noted, such a 'live out' situation would be unusual in domestic service work, but for Ethel it meant that she escaped the usual close supervision by employers of their servants' lives. It meant, in fact, that Ethel was able to have a social life, attend parties and dances, go out with friends of her own age and shop for clothes with other girls without being under the direct supervision of an adult. Thus Ethel, and the other young girls like her who left school in their midteens, experienced their youth in a setting other than a school one.

Mention has already been made of the fact that teenage girls would experience tensions and contradictions between adolescence and femininity, between the struggle for independence and expectations of dependence and passivity. As Ethel lived through these tensions and contradictions, she came to know what it was to be female in a patriarchal and capitalist world.

One night Ethel and her friend, Addie, attended a house party at the invitation of a married friend, Mrs Virgil. Because the party did not break up until 1.30 a.m., Virgil, ostensibly concerned about the girls' safety, encouraged them not to walk home alone in the dark and suggested they stay for the night. Shortly after Ethel went to bed, a male boarder in the Virgil home entered Ethel's bedroom uninvited and attempted to rape her. Ethel managed to escape and ran to her friend's bed for protection. The man, whose name was De Witt, followed Ethel and got into bed with both the girls and then, using substantial physical force, literally kicked Addie out of the bed.

On hearing the girls yell and scream, Virgil entered the room but reportedly did little to protect Addie or Ethel. In fact, she actually encouraged Ethel to 'give in' to De Witt and promised she would pay Ethel some money in the morning if she cooperated. Ethel, however, was outraged and refused such a proposition whereupon, in her words, De Witt

> took me by the feet and he took me by the arm and took me back to the other room, and he put me on the bed, and he tried to get the advantage of me, he had his underwear open and was holding it aside with his hand, then I fought and got him off and I went back to Addie. Then he goes and calls Lee Thomas, who was upstairs, and before that he said he would kick my teeth down my throat, and he hit me in the eye, so he goes and calls Lee Thomas and sayd [sic] 'Come on down, we're going to fix these girls, but don't let her sass you like this one has.[17]

The record of Ethel's testimony ends here so it is difficult to determine whether she was raped or not. However, her description of events is a vivid portrayal of male violence again women and the way in which individual men took it upon themselves to discipline women, to 'teach them a lesson'. And just in case Ethel did not learn the lesson, the court, too, engaged in some discipline of its own. In January 1917, and as a result of the sexual assault, sixteen-year-old Ethel appeared in Magistrate's Court in Edmonton charged with being a neglected child.

In making her a ward of the Department of Neglected Children, the magistrate lectured Ethel.

> I think you need a good sound thrashing . . . They say a thankless child is like a serpant's [sic] tooth, you are not returning your mother anything, but are bringing disgrace and shame oupon [sic] her . . . Now you have got to obey me, you have evaded your mother but you can't get away from me. I am going to make you a Ward of the Department and that means that you belong to the Court instead of your mother, and if you don't do as they [sic] tell you, and if you run around with those fast men, and with girls like Cutie Wade, they will lock you up. If you are not absolutely obedient, if you are flighty or stay out late at night, I shall know about it and you will be locked up.[18]

In other words, Ethel had become too independent and the state, like De Witt, was going to 'teach her a lesson'. Her manner of living was a challenge to the prevailing standards and dominant ideology of middle-class femininity and that challenge was to be met with close supervision and punitive correction. Under the control of neither father nor husband, Ethel was henceforward to become '*absolutely* obedient' to representatives of the patriarchal state.

Who was this unsympathetic magistrate with a desire to thrash, control and lock up a victimized teenage girl? *She* was Emily Murphy, a prominent Canadian 'maternal feminist'[19] and the first woman magistrate in the British Empire. Even as she disposed of Ethel's case Murphy was actively engaged in the struggle for women's suffrage and for the legal recognition of women as 'persons' under the British North America Act.[20] In this context how are we to understand the explosion of anger directed towards Ethel? How could someone who worked so hard for women's rights treat an individual woman so harshly?

Racism was a powerful factor in this case. Ethel was a black woman in a city that was overwhelmingly white and Emily Murphy like many other social reformers of the day, harboured serious concerns about the advisability of admitting immigrants other than those who were white and from western Europe or the United States. It was also argued that girls from the 'hot' countries were prone to sexual precociousness and promiscuity and were in particular need of control.

While Murphy was undoubtedly racist, it must be recognized her distaste for Ethel's way of life also had its genesis in class differences. Ethel moved around from job to job and from address to address. This was part of the life of a young woman trying to survive in the world without an education or a strong family or social support system but the magistrate may well have seen it as evidence of instability and incorrigibility. Furthermore, working-class girls were consistently condemned for their inappropriate and 'frivolous' concerns, for their love of a good time and their desire for fancy clothes. Ethel went to parties and dances, she stayed out late in mixed company and some of that company had had previous skirmishes with the law. In some sense, then, she was seen as in need of protection from herself for had she not authored her own misfortune by engaging in 'loose' behaviour?

Part of Murphy's anger may also be attributed to her belief that Ethel was 'a thankless child' who caused nothing but trouble for her mother. As we have seen, however, this is not an accurate description, for Ethel's mother acknowledged in the court room that her daughter had been supportive, had gone out to work to earn money for her family. Murphy appeared to ignore this and it is fair to conclude that in ascribing her own feelings to Ethel's mother, Murphy demonstrated not only a disregard for a working-class woman's views but also an abject failure to understand the hard choices which faced members of families living in poverty.

The harsh words of reprobation showered on Ethel were not unique to this case. Other girls also were thoroughly chastised by Murphy. For example, in 1921, a young woman serving time in the Fort Saskatchewan Gaol wrote to Murphy with the following plea.

> Mrs Murphy please don't order anymore whippings for me. Sargent gave me such a hard whipping I shall never forget it. I have come to the conclusion I have been a bad girl but will be a good girl when I get out . . . With lots of love from your little girl Margaret.[21]

Murphy's reply was unsympathetic. She had not ordered the whipping 'but if you got one, I have no doubt in the world that it was well deserved as apparently you are behaving yourself better'.[22]

In trying to understand this tough-minded approach to young women, we must remember that maternal feminists like Murphy based their claims for equality on arguments about women's moral superiority. Because of this they had a high stake in demonstrating the accuracy of their position.[23] Fear that evidence of 'moral slippage' would be drawn from cases such as Ethel's to challenge the very tentative grasp some (middle-class) women had gained on positions of power, might well explain why maternal feminists such as Murphy would respond aggressively to women who 'let down the side'.

It is not only the nature of the relationship between the young, black, working-class woman, Ethel T., and the middle-aged, white and middle-class feminist, Emily Murphy, which this case raises. Although recent studies[24] have begun to explore how women individually and collectively react and respond to one another while living in a male-dominated society, it remains extremely difficult to describe, let alone understand, the complex interplay of race, class, ethnicity, age, sexuality and other variables in the lives of Canadian women in general and young working-class women in particular. The voices of this latter group are especially muted because of their youth, sex and class.

Nevertheless, some sources suggest enough to allow a tentative exploration of the degree to which women offered mutual support on the basis of their shared femaleness. Any tendency to romanticize women's support for women must be dealt a blow when considering Virgil's role in the assault against Ethel. What are we to make of Virgil's refusal to respond to Ethel's plea for help? Did Virgil simply want to avoid trouble with her male boarder or perhaps even curry his favour? Was she herself a victim of De Witt's violence? Did she think that Ethel lived so close to the margins anyway that she might as well learn that a girl could earn more money by selling sex than by scrubbing floors? Did Virgil's offer to reward Ethel financially for 'giving in' to De Witt indicate that Virgil was in the business of recruiting young women to prostitution?

It is impossible to answer these questions with any certainty but it can be said that despite Ethel's experiences with Murphy and Virgil, it would not be appropriate to characterize relations between younger and older women as hostile or uncaring. Considerable evidence to the contrary can be found. For example, in Edmonton in the 1920s two institutions managed and staffed by older women provided important social services to younger women. The Beulah Home served young working women who became pregnant outside of marriage and the Good Shepherd Home housed girls who had been convicted of sexual immorality, incorrigibility and 'waywardness'. Although both institutions were forced to operate on very limited funds, attempts were made to provide job training or continuing education for the girls to enable them to secure paid employment when they left the homes. Insofar as possible the all-female staffs also helped girls find work and provided some follow-up support. As one of the nuns at the Good Shepherd Home explained, 'We are trying to help them to get on their feet again . . . They are practically all such nice girls— all they need is guidance, and someone to have faith in them.'[25]

The Beulah Home provided support of another kind for unwed mothers, the majority of whom chose to keep their babies. Recognizing that single mothers would find it difficult to care for children and work for pay, that the few child-care facilities available charged high rates and that other more casual arrangements would not guarantee an appropriate quality of care for babies, the Beulah Home provided child care to each of their clients for up to a year after birth. This type of practical assistance offered by women to women must have gone a long way towards helping young women 'make good' in the world.

The cases of the Beulah Home and the Good Shepherd Home suggest that for some girls at least, an all-woman environment was supportive and healing. One description of life at the Beulah Home shows the wide range of activities that were offered to the girls. Although they were all expected to work within the institution, whether in the kitchen, the nursery, the laundry or the garden, there were also birthday parties, events to celebrate special holidays, berry-picking excursions to the country, games and sing-songs. Girls worked together and played together, laughed and cried, supported each other through illness and the decisions that had to be made about the future of the babies.[26] A similar camaraderie seems to have existed for girls in the Good Shepherd Home as reports indicate that girls frequently returned to visit after they had been released.[27] It could be said that the Beulah and Good Shepherd Homes were for some young working-class women what private girls' schools were for the rich—a same-sex learning environment!

Young working women also established cohesive work and social groups of their own, groups which served to provide mutual help and support. Ethel, for example, found work through her friends and when she was ill and unemployed another young woman, Addie, shared her food and lodgings with Ethel, assistance which enabled Ethel to weather this rough spot in her life.

[. . .]

Young women lived in a world where paid employment opportunities were limited to a small range of personal service, clerical and 'light' manufacturing jobs, where they could never earn more than 40 to 60 per cent of a man's salary and where it was made clear to them that a period of paid work ought to be but a brief period before they began their 'real' (and unwaged) career of reproductive labour. Young women's daily lives provided personal experiences—low wages, long hours, repetitive labour, job insecurity, unsafe working conditions, sexual harassment—of the structural inequities of a male-dominated, capitalist marketplace governed by the profit motive and reliant on sources of cheap labour.

Social and friendship groups may well have provided a temporary and sometimes necessary refuge from the harsh realities of life but they did not signify a retreat from engagement with the outside world. The friends and co-workers of Ethel and Alice were more than gangs of girls talking about men, buying clothes and going to dances. They actually fulfilled many of the tasks of social service agencies by finding jobs, helping members over spells of unemployment, sharing knowledge about 'underground' medical services and generally sustaining one another. It was in groups that young women developed strategies to survive in the working world, engaged in strikes and slowdowns, attempted to control the pace of work and developed ways to deal with sexual harassment.[28] [Leslie Woodcock] Tentler may be unhappy because women's ways of trying to shape and control the world did not replicate male models but the objective circumstances of women's lives were, after all, quite different.

The life of Ethel T. was unique. The constellation of people and situations she experienced were, at one level, peculiar to her. At the same time, Ethel's life well illustrates the difficulties and indignities, the economic and physical violence, which all too often confronted young women as they tried to make their way in the world. It shows, too, how young women struggled, if sometimes only in small ways, to make their lives more worth living. Ethel's life is connected to the collective life, it is part of the history of women's suffering and women's strength.

[1989]

Notes

1. 'A testimony of one of the girls', *1925 Annual Report*, Beulah Home Records, file 1, box 1, acc. no. 71.47, Provincial Archives of Alberta (PAA).

2. William Ryan, *Blaming the Victim*, New York, 1976; Richard Sennett and Jonathan Cobb, *The Hidden Injuries of Class*, New York, 1972.

3. *Report of the Social Survey Commission of Toronto*, Toronto, 1915. See also, Veronica Strong-Boag, *The New Day Recalled: lives of girls and women in English Canada, 1919–1939*, Toronto, 1988, ch. 2, and Rebecca Coulter, Teen-agers in Edmonton, 1921–1931: experiences of gender and class, Ph.D. thesis, University of Alberta, 1987, ch. 3.

4. Strong-Boag, pp. 55–6.

5. See for example, Michèle Barrett, *Women's Oppression Today: problems in Marxist feminist*

analysis, London, 1980; Annette Kuhn and AnnMarie Wolpe (eds), *Feminism and Materialism: women and modes of production*, London, 1978; Veronica Beechey, *Unequal Work*, London., 1987; Pat Armstrong, *Labour Pains: women's work in crisis*, Toronto, 1984; Lydia Sargent, *Women and Revolution*, Boston, 1981; Bonnie J. Fox, 'Conceptualizing patriarchy', *Canadian Review of Sociology and Anthropology*, vol. 25, no. 2, 1988, pp. 163–82.

6. Women's Studies Group, Centre for Contemporary Cultural Studies, University of Birmingham, *Women Take Issue: aspects of women's subordination*, London, 1978, p. 10.

7. Joan Kelly, 'The doubled vision of feminist theory' in Judith L. Newton, Mary P. Ryan and Judith R. Walkowitz (eds), *Sex and Class in Women's History*, London, 1983, p. 265.

8. Geraldine Jonçich Clifford, '"Marry, stitch, die, or do worse": educating women for work' in Harvey Kantor and David B. Tyack (eds), *Work, Youth, and Schooling: historical perspectives on vocationalism in American education*, Stanford, 1982, p. 225.

9. All of the details used in this paper to describe the experiences of Ethel are drawn from 'Ethel T. case, 17 January 1917', Emily Murphy papers, file 15, box 1, MS2, City of Edmonton Archives (CEA).

10. Coulter, pp. 56–7.

11. Coulter, pp. 70, 113; Strong-Boag, pp. 54–5.

12. Coulter, pp. 70, 113; Strong-Boag, pp. 54–5.

13. Edmonton City Police Circulars, file 1300, acc. no. 66.166, Alberta Provincial Police files, PAA.

14. Barbara Hudson, 'Femininity and adolescence' in Angela McRobbie and Mica Nava (eds), *Gender and Generation*, London, 1984, pp. 31–53.

15. Alfred A. Hunter, *Class Tells: on social inequality in Canada*, Toronto, 1986; Elyce J. Rotella, *From Home to Office: U.S. women at work, 1870–1930*, Ann Arbor, 1981.

16. Graham S. Lowe, *Women in the Administrative Revolution: the feminization of clerical work*, Toronto, 1987, pp. 77–8.

17. This quote comes from the files cited in note 9.

18. See files quoted in note 9.

19. Linda Kealey (ed.), *A Not Unreasonable Claim: women and reform in Canada, 1880s–1920s*, Toronto, 1979; Alison Prentice, Paula Bourne, Gail Cuthbert Brandt, Beth Light, Wendy Mitchinson and Naomi Black, *Canadian Women: a history*, Toronto, 1988.

20. Christine Mander, *Emily Murphy: rebel*, Toronto, 1985; Byrne Hope Sanders, *Emily Murphy: crusader*, Toronto, 1945. The Persons case was one in which Murphy and four other women from Alberta, Henrietta Edwards, Louise McKinney, Nellie McClung and Irene Parlby, challenged the position that women were not persons in British law by taking a case through the courts and appealing adverse decisions all the way to the Judicial Committee of the Privy Council in Britain which ruled in 1929 that women were, indeed, persons under the British North America Act and thus could hold appointive positions including those in the Senate.

21. G. to Murphy, 5 June 1921, box 1, file 10, MS 2, Emily Murphy papers, CEA.

22. Murphy to G., 16 June 1921, box 1, file 10, MS 2, Emily Murphy papers, CEA.

23. See discussions of women's moral superiority as an argument for equality in Kealey, *A Not Unreasonable Claim*; Prentice et al., *Canadian Women*; Joan Sangster, *Dreams of Equality: women on the Canadian left, 1920–1950*, Toronto, 1989.

24. See for example, Janice Raymond, *A Passion for Friends: toward a philosophy of female affection*, Boston, 1986; Carroll Smith-Rosenberg, 'The female world of love and ritual: relations between women in nineteenth-century America', *Signs*, no. 1, 1975, pp. 1–29; Sheila Jeffreys, *The Spinster and Her Enemies: feminism and sexuality, 1880–1930*, London, 1985; Lillian Faderman, *Surpassing the Love of Men: romantic friendship and love between women from the Renaissance to the present*, New York, 1981; Lee Virginia Chambers-

Schiller, *Liberty a Better Husband: single women in America, the generations of 1780–1840*, New Haven, 1987; Patricia T. Rooke and R.L. Schnell, *No Bleeding Heart: Charlotte Whitton, a feminist on the right*, Vancouver, 1987.

25. *Western Catholic*, 4 September 1924, p. 3.

26. 'Problems and struggles of life at Beulah Home', file 1, box 1, Beulah Home Records, PAA.

27. *Western Catholic*, 4 September 1924, p. 3.

28. Strong-Boag, ch. 2; Prentice et al., ch. 9; Wayne Roberts, *Honest Womanhood: feminism, femininity and class consciousness among Toronto working women, 1896–1914*, Toronto, 1977.

Father? Master? Boss?

From *Royal Commission on the Relations of Labor and Capital* (1889)

MISS GEOGIANA LOISELLE, Cigar Maker of Montreal, sworn.
By MR HELBRONNER:

Q. In what factory do you work, Miss?
A. At Mr Fortier's.

Q. In what establishment did you serve your apprenticeship?
A. At Mr Fortier's.

Q. Were you beaten when at Mr Fortier's?
A. Yes, sir.

Q. Will you tell us in what way you were beaten?
A. It was Mr Fortier who beat me with a mould cover.

Q. Is it a tool such as you see before you on the table?
A. Yes; it was the cover.

Q. Why did he beat you?
A. I would not make one hundred cigars which he gave me to make. I refused to make them, and he beat me with the mould cover.

Q. Did he seize you before beating you?
A. I was sitting, and he took hold of me by the arm, and tried to throw me on the ground. He did throw me on the ground and beat me with the mould cover.

Q. Did he beat you when you were down?
A. Yes, I tried to rise and he kept me down on the floor.

Q. Were you able to rise at once after being beaten?
A. Yes.

Q. Did you suffer from the blows he gave you?
A. No, sir; I bore no marks.

Q. Were there young girls, workingmen or boys in the factory?
A. There were other girls, but I did not notice the girls. I noticed only the foreman, Mr Fournier.

Q. Mr Fournier said nothing?

A. No. . . .

Q. How old were you when you were beaten?

A. I was going on eighteen years.

Q. How long is it since you were beaten?

A. I am now twenty-three years old.

By MR WALSH: . . .

Q. Did you quit Mr Fortier after that?

A. Yes; after my apprenticeship was over.

Q. And you went back to work for him?

A. Yes; and I still work there for him. . . .

J.M. FORTIER, Cigar Manufacturer, called and sworn. . . .

Q. Do you know the age of the youngest apprentice at present employed in your factory?

A. I do not know; I have given strict instructions not to have any boy younger than fourteen years.

Q. How long is it since you gave that order?

A. That order was given a couple of years ago; but lately, since about a couple of months ago, I noticed there were a few who worked there that might not be of that age, and I have since given strict instructions to the manager to have nobody there of less than fourteen years.

Q. When you employ an apprentice you have an indenture passed, I believe?

A. Yes.

Q. Do you mention the age of the apprentice in the contract?

A. Yes.

Q. So that if you employ a child too young, it is either the fault of the father or the tutor?

A. Yes; because he wants to place the boy. It is generally the financial circumstances of the family that brings him to work so young.

Q. Under whose control are the apprentices?

A. They are under the control of the manager and foremen.

Q. Under whose control are they during the hours of work?

A. During the hours of work they are under the control of the foremen of the different departments and in general, of the manager.

Q. How are those apprentices treated by the foremen?

A. Those apprentices are treated by the foremen in the same manner as if they were his own children, or in other words, as they would be treated at school.

Q. Is it not to your knowledge that those children have been beaten?

A. It is not to my personal knowledge that those boys have been beaten, other than what they have deserved for wrongs they have committed, the same as a parent would punish his child, or I would punish my child, or a school master would punish a child who does not do what is right at school.

Q. I understand by your reply the children have been beaten?

A. They have been beaten in the same manner; they have been beaten for correction.

Q. Is it to your knowledge that those children have been beaten?

A. It is not to my knowledge that those children have been beaten.

Q. You have told us that the children have been beaten as they would have been by their parents, or at school, or for correction?

A. For correction.

Q. So it is to your knowledge that some have been beaten?

A. For correction.

Q. Do you believe it to be the duty of the foreman, or proprietor of a shop, to beat a child?

A. No.

Q. Why did the foremen of your establishment beat them?

A. They did not beat them to my knowledge.

Q. You have told us that the children have been beaten to correct them.

A. Yes. . . .

By MR HELBRONNER:

Q. Do you believe a foreman, or proprietor of a factory, has a right to strike a child?

A. I believe the foremen of departments, over a certain number of boys of low age, like apprentices, have a right to touch the children with a ruler, or with their hands to correct them.

Q. To your knowledge, then, correction has been applied in your establishment?

A. Yes.

Q. Please give us the method of correction applied by yourself, or by your foremen, in the factories?

A. For instance: a boy will disobey orders. He is told to do certain things and he will not do them. What I am now speaking of, we have not had any experience of for about a year. We have had a very noisy class of boys within a year or two, and it was very hard to get them to do what they were ordered, but this last year we have had no experience of correcting a boy by hitting him on the fingers. In previous years we had lots of trouble with them; it was during the agitation of the strike, and so forth, and if we told a boy to do certain things, and he did not do them, or if he did not do right by taking tobacco or destroying tobacco, the foreman would very likely hit him on the fingers with a ruler. . . .

Q. From whom did the foremen receive instructions to beat the children?

A. They have never been authorized by me to beat any children.

Q. Did you know they were touched?

A. I have given them instructions to correct them, and those instructions come from the Recorder down stairs. . . .

Q. Did you beat an apprentice, either boy or girl, yourself?

A. Yes.

Q. Will you give us the name of the person you struck?

A. Georgiana Loiselle.

Q. Were you present yesterday when Miss Georgiana Loiselle gave her deposition.

A. Yes.

Q. Can you tell us what you can offer in contradiction of what she said?

A. I cannot contradict what she said, for she told the truth, that I asked her to make one hundred cigars. It was in the afternoon or in the morning before the quitting hour, and she said she was not going to do it; and she spoke in a very impertinent manner. I had had several troubles with the same young lady previous to that, and I had seen her mother, and her mother had prayed me to do the best I could and to correct her the best way I could. So after receiving those instructions, and as I had three or four of her brothers working for me at the time, I took a great interest in the girl—the mother being alone and supported by her children—to see that the children were properly attended to. I took this young lady by the arm to have her sit down. She would not, so I turned her around and tried to sit her down. She would not. I took the cover of a mould and tried to sit her on my knee, but she was too heavy and fell on the floor. I held her on the floor and smacked her on the backside with the mould. I asked her if she would do it, and after a couple of strikes she said 'I will.' She got up and sat down at her table and made her one hundred bunches and went off quietly. She never lost one hour, and I think she is very glad to-day to have received the lesson she did, for she has been an obedient girl since then.

Q. Is this what you call a mould (pointing to a mould on the table)?

A. It was not exactly that kind; that is a little too heavy.

Q. Is it the same kind as that?

A. It is not the same as that; it is lighter than that.

Q. Give the dimensions of the mould you did use?

A. The cover may have been a little lighter than that one, one eighth of an inch thinner; it would be about the same width, not quite so long.

Q. How long ago is it since you beat her?

A. It must have been four or five years ago. I could not say exactly. . . .

Q. Do you mean to say you corrected her according to the instructions you received from the Recorder?

A. Yes. The Recorder spoke in this way; he said: 'Correct them the same as you would your own child. Hit them there because it cannot hurt them, and they will be corrected.'

Q. Do you correct your child with such a mould as this?

A. If he deserved it, it would not hurt him to hit him on the backside with that as much as with the hand.

Q. Would you allow the school-master to hit your child with such a machine as this?

A. Yes; if he did it the same as I did it. . . .

Q. You have said you held this girl down?

A. Yes.

Q. In what manner did you keep her down?

A. I held her down with my arm, like this, and struck her this way.

Q. Do you believe it is decent for a man to place a girl of eighteen in that position?

A. When she is very disobedient and there are about fifty or sixty other girls there, I think it is only right that she should be taught a lesson when she deserves it.

Q. One of the Commissioners is anxious to know would you allow one of your daughters, if you have any, to be placed in that position?

A. If she deserved it, I would.

Q. By a stranger?

A. By a person to whom I had entrusted her, the same as this girl was to me; she was bound to me, and I was to represent her father. It is very important you should know that these girls and boys are bound to me. They are engaged by indentures, and, of course, under the engagement the mother and father must help me along as much as they can. . . .

Q. Were you beaten during your apprenticeship?

A. No; I did not happen to need it, I suppose; otherwise I should have been. . . .

Q. Have you any special room in which you place them when you correct them?

A. No.

Q. Mr McGregor, your manager of the factory, told us yesterday of the fact that there was a certain room, which he styled an enclosure, in which children were locked up?

A. They were put away there for theft, or robbing, or anything of that kind. We have a system of searching the apprentices, and most of the men, and when they come down stairs—there are probably one hundred men—perhaps the tenth man has cigars about him that he should not have. Then this man goes to work and calls one of us, and says, 'Take care of that man, I will finish searching the hands, and take him to the station house.' Then the man is taken and put in the enclosure, this room or some other place.

Q. At what time is this searching done?

A. The searching is done at noon before they go out and in the evening when they leave.

Q. How long do you allow children to remain in this room?

A. I do not know; I have never put any there myself; I cannot tell you that we ever kept any children there longer than until the man got through with the searching, and was ready to take them away. I do not know, I could not say.

Q. Have all the children placed in that room, been brought before the Recorder?

A. No; in some instances they have been forgiven, for it was not very pleasant for the parents to hear of their children being brought before the Recorder and be sent for. They would be brought before me or the manager, and forgiven. . . . I must say that at that time most of the parents who could not get along with their children, because they were in bad order and were bad boys, came to me as a cigar manufacturer and put them in my hands, and I tried to do what I could with them. As they could not correct them themselves they put them in my hands. They had seen my name so often before the Recorder that they knew if there was great trouble with them I would put them into the Reformatory.

Q. The parents considered your factory as a species of Reformatory, or on the road to Reformatory?

A. It was on the road to the Reformatory; it was to reform those bad boys or any bad boys who came there.

[. . .]

[Canada, *Royal Commission on the Relations of Labour and Capital,* 1889]

Suggestions for Further Reading

Andrew, Sheila, 'The Gauthier Girls: Growing up on Miscou Island, 1841–1847' in Hilary Thompson, ed., *Children's Voices in Atlantic Literature and Culture: Essays on Childhood.* Guelph: Canadian Children's Press, 1995: 85–103.

Bradbury, Bettina, *Working Families: Age, Gender, and Daily Survival in Industrializing Montreal.* Toronto: Oxford University Press, 1993.

Bullen, John, 'Hidden Workers: Child Labour and the Family Economy in Late Nineteenth-Century Urban Ontario,' in Bettina Bradbury, ed., *Canadian Family History.* Toronto: Irwin, 1992: 199–219.

McIntosh, Robert, *Boys in the Pits: Child Labour in Coal Mining.* Montreal: McGill-Queen's University Press, 2000.

Parr, Joy, *Labouring Children: British Immigrant Apprentices to Canada, 1869–1924.* Montreal and London: McGill, Queen's and Croom Helm, 1980.

Strange, Carolyn, *Toronto's Girl Problem: The Perils and Pleasures of the City, 1880–1930.* Toronto: University of Toronto Press, 1995.

PART 4

Schools for the Nation, 1850–1923

In the nineteenth century, more children attended school. However, the development of mass schooling was neither smooth nor uncontested. These articles examine the politics of school expansion and the conflicting goals of school promoters and families. In the mid-nineteenth century, the supporters of the free-school movement believed that the economic, political, and moral development of the nation depended on an educated citizenry and that inadequate funding prevented universal attendance at schools because poor and working-class families could not afford to pay tuition fees. In his 1864 case for compulsory taxation to stabilize school financing in Nova Scotia, Theodore Rand argues that this monetary investment in the school system would encourage in the elite a commitment to improve the conditions of schools and the quality of education. The elite's investment would be repaid with a moral, industrious workforce. Ian Davey examines working-class children's school attendance in Ontario and the conditions that prevented regular attendance.

Class, social status, and race determined the value families placed on education. This value varied according to region and over time. Ontario agricultural families supported the free-school movement because dividing the land amongst male offspring would endanger their prosperous futures. Education allowed families another means of securing the social status of the family. In Black settlements, education, a privilege that had been denied to them in slavery, was highly valued. Community leaders promoted schooling to improve the opportunities of the next generation. Schools were also the key to self-reliance. In Buxton, Ontario, some Black educators believed that schools for Black children should be autonomous from the government. Segregated schools that excluded children in order to bolster white supremacy were very different institutions. Timothy Stanley finds that the Chinese community in early twentieth-century Victoria opposed the school board's attempt to segregate schools. Resistance to Chinese students' integration into the schools was linked integrally to immigration policies that defined the nation as 'white'.

Nancy Janovicek

The Rhythm of Work
and the Rhythm of School

Ian E. Davey

These returns present us with the painful and startling fact, of nearly one hundred thousand children of school age in Upper Canada, not attending any school. This awful fact furnishes a hundred thousand arguments to urge each friend of Canada, each friend of virtue, of knowledge and of civilization, to exert himself to his utmost until the number of children attending our schools shall equal the number of children of school age.

The average attendance of pupils, compared with the whole number, is little more than half . . . I doubt not but the provision of the present Act to distribute the school fund to the several school sections according to the average attendance of pupils in each school, (and not according to the school population as heretofore), the mean attendance of summer and winter being taken, will contribute very much to increase the regular attendance at the schools and to prolong their duration.[1]

Egerton Ryerson, writing in the chief superintendent's *Annual Report* for 1850, presented the challenge to the friends of educational reform in the province. The School Act of 1850 gave legislative recognition to property assessment for school purposes, making it possible for the individual school boards to introduce free schools. If the schools were free, then there was no reason why every child of school-age should not attend them. The task was to bring the children into the schools and, just as importantly, to ensure that they attended with sufficient regularity to gain the benefits of education. The goal was regular school attendance throughout the year for all school-age children, a remote possibility in 1850 when enrolments were low and average attendance even lower.

In the succeeding years Ryerson's chronicle of the progress of the free-school movement was based largely on the increasing proportion of the province's school-age (five to sixteen) children enrolled in the schools. Every year in his annual report he compared the number of children five to sixteen years old with the number of children enrolled in the schools, commented on the narrowing gap between the two figures and deplored, as a 'public blot and disgrace', the ever diminishing residual group of unschooled children. According to this criterion, the success of the free-school movement was easily demonstrated. In the two decades prior to 1871 virtually all cities, towns, and school sections abandoned the old rate-bill system in favour of property assessment and free schools, and at the same time, registered substantial increases in the number and proportion of children who enrolled in school.

The number of five- to sixteen-year-old children reported by the local superintendents as enrolled in the common schools rose from 158,159 in 1851 to 423,033 in 1871, an increase in the proportion of the growing school-age population attending school from 61.2 per cent in 1851 to 86.4 per cent in 1871. Moreover, the increase in the common school enrolment accounted for most of the increase in attendance as the enrolment in the various private schools and academies only increased from 6,753 in 1850 to 8,562 in 1871. The increase in enrolment was more spectacular in the cities but this was only because much lower proportions of urban school-age children attended the common schools in the earlier years. In 1851 over 62 per cent of the five- to sixteen-year-old children in the rural areas were enrolled in the common schools, compared to less than 38 per cent in the cities. (Of course, many city children attended private schools.) In 1871 over 85 per cent of the school-age children in both the cities and the rural areas were enrolled in the public schools of the province. Within two decades the free schools had become an accepted fact of life in Ontario and part of the experience of growing up for most children.[2]

However, the total yearly enrolment is a somewhat misleading measure of school attendance as it grossly exaggerated the number of children attending school at any one time. The figure was derived from all of those who registered in the public schools at any stage of the year. In consequence, the total enrolment included those children who were in a particular school for a week, a month, or six months, but who subsequently left. Thus, children who were working or had moved to another neighbourhood, city, town, or farming area were still counted as enrolled by the local superintendents in their annual reports to the chief superintendent.

At the same time that the total enrolment figure implied a much greater rate of attendance than actually existed, the success of the free schools was severely limited by the continuing irregularity of attendance of those enrolled. For the majority of children, schooling remained a part-time activity throughout the period. In 1856 fully 57 per cent of those who were enrolled in the common schools of the province attended for one hundred days or fewer. In 1871 the equivalent proportion was 56.5 per cent and in no intervening year did it drop below 54 per cent. The proportion of children who attended for one hundred days or less was much higher in the rural areas than in the cities. In 1856 the proportion of rural students in this group was 59 per cent and in 1871, 58.4 per cent; and in the intervening years their proportion never fell below 56 per cent. The proportion who attended for a similarly short time in the cities was much less although it fluctuated considerably. In 1856 it was 42.9 per cent and in 1871, 46.2 per cent. In the intervening years the proportion attending for one hundred days or less rose as high as 50.3 per cent in 1857 and dropped as low as 39.1 per cent in 1868.

It is paradoxical that at the same time the free-school system was being adopted throughout almost all of Ontario and the proportion of children enrolled was increasing rapidly, the actual number of days most children attended remained relatively low. It became increasingly clear in the local superintendents' reports of the

1860s that the real issue was not so much non-attendance but irregularity. The structure of a permanent school system had been erected remarkably quickly; by the end of the 1860s most areas were served by schools which were free and which were open throughout the year.[3] Furthermore, as Ryerson continually pointed out, the idea of schooling had been generally accepted as the increasing enrolments demonstrated. By 1871 the actual number of children reported as not attending any school had declined to 38,535 and less than one-third of those, 12,018, were between the ages of seven and twelve, during which years attendance was made compulsory by the 1871 Act. Even though the number of non-attenders was probably larger, given the fact that the enrolment figures exaggerated the number in school, only a small group of children were not exposed to any form of schooling and most of these resided in the rural areas. In the cities, where the fear of juvenile crime was greatest, the educators had come to recognize the existence of a permanent class of poor who were beyond the reach of the public schools and for whom special institutions, such as industrial schools, were needed.[4] Once most children had been gathered into the public schools, more and more attention was focused on the ways and means of keeping them there with sufficient regularity and for a long enough time for each child to learn the lessons the schools were designed to instil.

'Irregularity of attendance', one local superintendent declared in 1871, 'is the bane and curse of the public schools; it is a log and chain upon the progress of instruction for it blasts and withers the noblest purposes of the best of teachers.' Irregular attendance not only deprived the individual student of adequate schooling but disrupted the whole school. It made the school system inefficient as it meant that the teachers were 'unduly occupied in uncalled for repetition' thus retarding the progress of the class.[5] It also confounded attempts to grade the students by age as those who attended irregularly remained in the lower grades much longer.[6] From 1860 when Ryerson asked each local superintendent to report the reasons for non-attendance, much of each report was devoted to the causes and effects of irregular attendance. By the late 1860s, the local superintendents, following Ryerson's lead, called for a measure of compulsion because it was inconsistent to have compulsory property assessment and voluntary attendance.

Opponents of the free-school system argued that the system increased irregularity of attendance because the parents did not value what they did not pay for directly. 'Where a rate-bill is charged', one superintendent declared, 'the pupil, if present at all during the month, is sure to attend as often as possible, for the parents feel that non-attendance causes them a pecuniary loss; whereas under the free-school system any trifle is too often deemed sufficient to excuse the absence of the child.'[7] The free-school supporters, including most of the superintendents, were also inclined to lay the blame for continued irregular attendance on the 'criminal apathy and negligence of parents' who did not appreciate the value of an education to their children.[8] Yet, clearly, the extent of irregularity of attendance was such that parental indifference could hardly be the complete explanation. Besides, it was contradicted by the rapid increase in enrolments throughout the province which, plausibly, could be considered more an expression of parental concern. As one superintendent put it while rebuking his colleagues in 1861, the term 'parental indifference' was used to explain poor attendance by some because it was 'a convenient way of filling up the column' in the annual report. 'Not indifference', he continued, 'but the pressing care of providing for their bodily wants, is . . . the more general cause of non-attendance.'[9] Those other superintendents who went beyond 'convenient ways of filling up columns' agreed that material circumstance rather than criminal negligence was the root cause of low and irregular attendance.

> Compulsory attendance and the poverty of families, will scarcely ever harmonize. Indeed to carry out the provisions of the Free School System, we would require to furnish, either by the Legislature or the trustees, or by both combined, all the necessary books, and other things required for the school, together, with, in some, cases, even the clothes in which the children are to attend the school, or a proportion of the children, in the rural districts, as well as in the towns and cities, will be deprived of the benefits of a common school education.[10]

[. . .]

The most potent determinants of attendance patterns in both urban and rural areas were the same conditions which shaped the economic and social realities of nineteenth-century Canadian life. Attendance was naturally influenced by such ubiquitous features as harsh climatic conditions, bad roads, and sickness. However, those factors which contributed to poverty and economic insecurity—trade depressions, crop failure, transient work patterns, and seasonal employment—largely determined the regularity of school attendance throughout the province.

'Two successive years of failure in the productions of husbandry, attended by a large decrease in the public revenue, and an unprecedented stagnation in every branch of business, could not fail to be seriously felt in the operation of our school system.'[11] In these words Ryerson summed up the impact of the depression of the late 1850s on Ontario. Its effect was more devastating in the larger cities which were brought to a standstill, making it difficult for them to bear the cost of the school system at the same time that attendance was more irregular. In Toronto, in fact, the superintendent of schools in 1857 and a committee of the board in 1864 advocated a return to the rate-bill schools because the free-school system was financially burdensome and had not improved either the proportional enrolment or the regularity of attendance of children in the city.[12] Depressions increased the irregularity of attendance because they brought increased hardship for many people, particularly the poor who, lacking financial resources at the best of times, were often reduced to reliance on charity to survive. In Hamilton, for instance, the depression of the late 1850s brought widespread unemployment as many establishments were forced to close, and one observer reported that before 1857 'the common labourer could make almost as much in a day as he now can in a week'.[13] The Ladies Benevolent Society and the City Council distributed bread, wood, and soup in the winter months of the depression, and the ladies expressed relief that many of 'the lowest and unsatisfactory class of applicants' for aid had been forced to leave the city because it enabled them to assist 'those whose necessities are as great, but who are more diffident in making known their wants.'[14]

The effect of economic privation on school attendance during depression years was twofold. First, many children were withdrawn from school through dire necessity and scavenged for the means of keeping themselves and their families alive— stealing money, objects to sell, and coal or wood to keep them warm.[15] Second, many children were withdrawn from school when their parents were forced to leave the city in search of work. The population of Hamilton, for example, dropped rapidly during the depression of the 1850s and, as Superintendent Ormiston remarked in 1860, 'a large number of those returned as attending school only a short time, are removed from the city.'[16]

Depressed prices and bad crops had similar effects in the rural areas, reducing school expenditures and affecting the rates of attendance. As one superintendent in Haldimand County commented in 1861, 'Inferior crops and low prices for produce have caused some undertakings to be stationary and others to retrograde; but as soon as farmers are blessed with better harvests and more remunerative markets, the children will be more regular in their attendance, they will be sent longer to school, and far more attention will be given to furnishing the school-houses.'[17] Similarly, one inspector noted that the aggregate attendance was less in the first half of 1879 than in the corresponding period in 1878 while in the second half it was greater. 'It seems fair,' he concluded, 'to infer that the hard times forced people to seek help from their children, till the good harvest justified them in sending them back to school.'[18] In short, cyclical depressions and crop failures affected school attendance because in good times more parents sent more of their children to school and sent them more regularly. Yet, lower attendance during bad times resulted largely from a magnification of those factors which caused irregular attendance throughout the nineteenth century—transience and poverty.

Recent research has given us insights into the nature and extent of transience in the nineteenth century—large numbers of people in both urban and rural areas were on the move.[19] Labourers moved from farms to cities in winter and back to farms in the spring; farmers sought work in logging camps and elsewhere in the winter months; canal, railroad, and road construction workers worked their way through the countryside; skilled workers moved on when there was no more work to be found in a particular city or town; and people from all walks of life packed their bags when opportunities to better themselves seemed more probable in another neighbourhood, city, town, farming area, or county. The actual number of transients was immense. In Hamilton, for example, only about one-third of those recorded on the 1851 census were found on the 1861 census, and Katz has estimated that at least twice as many people lived in the city during a whole year as were there at any one time.[20] Those who left in the decade spanned the spectrum of Hamilton's occupational and ethnic structure, but they were less likely to be married and more likely to be young, poor, and to own no property in the city than those who stayed.[21]

The skilled workers who moved on may have drawn on past experience. Those artisans who came from England, for example, brought with them a tradition of 'tramping,' [. . .] At least the artisans had a portable skill to carry with them in their search for work. The position of labourers was even more precarious for they had only their brute strength to sell. Much of their work such as farm and lumber work was seasonal, or else it was institutionally transient in nature like canal and railroad construction. Labourers were forced to move on when the source of work dried up, although Thernstrom concludes that those who worked in the cities only left 'when the depressed state of the local labour market made it impossible to subsist where they were.'[22] Economic conditions forced workers to move on and, in a sense, it was a vicious circle. Transience bred transience and those on the tramp were usually the last to be employed and the first to be laid off.[23] [. . .]

The implications for school attendance of this widespread geographic mobility were profound. On the one hand, children who enrolled in school and later left the area exaggerated the degree of irregularity in any one school by inflating the enrolment and lowering the average attendance figures. On the other, the number of children whose schooling was interrupted must have been immense. If the distance of migration was small—from neighbourhood to neighbourhood within a city or from farming community to farming community within a school district—it was possible that a child's name would appear on more than one school register in the area. One inspector of schools in the County of Middlesex, for example, pointed out that he had 'found pupils reported from a school in Metcalfe as having attended less than 100 days also reported from a school in Lobo', as the family had moved from Metcalfe to Lobo during the year. It was possible, he suggested, that they might have attended for more than 100 days if their attendance at both schools was taken together.[24] For those who moved beyond the jurisdiction of a particular school board, it was impossible to gauge how many days each year they may have attended. Certainly, school superintendents remarked on the effect of transience on poor attendance rates in their schools. The fact that Collingwood's population was 'a floating one—continually changing', was given as the reason that the average attendance was much lower than the number enrolled on the books.[25] Similarly, the failure to increase the number of students in Ottawa in 1865 was 'caused by the number of mechanics and labourers who have migrated to the US, in consequence of the falling off of work at the public buildings here.'[26]

Some superintendents reported that the continual movement of parents from place to place was unsettling because 'many having recently come to the place, or expecting soon to go, feel . . . indisposed to go to the expense of a set of school books, and the trouble of sending their children for the short time they may remain.'[27] The unsettled character of the population was seen to be detrimental to the progress of education. As one superintendent in the County of Prescott wrote of the French Canadian majority in his school section: 'One great impediment is . . . they do not remain long enough in one locality for their children to be benefited by the schools.'[28] It was difficult to teach transient students whose movement in and out of the schools disrupted the efficient working of the system. How efficient and settled the school system would have been if its clientele was less mobile is a moot question because, particularly in the rural areas, the teachers themselves were not immune from the transient experience. In one county, for example, 'out of one hundred and one employed on the First of January, 1868, seventy-nine were not found in the same position in January, 1870, and of this large number, fifty-seven had either given up teaching or had left the County.'[29]

Although geographic mobility cut across all classes in the society, as a cause of irregular attendance it was usually associated with the working class and the poor. [. . .] Their insecurity stemmed from the practices of employing labourers by the day and journeymen irregularly throughout the year. In fact, the irregularity of employment probably contributed more to the poor economic condition of the working class than did the low wages.[30] In 1864 the editor of *The Workingman's Journal*, which was published in Hamilton, declared that the city's workers were likely to be on short-time amount to five days a week for eighteen weeks in the year. He was critical of the mayor's practice of declaring general holidays 'whenever a few individuals take a fancy to have it done', and pointed out that each holiday cost the 3,000 workers in Hamilton a minimum of $3,500.[31] It was a matter of necessity for the working man to earn as much as possible in the good seasons to ward off periods of unemployment in winter and during depressions. As one moulder put it, they went on strike because 'we felt we should have more wages when we were working in order to be able to live during those portions of the year when there was nothing to do.'[32]

Moreover, it is likely that in the second half of the nineteenth century the rise of industrial capitalism brought increasing irregularity of employment for skilled workers and made their work experience much more similar to that of the unskilled labourers. [. . .] Some artisans lost their jobs to children and 'greenhorns' who were able to operate the machines and were cheaper to employ. Those who kept their jobs were often forced to accept lower wages because of the increased competition for their jobs. The result of these processes was the weakening of the artisans' position as their hold on their employment became less secure and cyclical unemployment increased.

The plight of working people was aggravated as well by the method of wage payment. Some were paid in truck and thus forced to buy at prices set by the company store, while others who were paid monthly found themselves continually in debt to the local shopkeeper. Many workmen had 'to run monthly accounts and that puts them entirely at the mercy of the corner grocers . . . you have to take what he has got and you cannot go anywhere else . . . if a man could get his wages weekly he could run his business more on a cash basis and go where he pleased.'[33] [. . .] Plainly, the experience of most working-class families militated against the formation in their children of the virtues of orderly, regular, punctual industry. The irregularity of their work patterns made it difficult for them to commit themselves (and their children) to regular activities for any length of time.

[. . .]

An acquaintance with irregular income and periods of poverty was not confined to the urban working class and the agricultural labourers. Many of the province's small farmers, especially those who scratched out a living from the rocky soils of the shield in the eastern and northern areas of the province, experienced the same deprivations. In one sense, the problem of irregular attendance at school was rooted in the success of the free-school program itself. It had succeeded in enrolling most of the poor in both rural and urban areas. To expect regular and punctual attendance from them without a concomitant improvement and regulation of their life style, was to expect the impossible.

[. . .] The ordinary workman and the small farmer had little room for manoeuvre, and if the former lost his job or the latter's crops failed, their families were often thrown into poverty until conditions improved. These not infrequent occurrences had considerable influence on school attendance patterns. The 'hard struggles of the tillers of the soil' often meant that they either required 'the actual assistance of their children, or they are unable to clothe them sufficiently well to appear in school'.[34][. . .]

Much of the poverty was associated with the seasonal rhythm of work as the harsh winter swelled the ranks of the unemployed in the cities and brought work to a standstill on the farms. Not surprisingly, this had considerable impact on attendance patterns although its manifestations were quite different in the urban and the rural areas. In the cities and towns, the coming of winter meant increased misery for large numbers of people. Those who worked outside were likely to be laid off. Labourers, carpenters and joiners, painters and decorators, bricklayers and brickmakers, and seamen lost their jobs or competed among themselves (and with the large number of agricultural labourers who came to the cities in winter) for the small number of jobs available. Those who were skilled enough, or sufficiently lucky, to keep their jobs were often forced to work for reduced wages because of competition for work and the shorter working day. [. . .] The plight of the urban poor was further exacerbated because of the increased price of food and fuel in the winter months. As Judith Fingard has remarked, 'winter deprived the poor of their employment at the same time as it made the necessaries of life prohibitively dear; and it endangered their health by aggravating the plight of the sick and infirm by creating dietary problems for those at or below the subsistence level, and by causing disablement or death for others through exposure.'[35]

[. . .]

Undoubtedly, more children were able to find jobs in the summer months and contribute to the family income, but before industrialization, the commercial city did not provide large numbers of jobs for children. Some found work as messengers in the large stores, or deliverers of newspapers; girls found jobs in the sweated trades and in domestic service, and boys helped their fathers in their craft shops. Moreover, industrialization in Canada did not involve large-scale employment of young children in the factories. Only tobacco manufacturing and cotton and woollen mills provided employment for a great number of young children. Certainly, from the 1860s there was an increasing number of children working in factories and this affected school attendance. The superintendent for the village of Hespeler, for instance, complained of 'the ebb-and-flow' of attendance and suggested that: 'The irregularity is caused by the boys and girls, of almost all sizes and ages, staying out of School or going to it, according as their assistance is required or not at the factories.'[36] But the evidence suggests that most of those children who found work in industry were over the age of twelve.[37] It seems that irregular attendance in the cities and towns was not so much the result of large-scale employment of young children as of the lack or loss of jobs for their parents. In large part, irregular attendance patterns in the urban areas were the cumulative result of many personal disasters stemming from the instability of the labour market and the incidence of sickness—conditions which intersected most acutely during the winter months.

This was certainly not the case in the rural areas. The most important feature of school attendance patterns outside of the cities and towns was the pronounced seasonal variation. As the figures for 1850 to 1854 indicate, average attendance was higher in winter. Moreover, while more boys than girls attended in both summer and winter, the difference between the sexes was approximately twice as large in the winter months. That is, many more boys and fewer girls attended the rural schools in winter. [. . .] The shortage and high price of agricultural labour meant that the older children, particularly the boys, worked on the farm 'during the three-fourths of the year' and were only sent to school (or allowed to attend) in 'those months, when by the very nature of the season, the tiller of the ground is dismissed from his toil'.[38] The result, according to one of the local superintendents in York County, was that 'in summer seasons those children who are too young to labour are sent to school, and those whose labour is valuable are kept at home; in the winter this order is reversed, thus making two distinct sets of pupils in the year.'[39] The pattern of attendance, then, was determined by the seasonal demands of the farm; even the young children were called on to assist in the busiest periods and the schools were virtually emptied 'at the times of hay, wheat, oat, apple and potato harvests'.[40]

[. . .] In 1871, in the counties, 45.3 per cent of those enrolled were between five and ten years of age, 47.9 per cent between ten and sixteen, and over 6 per cent between sixteen and twenty-one. In contrast, in the cities, fully 58.5 per cent were in the younger age group of the school-age population and only 39.1 per cent were between ten and sixteen. Furthermore, the proportion of city students between sixteen and twenty-one was only 2.1 per cent. The much larger proportion of older students in the rural areas was a function of the older boys attending only for three or four months in the winter. As one superintendent remarked, 'a number of lads, who have outgrown their school-boy days, return to peruse old studies, and to make still further advancement.'[41] Fewer girls attended in winter. The younger children who attended in summer were often unable to go to school in winter because of the distance from the school and the severity of the weather. It would seem that many older girls were kept home in order to look after them.

[. . .]

The plethora of reasons that combined to cause continuing irregular attendance certainly went far beyond the original glib assertions of the local superintendents of 'parental indifference and negligence.' And yet, in one sense, the 'lack of appreciation of education' that they observed was rooted in the cultural reality of mid-nineteenth-century Ontario life. On the one hand, the extravagant claims of the free-school promoters regarding the benefits of education were not immediately observed in the society. Crime and vice had not been eradicated; militant trade union organization and strikes were unlikely indications of increasing social stability; and poverty was still an ever-present problem. On the other hand, although it was said that 'the public is beginning to appreciate the idea that a person without education must remain during life a "hewer of wood and drawer of water"', most people probably knew someone who was a living contradiction of that same idea.[42] As one superintendent complained in 1869:

A large proportion of our population consists of emigrants from nearly every clime and region of the earth. The majority of these came here with nothing but their sturdy thews and sinews, and their indomitable energy and perseverance. With their axes upon their shoulders, they marched boldly into the wilderness; and out of it, by stringent frugality and unremitting toil, they have carved for themselves an easy competence—a rude plenty. They have seen educated men settle around them, and decrease in wealth, whilst THEY the uneducated, have flourished and increased in it. Many of them, owing to the unavoidable force of circumstances—from sheer necessity—have been elected by those around them to situations of trust as school trustees and councillors . . . They have waxed haughty in their grandeur, they have become inflated with their official pomp, they utterly eschew alike, education, reason and common sense.[43]

Clearly, education was not a necessary component of success in farming, unlike 'unremitting toil' in an age when mechanization was not very far advanced.

Moreover, as Harvey Graff has demonstrated, illiteracy was not a complete stumbling block to an individual's progress in the urban areas either, for though most illiterates were labourers, many held skilled jobs and some even worked in non-manual occupations.[44] In fact, in the initial stages of industrial capitalism, the new opportunities for less skilled and child labour in the mechanized factories must have made it difficult for working-class people to appreciate the benefits of schooling. This was the concern of the superintendent for Guelph when he complained in 1873 that there were fewer children in the higher grades of the public system. The children left school early because of

the desire of parents to avail themselves at too early a period of the earnings which their children can make, and the opportunities which stores and manufactures afford for child labour, in the disposition of employers to engage children, because of the higher wages which must be paid for the labour of grown-up persons. Account ought, also, to be made, of the course of instruction that has been prescribed and rendered imperative in our Public Schools, embracing subjects which, while valuable in themselves, are not thought necessary by parents for their children, and who, consequently, grudge the time devoted to them, and the expense that must be incurred in the purchase of text-books.[45]

If farmers and working people could not readily discern the immediate advantages of sending their children to school regularly and for sustained periods of time, the type of education offered in the common schools was not likely to improve the situation. As the superintendent for Guelph suggested, much of the curriculum seemed irrelevant or unnecessary to those engaged in the business of making a living. Although Ryerson had emphasized the importance of practical education in his 1846 report, the initial battles to get the principles of free and compulsory education accepted in the province absorbed most of his energy prior to 1871. In consequence, the curriculum of the common schools remained oriented towards the tiny minority who went on to the grammar schools and the university, and little attention was paid to more practical subjects. Thus, while the children learned how to read and write and cipher, they were unlikely to learn much of practical use to them in their working lives. Ryerson remarked in 1869 when it had become obvious that a free and compulsory education system was generally accepted: 'the tendency of the youthful mind of our country is too much in the direction of what are called the learned professions, and too little in the direction of what are termed the industrial pursuits ... it appears to be very important, as the fundamental principles and general machinery of our School System are settled, that the subjects and teaching of the schools should be adapted to develop the resources and skilful industry of the country.'[46]

There was, then, a tension between the reality and the possibility of education as the school curriculum, grading up to the classical grammar school, bore little relation to the everyday world of most of the clientele. And this tension was exacerbated by the emergence of new industrial order in the 1860s as mechanized factory production increased economic insecurity at the same time that it devalued the importance of education. To keep children in school was to forgo the contribution of potential wage earners to the family income, a form of denial that many could not afford, particularly as much of the schooling seemed irrelevant. Adolescent labour in the factory or the sweatshop became like adolescent labour on the farm—a necessary factor in the family's struggle to make a living. For both the farmer and the working man, the family's welfare took precedence over the child's education. However, the impact on school attendance patterns was quite different. The seasonal pattern of farming meant that rural children attended school seasonally and stayed there well into their teens. In the cities, the years of attendance were more compressed, most children leaving school to go to work or help around the home after they were twelve. Thus, although from 1871 onwards the majority of children were in school, family circumstance, economic pressures, and physical conditions dictated the length of their stay and the seasonality and the regularity of their attendance.

In these circumstances it is not surprising that attendance remained irregular after 1871. The legislation for compulsory attendance, after all, had absolutely no effect upon the material conditions in which people lived. The inspector for the County of Renfrew made exactly that point in 1872:

> We must not expect to find our schools in a healthy and vigorous condition, or the claims of education properly respected, until pupils and parents learn to appreciate the importance of regular attendance . . . we cannot overlook the fact that there are, in many of our rural districts, obstacles which are simply insurmountable at present. When we take into consideration the difficulties in the way of many pupils getting to school at all; when we think of the requirements of the farm in the seasons of sowing and harvesting, in which the aid of children is indispensably necessary, we feel that these things must unavoidably interfere with School Attendance. When we take into careful consideration the claims of industry, of domestic service, and the necessary interference by sickness, we feel that considerable time must elapse before the attendance of pupils will come up to the required estimate . . .[47]

It was not that parents did not want to send their children to school—the almost universal enrolments deny that—rather the rigour and the rhythm of work made it difficult to keep them there for sustained periods of time.

[1978]

Notes

1. Upper Canada, Department of Public Instruction, *Annual Report of the Normal, Model, Grammar and Common Schools*, 1850, p. 12. (The titles of the chief superintendents' annual reports change from year to year, hereafter cited as *Annual Report* for the given year.)
2. The increase in enrolments resulted particularly from an influx of girls into the public schools, see Ian E. Davey, 'Trends in Female School Attendance Patterns', *Histoire sociale/Social History*, Fall 1975, pp. 238–54; and id. 'Educational Reform and the Working Class: School Attendance in Hamilton, Ontario, 1851–1891' (Ph.D. thesis, University of Toronto, 1975) especially chapters 3 and 5. It should be noted that Ryerson's figures for those enrolled in the common schools was an aggregate of those in the public and separate schools, although in the *Annual Report*, the number attending the separate schools is also listed separately.
3. In all but the most remote and poor areas, the schools were open throughout the year. As early as 1865, Ryerson remarked that 'the time during which schools are kept open in cities, towns and villages embraces, with scarcely an exception, the whole period required by law; and the average time . . . was 10 months and 2 days . . . about 2 months longer than the schools are kept open in any state of America.' *Annual Report* for 1856, p. 12.
4. See Susan E. Houston, 'The Impetus to Reform: Urban Crime, Poverty and Ignorance in Ontario, 1850–1875' (Ph.D. thesis, University of Toronto, 1974), Sec. III.
5. This aspect was often referred to by the local superintendents and, after 1871, the inspectors. See, for example, *The Second Annual Report of the Inspectors of Public Schools for the City of Ottawa, 1872* (Ottawa, 1873), p. 14.
6. For a discussion of this point, see Davey, 'Educational Reform', pp. 243–5.
7. The superintendent for the County of Durham in the *Annual Report* for 1864, Appendix A, p. 19.
8. 'Parental indifference' or 'criminal neglect' or 'carelessness' were the phrases most frequently used to explain non-attendance or irregular attendance, especially in the earlier years. Perhaps an extreme example of its use (misuse?) was that of the superintendent for Bruce County in 1865 who stated regarding non-attendance: 'The common cause given in almost every report is the indifference of parents. Extreme poverty, sickness and religious convictions I would excuse, but all put together does not make one case out of ten.' Ibid. for 1865, Appendix A, p. 46.
9. Superintendent for Wolfe Island, County of Frontenac, ibid. for 1861, Appendix A, p. 168.
10. *Annual Report* for 1868, Appendix A, p. 38.
11. *Annual Report* for 1858, p. 1.
12. Superintendent Barber's 1857 report surveyed the progress of the Toronto free schools in the 1850s. The board passed a no-confidence motion against him in 1858 and reaffirmed the commitment to the free-school system, as they did in 1864 despite the select committee's report. During the depression years of the early 1860s and the late 1870s, the City Council tried to reduce the board's estimates because of the financial drain they represented on the city's resources. The point is that the expense of maintaining the school system was most burdensome in depression times while, at the same time, poor attendance was most obvious. For a discussion of these reports, see Haley P. Bamman and Ian E. Davey, 'Ideology and Space in the Toronto Public School System' (paper presented to the Conference on Historical Urbanization in North America, York University, 1973).
13. See Thomas Hutchison, *City of Hamilton Directory, 1862–63* (Hamilton, 1862), p. 14. For the effect of the depression on the city see 'The City of Hamilton, Past, Present and

Future', a letter to the editor in the *Hamilton Spectator and Journal of Commerce*, 1 January 1861.

14. From the Hamilton Orphan Asylum and Ladies Benevolent Society, *Minutes*, Vol. 3, January 1859, Hamilton Public Library.

15. On one day, 21 May 1859, in Hamilton two boys aged eight and thirteen were charged with stealing iron to sell, another eight-year-old was charged with stealing coal and a nine-year-old with stealing $5. The latter on conviction was fined $10 or one month's gaol. See *The Weekly Spectator*, 21 May 1859.

16. *Annual Report* for 1860, p. 189.

17. Ibid., p. 180.

18. Inspector for York County, North, ibid., 1879, Appendix D, p. 66.

19. Historians have only recently become aware of the extreme geographic mobility in the nineteenth century. See Stephan Thernstrom and Peter B. Knights, 'Men in Motion: Some Data and Speculations about Urban Population Mobility in Nineteenth Century America', *Journal of Interdisciplinary History* I (1970), 7–36. For Hamilton, see Michael B. Katz, 'The People of a Canadian City, 1851–2', *Canadian Historical Review* L, No. 4 (1972), 402–26; and ibid., *The People of Hamilton, Canada West: Family and Class in a Mid-Nineteenth Century City* (Cambridge, Mass., 1975), especially the chapter on transiency and social mobility; for rural Ontario, see David P. Gagan and Herbert Mays, 'Historical Demography and Canadian Social History: Families and Land in Peel County, Ontario', *Canadian Historical Review* LIV, No. 1 (1973), 27–47.

20. See Katz's chapter on transiency and social mobility in *Hamilton* for an analysis of the rates of persistence in Hamilton and an analysis of the characteristics of those who stayed and those who left. It is important to note that rates for females are difficult to assess because it is hard to link those who got married in the interim period.

21. Ibid.

22. Stephan Thernstrom, *Poverty and Progress: Social Mobility in a Nineteenth Century City* (Cambridge, Mass., 1964), p. 87.

23. Erickson, *Invisible Immigrants*, pp. 249–50.

24. *Annual Report* for 1890, Appendix I, p. 182. Although this example is drawn from a later period, there must have been numerous examples of double reporting. The 600 children reported as moving from school to school in Toronto in 1852 would also have inflated the overall enrolment and lowered the average attendance.

25. Ibid. for 1866, Appendix A, p. 60

26. Ibid. for 1865, Appendix A, p. 65.

27. Superintendent for Petrolia village in ibid. for 1869, Appendix D, p. 116.

28. Ibid. for 1861, Appendix A, p. 159.

29. Superintendent for the County of Durham, ibid. for 1869, Appendix D, p. 69.

30. Erickson concludes that the main grievances for most of the immigrant artisans at first 'were not low wages or long hours but irregular employment and the difficulty of securing wages in cash'. *Invisible Immigrants*, p. 250.

31. *The Workingman's Journal*, 18 June 1864. This paper was published for a couple of years in the mid-1860s in Hamilton, although this is the only issue found. It is located in the Hamilton Public Library.

32. See the evidence of Fred Walters of Hamilton in the *Royal Commission on the Relations Between Capital and Labor*, p. 796.

33. Evidence of Thomas Towers, a carpenter for the Grand Trunk Railroad and Hamilton District Master of the Knights of Labor, *Royal Commission on the Relations Between Capital and Labour*, p. 875.

34. Superintendent for Dereham Township, County of Oxford, in *Annual Report* for 1861, Appendix A, p. 184.
35. The evidence in the *Royal Commission on the Relations Between Capital and Labour* is an excellent source of information on seasonal labour patterns. For the evidence of winter unemployment among moulders, see, for example, the testimony of Fred Walters of Hamilton, pp. 794–5.
36. Judith Fingard, 'The Winter's Tale: Contours of Pre-Industrial Poverty in British America, 1815–1860', Canadian Historical Association, *Historical Papers*, 1974, p. 67. It should be noted that seasonal poverty was not confined to 'pre-industrial' Canada. *The Palladium of Labour*, 1 December 1883, commented on the injustice of paying carpenters less in winter because of the shorter working day: 'Man's wants are greater in winter than at any season of the year. It costs more for fire, food and clothing and all the necessities of life, and more are consumed on account of the weather.'
37. *Annual Report* for 1874, Appendix B, p. 71.
38. Davey, 'Educational Reform', Chapter 4.
39. Superintendent for London Township, County of Middlesex, ibid. for 1863, Appendix A, p. 140.
40. In ibid. for 1859, p. 167.
41. Superintendent for Nelson Township, County of Halton, in ibid. for 1861, Appendix A, p. 176.
42. Superintendent for Huron County, in ibid. for 1863, Appendix A, p. 160. This facet of winter attendance is well captured in Charles William Gordon's [Ralph Connor] memories of his school days, *Glengarry School-Days* (Toronto, 1902). [. . .]
43. Superintendent for Welland County, in ibid. for 1868, Appendix A, p. 25.
44. Superintendent for Moulton Township, County of Haldimand, in ibid. for 1869, Appendix D, p. 86. The perception of the immigrants as ignorant was common in the reports; see the superintendent for Markham, County of York, in ibid. for 1862, Appendix A, p. 114, who remarked: 'The few discontented parties being ignorant persons from the old countries. . . . Happily the number is few . . . and in a few years I hope it will be esteemed as great a disgrace to be ignorant as it is now considered to be intemperate. The immigrant children are growing up in ignorance, a strong contrast to our native born Canadian children, not one of whom at the age of ten years and upwards but can read, write and cipher.'
45. Harvey J. Graff, 'Literacy and Social Structure in the Nineteenth Century', (Ph.D. thesis, University of Toronto, 1975).
46. *Annual Report* for 1873, Appendix B, pp. 77–8.
47. Ibid. for 1869, p. 24.
48. Inspector for the County of Renfrew, in *Annual Report* for 1872, Appendix B, p. 30.

An Argument for Assessment and Free Schools (Nova Scotia)

Theodore Rand

The Case for Free Schools

[One reason why I commend assessment as a] system of supporting common schools to your favourable consideration, is its cheapness to parents educating their children. I will select the example of one district, rather better than an average specimen; and the same mode of reasoning will apply to every district in Upper Canada, and with the same results. In one district there were reported 200 schools in operation in 1848; the average time of keeping open the schools was eight months; the average salaries of teachers was £45.7s. ld.; the total amount of the money available for the teachers' salaries, including the legislative grant, council assessment and rate-bills, was £7,401.18s.4½ d.; the whole number of pupils between the ages of five and sixteen years on the school registers, was 9,147; the total number of children between those ages resident in the district, 20,600; cost per pupil for eight months, about sixteen shillings. Here it will be seen that more than one-half of the children of school age in the district were not attending any school. Now, suppose the schools be kept open the whole year, instead of two thirds of it; suppose the male and female teachers to be equal in number, and the salaries of the former to average £60, and those of the latter £40; suppose the 20,600 children to be in the schools instead of 9,147 of them. The whole sum required for the salaries of teachers would be £10,000—the cost per pupil would be less than ten shillings—less than five shillings per inhabitant—which would be reduced still further by deducting the legislative school grant. Thus would a provision be made for the education of every child in the district for the whole year; there would be no trouble or dispute about school-rate bills; there would be no difficulty in getting good teachers; the character and efficiency of the schools would be as much improved as the attendance of pupils would be increased; every child would be educated, and educated by the contribution of every man according to his means.

This is also the most effectual method of providing the best, as well as the cheapest, school for the youth of each school section. Our schools are now often poor and feeble, because a large portion of the best educated inhabitants stand aloof from them, as unworthy of their support, as unfit to educate their children. Thus the Common Schools are frequently left to the care and support of the least instructed part of the population, and then are complained of as inferior in character and badly supported. The Free School system makes every man a supporter of the school according to his property. All persons—and especially the more wealthy—who are thus identified with the school, will feel interested in it; they will be anxious that their contributions to the school should be as effective as possible, and that they themselves may derive all possible benefit from it. When all the inhabitants of a school section thus become concerned in the school, its character and efficiency will inevitably be advanced. The more wealthy contributors will seek to make the school fit and efficient for the English education of their own children; the Trustees will be under no fears from the disinclination or opposition of particular individuals in employing a suitable teacher and stipulating his salary; and thus is the foundation laid for a good school, adapted to all the youth of the section. The character of the school will be as much advanced as the expense of it to individual parents will be diminished; the son of the poor man, equally with the son of the rich man, will drink from the stream of knowledge at the common fountain, and will experience corresponding elevation of thought, sentiment, feeling and pursuit. Such a sight cannot fail to gladden the heart of Christian humanity.

The Free School system is the true, and, I think, only effectual remedy for the pernicious and pauperising system which is at present incident to our common schools. Many children are now kept from school on the alleged grounds of parental poverty. How far this excuse is well founded, is immaterial to the question in hand; of the fact of the excuse itself, and of its widespread, blasting influence, there can be no doubt. Now, while one class of poor children are altogether deprived of the benefits of all education by parental pride or indifference, the other class of them are educated as paupers or as ragged scholars. Is it not likely that children educated under this character will imbibe the spirit of it? If we would wish them to feel and act, and rely upon themselves as freemen when they grow up to manhood, let them be educated in that spirit when young. Such is the spirit of the Free School system. It banishes the very idea of pauperism from the school. No child comes there by sufferance, but every one comes there upon the ground of right. The poor man as well as the rich man pays for the support of the school according to his means; and the right of his son to the school is thus as legal as that of the rich man's son.

But against this system of Free Schools certain objections have been made, the principal of which I will briefly answer:

First objection: 'The common schools are not fit to educate the children of the higher classes of society, and therefore these classes ought not to be taxed for the support of the common schools.'

Answer: The argument of this objection is the very cause of the evil on which the objection itself is founded. The unnatural and unpatriotic separation of the wealthier classes from the common school has caused its inefficiency and alleged degradation. Had the wealthy classes been identified with the Common Schools equally with their poorer neighbors—as is the case in Free School countries—the Common

School would have been fit for the education of their children, and proportionally better than it now is for the education of the children of the more numerous common classes of society. In Free School cities and states, the Common Schools are acknowledged to be the best elementary schools in such cities and states; so much so, that the Governor of the State of Massachusetts remarked at a late school celebration, that if he had the riches of an Astor, he would send all his children through the Common School to the highest institutions in the State.

Second objection: 'It is unjust to tax persons for the support of a school which they do not patronize, and from which they derive no individual benefit.'

Answer: If this objection be well founded, it puts an end to school taxes of every kind, and abolishes school and college endowments of every description; it annihilates all systems of public instruction, and leaves education and schools to individual caprice and inclination. This doctrine was tried in the Belgian Netherlands after the revolt of Belgium from Holland in 1830; and in the course of five years, educational desolation spread throughout the kingdom, and the Legislature had to interfere to prevent the population from sinking into semi-barbarism. But the principle of a public tax for schools has been avowed in every school assessment which has ever been imposed by our Legislature, or by any District Council; the same principle is acted upon in the endowment of a Provincial University—for such endowment is as much public property as any part of the public annual revenue of the country. The principle has been avowed and acted upon by every Republican State of America, as well as by the Province of Canada and the countries of Europe. The only question is as to the extent to which the principle should be applied—whether to raise a part or the whole of what is required to support the public school. On this point it may be remarked, that if the principle be applied at all, it should be applied in that way and to that extent which will best promote the object contemplated, namely, the sound education of the people; and experience, as well as the nature of the case, shows that the free system of supporting schools is the most, and indeed the only, effectual means of promoting the universal education of the people.

I observe again on this second objection, that what it assumes as fact is not true. It assumes that none are benefited by the Common School but those who patronise it. This is the lowest, narrowest, and most selfish view of the subject and indicates a mind the most contracted and grovelling. This view applied to a Provincial University, implies that no persons are benefited by it except graduates; applied to criminal jurisprudence and its requisite officers and prisons, it supposes that no persons are benefited by them except those whose persons are rescued from the assaults of violence, or whose property is restored from the hands of theft; applied to canals, harbors, roads, &c., this view assumes that no persons derive any benefit from them except those who personally navigate or travel over them. The fact is, that whatever tends to diminish crime and lessen the expenses of criminal jurisprudence, enhances the value of the whole estate of a country or district; and is not this the tendency of good common school education? And who has not witnessed the expenditure of more money in the detection, conviction, and punishment of a single uneducated criminal, than would be necessary to educate in the common school half a dozen children? Is it not better to spend money upon the child than upon the culprit—to prevent crime than to punish it? Again, whatever adds to the security of property of all kinds increases its value; and does not the proper education of the people do so? Whatever also tends to develop the physical resources of a country, must add to the value of property; and is not this the tendency of the education of the people? Is not education in fact the power of the people to make all the resources of their country tributary to their interests and comforts? And is not this the most obvious and prominent distinguishing feature between an educated and uneducated people—the power of the former, and the powerlessness of the latter, to develop the resources of nature and Providence, and make them subservient to human interests and enjoyments? Can this be done without increasing the value of property? I verily believe, that in the sound and universal education of the people, the balance of gain financially is on the side of the wealthier classes. If the poorer classes gain in intellectual power, and in the resources of individual and social happiness, the richer classes gain proportionally, I think more than proportionally, in the enhanced value of their property. As an illustration, take any two neighbourhoods, equal in advantages of situation and natural fertility of soil; the one inhabited by an ignorant, and therefore unenterprising, grovelling, if not disorderly, population; the other peopled with a well educated, and therefore enterprising, intelligent, and industrious class of inhabitants. The difference in the value of all real estates in the two neighbourhoods is ten if not a hundredfold greater than the amount of school-tax that has ever been imposed upon it. And yet it is the school that makes the difference in the two neighbourhoods; and the larger the field of experiment the more marked will be the difference. Hence, in Free School countries, where the experiment has been so tested as to become a system, there are no warmer advocates of it than men of the largest property and the greatest intelligence; the profoundest scholars and the ablest statesmen.

[From Nova Scotia *House of Assembly Journals*, 1865. App. 9. Education Report for 1864, App. A.]

White Supremacy, Chinese Schooling, and School Segregation in Victoria: The Case of the Chinese Students' Strike, 1922–1923

Timothy J. Stanley

In September 1922, the Victoria School Board moved to segregate the Chinese students enrolled in the district. On September 5, the first day of classes, the principals of the Boys' Central and the George Jay Schools called the Chinese students out of their classes, lined them up, and marched them down to the schools which had been set aside for the Chinese only.[1] Much to the surprise of the Victoria School Board and its officials, the Chinese community did not passively acquiesce to this discriminatory move. When Principal J.A. Cunningham of Boys' Central School and his charges reached the segregated King's Road School,

> a Chinese boy holding the reputation of being the quietest and most studious in the class shouted something in the Oriental lingo, and like a flash the parade disbanded, leaving Principal Cunningham in the middle of the roadway and wondering how he could overcome the difficulties of the situation.[2]

Similar events took place with the students from the George Jay School.[3] The Chinese community had organized a student strike against the public school system of Victoria in an effort to pressure the school board into allowing their children to return to their former schools. Despite various attempts at resolution in the coming months, the deadlock between the Chinese community and the Victoria School Board lasted for the rest of the school year. To maintain the strike, the Chinese community even established its own school for the children involved. Consequently during the 1922–23 school year, 'less than six' Chinese students attended the public schools in Victoria, compared to 216 the previous year.[4]

School segregation can be seen as a particular instance of white supremacy: the political and social system predicated on the supposed existence and natural dominance of a white 'race'.[5] In British Columbia, white supremacy was often expressed in the notion that BC was, and should be, a white man's country. Non-whites, including the Chinese, were by definition alien to this country. White supremacist opinion consequently represented the Chinese to be morally, culturally, and biologically different from whites. For example, shortly before World War One, a commentary in *British Columbia Magazine* presented its readers with the following characterization of the 'Oriental'.

> Racially he is as opposite to the Anglo-Saxon in life, thought, religion, temperament, taste, morals, and modes, as ice is to fire. AND HE CAN NEVER BE OTHERWISE. There is the test; this is the touchstone that irrevocably fixes the difference. He cannot be changed, even by centuries of contact, any more than the leopard can change his spots. He may adopt certain of the white man's vices, because to him these seem virtues; but he will not take up any of the white race's virtues, because these seem, either as vices to him or negligible trifles. So that, to begin with, in this review you may set it down as unalterable that, racially, the yellow man can never become a white man.[6]

Opinions of this sort made socially constructed divisions of the human species into groups such as 'Anglo-Saxons' and 'Orientals' appear natural, at the same time that they rationalized the dominance of one over the other. Such opinions were often used to exclude the Chinese and members of other groups from participation in white society and to justify discriminatory measures directed against them. For example, in 1885, in order to defend extending British Columbia's disenfranchisement of the Chinese to the federal level, Sir John A. Macdonald told the House of Commons that the Chinese immigrant 'has no British instincts or British feelings or aspirations', and that the Chinese in Canada constituted 'an Asiatic population, alien in spirit, alien in feeling, alien in everything'.[7] Discriminatory measures, like disenfranchisement, in turn codified and reinforced representations of the Chinese as Other.[8]

The result was that, by the turn of the century, a patchwork of discriminatory legislation, petty regulations, and racist social practices effectively circumscribed the daily lives of the Chinese residents of British Columbia. Amongst other things, these measures limited their sectors of economic activity, sanctioned their places of residence, and deprived most of them of family life.[9] The Chinese lived in 'A World of Their Own',[10] more often than not, effectively isolated from meaningful interaction with white society. Thus, for some whites, like the *Victoria Daily Colonist*'s 1902 labour columnist, T.H. Twigg, school segregation seemed to involve little more than 'carrying into the schools what already exists in every other institution of society— the branding of Chinese as Ishmaelites'.[11]

Even though it was not the only instance in which Chinese children attending public schools in British Columbia were segregated,[12] the 1922–23 dispute between the Chinese community and the Victoria School Board poses some of the most important questions for our understanding of how white supremacy functioned. The sustained and organized response of the Chinese community evident in this dispute suggests that white supremacy should not be seen as a static, one-way system. Rather it points to the fact that discriminatory legislation, government regulations, and racist social practices were continually being challenged by affected groups. For example, racist legislation was at various times in full effect, suspended pending court challenges, unenforceable, or being systematically ignored.[13] Far from being static, white supremacy, therefore, needs to be understood as a dynamic system continually in flux. The advantages of such an understanding become apparent through an examination of the factors shaping the response of the Chinese community during the 1922–23 Victoria school segregation controversy as well as those shaping the actions of the school board.

The ever-changing nature of white supremacy would have been readily apparent to Chinese children attending Victoria public schools before 1922. Few of these children could have escaped school segregation, or threats of school segregation, at some point in their careers. School segregation was first proposed in 1901, and put into effect for all the Chinese students in the district between 1902 and 1905.[14] Partial school segregation in the lower grades, either for all Chinese students, or for those who were older than the average for their grade levels, was in effect during much of the period between 1908 and 1922.[15]

Chinese resistance to school segregation in large measure accounts for this shifting pattern. As early as 1902, Chinese merchants whose children attended public schools in Victoria directly intervened with the school board to respond to calls for school segregation.[16] Segregated classes had to be closed, due to lack of enrolment, in 1904 and again in 1916.[17] In 1907 and 1908, legal challenges were made to segregation and exclusion of Chinese students from the district.[18] In 1921–22, older Chinese students in segregated schools may have deliberately subverted school discipline to protest segregation.[19]

Pressure for school segregation also varied in its intensity and in its nature. Most often calls for school segregation were motivated by the supposed moral and physical threat that the Chinese posed to white children. For years Chinatown had been vilified as the moral opposite of white society, as a breeding ground for depravity and disease.[20] Chinese children, it was often feared, would spread the contagions of Chinatown to white children.

The moral and physical threat to their white classmates that Chinese students could supposedly transport from Chinatown was well summarized by Vancouver City Council in 1914 when it called for school segregation. This call was in response to an incident in which a Chinese servant, who was also a public school student, was accused of murdering the white woman who employed him. Council stated that

> by being indiscriminately thrown into association with Orientals many years their senior, our children are wantonly exposed to Oriental vices at an age when revolting incidents may be indelibly stamped upon their minds. Furthermore the health of our children is endangered by such close association with Oriental children, many of whom hail from habitations where reasonable sanitation and cleanliness are not only despised but utterly disregarded. In some cases, these Orientals come into our public school classrooms with their apparel polluted with the fumes of noxious drugs and germs of loathsome diseases on their persons.[21]

School segregation, it was argued, was essential for the protection of white children.

The physical threat of disease probably motivated residents in the area of Victoria's Rock Bay School to call for school segregation in 1901,[22] while the threat posed by alleged improper sanitation was certainly an issue when the Victoria

Trades and Labour Council resurrected the matter the following year.[23] This theme was returned to in 1922 by Municipal School Inspector, George H. Deane, when he reintroduced the subject to the Victoria School Board. 'There is a danger in these Chinese boys, many of whom cannot even speak English, coming from the unsanitary living quarters downtown and mixing with other children with no attempt at segregation', he told the board. 'We know that it is not only a tendency with the Chinese to live in unsanitary quarters, but a practice.'[24]

What most captured the imaginations of white parents was the moral threat posed by older Chinese students in the lower grades.[25] Thus, school segregation again became an issue in Victoria in 1908 when white residents threatened to pull their children out of the Rock Bay school[26] after one of the older Chinese students was expelled for 'employing his spare-time in drawing obscene pictures in the exercise books of little white children'.[27] White girls were believed to be particularly vulnerable to the threat of older Chinese boys. There was a brief scare in 1909 over the risks facing white girls teaching English in Chinatown,[28] and similar concerns motivated the Vancouver City Council's call for school segregation in 1914. But the fears that underlay these concerns were made the most explicit in popular fiction. One novel, published in serial form in the *Vancouver Sun* in 1921, described the unusually 'hopeless despair' felt by two parents who woke up one morning to discover that their daughter had eloped during the night:

> Pretty Eileen Hart, the pride of her mother, the apple of her father's eye, and only eighteen years old, had run away and married—a Chinaman. The horror of it turned them sick. She had been better dead. Eileen, with her beauty, her daintiness, her originality—they had always been specially proud of this and her daring—was now Mrs Wong Fu![29]

Since Eileen had met Wong Fu, an older student, at school, where she was seduced by his more worldly ways, the distraught father placed the blame squarely on 'this *damned system of co-education*' and 'co-education with the spawn of these yellow dogs'.[30]

However, not all white British Columbians accepted that the Chinese constituted a real physical and moral threat. School personnel in particular questioned this notion. For example, in 1902 in response to the Trades and Labour Council's pressure to effect school segregation, Victoria's Superintendent F.H. Eaton noted that far from causing problems, the Chinese children were 'getting on very well' and that 'they were obedient, attentive, and studious, and often set a good example in these things to the other children of the various rooms'.[31] According to the *Victoria Daily Colonist*, he was using even stronger language a few months later when he referred to reports that the Chinese were causing problems as 'pure fabrications'.[32] In 1914, Principal Cunningham of the Boys' Central School questioned the school board's policy of segregating primary students. He noted that the Chinese students 'make good use of the educational chances available in the higher grades, and are docile and easy to teach', but pointed out that they entered the higher grades with little fluency in English. 'Hence', he informed the board, 'it is no remedy to establish a separate graded school for the Chinese, who would thus never thoroughly learn English or western ways.'[33]

In fact, white attitudes towards the Chinese were to a large extent class-based. Before the First World War, it was mainly working-class organizations, and politicians pandering to the working-class vote, who called for school segregation.[34] The drive towards school segregation in 1902 was spearheaded by the Victoria Trades and Labour Council. In 1907–8, it was the Asiatic Exclusion League, an organization actively supported by white trade unions, that pressured for action against Chinese students who were supposedly using schools to evade the immigration head tax. These concerns were motivated by fears that the Chinese were cheap labourers who were undercutting the wages of white workers. Indeed, working-class opinion was so inimicable to the Chinese that it is likely that otherwise class-conscious white workers did not see their fellow Chinese workers as workers at all.[35] During the summer of 1907, fears that Chinese labourers were using the school system to circumvent the immigration head tax led the Victoria School Board to refuse admission to Chinese students unless they spoke sufficient English as 'to be amenable to the ordinary regulations of school discipline',[36] thus effectively barring recent Chinese immigrants from the district. In January 1908, it ruled that it would admit only native-born Chinese students who met the English test.[37] Fear of competition from cheap Chinese labour even led the provincial government to pass an order-in-council complaining that Chinese students were only using the educational system 'to increase their efficiency and to render them better able to compete with white labour'.[38] By contrast, upper-class whites living in Victoria, themselves often the employers of Chinese servants and industrial workers, probably saw the Chinese as no threat at all, but merely a rather exotic aspect of life in British Columbia.[39] They may well have been somewhat bemused by calls for school segregation.[40]

However, even those whites who opposed the excesses of white supremacist opinion shared the view that the Chinese were alien. They, too, took for granted that BC was a white society. For example, when he criticized the board's policies in 1914, Principal Cunningham commented that the problem of how best to provide for the Chinese students was one 'which is inevitable with so many children of Chinese nationality residing and growing up in a white country'.[41]

Class-based attitudes began to shift during the First World War. Increasingly, it was the white middle classes, rather than the working class, which saw the Chinese as a threat.[42] The problem for white opinion was that the Chinese were no longer just cheap labour, but were entering other fields of endeavour. The contradiction was summarized by *The Daily Colonist* in 1922: 'So long as Orientals, or the members of any foreign race, are property owners in British Columbia our municipalities cannot refuse to provide for the education of their children.'[43] In a political and social system predicated on the rights of property-owners, the Chinese, although a 'foreign race', were now property-owners. This posed more of a problem for white property-owners than white workers. In this respect it should be noted that it was the Board of Trade and the Chamber of Commerce whose calls for school segregation, and laws barring the Chinese from owning land, led to the actions of the school board in 1922.[44] As the *Daily Colonist* editorial pointed out, it was the children of Chinese property-owners who were being segregated. Most of the Chinese children in the public schools of British Columbia during this era were likely the sons and daughters of merchants or professionals. This was for the simple reason that most of the Chinese children in Canada by this time came from this class.

Discriminatory immigration measures maintained male Chinese workers as cheap labour by transferring the costs of reproducing their labour to China. This was primarily achieved through the head tax on Chinese immigration (raised to $500 by 1904) which, however much it inhibited male labourers from entering Canada, effectively barred their wives and dependent children from immigrating.[45] Merchants and their families, by contrast, were specifically excluded from the head tax provisions. The net effect of these measures was that most of the Chinese families in Canada, and much of the second generation, would have been from the merchant class.[46]

That school segregation was primarily directed against the children of Chinese merchants becomes apparent from the response of the Chinese community in Victoria to the school board's decision to impose segregation. From the very beginning of the 1922–23 school segregation controversy, the Chinese Consolidated Benevolent Association (CCBA) played a key role in organizing this response. The CCBA, whose membership theoretically included all the Chinese living in Victoria, had always been controlled by the merchant-elite of the community. It was formed in 1884 by a group of Victoria merchants who received a charter from the Chinese Consulate in San Francisco, and a year later it incorporated under the BC statutes.[47] It functioned as 'a *de facto* Chinese government in Canada',[48] not only operating welfare institutions such as a Chinese hospital, but also resolving disputes internal to the community and providing support for those Chinese caught in disputes outside the community.[49] It was in this latter role that it first became involved in the 1922–23 school segregation issue. At a school board meeting early in 1922, the CCBA directly challenged Inspector Deane's charges of improper sanitation on the part of Chinese students.[50] During the summer, after the board announced its plans to proceed with segregation, the CCBA, this time in conjunction with other Chinese organizations, again protested.[51] It was the CCBA that organized the students' strike and established the Victoria Overseas Chinese Resist School Segregation Association (*Weiduoli Huaqiao Kangzheng Fenxiao Tuantihui*), an *ad hoc* organization which was to coordinate the fight against the school board in the coming months.[52]

The students' strike and ensuing deadlock must have come as a surprise to the trustees of the Victoria School Board. While they were well aware that the Chinese were opposed to segregation,[53] from their point of view they were merely extending to the middle grades an existing system of partial segregation already in effect in the lower grades. The response of the Chinese must have seemed extreme to say the least. Indeed, throughout the segregation dispute, the Victoria Chinese community demonstrated a high degree of solidarity. When segregation was first proposed, the school inspector granted special permits which allowed twenty Chinese students to attend integrated classes on the grounds that their English was good enough.[54] Despite this, the twenty children granted permits also boycotted classes.[55] For a time in October, five Chinese students showed up for class at the King's Road School, but they too withdrew after a while.[56]

What the school board had not taken into account was the depth of Chinese resentment of school segregation. In particular, second-generation Chinese Canadians, who may have made up to 85 per cent of the students attending Victoria schools,[57] had a great deal to lose. The stakes involved for them were made clear by Low Kwong Joe, the President of the Chinese Canadian Club, an organization of second-generation people. In a letter to the *Victoria Daily Times*, he admitted that for several years Chinese in Victoria had accepted the principle of separate classes for the Chinese students in the lowest grades on the grounds that 'segregation would enable the children better to acquire a knowledge of English'. Quite the contrary had proved to be the case, however. Now the Chinese were being asked to accept segregation up to the level of the high school entrance class. According to Joe,

> If we accept this we have no reason to expect any better result, so the next step will be on the grounds of imperfect knowledge of English we will be prevented from the entrance classes or the High School. You can therefore see, Mr. Editor, how serious the question is for us. It is not the 200 children now affected that we have to think of, but the whole of our future is involved in this question. We cannot afford to take any other attitude than the one we have taken.
>
> We ask ourselves this question: What can be the purpose behind this movement? Can it be the intention to prevent us securing an English education so that our children can be permanently ignorant, so that they must remain labourers to be exploited? Being ignorant of the language we will be unable to take our part by the side of other Canadians, and we will then be pointed out as those who refuse to learn the customs or social life of the country—in fact, refuse to assimilate. It will have been forgotten by then that it was not because we did not want to learn, but because certain narrow-minded autocrats have taken upon themselves the responsibility of preventing our learning.[58]

In other words, second-generation Chinese Canadians saw school segregation as an attempt to prevent them from learning English. This not only threatened to maintain their separation from white society; it also threatened to make the second-generation children of merchants into cheap labour like most of the first generation. In addition, by maintaining the pariah status of the Chinese, it also laid the basis for their potential expulsion from Canada.[59]

Throughout the 1922–23 school segregation crisis, the Chinese Canadian Club played an important role in exposing the school board's agenda. The racist nature of the school board's actions had been evident to the Chinese in Victoria from the beginning of the dispute. This was apparent in several letters to the editor published in the English-language papers. For example, one Chinese letter-writer saw the school board's actions as 'purely and simply a matter of discrimination', while another asked what the reasons for the board's actions were: 'Surely they are not moved to act simply out of racial prejudice', he commented ironically.[60] However as the deadlock continued, it was the Chinese Canadian Club that took on the role of responding to the school board's allegations in the white newspapers. For example, when the school board claimed that segregation was necessary because Chinese students were retarding the progress of white students, the Chinese Canadian Club published a list of the names, ages, and class rankings of ninety-four Chinese students, formerly attending non-segregated schools, who were above their class averages. In addition it published the names of another seventeen students who were below their class averages but were two years younger than their classmates. It pointed out that in these classes 'all questions and answers are given in English, and that the Chinese children could not stand so high up in their classes unless they understand the questions asked them, and could answer intelligently.'[61]

Collecting the kind of information that the Chinese Canadian Club used to respond to the school board indicates that there was a high degree of organization and solidarity within the Chinese community. This organization and solidarity is also apparent in the other element of the Chinese community's response to segregation: the creation of a Chinese-language school for the children involved in the strike. Plans for the creation of the *Weiduoli Bu Zhonghua Yixue* (Victoria Chinese Free School) were first discussed on October 5, 1922, when some of Victoria's most 'prominent Chinese residents' met to discuss the formation of a Chinese-language school since 'the school board persists in upholding school segregation'.[62] By the end of October, quite detailed plans for the Chinese Free School were announced. The school, which would not charge tuition, had been 'specially established to support the students on strike against school segregation'. It would hold classes in the CCBA building and be divided into two grades—a 'national grade' for students ages seven to twelve, and a higher grade for students thirteen to eighteen. Its staff of seven teachers and one principal would teach a curriculum which would 'normally' include Chinese language, calligraphy, arithmetic and English.[63]

Chinese nationalism was an integral element in the school. This was evident in its 'Guiding Principles' which stated, 'Established in order to support understanding of Chinese [language] amongst the students of the western schools on strike to resist school segregation, the school will nourish knowledge amongst the overseas people of the homeland's common written characters and stimulate the overseas people to have the idea that patriotism wipes out shame.'[64] In other words, the school was primarily intended to instil Chinese nationalist feeling and knowledge of written Chinese amongst the striking students in order to strengthen their resolve while the strike lasted.

It may be that the nationalist character of this school was the result of expediency. A white sympathizer of the Chinese, Harry Hastings, claimed that the Chinese had 'no intention of establishing their own English schools at an additional cost to themselves when they are already paying more than their share through the school tax.'[65] In addition, the Chinese would have drawn upon readily available resources to create such a school. At this time the Chinese community of Victoria had its own network of day and evening Chinese-language schools.[66] The existence of this network of Chinese schools was even apparent in the announcement of the creation of the Chinese Free School which made careful provision to insure that the school would not take away students from any existing schools.[67] Because of this network, a Chinese-language school would have been easier to establish. But the nature of the school also points to the fact that, during this era, the Chinese community used Chinese nationalism instrumentally to challenge white hegemony. Indeed the Chinese community had invented a common identity as Chinese largely in response to the threat of white-supremacist exclusion.

Although white opinion portrayed the Chinese in Canada as monolithic, they did not see themselves as such. Most of the Chinese immigrants to Canada came from

Guangdong province in South China. However, they spoke several, often mutually unintelligible, dialects of Cantonese and Hakka. Their loyalties tended to be based on their county of origin, rather than any broader identification.[68] Settlement patterns in Canada further compounded these centrifugal tendencies as people from the same districts, speaking the same dialects, grouped together in certain localities, or else established monopolies in certain industries or trades, in order to survive in the new world. It was only very slowly that institutions such as the CCBA, or pan-local organizations such as the clan associations, 'invented' a common identity as Chinese.[69]

The promotion of literacy in written Chinese was an important element in overcoming the barriers of dialect and home origin. For over two thousand years written Chinese had made possible the political unification of China. Through written texts, officials, who would need interpreters to speak face to face, could communicate effectively. Written Chinese fulfilled the same function amongst the Chinese communities of Canada. As written Chinese could be understood without reference to spoken languages, it provided a common language accessible to all the Chinese in Canada.

Life in a country like Canada placed a premium on literacy. The ever-changing nature of white supremacy meant that previously barred areas of endeavour might suddenly open up, thus providing work or new opportunities for investment. By the same token, a district, or economic sector, that had earlier welcomed the Chinese might suddenly become hostile. In the former case one's economic well-being could depend upon accurate information and in the latter case, one's very survival might depend upon it. Chinese-language newspapers, like *The Chinese Times*, provided this kind of information.[70] The fact that literacy in Chinese allowed for confidential communications with family or business partners in China would have provided an added incentive to learn how to read and write.

At the same time, the periodic efforts of white supremacy to further restrict the Chinese provided an incentive to organize beyond the local level. Such organization in turn presupposed a common identity and a common language. The utility of organizing beyond the local level was apparent in the 1922–23 school segregation dispute. One of the first acts of Victoria's Resist School Segregation Association was to write to other communities, and even China, to request support.[71] In response, the Vancouver Chinese Benevolent Association established the Vancouver Resist School Segregation Rear Support Association to raise money and provide moral support to the Chinese in Victoria. It also held several public meetings which claimed that unless school segregation was stopped in Victoria, it would not only spread to Vancouver schools, but all sectors of Chinese endeavour in Canada.[72]

Knowledge of written Chinese thus became a resource for survival in the new world at the same time that it provided a common language and common identity. Chinese-language schools, therefore, were inseparably nationalist and anti-racist institutions. This is apparent in the case of the Chinese Public School, the most important and oldest of the Chinese language schools in Victoria. The Victoria Chinese Public School had originally been established under the auspices of the CCBA as the Lequn Yishe (Happy Masses Free School) in 1899.[73] The school itself was formed as the result of a burgeoning consciousness of being Chinese amongst the merchant class. Quoting an anonymous Chinese, the *Victoria Daily Colonist* claimed that the school was created because 'we are Chinamen wherever we go . . . and find that, in view of the international commercial relations now opening up, it is necessary to have an education in Chinese as well as English.'[74] In 1907–8, this school was called upon to provide for the schooling in Chinese and English of those students who were refused entry into the Victoria public school system. Consequently it became overcrowded and a new building was established, this time with the help of the Imperial Qing government. For a short time it was called the Imperial Chinese School, although the name subsequently was changed to the Chinese Public School.[75]

The school's importance is indicated by its enrolment. From 1908 to 1923, between 43 and 127 students a year attended the school.[76] For example, in 1914–15, it enrolled ninety students in six classes. The four upper classes were held during the evening as they were made up of students who attended the white public schools during the day. The two lower classes were held during the daytime.[77]

For the Chinese, this school was a 'public' school in the true sense. This was not only reflected in its name but also in its practices. It charged no tuition, was open to all Chinese children, and its activities were regularly followed in the Chinese-language press.[78] It was financed through the revenues of, and answerable to, the local Chinese government: the Chinese Consolidated Benevolent Association. In addition, it sought to instil in its students a collective consciousness through public speaking and observance of Chinese holidays such as Confucius' birthday. Its teachers were brought over from China and its language of instruction was Cantonese, even though most of its students spoke local dialects.[79] Its curriculum also appears to have been closely modelled on that of schools in China, as the school was inspected by official educational delegations from China on a number of occasions and pronounced up to standard each time.[80]

White supremacy provided an additional incentive for Chinese-language schools in Canada to be similar to their counterparts in China. The conditional nature of the Chinese presence in Canada meant that Chinese entrepreneurs or professionals might easily find their ambitions blocked in Canada, in which case, China could provide the best area of endeavour. It is likely that both white society and first-generation Chinese pressured second-generation children to seek fame and fortune in China.[81]

White supremacy is also important in explaining an additional feature of the Chinese Public School. In comparison to the Chinese attending the white public schools, the Chinese Public School appears to have enrolled a higher proportion of girls. In 1915, for example, of the school's ninety students, sixty-two were boys and twenty-eight girls. In 1914–15, the segregated school board school on Fisguard Street enrolled eighty-one boys and only seventeen girls. The next year at Rock Bay, there were forty boys and five girls.[82] Although it is no doubt true that some Chinese girls did not attend schools of any kind during this era,[83] and that the schooling of girls was devalued by Chinese patriarchy, it appears that the Chinese schools may well have been less hostile to Chinese girls than white schools. This points to the fact that white supremacy had a different effect on Chinese males compared to

Chinese females. This differential effect can be seen in the gender imbalance created by immigration patterns.[84] It can also be seen in the discussions of school segregation which, as should be apparent, were gendered. Thus school segregationists often spoke of 'Chinese boys' in contrast to 'white boys and girls' and since white girls were perceived to be particularly at risk from Chinese boys, for example, the City of Vancouver had called for segregation in 1914.

Much of the gender imbalance amongst Chinese students in the white school system can only be accounted for by the racist violence which was a constant reality facing the Chinese in British Columbia. Women and children, the Chinese believed, were especially vulnerable to this violence. As the market gardener Sing Cheung Yung explained to the 1902 Royal Commission on Chinese and Japanese Immigration when asked why he left his family in China, 'the people in this country talk so much against the Chinese that I don't care to bring them here.'[85]

Racist violence was certainly a constant reality confronting Chinese students in the white public schools. A number of incidents of such violence are reported in the English and Chinese-language newspapers throughout this era. At the turn of the century assaults on Chinese occasioned negative newspaper comments in both Vancouver and Victoria.[86] These assaults could have tragic results as was evident in 1904 when a Victoria Chinese youth had to have his leg amputated after being run over by a streetcar following an assault by a group of white boys.[87] In 1908, white boys were reported to be making 'an organized attempt to prevent Chinese pupils from attending the Rock Bay and Central Schools'.[88] Again in 1915, a Chinese schoolgirl was so seriously injured when she was stoned by a group of white boys that she required major surgery to save her life.[89] In 1922, tensions were sufficiently high in Vancouver that a snowball fight at Lord Strathcona School, on the edge of Chinatown, ended in the stabbing of a white boy.[90] Several years later, going to and from school was still an ordeal for Chinese students. One student who attended school in Vancouver recorded in his autobiography: 'We had trouble with the white kids on our way to and from school. We walked in groups for protection, the small kids following closely behind the bigger, stronger boys.'[91] Given this kind of violence, the Chinese community inevitably kept its youngest children and girls out of the white public schools, but allowed them to attend Chinese institutions in the relative safety of Chinatown. Therefore it is not surprising that the Chinese Public School's classes for its youngest students were day classes, nor that more Chinese girls attended it proportionally than attended the white public schools.

From the foregoing it is apparent that white supremacy needs to be understood as a complex system, one whose many dimensions were continually being challenged by the Chinese and other groups. School segregation was an on-again, off-again phenomenon as it swung back and forth between Chinese resistance and white opinion. White opinion about the Chinese itself was in constant flux as it varied considerably in intensity and content with time and class origins.

To acknowledge that white supremacy was in constant flux is not to render it any more palatable as a system. Rather it is to try to come to terms with its true horror: to recognize that for Chinese Canadians, their presence in British Columbian society was always contingent, and subject to potential renegotiation and exclusion. For the Chinese in Canada, coming to terms with white supremacy at least in part involved the creation, through the devices of literacy and Chinese-language schooling, of a domain separate and distinct from that of white society. This domain existed largely beyond the ken of white society and proved to be the greatest resource available to the Chinese in resisting white oppression. Its existence made possible their invention as a community, and enabled organized, community-wide, politically conscious challenges to white domination such as the 1922–23 students' strike. The fact that this Chinese domain, and its institutions such as *The Chinese Times* and the Victoria Chinese Public School, are still present in British Columbia is a testament to the persistence of the Chinese community in challenging supremacy. It is also a testament to the fact that the creation of a realm open to the full participation of all the peoples of Canada remains unfinished.

[1990]

Notes

An earlier version of this paper, 'White Supremacist Fictions and Schooling in British Columbia, 1900–1925: The Case of Chinese School Segregation in Victoria', was presented at the Fifth Biennial Conference of the Canadian History of Education Association/Association canadienne d'histoire de l'éducation, University of Western Ontario, London, Ontario, October 1988. I am particularly indebted to J. Donald Wilson for his careful reading of this paper and for providing me with the benefit of his profound knowledge of the field. I would also like to thank Frances Boyle, Vincent D'Oyley, Bill Maciejko, and Celia Haig-Brown for their comments on various drafts of this paper, as well as for their continuing encouragement.

1. 'Chinese Pupils Start "Rebellion"', *Victoria Daily Times*, Sept. 6, 1922, 2.
2. Ibid.
3. Ibid.
4. British Columbia, Department of Education, *Annual Report of the Public Schools of the Province of British Columbia, 1922–1923* (Victoria: King's Printer, 1923) [henceforth *Annual Report*], F45, and 'Orientals Health Menace in Schools, Inspector Asserts', *Victoria Daily Times*, Jan. 12, 1922, 18.
5. White supremacy is in this respect a particular form of racism. In this paper, the usage of the term 'racism' is intended to follow that of Robert Miles, who has argued that 'racism "works" by attributing meanings to certain phenotypical and/or genetic characteristics of human beings in such a way as to create a system of categorization, and by attributing additional (negatively evaluated) characteristics to the people sorted into these categories.' See Robert Miles, *Racism* (London: Routledge, 1989), 3. 'Races' should be understood as 'socially imagined rather than biological realities' (Ibid., 71). See also Ashley Montagu, ed., *The Concepts of Race* (New York: Free Press, 1964).
6. Ernest McGaffey, 'British Columbia and the Yellow Man', *British Columbia Magazine* 8, 3 (Mar. 1912): 198.
7. Canada, House of Commons, *Debates, Vol. XVIII* (Ottawa: King's Printer, 1885), 1582, 1589.
8. For a discussion of how European representations of the people of the Near East have made them Other, see Edward W. Said, *Orientalism* (New York: Vintage, 1979).

9. These measures and many of their consequences are documented in several histories of the Chinese in Canada and histories of racist discourse in BC. See David T.H. Lee (Li Donghai), *Jianada Huaqiao shi [A history of the Chinese in Canada]* (Taibei: Zhonghua Da Dian Bianyin Hui, 1967); W. Peter Ward, *White Canada Forever: Popular Attitudes and Public Policy Toward Orientals in British Columbia* (Montreal: McGill-Queen's University Press, 1978); Harry Con et al., *From China to Canada: A History of the Chinese Communities in Canada*, ed. Edgar Wickberg, *Generations: A History of the Canada's Peoples* (Toronto: McClelland and Stewart Ltd., 1982); Anthony B. Chan, *Gold Mountain: The Chinese in the New World* (Vancouver: New Star Books, 1983); Peter S. Li, *The Chinese in Canada* (Toronto: Oxford University Press, 1988); Patricia E. Roy, *A White Man's Province: British Columbia Politicians and Chinese and Japanese Immigrants, 1858–1914* (Vancouver: University of British Columbia Press, 1989). Two important doctoral dissertations are: Gillian Creese, 'Working Class Politics, Racism and Sexism: The Making of a Politically Divided Working Class in Vancouver, 1900–1939' (Ph.D. diss., Carleton University, 1986), and Kay Anderson, '"East" as "West": Place, State and the Institutionalization of Myth in Vancouver's Chinatown, 1880–1980' (Ph.D. diss., University of British Columbia, 1987). Paul Yee's *Saltwater City: An Illustrated History of the Chinese in Vancouver* (Vancouver: Douglas & McIntyre; Seattle: University of Washington Press, 1988), while intended for a non-academic audience, provides superb insights into the historical experiences of the Chinese in Canada.
10. Roy, *A White Man's Province*, 13.
11. Cited by Mary Ashworth, *The Forces Which Shaped Them: A History of the Education of Minority Group Children in British Columbia* (Vancouver: New Star Books, 1979), 58.
12. School segregation was also in effect at various times in Vancouver, New Westminster, and Nanaimo. Two excellent studies are Ashworth, 'Chapter Two, The Chinese', in *The Forces Which Shaped Them*, 54–90 and David Chuenyan Lai, 'The Issue of Discrimination in Education in Victoria, 1901–1923', *Canadian Ethnic Studies/Études Ethniques au Canada* XIX, 3 (1987): 47–67. Lai provides a particularly detailed account of segregation in Victoria. See also Lee, *Jianada Huaqiao shi*, 357–8; Ward, *White Canada Forever*, 62–4, 127–8; Wickberg, *From China to Canada*, 128–30; and Roy, *A White Man's Province*, 24–7, 276n31. On segregation in Victoria, see also Liu Guangzu, 'Weibu Huaqiao sanshi nian fendou shiji', [The record of accomplishments of thirty years of struggle by the Victoria Overseas Chinese] in *Jianada Weiduoli Zhonghua Huiguan/Zhonghua Xuexiao chengli qishiwu/liushi zhounian tekan* [Special publication commemorating the seventy-fifth anniversary of the founding of the Victoria Chinese Consolidated Benevolent Association and the sixtieth anniversary of the founding of the Chinese School] (Victoria: Chinese Consolidated Benevolent Association, 1960), Part IV, and on Nanaimo, see 'Jishi Dong Ya xuetong', [Angry glares at East Asian students] *Chinese Times (Da Han gongbao)*, Nov. 8, 1921, 3. Since 1907, the *Chinese Times* has been published in Vancouver by the Zhigongdang, a.k.a. the Chinese Free Masons. During the era under consideration here, it was continually publishing news about the Chinese communities across Canada. It paid particular attention to racist violence, anti-Asian discrimination, and calls for exlusion. This makes it one of the most important sources on white supremacy during this era. Fortunately, an English-language index of the paper's news columns on the Chinese communities of Canada, including some translations of variable quality, are available through the Chinese Canadian Research Collection (CCRC) located at UBC Special Collections. The CCRC contains much of the background research for *From China to Canada*.
13. Such was the case with the Coal Mines Regulations Act, which supposedly kept the Chinese out of the coal mines. See Roy, *A White Man's Province*, 77–81, 134–42, and 167–72.

14. 'Chinese Pupils Will Sit Alone', *Victoria Daily Colonist*, Nov. 13, 1902, 3, and Ward, *White Canada Forever*, 63.
15. See 'Chinese Question to Again be Considered', *Victoria Daily Colonist*, Oct. 14, 1908, 7; 'Secures Quarters for Chinese Pupils', *Victoria Daily Colonist*, Oct. 15, 1908, 2; 'Chinese Problem Solved', *Victoria Daily Times*, Oct. 15, 1908, 3; and 'Education of the Chinese Arranged', *Victoria Daily Colonist*, Oct. 24, 1908, 3. On its first day of opening, only six-teen out of an expected forty students showed up at segregated facilities rented in Chinatown. 'Chinese School is Opened Today', *Victoria Daily Times*, Nov. 2, 1908, 2. At this time there were fifty-four Chinese and two Japanese enrolled in the district. See 'Chinese Question to Again Be Considered', *Victoria Daily Colonist*, Oct. 14, 1908, 7. This 'Fisguard Street School' remained in operation from 1908 through to 1915. See British Columbia, Department of Education, *Annual Report, 1908–1909*, A XX; *Annual Report, 1909–1910*, A XXI; *Annual Report, 1910–1911*, A XXV; *Annual Report, 1911–1912*, A XXIX; *Annual Report 1912–1913*, A XXXIV; *Annual Report, 1913–1914*, A XXXVI; *Annual Report, 1914–1915*, A XXXVIII. In 1915–16, this school was closed and the Chinese students moved to Rock Bay School which was closed quite quickly due to 'a lack of enrol-ment'; see *Annual Report, 1915–1916*, A 43 and A XLI. The Rock Bay School re-opened in 1919, with 44 Chinese students (43 boys, 1 girl) and by 1921 had 171 (167 boys, 4 girls) students in 3 divisions. See *Annual Report, 1919–1920*, C12; *Annual Report 1920–1921*, C12; and *Annual Report, 1921–1922*, C15. The annual reports do not make clear whether these segregated classes applied to immigrant Chinese or the native-born. In fact there are some indications that the Rock Bay School may have contained both while earlier schools had not. See, for example, 'Chinese Segregation', *Victoria Daily Colonist*, Oct. 11, 1922, 4.
16. 'The Chinese Enter a Protest', *Victoria Daily Colonist*, June 11, 1902, 3.
17. See Ward, *White Canada Forever*, 63 and *Annual Report, 1915–1916*, A 43.
18. See, for example, 'Victoria West School Plans', *Victoria Daily Times*, Sept. 24, 1907, 6 and 'Government to Defend Action', *Victoria Daily Colonist*, Sept. 24, 1907, 7.
19. See 'Says Chinese Are Menace in Schools', *Victoria Daily Colonist*, Jan. 12, 1922, 9 and 'No More Chinese Teachers Here', ibid., Aug. 30, 1922, 5. This report of disciplinary problems is in such contrast to other assessments of the Chinese that it suggests an unusual prob-lem. Chinese schoolchildren were under tremendous pressure from their own commu-nity to act properly in school. On a number of occasions the Chinese Benevolent Association in Vancouver held meetings with Chinese students attending white public schools at which no less a person than the Chinese Consul lectured them on the need to behave. See 'Zhonghua Huiguan zhixun xuesheng jishi' [Chinese Benevolent Association instructs students in important matters], *Chinese Times*, Sept. 7, 1920, 3. See also 'Lin Lingshi Bugao' [An Announcement from Consul Lim], ibid., Nov. 8, 1922, 2–3.
20. Anderson, '"East" as "West"', thoroughly documents how Vancouver's Chinatown was constructed in white opinion as the antithesis of white society.
21. City of Vancouver, *Council Minutes*, City of Vancouver Archives, Vol. 10, Apr. 8, 1914, 122, cited by Anderson, '"East" as "West"', 152.
22. 'To Exclude the Chinese', *Victoria Daily Colonist*, Feb. 14, 1901, 8. On the issue of moti-vation, see Roy, *A White Man's Province*, 24.
23. 'Chinese in Schools', *Victoria Daily Colonist*, Mar. 13, 1902, 2. See also, 'The World of Labour', ibid., Apr. 20, 1902, 9.
24. 'Says Chinese are Menace in Schools', ibid., Jan. 12, 1922, 9 and 'Orientals Health Menace in Schools, Inspector Asserts', in *Victoria Daily Times*, Jan. 12, 1922, 18.
25. Older Chinese boys in the public school were a recurring issue. These were English as a

Second Language students who were placed in primary classes. Most often, they were only one or two years older than the average white student in the class. In some instances, however, they were as much as ten years older, being sixteen- to eighteen-year-olds.

26. 'Will Have Separate School for Chinese', *Victoria Daily Colonist*, Apr. 4, 1908, 2.
27. 'Orientals in the Schools', ibid., Mar. 28, 1908, 3. See also ibid., Mar. 28, 1908, 1 and 3.
28. 'Says Danger Has Been Magnified', ibid., July 30, 1909, 7. See also Lai, 'Discrimination', 54.
29. Hilda Glynn-Ward, *The Writing on the Wall*, with an introduction by Patricia E. Roy (Toronto: University of Toronto Press, 1974), 85. This novel has been called the worst piece of literature in Canadian history. See Terrance Craig, *Racial Attitudes in English Canadian Fiction* (Waterloo, Ontario: Wilfrid Laurier University Press, 1987).
30. Glynn-Ward, *The Writing on the Wall*, 84–5. Emphasis in the original.
31. 'Chinese in The Schools', *Victoria Daily Colonist*, Mar. 13, 1902. 2.
32. 'Chinese in the Schools', 'ibid., Nov. 12, 1902, 6. The teachers in the district also felt the Chinese caused no problems. See also Eaton's comments at the Nov. 12, 1902 meeting of the school board to the effect that the case for segregation had not been proven. See 'Chinese Pupils Will Sit Alone', *Victoria Daily Colonist*, Nov. 13, 1902, 3. Similar opinions were expressed by officials of the Vancouver School District in 1907 in response to calls for segregation. The *Vancouver Daily Province* reported 'the opinion of the school authorities' that 'the Oriental children are model pupils and exceedingly apt. It is stated that they are well dressed and cleanly, and give practically no trouble to the teaching staff.' See 'Orientals in City Schools Do Not Exceed 150', *Vancouver Daily Province*, Sept. 13, 1907, 1.
33. 'Chinese Children in Public Schools', *Victoria Daily Times*, Feb. 2, 1914, 12.
34. This was apparent in the platforms of the Labour candidates in the 1902 local elections in Victoria. See 'With the Labor Candidates', *Victoria Daily Colonist*, Dec. 21, 1902, 3.
35. Gillian Creese, 'Exclusion or Solidarity? Vancouver Workers Confront the "Oriental Problem"', *BC Studies*, 80 (Winter 1988–89): 24–51.
36. 'Chinese and City Schools', *Victoria Daily Times*, Aug. 31, 1907, 1.
37. 'Again Urges Claims of Chinese Scholars', *Victoria Daily Colonist*, Aug. 13, 1908, 2, and 'Chinese Question Is Knotty Proposition', ibid., Sept. 11, 1908, 2.
38. 'Takes Action in Chinese Question', ibid., Nov. 15, 1907, 7. The same issue was also raised in Vancouver during this era largely under the inspiration of the Asiatic Exclusion League. Ironically, the anti-Chinese and anti-Japanese riot of Sept. 7, 1907 may have moderated demands for segregation. It is also apparent most Asian students were concentrated in schools bordering Chinatown and the Japanese quarter. See 'Orientals in City Schools Do Not Exceed 150', *Vancouver Daily Province*, Sept. 13, 1907, 1. However, older Chinese students in the junior grades were segregated in a special class at Central School. See Ashworth, *The Forces Which Shaped Them*, 72 and 'Oriental Pupils in the Schools', *Vancouver Daily Province*, Feb. 12, 1908, 4.
39. Margaret A. Ormsby, *British Columbia: A History* (Vancouver: MacMillan of Canada, 1958), 303.
40. For example, when segregation was first proposed in Victoria, one trustee reportedly commented that 'if our Anglo-Saxon civilization could not withstand the effects of educating a hundred or so of Chinese, it was time that the school board should be abolished.' See 'To Exclude the Chinese', *Victoria Daily Colonist*, Feb. 10, 1901, 8.
41. 'Chinese Children in Public Schools', *Victoria Daily Times*, Feb. 2, 1914, 12.
42. For example, in the late 1910s and early 1920s, white merchants led a campaign to keep Vancouver's Chinese community from expanding into the Grandview-Woodlands area of East Vancouver. See Anderson, '"East" as "West"', 206–9.
43. 'Segregation in Schools', *Victoria Daily Colonist*, Oct. 14, 1922, 4.

44. See 'Aim Resolutions Against Orientals', *Victoria Daily Colonist*, Nov. 29, 1921, 3; Wickberg, *From China to Canada*, 137.

45. The role of immigration regulations in maintaining a split labour market is explained by Li, *Chinese in Canada*, 33–52. An important discussion of the differential effect of immigration laws and the nature of work for Chinese women and men is provided by Tamara Adilman, 'A Preliminary Sketch of Chinese Women and Work in British Columbia 1858–1950', in *Not Just Pin Money: Selected Essays on the History of Women's Work in British Columbia*, ed. Barbara K. Latham and Roberta J. Pazdro (Victoria: Camosun College, 1984), 52–78.

46. Intermarriage with white women would have been virtually impossible for bachelor Chinese males. Often there were legal hurdles. See, for example, 'Sheng Zhengfu quid huang bai tonghun' [Provincial Government outlaws yellow white intermarriage], *Chinese Times*, Apr. 10, 1917, 2–3.

47. Lee, *Jianada Huaqiao shi*, 176–8.

48. See Chan, *Gold Mountain*, 89.

49. Ibid., 86–89.

50. 'Weibu Zhonghua Huiguan shang xuewubu shu' [Victoria Chinese Consolidated Benevolent Association sends letter to school board], *Chinese Times*, Feb. 22, 1922, 3. See also Lai, 'Discrimination', 55. One of the strengths of Lai's study is that he had access to the CCBA archives.

51. 'Oppose Plan of Segregation', *Victoria Daily Colonist*, Sept. 9, 1922, 1. The fact that the CCBA joined with the Chinese Chamber of Commerce and the Chinese Canadian Club in making this protest suggests that merchants and second-generation Chinese were particularly concerned about school segregation. See also, 'Showdown in School Crisis', *Victoria Daily Colonist*, Oct. 8, 1922, 3.

52. Lai, 'Discrimination', 57. Formation of such *ad hoc* organizations was quite common during this era. For example, in 1923 many such groups were formed across Canada to protest the federal government's proposed Chinese Immigration Act. See Chinese Canadian Research Collection, Box 4, folder for 1923.

53. See 'Board Does Not Yield to Plea', *Victoria Daily Colonist*, Aug. 30, 1922, 5.

54. Strike supporters firmly denounced the permit system as 'one of favoritism, permits being granted to the wealthier ones with the intention of preventing cohesion amongst the Chinese'. See 'Chinese Segregation', *Victoria Daily Colonist*, Oct. 15, 1922, 4. Apparently one permit had been granted to the Inspector's insurance agent.

55. 'Chinese Picketing Schools; Five Boys Start Work To-Day', *Victoria Daily Times*, Oct. 9, 1922, 1.

56. Ibid., Oct. 9, 1922.

57. Letter from P. Lee, 'Chinese Segregation', *Victoria Daily Colonist*, Oct. 15, 1922, 4.

58. 'Chinese Segregation', *Victoria Daily Times*, Oct. 11, 1922, 4.

59. Lack of English had often been used to justify differential treatment. This was not only evident in school segregation but in other areas. For example, it was claimed that since the Chinese did not speak English, they were a safety threat in the mines. During World War I, by studying English the miners of Cumberland circumvented an attempt by the provincial government to get the Chinese out of the mines. See, for example, 'Yaoyinmi kuanggong zhizhao zhi shencha' [Examination of Cumberland miner's certificates], *The Chinese Times*, Sept. 5, 1916, 3.

60. See 'School Problem', 'Chinese in Schools', and 'Chinese in Schools', three letters to the editor in the *Victoria Daily Colonist*, Sept. 10, 1922, 4. See also 'Segregation', *Victoria Daily Times*, Sept. 14, 1922, 4.

61. 'Chinese Segregation', *Victoria Daily Colonist*, Nov. 26, 1922, 14. For other interventions, see the letters, 'Chinese Segregation', *Victoria Daily Colonist*, Oct. 15, 1922, 4 and 'Chinese Segregation', *Victoria Daily Times*, Nov. 2, 1922, 4.
62. 'Huaren kangzheng fenxiao zhi judong' [Activities of Chinese resisting school segregation], *Chinese Times*, Oct. 7, 1922, 3.
63. 'Weiduoli bu Zhonghua Yixue zhaosheng jian zhang' [Brief rules of the call for students of the Victoria Chinese Free School], reproduced by Lai, 'Discrimination', 61.
64. Ibid.
65. 'Chinese Segregation', *Victoria Daily Colonist*, Oct. 13, 1922, 4.
66. See Lee, *Jianada Huaqiao shi*, 312–47, for a discussion of Chinese-language schooling amongst the Chinese communities of Canada.
67. 'Zhonghua Yixue zhaosheng' [Call for students of the Chinese Public School].
68. This, for example, accounts for the stormy reception of Sun Yat-sen in 1910 when he spoke in Vancouver's Chinatown. He spoke a different dialect from the Sye-Yip people who were the majority there. See Chang Yung Ho's account of this meeting in Yee, *Saltwater City*, 40–1, 44–5.
69. Chuen-Yan David Lai, 'Home County and Clan Origins of Overseas Chinese in Canada in the Early 1880s', *BC Studies* 27 (Autumn 1975): 3–29. On the use of the term 'invent' here, see Roy Wagner, *The Invention of Culture* (Chicago: University of Chicago Press, 1981).
70. See Chinese Canadian Research Collection, Box 4.
71. See 'Zhonghua Huiguan suo jie zhongyao wenjian' [Chinese Benevolent Association office receives important letter], *Chinese Times*, Oct. 3, 1922, 3. Such activities led to fears amongst the whites of Victoria that a boycott of Canadian goods would be effected in China; see, for example, 'Chinese Here May Retaliate', *Victoria Daily Colonist*, Oct. 16, 1922, 1.
72. For example, 'Bokuan ju Weibu Kangzheng Fenxiao Tuan' [Funds assist Victoria Resist School Segregation Association], *Chinese Times*, Dec. 20, 1922, 2.
73. Previously, Chinese schools in Canada were really little more than spaces in the backs of shops where merchants taught basic literacy. Lee, *Jianada Huaqiao shi*, 323.
74. 'A Chinese School', *Victoria Daily Colonist*, Jan. 18, 1899, 6.
75. Lim Bang, 'Weibu Zhonghua Huiguan zhi yuange ji qiaoxiao chuangli zhi yuanqi' [The origins of the Victoria Chinese Consolidated Benevolent Association and the reasons for the creation of overseas schools], *Zhonghua Huiguan/Huaqiao Xuexiao jinian qikan*, Part IV, 1–5; Guan Qiyi, 'Jianada Huaqiao jiaoyu shilue' [A short History of Overseas Chinese Education in Canada], ibid., Part IV, 17–18. See also 'Benxiao xiaoshi' [A history of our school], ibid., Part III, 54–8.
76. Ibid., Part V, 26.
77. 'Weibu Huaqiao Gongxue baogao ce' [Text of the report of the Victoria Chinese Public School], *Chinese Times*, July 13, 1915, 1.
78. Even though it was based in Vancouver, the *Chinese Times* regularly reported on the activities of the school, its graduation ceremonies, and social events. See, for example, 'Weibu Huaqiao Gongxiao dierci qingyou jicheng' [Victoria Chinese Public School holds second annual picnic], *Chinese Times*, July 20, 1920, 3.
79. The *Chinese Times* reported that 'every girl and boy who graduates from the first class can leave behind their local dialects and are fluent in Cantonese when reading and speaking.' 'Weibu qikao zhuzhong Shenghua Guoyu ying sheng zhi tese' [Special characteristics of the pronunciation of Cantonese and Mandarin at the Victoria end of term examinations], *Chinese Times*, July 17, 1915, 3. The writer complained that Victoria's Cantonese was not standard as it 'suffered from the influence of the students'.

80. For example, Cai Yuanpei, the principal of Beijing University, led such a delegation which inspected schools in Victoria and Vancouver in 1918.
81. See, for example, "'All For China'", *Victoria Daily Colonist*, Aug. 13, 1909, 4.
82. *Annual Report, 1914–15*, A XXXVIII and *Annual Report, 1915–1916*, A XLI.
83. See Yee, *Saltwater City*, 44–6.
84. During this era the male/female ratio amongst Chinese in Victoria was six to one; in other centres in BC it was as high as twenty to one. See *Census of Canada*, 1921., Vol. 1, 542.
85. Cited by Chan, *Gold Mountain*, 129.
86. 'Youthful Viciousness', *Victoria Daily Colonist*, Nov. 16, 1899, 5 and 'Ill Mannered Boys', *Vancouver Daily Province*, Jan. 15, 1901, 4.
87. 'The Injured Chinaman', *Victoria Daily Colonist*, Apr. 6, 1904, 4.
88. *Victoria Daily Times*, Nov. 4, 1908, 5. This report was untitled.
89. 'Huanu beiwu' [Chinese girl assaulted], *Chinese Times*, Feb. 26, 1915, 3.
90. 'Huatong cishang xitong' [Chinese youth stabs western youth], *Chinese Times*, Feb. 4, 1922, 3.
91. Sing Lim, *West Coast Chinese Boy* (Montreal: Tundra Books, 1979), 23.

Suggestions for Further Reading

Axelrod, Paul, *The Promise of Schooling: Education in Canada 1800–1924*. Toronto: University of Toronto Press, 1997.

Barman, Jean, Neil Sutherland, and J. Donald Wilson, eds, *Children, Teachers and Schools in the History of British Columbia*. Calgary: Detselig Enterprises, 1995.

Conrad, Margaret, 'An Abiding Conviction of the Paramount Importance of Christian Education: Theodore Harding Rand as Educator, 1860–1900,' in Robert S. Wilson, *An Abiding Conviction—Maritime Baptists and their World*. Saint John: Acadia Divinity College, 1988: 155–95.

Curtis, Bruce, 'Schoolbooks and the Myth of Curricular Republicanism: the State and the Curriculum in Canada West, 1820–1850,' *Histoire sociale/Social History* 16, 32 (November 1983): 305–29.

Houston, Susan and Alison Prentice, *Schooling and Scholars in Nineteenth Century Ontario*. Toronto: University of Toronto Press, 1988.

Prentice, Alison, *The School Promoters: Education and Social Class in Mid-Nineteenth Century Upper Canada*. Toronto: Oxford University Press, 1999.

PART 5

Defining 'Bad Homes' and Delinquent Children, 1890–1955

Middle-class values informed initiatives to protect abused children and to prevent young people from activities deemed immoral. The following articles discuss the social and economic politics that defined 'bad families' and 'delinquent children'. The child-saving movement believed that children's health, morality, and respectability depended on the quality of their homes. How closely a home conformed to middle-class values determined its quality. Prescriptively, good homes were led by a sober, Christian patriarch; mother tempered father's authority and managed an orderly home with love and thrift. Emily Carr's juxtaposition of paternal authority and maternal love captures the Victorian ideal, but her memories of family life show that the ideal was not always practised in daily life.

Legal definitions of cruelty toward children and state-sanctioned intervention have changed over time. Power struggles within families and among social groups have influenced social conceptions about neglect and appropriate discipline. Infamous cases of child abuse became parables for anxieties about the nation. Peter Gossage shows how the tragedy of Aurore Houde became a metaphor for future manifestations of Quebec nationalism. Too often, caring for the abused child became less important than protecting the nuclear family and defending gender, class, and race hierarchies. In her study of the evolution of legal definitions of incest, Joan Sangster argues that young women who sought justice through the criminal justice system rarely overcame stronger social discourses that protected paternal authority and familial privacy and asserted that incest did not occur outside of poor families.

The legal regulation of childhood institutionalized Anglo-Saxon, middle-class values. Children from poor families appeared in family courts more often than children from more influential families. There were different standards for girls and boys. Dorothy Chunn examines how perceptions about the 'natural' differences between girls' and boys' sexuality and anxieties about girls' morality influenced more punitive sentences for girls. Other historians have found that many working-class families adopted dominant notions of respectability and sexual morality, and used the courts to control their daughters' behaviour. Roderick Haig-Brown argues that too many young people were being punished for actions that were merely normal youthful challenges to social mores.

Nancy Janovicek

La marâtre: Marie-Anne Houde and the Myth of the Wicked Stepmother in Quebec

Peter Gossage

There is a well known story in Quebec about an ugly incident of child abuse. The victim was Aurore Gagnon, a young girl who was battered and neglected by her father and stepmother, Télesphore Gagnon and Marie-Anne Houde. The mistreatment was so severe that the child died, at the age of ten years, on 12 February 1920. Both father and stepmother were soon brought to public account for their roles in the mortal abuse. Separate trials in Quebec City's Court of King's Bench in April of the same year made headlines all over the province. Both defendants were convicted and sentenced. Gagnon, guilty of manslaughter, was to be imprisoned for life. Houde, convicted of murder, was condemned to hang.

In the ensuing seventy-five years, this tragic tale became a classic of French-language popular culture in Quebec. The drama was played out time and time again, first in the theatre of the courtroom and in the pages of the popular press, then over the years in a series of fictionalized accounts, including plays, novels, a successful film produced in the early 1950s, and, most recently, a popular television dramatization.[1] Though the details vary from one interpretation to the next, two motifs always stand out: the victimization of the innocent child, Aurore, and the shocking cruelty of her stepmother, Marie-Anne Houde.

Academic interest in the Gagnon tale has focused largely on the victim in the story, the child Aurore, known universally as 'l'enfant martyre', or the martyred child. Theatre historian Alonzo Leblanc, for example, sees in Aurore a political metaphor: 'a symbol of the alienation of the Quebec collectivity, deprived early on of her own mother (France), and mistreated by her stepmother (England), under the complicit eye of her father, holder of authority, abetted by the impotence of the political and religious powers'.[2] Film historian Heinz Weinmann, in a similar vein, argues that audiences of the 1952 film *La petite Aurore l'enfant martyre* identified massively with the child because her sad life constituted an 'imaginary projection of the history lived and suffered by French Canadians'. She was a 'helpless child, abandoned by her parents, as at one time Canada had been by France, then by

England'.[3] Such political readings, in treating *Aurore* as a symbol of French Canada's historic 'victimization', sidestep most of the story's rich social and cultural content.[4] Much more helpful is Danielle Tremblay's suggestion that the stage show inspired by these events played a role in 'the functioning of popular morality' in Quebec, that it united 'the spontaneity of the mass phenomenon with a folklore renewed through its contact with the urban world', and that it found 'its source of inspiration (and the source of its audience) in a recreation of collective myths'.[5]

In studies of the cultural significance of the Gagnon story, the sympathy Quebec audiences felt towards the innocent 'martyr', Aurore, has been well established. Less attention has been paid to the villain in the piece, Marie-Anne Houde. Just as strong as the pity aroused in audiences by the plight of the youthful, innocent Aurore was the revulsion and outrage engendered by Houde. As I will argue here, the story of the Fortierville tragedy achieved its enormous popularity at least in part because it drew on and reinforced some deep-seated misgivings about that most mistrusted of domestic archetypes, the 'wicked stepmother'.

Negative views about stepmothers are centuries old. In former times they found expression in proverbs, fairy tales, and other forms of popular culture.[6] If nothing else, the tale that grew up around Marie-Anne Houde certainly illustrates the persistence of anti-stepmother feeling in twentieth-century Quebec. More than this, I will argue, the popular construction of Marie-Anne Houde as *la marâtre* underscored dominant notions of motherhood and family life. By appearing to subvert a widely held ideological construct, maternal love, the Gagnon story in all its tellings helped to define and reify it.

[. . .]

Crime and Punishment

Aurore Gagnon died in Saint-Philomène-de-Fortierville, in the county of Lotbinière, Quebec, in the farm house where she had lived with her father, her stepmother, and four other children: her older sister, Marie-Jeanne, her younger brother, Georges, her stepbrother, Gérard, and her infant half-sister, Pauline. Aurore's death aroused strong suspicions in the small community. Neighbours, such as Exilda Lemay, had recently expressed concern for the girl; she had not been seen outside the house for some time. When Lemay decided to visit the Gagnon home just two days before the child's death, she found Aurore in a pitiful state, lying 'in a corner of the attic on a pallet consisting of a small grey blanket and a pillow. Beside her on a small table was a plate containing two potatoes and a knife. Seeing me approach, [Aurore] leaned up on her elbow, but could barely support herself. She told me that her knees hurt a great deal, but that as usual she had complained to no one about it. I hadn't asked her about it either.'[7] On 12 February, the day of the child's death, Marie-Anne Houde telephoned Dr Andronic Lafond of the nearby village of Parisville, who arrived at the house that afternoon. By that point, however, the child was already in a coma and beyond medical help. According to Lafond's subsequent account, her body was a mass of bruises, sores, infection, and scar tissue; her eyes were blackened and there was a particularly nasty contusion on her forehead.[8]

By the next day, authorities in Quebec City had been alerted to the suspicious death. On 13 February three officials arrived in Fortierville from the provincial capital, some 100 kilometres away. Provincial police constable Lauréat Couture went to the Gagnon house to take possession of the child's body, which he then transported to the sacristy of the nearby Catholic church. Dr Albert Marois, who had accompanied him from Quebec, used that sacred space as the operating theatre for an autopsy. In his chilling report, Marois identified dozens of grotesque injuries to the child's legs, face, feet, and virtually every other part of her body, speculating that some of them could have been caused by blows with a whip or a narrow piece of wood.[9]

The third official to arrive that day was Dr George William Jolicoeur, the provincial coroner whose inquest would determine whether charges should be laid in the matter.[10] Exilda Lemay and Albert Marois were two of the seven witnesses to appear before the coroner and six locally appointed jurors. Andronic Lafond, the attending doctor, also testified. Two local farmers reported having seen the child near death the day before, but neither knew anything about the cause of her injuries. The remaining two witnesses knew the case more intimately, though they revealed relatively little to the inquest. Marie-Jeanne Gagnon denied knowing anything about any beatings; she claimed that the marks on her sister's body had begun to appear some three weeks earlier and had worsened in the preceding five days.[11] The children's father, Télesphore Gagnon, a thirty-seven-year-old farmer, agreed that the marks on Aurore's arms, legs, and body had materialized some three weeks previously, but stated that he had not examined these lesions, which he referred to as 'bobos', very closely. 'It was my wife who took care of the child; I wasn't involved,' he told the coroner.[12] Questioned about whether the child had ever been mistreated, Gagnon responded that 'the child was difficult to raise and I punished her a number of times with a whip, and on other occasions with a wooden stick. I punished her in this way when I discovered she had misbehaved or when my wife reported her misdeeds to me.'[13]

All this evidence convinced the coroner and jury that the death of Aurore Gagnon was a matter for the criminal courts. Their inquiry pointed in the direction of both Télesphore Gagnon and his wife, Marie-Anne Houde. Constable Couture arrested the couple the next day as they made their way home from Aurore's funeral. The initial charge against both parties was manslaughter, but after preliminary hearings were held in Quebec City's Court of Quarter Sessions of the Peace, Justice P.A. Choquette concluded that there was sufficient evidence in the matter to charge both Gagnon and Houde with murder.

Télesphore Gagnon and Marie-Anne Houde were tried separately before the Court of King's Bench in Quebec City in the April term of 1920. Houde's trial got under way first, on Tuesday, 13 April. She was charged with having 'killed and assassinated Aurore Gagnon, a minor aged sixteen years [sic], by inflicting, during the twelve months preceding the death of the said Aurore Gagnon, blows, injuries, and other ill treatments which she, the said Marie-Anne Houde, knew to be of such a nature as to cause death and from which the said Aurore Gagnon died the twelfth day of February in the year of our Lord 1920.'[14] During the trial, Houde's lawyer, J.N. Francoeur, first attempted to argue that the child had died of natural causes and that the lesions and infections that covered her body were the result of some disease, such as tuberculosis or meningitis, rather than physical abuse. The Marois autopsy seemed conclusive on this point, but Francoeur tried to call it into question by arguing that the doctor had not examined the child's spinal cord in sufficient detail and therefore had failed to rule out certain diseases.[15]

By the end of the week, however, it had become clear from the sworn testimony of witnesses, including Houde's own eleven-year-old son, Gérard, that she had in fact participated in a series of tortures that had led to Aurore's death. Gérard and Marie-Jeanne Gagnon were the key witnesses for the prosecution. They testified that Houde had not only beaten the child with such instruments as whips and axe handles, but had restrained her with ropes and deliberately burned her with a poker, heated red-hot on a wood stove.[16] In the face of this damning testimony, Francoeur's original defence broke down completely. He attempted to recover by changing Houde's plea from 'not guilty' to 'not guilty by reason of insanity'. But this strategy succeeded only in prolonging the trial into the following week, the time needed to assemble a panel of medical experts and to hear their divergent opinions on Houde's mental state. Much of this discussion turned on Houde's 'delicate condition'—she had been four months pregnant at the time of Aurore's death—and the impact it might have had on her mental equilibrium. Defence arguments relied in part on the testimony of two doctors and in part on that of Télesphore Gagnon, who observed that when his wife was pregnant she became agitated very easily, so that 'you had to be very sure not to cross her'.[17]

The trial judge, Louis Pelletier, was not at all swayed, either by the men who testified to Houde's instability while pregnant or by the insanity defence in general. He believed the defendant had acted wilfully in accordance with a consciously formed intent to bring about the child's death: the requirement for a murder conviction. On Wednesday, 21 April, in his charge to the jury, he told them as much, suggesting that 'the defence's case on the question of insanity is so weak—if it exists at all— as to confirm the idea that the insanity plea was concocted at the last minute as a last ditch effort, a desperation measure'.[18] That same day, these twelve men found Houde guilty of murder, a crime which, as they well knew, called for the death penalty. Newspapers reported that Pelletier, who clearly agreed with this verdict, nonetheless had difficulty containing his emotion as he sentenced Houde to hang in October of that year.[19] The delay is significant. Marie-Anne Houde's pregnancy during her murder trial, which Pelletier had instructed the jury to ignore in assessing her guilt or innocence, moved him to postpone the execution to allow Houde time to give birth to the child she was carrying.[20] The 'child' turned out to be twins, a boy and a girl, born on 8 July 1920 in the Quebec City Jail.[21]

[. . .]

Houde lived most of the rest of her life in the Kingston Penitentiary. By all accounts a model prisoner, she was an indefatigable letter writer who relentlessly petitioned federal authorities for early release. Interestingly, she consistently cited her maternal feelings and duties as grounds for further clemency. In a letter to the minister of justice written in October 1923, for example, she wrote: 'I am not responsible for what I was accused of three and a half years ago . . . I suffer for all of my children . . . [T]his separation is so great for me that it affects my heart and I know you will understand what a mother can suffer from such a cruel separation and especially from hearing these poor children ask when they will see their mother again.[22] When she ultimately was released in July 1935, it was only after the cancer that had cost her a breast two years earlier had spread to her lung and reduced her life expectancy to less than a year. She died in Montreal in May 1936, at the age of forty-five.[23]

The trial of Marie-Anne Houde had created a sensation in the province of Quebec, and particularly within its francophone majority. In its wake, her husband's trial was anticlimactic, though his acts had been dramatic enough. The court began hearing testimony in the *King v. Télesphore Gagnon* on Friday, 23 April 1920. In the spirit of Quebec civil law, which placed a married woman under the legal tutelage of her husband,[24] the dual nature of Gagnon's offence was emphasized. He was charged not only with inflicting some of the mistreatments that had led to the child's death but 'with criminally permitting his wife, Marie-Anne Houde, to inflict' such treatment.[25] Witnesses testified that the man had brutally beaten Aurore with horsewhips, axe handles, and other weapons. Some reported conversations in which Gagnon had mentioned his preference for the attic as the site of these abuses; apparently, he had more room there to swing his weapons.[26] It was also reported during the trial that the man had beaten his daughter on the flimsiest of pretences, and particularly on the basis of apocryphal stories his wife had told him about the child's misbehaviour.[27]

The trial lasted four days, at the end of which Gagnon was found guilty of manslaughter, rather than murder. Far from holding him responsible for his wife's malevolence, jurors apparently believed defence arguments according to which Gagnon had been the 'unconscious victim' of his wife's cruel designs. As one well-placed observer put it, the defence case had rested on the notion that 'the abominable tortures that the father himself inflicted on his child were the result of the odious lies his wife told him'.[28] Judge Désy delayed sentencing until 5 June, at which time he gave Gagnon the maximum penalty: life imprisonment. But after serving only five years in prison he was released, apparently for good behaviour, though some accounts suggest there were also medical reasons.[29] Télesphore Gagnon then returned to Fortierville and managed to reintegrate into the community, marrying for a third time, working steadily as a carpenter, and dying there in 1961 at the age of seventy-eight.

[. . .]

Popular Classic

This courtroom drama certainly spawned sensationalist newspaper accounts, particularly in mass-circulation French-language newspapers such as *La Presse*. But the cultural reverberations of the tale did not end there. In early 1921, not even a year after the trial, an obscure Montreal theatre troupe led by Léon Petitjean and Henri Rollin used it as the inspiration for a play, *Aurore l'enfant martyre*.[30] In its original form, this was a two-act melodrama dealing with events leading up to the child's death. Some time later, apparently in 1927, the piece was expanded to five acts; it now included an interpretation of the courtroom drama.[31]

Aurore l'enfant martyre became an enduring classic of French-language popular theatre.[32] Thirty years after it was first staged, members of the Petitjean-Rollin troupe claimed it had been performed between five and six thousand times.[33] It played to packed houses in major centres such as Montreal and Quebec City; but it also toured to rural regions of the province, and to the French-speaking areas of Ontario and New England. Despite the mass appeal it clearly enjoyed, high-minded theatre critics were less enthusiastic about *Aurore l'enfant martyre* than the general public. Some even suggested that the play should be banned, as it was in Lowell, Massachusetts, in 1930.[34] In 1921, reacting to news of the first performances of the piece (which he obviously had not yet seen), one Montreal theatre critic wrote: 'We have learned that a group of amateurs has performed this week, somewhere in Montreal, a play built around the sorry Gagnon affair of Quebec City. And that the receipts must have been considerable since the theatre has been full every night. . . . It will be admitted that there is nothing in these kinds of spectacles likely to honour our race, and that they should on the contrary be prohibited as being more immoral than many others that have been banned in the past.'[35] A decade later, playwright Henri Letondal, commenting in *La Patrie*, denounced the base, commercial motives of the Petitjean-Rollin troupe. 'No artistic sentiment . . . presided at the composition of this play. It was designed only to strike at the popular imagination and curiosity. As to the interpretation, I'll let you guess what it must have been like, with a script worthy of the worst pulp novel [*roman-feuilleton*]. Would it

Part of the front page of *La Presse's* 20 April 1920 edition, with a rare photograph showing the veiled figure of Marie-Anne Houde. The caption reads, 'The Gagnon woman (Marie-Anne Houde) carefully veiled as always, photographed yesterday afternoon as she hurriedly entered the Quebec City courthouse.'

Thérèse Mackinnon (the stepmother) and Yvonne Laflamme (Aurore) in a scene from the Jean-Yves Bigras film *La petite Aurore l'enfant martyre.* Mackinnon became so closely associated with the character of Aurore's stepmother that she difficulty finding other acting work.

please you to know that the martyred child has delivered to her authors a small fortune?'[36] Although critics both denounced and ridiculed it, the play clearly had a great deal of success appealing to the popular imagination and curiosity.

[. . .]

In the early 1950s the story gained new popularity with the publication of at least two new novels, and particularly the release of the Jean-Yves Bigras film, *La petite Aurore l'enfant martyre.*[37] This motion picture was produced in Montreal in the summer of 1951. It was financed by J.A. DeSève, who had recently acquired the rights to the play and who had commissioned Emile Asselin, a member of the Petitjean-Rollin troupe, to write a novel and a screenplay based on the Fortierville events. DeSève was a prominent theatre impresario who owned several playhouses and who had recently branched out into film production. His reputation as the 'king of melodrama' was well known, as was his philosophy of show business: 'Make them cry.'[38]

The Fortierville tragedy seems to have met this criterion. Originally scheduled for release in November 1951, the film was not presented in Quebec theatres before April 1952, when it premiered at the Théâtre St-Denis in Montreal.[39] Like the play upon which it was based, *La petite Aurore* was enormously popular with the public, but a target for the derision of many critics. The comments of Roland Côté in *Le Canada* are particularly interesting because they convey a sense of the way crowds reacted to this highly melodramatic film.

Two shows for the price of one, that's what you can see at the Théâtre St-Denis this week. Indeed, those who are unable to swallow *La petite Aurore l'enfant martyre* will be amused to watch the spectators react to the sufferings endured by Yvonne Laflamme, who plays the role of the little Aurore. For me, this side-show was much more interesting than the one presented on the screen. Because most of the time, the audience performs as well as the actors. They cry, they scream, they call the step-mother's husband an imbecile because he's too stupid to discover the harm being done to Aurore. They applaud when Jeannette Bertrand takes it upon herself to go and inform the parish priest, and when the stepmother is condemned to be hanged by the neck until dead.[40]

Crowds must have continued reacting with such emotion, as the commercial success enjoyed by the film version of the Gagnon story was unprecedented in the history of Quebec cinema to that point. *La petite Aurore* was certainly one of the most popular movies, if not *the* most popular movie, produced in the province in the 1950s. Many people watched it, whether in the ornate cinemas of Montreal or Quebec City shortly after its release, or a year or two later in the Saturday afternoon movie sessions held in rural parish halls all over the province, or over the course of the following ten or twenty years on television late shows, or more recently, on rented video cassettes.

During the 1960s and 1970s interest in the story seems to have waned; there was certainly a hiatus in the production of new material based on the events in Fortierville. But since the early 1980s there has just as certainly been a revival. In 1982 the script of the Petitjean-Rollin play was published for the first time, making the original text available to scholars and would-be performers.[41] There have been other dramatizations of the events, including a 1986 radio play dealing with Marie-Anne Houde's imprisonment and her alleged insanity. In 1990 André Mathieu published his attempt to reconstruct the events surrounding Aurore Gagnon's death realistically in a novel entitled *Aurore: la vraie histoire*. And in the fall of 1994 a one-hour drama-tization of the Marie-Anne Houde trial aired on the Quebec network TVA as part of a popular television series on famous criminal cases in Quebec history.[42]

Without question, the story of Aurore Gagnon, Marie-Anne Houde, and Télesphore Gagnon has, in the three-quarters of a century since the events occurred, become embedded in the popular imagination of francophone Quebec. Even the word 'Aurore' has acquired a clear connotation in the Quebec vernacular. To say '*fais pas ton Aurore*' to a child is to chide him or her for acting in such a way as to attract pity, as if a victim of great suffering.

Between History and Fiction

Why the great and persistent interest? Why did the story of Aurore Gagnon and Marie-Anne Houde, in one form or another, remain so prominent in the collective memory of French-speaking Quebec? The short answer is that someone recognized a good, melodramatic story when they saw it. In other words, someone understood the mass appeal of this frightful tale and wagered, correctly, that a good deal of money could be made by telling and retelling it. This is true whether we are discussing the publishers of *La Presse*, the rag-tag theatre troupe that first dramatized the events in the 1920s, the Quebec motion-picture mogul DeSève in the 1950s, or the TVA programming executives in the 1990s. This is fine, as far as it goes. But where did the mass appeal come from? Why was the story so unforgettable?

To answer this question, one might first situate the tale within the genre of 'crime stories'. [. . .] [S]tories of violent crimes committed by women seem to be particularly fascinating. Lizzie Borden's hatchet work, Karla Homolka's complicity in the Bernardo killings, Lorena Bobbitt's punitive surgery, Susan Smith's child drownings: all drew a great deal of attention partly because they involved violent acts and partly because these women stepped so far outside socially prescribed female gender roles.

One might further argue that the normative discourse upholding a definition of women as nurturers, homemakers, life givers, and submissive sexual partners was particularly rigid in Quebec in the period prior to 1960. Marital fertility rates fell much more slowly in the province than in most other parts of North America. Quebec women could not vote in provincial elections until 1940. And the influential Catholic Church was one of the many defenders of a definition of the family in which wives were subordinate to their husbands and in which women's child-bearing and child-rearing roles were paramount.[43] In abusing her husband's daughter, Marie-Anne Houde not only committed a violent crime but also challenged hegemonic notions of a woman's 'natural' role as nurturer and care-giver, particularly where children are concerned. This is certainly part of the reason why the abuse she inflicted on the young Aurore has been permanently etched into the collective memory of Quebeckers, while the similarly brutal treatment the child received at the hands of her father has been all but forgotten.

Marie-Anne Houde's deviation from prescribed female roles, and particularly maternal roles, also resonated with a particularly tenacious 'collective myth', to use Danielle Tremblay's phrase: the myth of the wicked stepmother. By brutalizing her husband's child, the historical Marie-Anne Houde played directly into this ancient cultural stereotype. The popular-culture versions of the Fortierville story drew on her violence to recreate a myth that was centuries old. Here was a new telling of the stepmother tale that would continue to do what others had done for generations: to build an impenetrable wall around acceptable patterns of maternal behaviour.[44]

To understand this process, it is useful to examine the popular literature inspired by this case against the backdrop of the events reported in the court records and newspaper accounts of the 1920s. How did those who told the Gagnon story edit or embellish it? What elements were left out, and what wrinkles were added by the various authors who embraced these events as their theme? And how, if at all, did these revised narratives reflect and reinforce societal attitudes about stepmothers?

In the first place, the structure of the household described in the popular versions of the Gagnon story never varies. There is always a father, a daughter, and a stepmother, living on a farm somewhere in the Quebec countryside. Readers and viewers can scarcely avoid the inference that the stepfamily itself, combined with the hardships of rural life, created conditions in which child abuse was possible. Beyond these facts, however, there is a good deal of variation. The historical Gagnons lived with three children from Télesphore's previous marriage, one from Marie-Anne's, plus their infant child, born ten months or so before Aurore's death. In most of the literary versions, the situation is less crowded; children who are not central to the story of the abuse are simply left out. In Benoît Tessier's 1952 novel, for example, Aurore is the only child in the household. And in the Asselin-Bigras film, the girl finds an ally in Maurice, her stepbrother, but there are no other children on the premises.[45]

In every telling of the tale, the two female figures stand out: the wretched, sadistic stepmother and the innocent, martyred child. The father is almost always a background figure, at worst an object of derision for his inability to control his wife, at best the innocent victim of a conniving woman. In most of the popularized versions, Marie-Anne Houde not only subverts the prescribed maternal role by abusing the child; she also dominates her husband to such an extent that he, too, more or less unwittingly, participates in the abuse. What a travesty of the dominant ideology of family relations in the period, in which fathers wielded authority and commanded respect, and in which mothers selflessly tended to house and children!

The character of Aurore, her youth, her innocence, and her pitiful victimization: these things too are consistent. Generally, the young girl identifies very strongly with and mourns deeply for her late mother. The historical child would have been eight years old when her mother died, so this seems realistic. The fact that the child's mother, Marie-Anne Caron, had been an inmate at the Saint-Jean-de-Dieu asylum for some time before her death is always overlooked. Such a disclosure would certainly have detracted from Aurore's, and the public's, idealization of Caron as the 'good' mother (godmother?).[46] The Petitjean-Rollin play is as melodramatic on this point as it is on other aspects of the story. As the child dies, she makes the following speech, which must have brought tears to the eyes of many an audience member: 'Soon before God. The heavens are opening. The Angels are smiling. Oh! Such beauty! *Maman*, my little *maman*, come and get me! I want, I want a better fate. (She dies.)'[47] This idealization of the lost mother sometimes takes the form of a refusal to address the stepmother as *maman*. This is the source of much of the woman's fury in the Asselin-Bigras film, in which the young Aurore stubbornly addresses her stepmother as *madame*, as she does in the Tessier novel. Interestingly, during the trial of Marie-Anne Houde, the young Marie-Jeanne Gagnon had no difficulty in referring to her stepmother as *maman*, even as she testified against her.[48]

Another consistent element is that the child is always called 'Aurore', which means dawn or first light, even though the names of the other characters vary.[49] The imagery of light and darkness is obvious here; the bright young child is ultimately extinguished by the dark figure of her stepmother. Furthermore, and more significantly, little Aurore is never identified as the 'battered' child or even as the 'murdered' child, but almost always as the 'martyred' child (*l'enfant martyre*). This expression appears first in the newspaper accounts at the time of the original events; *La Presse*, in particular, used it consistently. The usage certainly reflects the centrality of Catholicism in French-Canadian popular culture in the period. Stories of martyred saints and their stoic acceptance of unthinkable tortures would have been important reference points in the popular imagination. In the 1920s, the campaign for the canonization of seventeenth-century Jesuits who had served as missionaries to the Huron and died as Iroquois prisoners was in full swing.[50] From this perspective, Aurore emerges not just as a particularly unfortunate young girl: she is a mystical martyred figure whose suffering and death are to be understood not as a senseless tragedy but as a religious sacrifice in the battle of good against evil, and whose very innocence confers upon her a kind of beatific, even saintly quality.[51]

This powerful symbol of light and innocence is pitted against a formidable representative of darkness and evil. Indeed, the highly publicized cruelty of Marie-Anne Houde dominates every telling of the table. In most of the narratives, the stepmother is so cruel as to become dehumanized, a monstrous shrew rather than a human being. Already in the newspaper accounts of the 1920s, this process of dehumanization had begun. Thus, in its coverage of the Marie-Anne Houde trial, *La Presse* consistently referred to the defendant as *la marâtre* (the cruel stepmother, for lack of a better translation) or *la mégère* (the shrew), rather than by her name.[52] This usage carried over into the fictionalized versions. The term *marâtre* appears in virtually every account; and in the 1920s play the stepmother character remains nameless.

[. . .]

The stepmother's cruelty finds many other avenues of expression in this popular literature. In virtually every version, the young Aurore, like Cinderella, is badly overworked and underfed. In the Tessier novel, for example, on the first morning of their life together, the stepmother forces the pitiful child to perform what seems like a week's worth of chores, including carrying water, chopping wood, scrubbing the floor, washing the clothes, and preparing the mid-day meal. But would she share in this meal? Certainly not. She is forced to eat a crust of stale bread instead, a punishment for not working hard enough. She must also watch her cruel stepmother gorge herself on stew.[53] Perhaps even worse, the cunning woman has devised an elaborate form of blackmail to prevent Aurore from reporting these abuses to her kindly, if rather shortsighted father. She has stolen a five dollar bill from her husband's trousers. Should Aurore complain to her father about the mistreatment, she threatens to produce the money and to claim to have found it among the child's things.[54]

In the ostensibly realist 1990 novel by André Mathieu, the malevolence of the Marie-Anne Houde character is established early on, well before she meets Télesphore Gagnon. On the morning of her first wedding, annoyed by young birds singing outside her bedroom window, she interrupts her bridal preparations to destroy a nest full of chicks. Much later, shortly after she has married Télesphore, she poisons the little dog that Aurore has brought into the household, telling the girl the dog has died of Spanish flu (this was 1918, after all). Clearly the capacity for cruelty to animals and cruelty to children coalesce in the mind of this author, as he ponderously foreshadows the tragedy that is to befall the young Aurore.[55]

In his effort to tell the 'real story', however, Mathieu probably provides more graphic descriptions of the real-life abuses inflicted on Aurore Gagnon than any other account in popular literature. He even includes a warning to readers approaching the section in which the child is branded with the red-hot poker, an incident that has been left out of many other versions. Mathieu's, moreover, is one of very few versions to suggest the extent to which the historical Télesphore Gagnon participated in the abuse of his daughter. In this book, Gagnon regularly inflicts lashings upon all his children, and his wife's offspring as well. Aurore's punishments, however, are the severest of all.[56]

In other versions, Aurore's father is portrayed as much more passive, perhaps even as a secondary victim of the woman's cruel designs. If he is to be reproached it is for his inability to control his wife's brutality, rather than for any violent acts of his own. In the Tessier novel, for instance, the father never lays a hand on his daughter; the stepmother alone is responsible for the beatings and the other physical abuse. In the end, the father even testifies against his wife in court.[57] In the Asselin-Bigras film, the father is absent much of the time, but at one point he does punish the child physically, at his wife's insistence. Marie-Anne has instructed him to punish his daughter for an innocent kiss she has shared with her stepbrother: the suggestion of anxiety over sexual impropriety is unmistakable. The father's moment of violence is short but brutal. He strikes Aurore over the head with an axe handle as punishment for the immorality imputed to her by her stepmother. The blow knocks the girl unconscious; the audience is manipulated into assuming, if momentarily, that she is dead. Yet in the context of the film, the act seems out of character—the father up to this point has seemed passive, almost kindly—and it is followed immediately by remorse. Télesphore is so shocked at what he has done that he immediately turns on his wife, slapping her and demanding that she never ask him to strike the child again, thus re-establishing, if temporarily, the domestic hierarchy.[58]

The innocence of the father is a particularly important element of the popular treatment of the subject. Broadly speaking, if Télesphore participates in the abuse at all it is because he is deceived and beguiled into doing so by his wife. Her cruelty, then, is compounded by her cunning and her ability to manipulate—one might say almost bewitch—her husband. These motifs draw on the arguments made in Télesphore Gagnon's defence at his trial. As one newspaper reporter put it, Gagnon 'would not have ill-treated the child had it not been for the false stories told him by the step-mother'.[59] The most disturbing of the stories attributed to the historical Houde was that the child had soiled her father's best suit of clothes with her excrement. Testimony by Marie-Jeanne Gagnon convinced the jurors that it was in fact the child's stepmother who had soiled her husband's clothes, and then blamed Aurore to induce a beating.[60]

Nowhere in any of the popular literature, except in the recent television drama, is there any reference to this incident. But the notion that Télesphore Gagnon, who in 'real life' used axe handles and whips on the child, was somehow duped into doing so by a sadistic, deceitful wife is a recurrent one. The fact that Gagnon was able to return to the community where these events occurred and 'get on with his life' after a very early release from jail is also interesting in this context, not least to Marie-Anne Houde herself. When in September 1932 she wrote, as she often did, to the minister of justice to plead for early release, she put her appeal in the following terms: 'I feel, Dear Sir, that I have a complaint to make to the Department of Justice and that is, my husband had Life [imprisonment], and only done (sic) five years and has had his freedom seven years, and since his release has not even seen his own daughter who was in the convent. He drove his own wife insane, whom [sic] died in an Asylum. I consider, Dear Sir, that he drove me crazy by his neglect and inhuman conduct during my pregnancy.'[61] Whatever else one makes of this letter—and Houde's own reiteration of the pregnancy/insanity defence is interesting—it seems clear that the historical Marie-Anne was sensitive to the asymmetrical treatment she and her husband had received at the hands of the criminal justice system. Was she equally aware of the extent to which she, much more than her husband, had been vilified in the popular imagination? It seems virtually certain that she was. 'The public has been extremely hard on me, in every way', she wrote in one of her letters to authorities from Kingston Penitentiary.[62] And as the prison chaplain put it, were she to be released, as he hoped she would be, there would be 'punishment aplenty, God knows, in the stigma she must always bear'.[63] Surely Houde herself would have agreed.

[. . .]

Marie-Anne Houde and the Stepmother Myth

The hugely popular Gagnon story, then, drew on and perpetuated the perennial myth of the wicked stepmother in twentieth-century Quebec. Like other literary stepmothers, the Marie-Anne Houde character does and feels exactly the opposite of what 'good' mothers are supposed to do and feel. Quebec mothers in the 1920s, as in other times and places, were expected to provide food and nourishment to their children. The Marie-Anne Houde character draws attention to this norm as she subverts it, by withholding food from her stepdaughter, in some accounts to support her own gluttony, in others to horde nourishment for her own son. Most accounts also made much out of the fact that the historical Houde was convicted of forcing Aurore to drink soapy water and to eat pieces of bread spread with lye soap rather than butter.[64] Rather than nourishing the child, then, there is a sense in which the stepmother was poisoning her. This is a gendered kind of violence that is perfectly consistent with the methods of mythical stepmothers (like the wicked queen in Snow White), and to which there are many other allusions in the popular literature on the case.

Quebec mothers in the 1920s, particularly in rural communities, were also expected to be hard-working managers of the family economy, responsible for innumerable duties in the house, garden, stables, and barn. Children Aurore's age were expected to contribute to the extent that they were able. Does the Houde character fulfil her prescribed role as household manager? No. In most versions, she forces her stepdaughter to do work that is well beyond her abilities, sometimes (as in the film) falling back on her pregnancy as an excuse for overworking the child, sometimes simply using work as a means of enforcing her arbitrary control. She is vilified as an overly authoritarian household manager who sloughs off part of her responsibilities onto a fragile young girl.[65] An overworked, underfed stepchild, Aurore's position is not unlike Cinderella's, with the sad exception that there will be no Fairy Godmother to rescue her. She can only dream of the kinder treatment she would have received had her own mother survived.

Mothers are also expected to be care-givers in the face of injury and illness, guarantors (well before the medical profession) of the health of children. Marie-Anne Houde and the characters she inspired subverted this aspect of the maternal role more than any other. The historical Houde was implored by Exilda Lemay to call a doctor in to attend the child just days before her death. She refused. Indeed, her failure (and that of her husband) to secure necessary medical attention for the child was an important part of the legal case against them.[66] Beyond this, Marie-Anne Houde's active role in the beatings, brandings, and other physical abuse of the child was not only a crime against the society and the state, not only a sin against the Catholic God and His Church, but an inversion of the 'natural' order of things, an order in which mothers were sources of comfort and security for children, the trustees of their health and safety, not their executioners.

Houde's status as a stepmother was central to the public construction of her 'unnatural' behaviour towards her husband's child; a 'real' mother could not possibly have been so cruel. Literary stepmothers, moreover, are often portrayed as selfish and avaricious, a reversal of the powerful ideal of maternal selflessness and generosity. In some of the fictional versions of the Gagnon story, Marie-Anne Houde's motive for murdering Aurore has to do with the child's position as a competitor, not only for Télesphore Gagnon's affection, but for his wealth.[67] Significantly, the judge who sentenced Houde to death saw the domestic situation in precisely these terms. Louis Pelletier's stated reason for rejecting the insanity defence was that, in his view, Houde had rationally formulated the intent to murder Aurore, based on that most venerable of all motives, greed. In his unfavourable report to the minister of justice on the prospect of commuting Houde's sentence, Pelletier pointed out that Télesphore Gagnon, who owned 'three plots of land and a large number of animals', was relatively well off by the standards of his community. Marie-Anne Houde,

> had found a way to arrange for herself a marriage contract by which the children of the previous marriage were disinherited to her benefit.
>
> But her cupidity did not stop there. The first wife had been married in community of property with her husband and, as a result of her death, the children of this union became their mother's heirs. Were one of these children to die, the father would be one of the beneficiaries and the inheritance of Marie-Anne Houde—given the marriage contract—would become that much better.[68]

Rather than as a disturbed woman who could not be held responsible for her actions, the judge in the case chose to see her as a scheming stepmother, a woman who would stop at nothing, not even murder, to satisfy her avarice.

The popularity of the Gagnon story reflected prevailing cultural assumptions, not only about stepmothers, but about marriage, family life, and motherhood more generally. In helping to 'martyrize' her husband's child, Marie-Anne Houde had subverted one of her society's most treasured assumptions—that mothers can be trusted to love their children. The fact that she was not the child's 'real' mother made her acts comprehensible to contemporaries, if no less reprehensible. Here was a stepmother whose behaviour fit precisely with a dark, fundamentally misogynist prejudice. Here at the same time was a radical inversion of the domestic ideal: an attack on the dominant ideology of family relations that, once defeated, would ultimately serve to reinforce that ideology.[69]

The ebb and flow of the story's appeal since the 1920s can be best understood in this light; the persistent popularity of the stage play in the 1930s and 1940s and the renewed interest generated by the new novels and the movie in the 1950s; the apparent decline in the popularity of the story as the structure and ideology of family life began to change in the 1960s and 1970s, and the resurgence of interest as a conservative 'family values' agenda emerged in the 1980s and 1990s. Apparently, this particular wicked stepmother was an especially important cultural icon in periods, such as the 1950s, in which family life and women's maternal role were most vigorously championed. The archetype lost some of its relevance in periods, such as the 1960s and 1970s, when ideological constraints on family formation, maternity, and private life in general were more relaxed.

One can also see these trends in more explicitly religious terms. Prior to the 1960s, from this perspective, religion provided the main conceptual framework for the Fortierville tragedy. Aurore was a Catholic martyr, and her stepmother nothing more (nor less) than the embodiment of evil. In the 1960s and 1970s, as Quebec society modernized and religious observance declined, the pitiful scenes depicted in print and on the screen lost much of their resonance. Only with the discovery of child battering as a societal problem in the 1980s did interest in the story revive. But the story now reminds its viewers and readers less of the lives of the saints than of the thousands of similar domestic tragedies that occur each year.[70]

However one interprets these trends, the sustained popularity of the Aurore Gagnon–Marie-Anne Houde story certainly illustrates the persistence of the age-old myth of the wicked stepmother in twentieth-century Quebec. The courtroom drama, the newspaper accounts, the plays, the novels, the film: all served to transmit negative stereotypes about women who married widowers and took on the task of raising their children. Like the fairy stories of an earlier time, these narratives exploited widely held prejudices about stepmothers. In so doing they articulated dominant ideologies of family life, essentially by holding up for public condemnation an inverted example of the prescribed maternal role.

The many tellings of the Gagnon story also provide a compelling example of the rich, if slippery, relationship between history and fiction. Historians often dismiss literary accounts for their 'imaginary' content; yet these imaginary elements can provide the means to illuminate historical events in significant new ways. With each retelling of the Gagnon story, successive generations of Quebeckers—myself now included—have projected something of their own culture and expectations onto the past, layering it with revisions that married their own agendas to the 'real story' of past events. These changing interpretations of and reactions to this family tragedy provide unexpected insights into the popular construction of gender roles and family ideals in contemporary Quebec. Each decoder of the story has left a palimpsest of his or her own culture, painting a vivid picture of how mothers—and families—ought not to be.

[1995]

Notes

1. The film has been described as the 'archetype of cinematic melodrama' in Quebec. Christiane Tremblay-Daviault, *Un cinéma orphelin: Structures mentales et socials du cinéma québécois, 1942–1953* (Montreal: Québec/Amérique, 1981), 224. According to Danielle Tremblay, more recent treatments of the theme even include a puppet show. See Danielle Tremblay, 'Un cas québécois de paralittérature: *Aurore l'enfant martyre* (1921–1936)' (MA thesis, Université de Sherbrooke, 1987), 129.

2. Alonzo Leblanc, *Aurore l'enfant martyre: Histoire et présentation de la pièce de Léon Petitjean et Henri Rollin* (Montreal: VLB éditeur, 1982), 111. This translation from a French-language source is my own, as are all the other translations in this article.

3. Heinz Weinmann, *Cinéma de l'imaginaire québécois: De la petite Aurore à Jésus de Montréal* (Montreal: L'Hexagone, 1990), 28.

4. I suspect Jean Gaudreau, who has recently discussed the Aurore Gagnon story from a psychological perspective, would agree with this assessment. In response to Weinmann, who takes the regime of abuse endured by Aurore as a symbol of *la grande noirceur* of the Duplessis years, Gaudreau writes, 'This interpretation . . . seems fanciful and, what is more, totally anachronistic.' Jean Gaudreau, 'Aurore, l'enfant martyre: Essai sur la violence faite aux enfants', *Santé mentale au Québec* 17, 1 (1992): 64.

5. Tremblay, 'Un cas québécois de paralittérature', 126–9.

6. The wicked stepmother myth has deep roots in European oral and written traditions. It was present in classical Rome, and has been detected by cultural historians of Early Modern Europe. See David Noy, 'Wicked Stepmothers in Roman Society and Imagination', *Journal of Family History* 16, 4 (1991): 345–61; Peter Laslett, *The World We Have Lost: England before the Industrial Age*, 2nd ed. (New York: Charles Scribner's Sons, 1973), 99–100; Robert Darnton, 'Peasants Tell Tales: The Meaning of Mother Goose', in *The Great Cat Massacre and Other Episodes in French Cultural History* (New York: Vintage Books, 1985), esp. 32; Natalie Zemon Davis, *Fiction in the Archives: Pardon Tales and Their Tellers in Sixteenth-Century France* (Stanford: Stanford University Press, 1987), 102.

7. Lemay continued: 'Returning downstairs, I said to her stepmother, Mme Télesphore Gagnon, that the deceased was very sick and in need of treatment. She answered: "She's my husband's child; if he wants her treated he should take care of it; and if he brings me medicine, I'll administer it." I did not return to the house before yesterday when I went at Mme Gagnon's request—she had telephoned to say that the deceased had grown worse. I found the deceased in bed in one of the downstairs rooms; she was unconscious. Mme Gagnon had telephoned the doctor and I took it upon myself to telephone *M le Curé.*' Archives Nationales du Québec, Quebec district (ANQ), Cour supérieur (Coroner). *Enquête tenue sur le cadaver d'Aurore Gagnon*, 13 Feb. 1920, testimony of Exilda Lemay.

8. Ibid., testimony of Andronic Lafond.

9. Ibid., testimony of Albert Marois.

10. André Lachance explains the role of coroners in twentieth-century Quebec in the following terms: 'The coroner . . . has the responsibility for conducting an inquiry into all suspicious deaths that are reported to him. In the first place, he may make observations and conduct research on his own, and draw his personal conclusions, if warranted. At the same time, he may on the basis of the seriousness of the death decide that Justice should pay particular attention to it. In these cases he constitutes a jury and conducts with it an inquiry into the causes and circumstances of the death.' This latter procedure was followed in the Gagnon case. André Lachance, 'La mort violente dans les Cantons de l'Est dans la première motié du xxe siècle', (unpublished manuscript, Université de Sherbrooke 1994), 3–4.

11. In fact, as testimony she gave two months later shows, Marie-Jeanne knew a great deal about the abuse that had led to her sister's death; she had no doubt been instructed to say nothing about it.

12. '*Je m'en occuppais pas*', Ibid., testimony of Télesphore Gagnon.

13. Ibid. It is revealing that Gagnon would make such frank admissions to an officer of the crown. Apparently, he considered that such forms of physical punishment were within his province, as the child's father. According to Gagnon's testimony, his wife, Marie-Anne Houde, had never inflicted similar punishments on the child, at least in his presence.

14. ANQ, Cour du Banc du Roi, Juridiction Criminelle, Québec, Session d'avril, 1920. *Le Roi v. Marie-Anne Houde* Acte d'accusation de meurtre.

15. In Marois's view, the cause of death was 'exhaustion (*épuisement*) in the aftermath of numerous injuries and the infection resulting from these injuries, this produced a sort of exhaustion, a general weakening, without there being, among any of the injuries, a directly mortal injury'. ANQ, *Le Roi v. Marie-Anne Houde*, Preuve de la part de la couronne, reçu par le Greffier de la Couronne le 19 juin 1920.

16. ANQ, *Le Roi v. Marie-Anne Houde*, testimony of Marie-Jeanne Gagnon and Gérard Gagnon, 15–16 April 1920. Gérard Gagnon was ill at the time of the trial, and his testimony was given from his sickbed in a Quebec City hospital.

17. In French, '*il y avait bien de l'attention à y faire pour ne pas la contrarier*', ANQ, *Le Roi v. Marie-Anne Houde*, testimony of Télesphore Gagnon, 19 April 1920.

18. National Archives of Canada, Department of Justice, Capital Case Files, RG 13, box 1507, file: Marie-Anne Houde (NA, Houde file) vol. 2, part 2, 88–9.

19. ANQ, *Le Roi v. Marie-Anne Houde*, copy of the sentence.

20. Ibid., 86.

21. NA, Houde file, vol. 1, Part 1: Cléophas Blouin (sheriff of Quebec) to the Office of the Secretary of State, 8 July 1920.

22. Ibid., Houde to minister of justice, 3 Oct. 1923. Already in April of that year, officials in the ministry had decided that Houde had no reason to expect parole before she had served at least fifteen years. M.F. Gallagher to J.D. Clarke, 25 April 1923.

23. These events were reconstructed from various documents in NA, Houde file, vol. 1, part 1.

24. For discussions of married women's legal rights in Quebec, see Bettina Bradbury, Peter Gossage, Evelyn Kolish, and Alan Stewart, 'Property and Marriage: The Law and the Practice in Early Nineteenth-Century Montreal', *Histoire sociale/Social History* 26 (1993): 9–39, and Micheline Dumont et al. (Collectif Clio), *L'histoire des femmes au Québec depuis quatre siècles*, 2nd ed. (Montreal: Le Jour, 1992): 355–6.

25. ANQ, Cour du Banc du Roi, Juridiction Criminelle, Québec, Session d'avril, 1920. *Le Roi v. Télesphore Gagnon*. Acte d'accusation de meurtre.

26. *La Presse*, 26 April 1920.

27. Ibid., 27 April 1920.

28. NA, Houde file, vol. 1, part 1. The observer was Judge Louis Pelletier, who had tried the Marie-Anne Houde case. Louis Pelletier to C.J. Doherty, minister of justice, 20 July 1920.

29. Leblanc, *Aurore l'enfant martyre*, 91.

30. The first confirmed performance of the play took place in Montreal's Alcazar Theatre during the week of 17 January 1921. See Leblanc, *Aurore l'enfant martyre*, 52.

31. Ibid., 61.

32. Danielle Tremblay provides a useful description of this genre, one of a number of new forms of popular culture in Quebec in the early twentieth century. It was quite distinct from 'serious' theatre in that it appealed directly to a working-class audience and drew on popular American forms, such as burlesque. Tremblay, 'Un cas québécois de paralittérature', 81–7.

33. Leblanc, *Aurore l'enfant martyre*, 92–3.
34. Ibid., 118.
35. *La Patrie*, 12 March 1920, cited ibid., 98–9.
36. *La Patrie*, 8 March 1930, cited in Tremblay, 'Un cas québécois de paralittérature', 118.
37. The less well known of these novels is Benoît Tessier, *Le drame d'Aurore, l'enfant martyre* (Quebec: Diffusion du livre, 1952). 'Benoît Tessier' is a pseudonym, generally attributed to the respected Quebec novelist Yves Thériault (*Agaguk*). The better-known book is Émile Asselin, *La petite Aurore* (Montreal: Alliance cinématographique canadienne, 1952). It served as the basis for the film directed by Jean-Yves Bigras, *La petite Aurore l'enfant martyre* (Montreal, Collection Cinémathèque québécoise 1951–2). On the novels, see Maurice Lemire, ed., *Dictionnaire des oeuvres littéraires du Québec*, vol. 3 (Montreal: Fides, 1982), 749–50. On the film, see Tremblay-Daviau, *Un cinéma orphelin*, 209–25; Pierre Véronneau, *Histoire du cinéma au Québec*, vol. 2: *Le cinéma de l'époque Duplessiste* (Montreal: Cinémathèque québécoise, 1979), 105–13; Yves Lever, *Histoire générale du cinéma au Québec* (Montreal: Boréal, 1988), 105 and 482; Weinmann, *Cinéma de l'imaginaire québécois*, 27–50.
38. Véronneau, *Le cinéma de l'époque Duplessiste*, 108.
39. The delay is interesting. It came about because Télesphore Gagnon, now a sixty-nine-year-old carpenter, sought a court injunction against the presentation of the film, and damages for the affront to his honour and that of his family which the publicity for the movie had already caused. The courts settled the matter in the filmmakers' favour in March 1952. No damages were awarded, but one account suggests that DeSève voluntarily paid a substantial sum to Gagnon. Véronneau, *Le cinéma de l'époque Duplessiste*, 109–10; Leblanc, *Aurore l'enfant martyre*, 87–96.
40. *Le Canada*, 28 April 1952, cited in Véronneau, *Le cinéma de l'époque Duplessiste*, 112.
41. Leblanc, *Aurore l'enfant martyre*.
42. The radio play, by Denis Giguère, is entitled *L'obsession de Marie-Anne G.* The author was kind enough to provide me with a copy of the script, for which I thank him. The recent novel is André Mathieu, *Aurore: la vraie histoire* (Saint-Eustache: Éditions du Cynge, 1990). The television play is Blandford's *L'affaire de la petite Aurore*.
43. See Andrée Lévesque, *La norme et les déviantes: Les femmes au Québec pendant l'entre-deux-guerres* (Montreal: Éditions du remue-ménage, 1989), esp. chapter 2, 'La maternité', 25–59. For Lévesque, social commentators in Quebec, more than in any other province, were virtually unanimous in their promotion of a maternal ideal (33). Further information on women's prescribed roles in Quebec prior to 1960 can be found in Denise Lemieux and Lucie Mercier, *Les femmes au tournant du siècle, 1880–1940* (Quebec: Institut québécois de recherché sur la culture, 1989), and in Dumont et al, *L'histoire des femmes au Québec*.
44. The recurrent cultural archetype of the 'bad mother' is examined by a number of authors in Elisabeth Ravoux-Rallo, ed., *La mère mauvaise* (Provence: Centre d'études féminines de l'Université de Provence, 1982). 'Bad' mothering practices were certainly the target of a good deal of reformist zeal in early twentieth-century Canada, and there is a growing literature on the campaign to reinvent 'mothercraft' in this period. See Veronica Strong-Boag, *The New Day Recalled: Lives of Girls and Women in English Canada, 1913–1939* (Toronto: Copp Clark Pitman, 1988): 145–77; Cynthia R. Commachio, 'Nations Are Built of Babies': Saving Ontario Mothers and Children, 1900–1940* (Montreal and Kingston: McGill-Queen's University Press, 1993); Nathalie Côté, 'Le rôle central des femmes-bénévoles au sein de l'Assistance maternelle et de la Goutte de lait à Sherbrooke (1922–1960)' (MA thesis, Université de Sherbrooke, 1993); Katherine Arnup, *Education*

for Motherhood: Advice for Mothers in Twentieth-Century Canada (Toronto: University of Toronto Press 1994).

45. Tessier, *Le drame d'Aurore*; Bigras, *La petite Aurore l'enfant martyre.*
46. ANQ, *Le Roi v. Marie-Anne Houde*, testimony of Exilda Lemay, 14 April 1920.
47. Leblanc, *Aurore l'enfant martyre*, 194.
48. ANQ, *Le Roi v. Marie-Anne Houde*, testimony of Marie-Jeanne Gagnon, 15 April 1920.
49. I am referring to the father and stepmother characters by their historic names in this section, even though the authors of many of the texts in question deliberately did not, probably to avoid lawsuits.
50. Weinmann, *Cinéma de l'imaginaire québécois*, 47.
51. The comments of one of the CHR's anonymous readers were particularly helpful on the religious aspects of the story. They are gratefully acknowledged. According to the literature published to accompany the recent television show, Aurore's grave in Fortierville is something of a pilgrimage site. A cousin, Anthyme Gagnon, has created a foundation that is collecting funds for a canonization campaign. 'Une stèle pour Aurore', in *L'affaire de la petite Aurore*, 8.
52. My thanks to Jean-Pierre Audet for this observation.
53. In her study of the representation of children in Quebec novels, Denise Lemieux has pointed out the importance of food as a symbol of mothers' affection for their children, in a universe in which the overt expression of such feelings was relatively rare. A loving mother would, as a matter of course, provide good things to eat for her children, even at the risk of going hungry herself. Here again, the Marie-Anne Houde character turns the 'natural' order of family relations on its head. See Lemieux, *Une culture de la nostalgie: L'enfant dans le roman québécois de ses origins à nos jours* (Montreal: Boréal Express, 1984), 187–92.
54. Tessier, *Le drame d'Aurore.*
55. Mathieu, *Aurore: la vraie histoire.*
56. Ibid.
57. As we have seen, the historical Télesphore Gagnon actually was a witness at his wife's trial, but on behalf of the defence and its attempts to establish her mental incapacity, rather than on behalf of the prosecution.
58. Asselin, *La petite Aurore*; Bigras, *La petite Aurore l'enfant martyre.*
59. *The Gazette*, 27 April 1920.
60. The story of the soiled clothes had also been told at Marie-Anne Houde's trial, ANQ, *Le Roi v. Marie-Anne Houde*, testimony of Marie-Jeanne Gagnon, 15 April 1920.
61. NA, Houde file, vol. 1, part 1: Houde to Hugh Guthrie, minister of justice, 29 Sept. 1932 (English in the original).
62. Ibid., Houde to M.F. Gallagher, 22 Oct. 1931.
63. Ibid., Wilfrid T. Kingsley to Ernest Lapointe, minister of justice, 7 Sept. 1925.
64. See the account in the *Montreal Daily Star*, 17 April 1920.
65. Not surprisingly, the historical Marie-Anne Houde did not see herself in this light. Pleading for her release only four years after her conviction, she emphasized her qualities as a hard-working woman who, 'on the outside', had done a double day in the interest of her family: 'When I was on the outside, I worked not like a woman but like three women, during the day outside the house and at night I worked at the upkeep of the house and the children and it was out of good will and today it is still my greatest desire to get out and to work towards their education.' Translated from NA, Houde file, vol. 1, part 1: Houde to solicitor general of Canada, 1 Dec. 1924.
66. Parents had the legal right to 'correct' their children physically, within certain limits that

in this case had been exceeded. They did not have a right, under any circumstances, to fail to provide necessary medical care for a child whose life was in danger.

67. This is the case in Tessier, *La drame d'Aurore*, for example. Evidence from other contexts suggests that remarriage can indeed create tensions between a widower's children and his second wife over the issue of inheritance. To place the blame for these tensions on the shoulders of stepmothers, though often unfair, was certainly typical. Stephen Collins has recently examined this issue for Early Modern England. See Collins, 'British Stepfamily Relations'. Based on a preliminary look at Quebec's nineteenth-century case law, inheritance seems to have been a flash point in relations among people related through remarriage in North America as well. For methodological aspects of this ongoing work, see Eric Whan, Tamara Myers, and Peter Gossage, 'Stating the Case: Law Reporting in 19th-Century Quebec', in Donald Fyson, Colin M. Coates, and Kathryn Harvey, eds, *Class, Gender and the Law in Eighteenth- and Nineteenth-Century Quebec: Sources and Perspectives* (Montreal: Montreal History Group, 1993), 55–79.

68. NA, Houde file, vol. 1, part 1: Louis Pelletier to C.J. Doherty, minister of justice, 20 July 1920. On the implications of marriage regimes for inheritance in Quebec, see Bradbury et al., 'Property and Marriage'.

69. Bruno Bettelheim sees the stepmother myth, as presented in fairy tales, as a symbolic 'splitting of the mother into a good (usually dead) mother and an evil stepmother'. This division acts 'not only a means of preserving an internal all-good mother when the real mother is not all-good, but it also permits anger at this bad "stepmother" without endangering the goodwill of the true mother, who is viewed as a different person'. Bettelheim, *The Uses of Enchantment: The Meaning and Importance of Fairy Tales* (New York: Knopf, 1976), 69.

70. Again, my thanks to the CHR reader for these insights.

A preliminary version of this paper was presented to the Popular Culture Association, Chicago, 9 April 1994. My thanks to Louise Dechêne for bringing the story of Marie-Anne Houde to my attention, to Hélène Martin, Diane Larochelle, and Lorraine Gadoury for putting me on the trail of the judicial records surrounding the case, to the CHR's anonymous readers for their careful readings and useful criticism, and to Annmarie Adams for her insights and encouragement.

Incest, the Sexual Abuse of Children, and the Power of Familialism

Joan Sangster

Evidence that sexual relations have been defined, regulated, and punished in markedly different ways over time is starkly apparent with the example of incest in twentieth-century Canada. Placed officially in the Canadian Criminal Code in 1890, incest was explained and analyzed within changing paradigms of legal, medical, and social discourse that are strikingly different today than they were a century earlier. Indeed, we might employ different terminology today, putting more emphasis on those kinds of incest that fall under the broader framework of the 'sexual abuse of children'.

This chapter explores the evolution of these changing understandings of incest, particularly relating to parents and children, and how they worked themselves out in legal contests in Ontario from the inception of the new Criminal Code of 1890 to World War II. The precise legal definition of incest remained almost completely unchanged until minor revisions in 1954 altered the definitions for its prosecution. [. . .]

The evolution of incest in law, between its definition in 1890 and the post–World War II period, indicates how changing notions of sexuality, reproduction, and the family intersected to shape the dominant understandings of incest held by the legal, medical, and social work experts who exercised the power to define, discipline, and punish this crime. While the social and legal *construction* of incest assumes most visibility here, some indication of victims' resistance to sexual abuse also emerges from incest trials and from the case files of incarcerated females claiming incest in their background. Even if medical experts concentrated their ire on the eugenic and reproductive evils of incest, some complainants spoke of the domination and fear shaping their own experiences of abuse. Even if acceptance of familial privacy or rationalizations of 'individual pathology' curtailed legal prosecution, victims might later complain of the deep injuries incest had caused them. While an understanding of official definitions and rulings may outweigh our ability to understand actual human experience, this contrast between official discourses and personal narratives

nonetheless provides a chilling and sobering recognition that human suffering may not be easily understood or compensated for by the processes of the law.
[. . .]

Incest in Law and Appeal

The law specifically prohibiting incest was first introduced into the Canadian Criminal Code in 1890, extending the laws existing in some provincial jurisdictions to create a consolidated, federal definition of the crime.[1] Introduced within a package of laws on sexual immorality, the incest provision offered severe punishment for 'sexual intercourse' and 'cohabitation' between parents and grandparents and children, brothers, and sisters who were 'aware of their consanguinity', though the Code noted that the female would not be punished if she had intercourse under 'restraint, fear, or duress'.[2]

Other relations could be prosecuted under the criminal prohibitions against rape or having carnal knowledge of a girl under 16; indeed, these were the laws used to deal with incest in Ontario before 1890. Step and foster parents might be dealt with quite separately under Criminal Code sanctions prohibiting the 'seduction' of or sexual intercourse with these young women.[3] Presumably, the later 1908 Juvenile Delinquent Act might have been invoked for sexual assaults against children, as it contained clauses prohibiting parents from encouraging immorality in their children. The latter, however, was not routinely employed for this purpose, perhaps, as Tamara Myers argues, because the courts did not see incest as a direct cause of delinquent behaviour.[4]

The 1890 definition of incest reflected legal and social thinking of the late nineteenth century. As Vikki Bell has argued in the British context, lawmakers at this time feared inbreeding and emphasized the eugenic, health, and reproductive dangers of incest, though they also argued that incest was a violation of children and was immoral and sinful. All these points of view were articulated by Canadian parliamentarians in 1890, but most telling was that they were far more concerned with 'designing women' who might exploit the proposed prohibitions against seduction[5] than they were with the incest provisions, even though the Minister of Justice claimed that incest was 'not an uncommon' occurrence. In his presentation of the bill, the minister offered an example of incest in which a father cohabited with his own child 'and produced twelve offspring by her', an illustration undoubtedly meant to incite alarm about the reproductive consequences of continued legal inaction.[6]

His fellow legislators seemed to concur that incest was a 'gross offence',[7] and the only contentious issue was the concern that the whipping provision in the bill not be applied to women who were convicted. A small number of MPs also warned of the dangers of criminalizing the victim, as women were liable to punishment under the law. Echoing emerging feminist and temperance critiques of violent familial abuse by male patriarchs, they recoiled at the thought of fathers forcing themselves on their young daughters. 'These outrages', one MP noted, 'are generally upon very young girls who are absolutely under the power of their fathers.' Such 'helpless parties', he warned, 'should not be liable to the same prosecution.'[8] Indeed, the Liberal leader Edward Blake astutely warned that the 'liability of the child to imprisonment' might simply set up 'obstacles to securing the necessary evidence' to convict the father.[9] Their concerns, however, were allayed by limiting whipping to men and by reassurances that judges would use discretion in their 'provision of punishment'[10] to any female.

This 1890 definition of incest remained largely unchanged for decades. Familial sexual abuse, as a more broadly defined term encompassing all family members, both biological and step, and all kinds of sexual touching relations, was not fully integrated into legal and social thinking at this time.[11] In 1934 the only amendment added half-brothers and half-sisters to the list of those who could be prosecuted. Over the next four decades, case law across Canada both reinforced the emphasis on the reproductive concerns at the heart of the initial bill and reaffirmed stringent parameters for conviction. Judges appeared reluctant to favour arguments and appeals that in any way infringed on the defendant's right to due process, thus ignoring the context of power and inequality already framing his relationship to the complainant.

Cohabitation, it was decided, had to be accompanied by intercourse, and occupation of the same bed was inadequate proof of incest; rather, the Crown must show 'corpus delicti'.[12] Though an attempt to have 'emission of seed'[13] a *sine qua non* for a conviction failed on appeal, the fact that lawyers often used this argument attests to the anxieties about reproduction behind incest charges. One appeal even tried to argue that only if children resulted could incest be proven. Other appeals concentrated on the question of whether there was legal proof of either marriage or blood relations—other than the 'mere' testimony of the victims or others who knew the parents.[14] If ignorance of consanguinity could be proven, charges could be dismissed. Using a familiar defence in wife-battering trials, one appeal argued that the father was 'drunk' and therefore did not know he was having sex with his own daughter—though this was too much for the judge, who announced that 'if he was not too drunk to have sexual relations then he was not too drunk to know Hetty was his daughter.'[15]

The law was also contentious when it tackled issues of consent, complicity, and corroboration of evidence. Although it was established that minors need not produce corroborating evidence, in practice this did become an issue in some jury trials, and it became *de rigueur* for women 16 and over.[16] The technicality of age, not an understanding of the daughter's situation in the household—perhaps living alone with a father, relying on him for financial support—was thus the important measuring stick. Clearly, courts had trouble believing non-consensual incest occurred when women were older or when they were sisters to the defendant. If a brother is guilty, as one lawyer attempted to argue, the sister, if over 16, must *by definition* be guilty too; there must be dual convictions or none at all.[17] While power relations between siblings were generally slighted, a youthful victim of paternal incest could spark outrage from the court. When a Toronto man attempted incest with his seven-year-old and was convicted on the testimony of her and a four-year-old girl, the court acknowledged that the crime had technically not transpired but used another statute to imprison him for seven years.[18]

Prosecuting attorneys also had to be careful how they used corroborating evidence and witness accounts of previous or subsequent instances of incest; the jury might be 'warned against'[19] these being key to the case. Moreover, a girl's role as 'accomplice' could be confirmed by her failure to report the crime 'at the first opportunity'.[20] In one appeal, for example, a 15-year-old claimed her father came to her bed at night and threatened her, saying that 'if she called out, her brothers would wake up and they would all go to jail'. Six days later she told her stepmother about the incest and two days after that, her sister. Yet, this time lag was used to launch an appeal against his conviction; at that appeal, the defendant's lawyer also claimed her 'seventy year old' father was unlikely to commit such a crime due to his age.[21]

[. . .]

Ontario Criminal Assize Cases, 1890–1929

The reasons for the paucity of formal criminal charges for incest emerged from the nature of the crime, its effect on the victims and other family members, and its perception by society.[22] Victims felt shame and humiliation, and sometimes projected guilt onto themselves. They were reluctant to expose their experience to public view and were often pressured by the perpetrators with rewards and/or threats, including physical violence. Girls, who comprised the majority of victims,[23] were always caught in an inescapable contradiction: to fulfil their daughterly and feminine roles, they should be passive, accept paternal authority, and remain within the family, all of which precluded an escape from sexual relations they were also told made them immoral and sinful. Moreover, other family members, including mothers, might reject victims' stories, urging them not to precipitate family disintegration and shame with public charges. As in the present, economic, social, and psychological factors created a 'conscious and unconscious need *not to see* that could blind mothers to paternal incest'.[24] It is not surprising that some girls confided their stories first to neighbours, for they feared the implosion that would follow a confession within the family circle. Many girls ultimately used other strategies to escape sexual abuse, such as running away, leaving home to work, or marrying and establishing their own households. In her research on Quebec incest cases, Marie-Aimée Cliche found the average age of abused girls to be 11–15; after 16, she surmises, they could more effectively rebel against the unwanted advances of male relatives.[25] Her conclusions, along with Dorothy Chunn's research on British Columbia, suggest that regional variations in the application of the incest law were often outweighed by shared patterns and problems across the country.[26]

If a jury was involved, they were reluctant to convict without incontrovertible evidence, such as a confession, given the 'heinous'[27] shame of the crime and the severity of punishment. Like other criminal cases involving violence against women, the complainant had to fulfil the role of the 'ideal victim' if the court and jury were to take her charge seriously. Subsequent sexual relations out of wedlock, a lack of shame and guilt on her part, and a delay in coming forward with the accusations, or the father's respectability, were all seen as indications of her complicity or a false accusation.

All of these problems surfaced in the cases tried across the province in the county criminal assizes between 1890 and 1929. Incest often occurred over a long period of time, and a woman's failure to go to the authorities after the first instance cast suspicion on her claims. Women who were not minors, it was believed, had the ability to act completely independently; their material dependence on the family or even continued threats of violence from a father were not considered relevant to the context of their 'acquiescence' to sexual relations. Thus, even in a case where a 33-year-old woman was presented by the prosecution as 'rather simple', and therefore easily pressured, the jury did not believe her claims that unwanted sexual relations occurred with her father. She lived alone with her widowed father, who allowed her only two dresses, told her to 'stay in [behind a] locked door', and isolated her from the outside world, but her age and delay in reporting undoubtedly worked against her, and her father was acquitted.[28]

Two women who subsequently married were not believed, even in one case when a sibling verified that an assault occurred after her sister's marriage.[29] One 20-year-old woman testified that her father repeatedly raped her and threatened to 'kill' her if she told. Despite the fact that her new husband encouraged her to lay the charge, despite testimony from a sister and a neighbour about his assaults, her year-long delay in reporting the last incident due to pressure from her mother not to tell anyone, along with her age and marital status, cast doubt on her story. The fact that mothers sometimes doubted their daughters' claims, or repudiated them, fearing their husbands' violence visited upon them, social shame, family disintegration, the loss of other children to the Children's Aid Society (CAS), or their own impoverishment with the jailing of a breadwinner, created a wall of denial that some victims could not overcome.

Moreover, even when siblings or a mother supported the girl's story, the court might reject it. When a respectable locomotive engineer was tried in 1923 in St Catharines, the judge urged the jury to 'give him the benefit of the doubt', thus pressuring them to accept the 'veracity of the father's story, as opposed to the girl's'.[30] This was the second trial for the man, as the first jury could not reach a verdict, despite the fact that the mother herself laid the complaint and neighbours offered supporting accounts of the father 'with his hands up [the daughter's] clothes'. The father's letter to the mother, pleading with her not to allow the daughter on the stand, declared 'drink was my downfall' and asked for 'forgiveness' and the opportunity to 'change', certainly implying his guilt. However, the jury clearly sympathized with him rather than the daughter who claimed the father threatened to kill her if she told on him; perhaps they bought the defence argument that these 'are respectable working-class people', thus incapable of such crimes.[31] With incest perceived to be a vice of the underclass, a useful defence strategy was to distinguish one's respectable client from such immoral people.

Witnesses could also be discredited due to other family conflicts. In one case, two younger sisters who shared their bed with a 17-year-old sister corroborated her story that their father 'laid on top of her' in the bed, yet the father was still found not guilty. Presumably the sisters' youth made their testimony suspect; moreover, the mother, who laid the complaint, was accused of trying to get rid of a difficult, non-supporting husband.[32]

A similar defence strategy was employed in a Hastings County trial in which the husband was charged with incest against his nine-year-old daughter. It was claimed that the wife was trying to 'put him away' because he did 'not use her right'.[33] He was subsequently found guilty of the lesser charge of assault. In these scenarios, mothers were placed in a difficult double bind: if they supported their daughters' stories, they might also be blamed for failing to safeguard the morality of the home and to protect their daughters adequately.[34]

A girl's presumed intelligence level and her moral character (as well as her family's standing in the community) conditioned how her case was treated. In one case where a stepfather was tried for carnal knowledge, for instance, the girl's subsequent sexual relations were probed by the defence as a means of discrediting her. Ruby testified that her stepfather, who married her mother when she was three, began having sexual relations with her when she was nine, later encouraging her brother to do the same. He came to her 'crib' to fetch her when she was almost 10, she claimed, and her mother also put her in her stepfather's bed sometimes, though she begged her not to. The abuse ceased when, as a 15-year-old, she left home to work for another family. Her stepfather had originally taken her 'to a man he knew in town, and he used her wrongly when his wife was away.' This relationship, however, became the focus of great scrutiny, and the older man's romantic postcards to her were introduced as evidence by the defence. Since the second man was comparatively 'nice' to her, even taking her on a trip, Ruby did not complain about his sexual advances. Moreover, the medical exam ordered by the court was inconclusive. Her subsequent 'immorality' thus discredited her stature as a true victim, a common problem in many incest trials.[35]

Some juries also clearly worried that children, perhaps under pressure, would fabricate stories. Favouring an adult's over a child's story, many courts wanted some corroboration from other witnesses (despite what the law said), a difficult requirement for a crime often committed in secrecy. Incest might also leave no visible traces of physical violence, and juries were thus unconvinced that sex was forced upon the girl. Even if the man admitted having intercourse with the daughter, the Crown might accept a reduced plea of assault, which could be dealt with more expeditiously.[36] The difficulty of proving that intercourse had occurred sometimes meant doctors were called in to examine the girl to see if the hymen was broken. If they claimed it was not, then incest was doubted; but if it was broken, they might find other explanations, casting doubt on the girl's story, as with the doctor who commented that this might simply be 'due to masturbation'.[37]

Those on trial usually had lawyers, but the accusers were less vigilantly protected by counsel in what must have been traumatic courtroom encounters, particularly if they had been physically threatened by the abuser. A 14-year-old, with only a teenage sister (who was also accusing the father) to stand by her, suddenly refused to speak against her father once on the witness stand and, consequently, was given a contempt charge.[38] In another case, which seemed to confirm the fears of Edward Blake that victims would be criminalized, 14-year-old Josephine was charged with incest, along with her father, but, confused about times and places, she admitted she made a 'false statement'. The father was acquitted, despite her brother's testimony supporting her claims. Two years later he was charged with incest again, after Josephine claimed his paternity for the child she bore in the school outhouse and disposed of there. The father's lawyer, however, secured the jury's sympathy by reminding them of her previous admission of 'false statements'. Josephine pleaded guilty to manslaughter and was sent to the reformatory for two years.[39]

The contentious cases represented in the Criminal Assizes were more likely to result in acquittals, but some did not. Guilty pleas were entered or returned when the accused admitted to the crime, when corroboration and the incontrovertible 'youthful innocence' of the victim seemed irrefutable, or perhaps when a pregnancy helped to confirm the girl's story.[40] In a famous case described by Karen Dubinsky, repeated pregnancies of three daughters and double infanticide committed by the mother were the catalysts exposing long-standing sexual assaults by a father on his daughters. The father was convicted of incest, the mother of infanticide, and her death sentence was only commuted after a concerted campaign for her release by women's groups—perhaps indicating their underlying sympathy for females caught in the maelstrom of violent and patriarchal families.[41]

[. . .]

Persisting Themes in the Legal and Medical Treatment of Incest

. . . During the 1930s and 1940s, courts continued to focus on the blood relation of the father to the complainant, often searching out birth certificates to establish paternity,[42] rather than concentrating on the social relations of power within the family. Equating incest only with intercourse, the courts relied on gynecological exams of girls, which might obscure as much as they revealed. Moreover, the prosecution might settle for a lesser charge if incest was difficult to prove.

Appeals to higher Canadian courts concerning the incest law became less frequent, and defence lawyers often resurrected conventional arguments. Lawyers pressed for the corroboration of girls' testimony, though the higher courts firmly defended the view that girls could not be 'accomplices' if they were under the age of consent.[43] A girl's 'moral character', including subsequent illicit relations with boys, might be also raised by the defence to cast doubt on her story. Some even tried the long-rejected argument that 'emission of seed' and 'proof in the form of children' were necessary to conviction.[44]

The crime itself was also portrayed as so aberrant that more than one court appearance by a defendant resulted in a doctor's assessment to see if the man could be declared legally insane. After finding one father guilty, the judge rationalized that the case was so 'disgusting . . . it would indicate the man was suffering from some mental trouble as a result of his service overseas.'[45] Playing to similar ideas, men told the courts they were not responsible for their actions, as they were 'out of control'—much like the arguments used in some sexual assault cases. One 46-year-old tool-and-die maker, for instance, described the setting of his sexual relations with his daughter in detail. Yet, in his police statement, he also excused his actions as uncontrollable and irrational: 'something came over my mind . . . I can't explain it', he claimed about his first assault of his 13-year-old daughter. 'A devilish feeling came over me', he added about another assault, projecting the blame into a realm of inevitable evil. Echoing the biases of the medical literature, he described incest using a language of passivity with reference to his daughter, clearly to imply consent: 'I asked her if she would do it . . . and she took off her clothes and lay on the couch.'[46] Moreover, he offered reassurance that he usually avoided full penetration or practised 'withdrawal' as if to allay concerns about reproduction. His police statement could well have been written by a lawyer who knew all the standard legal buttons to push.

As in the earlier period, brother/sister incest was viewed sceptically, even if the sister was younger. In a rare instance, a Toronto Juvenile Court judge used his discretion under the Juvenile Delinquent Act to transfer a case to adult court, feeling the boy, who was over 14, fully understood the crime against his sister. After hearing the boy's claim that it was an accident of communal sleeping arrangements and that 'he did not even know what made me do it', the criminal court judge directed a verdict of not guilty.[47]

Some girls' claims about their brothers' forceful advances were simply disbelieved, or girls were presumed to be equally guilty despite age and strength differences. A young woman who gave birth to her brother's child at 13 testified that her 15-year-old brother 'came into her room and held her down' but that she was too frightened to scream or tell her parents. The judge admitted that she didn't even understand the term 'immorality', nor had she known what intercourse was, though ultimately this was attributed to her slow mental capacity. Her brother was charged but given a suspended sentence and returned to the family, leaving his sister no option after her sentence in the Ontario Training School for Girls (OTSG) at Galt, Ontario, except to forsake her family to which she had strong ties or return and live with him.[48] Because the prescription for recovery offered by medical experts was often for girls simply to forget incest, the emotional trauma they faced upon return home was little understood by social workers or doctors.

In this later period, girls also remained especially vulnerable to incest when they were young, isolated, and relied solely on their fathers for support, or when they endured especially authoritarian fathers. One widowed man and new immigrant, for example, brought his daughter, who may not have spoken English, to a rooming house and occupied the same bed, claiming she was his wife.[49] In another instance a daughter, who was the eldest in the family, helped to care for younger siblings and her widowed father, and became easy prey for his threats of isolation and violence; police intervention may have come only when she was badly beaten by him.[50]

Although some men professed shame, or blamed alcohol, others could not relinquish their sense of entitlement to complete control, including sexual access, to their daughters. One father, even though he had been convicted of her indecent assault, demanded to see his daughter who had been sent to the OTSG. Writing to the federal Department of Justice, he railed that, as a 'Scotsman, a veteran, a Christian, a Salvation Army' member, he had a right to visit. His claim to respectability did not impress provincial officials, who denied his request. Tragically but predictably, the training school did not help his daughter, who was described as 'worse than before she was committed.'[51]

Training school records offer compelling evidence that incest was often hidden from legal and social view. It was not uncommon for judges to send victims of sexual abuse to training schools, even if the social workers and judges felt the girl was 'more sinned against than sinning'.[52] Because she was perceived to be morally polluted and potentially promiscuous, the solution was to isolate her from her family and society in order to reinscribe *her* moral conscience. One judge blithely disregarded a girl's court-appointed lawyer, who protested her sentence to the training school, pointing to the fact that *she* was the victim and should not be mixed with 'incorrigibles'.[53]

In another court judgement a young girl, 'Eileen', who was apparently pregnant by her father, was sent to the training school because of her 'immorality'. She had witnessed her mother's murder by a boarder when she was only seven, then went to live with her father in a lumber camp, where she had to share his bed. Pregnant at 13, she was sent to the OTSG to receive an 'education and moral training'. In a bland euphemism, her pregnancy was described as the result of her 'unhappy home', presumably because paternal incest could not be legally proven.[54]

Some girls did not even talk about incest until they were examined by OTSG psychiatrists; a veil of shame and anger had shielded relatives from prosecution. Others made references to their ill treatment by male relatives in ways that suggested they were victims of abuse, but they could not bring themselves to talk to the psychiatrist about it. Doctors, psychologists, and social workers involved in the juvenile justice system, as well as local CASs, believed girls should be removed from violent, sexually abusive adults, but this solution was sometimes experienced by the girls as *their* punishment. Also, experts working for the courts and penal system had trouble believing girls' stories unless the family fitted the incest stereotype, and they interpreted girls' confused retreats back to these families as evidence that incest had not happened or had not been serious. Some girls' stories were simply dismissed as fabrications, and even if they were believed, their moral complicity, at some level, was assumed.[55] Moreover, doctors' physical descriptions of incest victims betrayed the lingering potency of eugenic theories: they are described as 'big stupid' girls, or 'a [girl] with an unhappy . . . hangdog expression that almost makes her look defective.'[56]

A case that surfaced during World War II indicated how [blaming girls for] incest had clung tenaciously in legal and medical minds. A 15-year-old, 'Priscilla', was sent to the Training School by a judge because she was 'sex obsessed', having intercourse with boys and men, and she had contracted a venereal disease. Years before, the girl had claimed she was sexually used by her (widowed) father and older brothers, from the age of six, but she was not believed until the school later became alarmed at her sexual awareness and 'amorality'. Nonetheless, her father's initial denials were accepted by the local police. Later, however, the father was sent to the penitentiary for incest after it was clear the girl's story was true.

The interpretative gloss on Priscilla's life proffered by local CAS officials sounded all too familiar. 'The home conditions are appalling', they wrote. These were 'subsistence farmers in the backwoods of [northern] Ontario, parents below normal intelligence, only one child normal, one in Orillia [the hospital for the mentally retarded].' The doctor who examined Priscilla at the Hospital for Sick Children in

Toronto referred to her as a 'moral delinquent' and concluded that the 'environment she was brought up in was so bad it was impossible to say yet whether this is secondary to the environment, or if due to some *inherent defect*.'[57] In and out of foster homes and the OTSG, isolated, desperately wanting some kind of family, hostile, unhappy, violent and abusive to others, Priscilla was ultimately deemed unreachable by the institution. Asked to look into the future, her last words to the OTSG board, at age 17, may sum up her damaged psyche: 'it doesn't matter.'[58]

Combined with criminal court files, training school records also demonstrate how girls and sometimes their allies within families, attempted to resist incest. Older sisters sometimes actively intervened to protect younger sisters. One 16-year-old in the late nineteenth century, already working and living away from home, returned to aid her 14-year-old sister who, like her, had been sexually assaulted by their father. From her testimony it seemed clear she had previously tried to shield her sister from her own fate when they shared a bed. 'My father', the younger girl testified, 'tried to do the same thing [have intercourse] to Katie when she and I were sleeping together. Before that . . . Katie would put me to the front of the bed.'[59]

Mothers might also aid their daughters' attempts to secure justice through the courts, and the courage needed to brave a courtroom with incest charges should not be underestimated. By the 1930s, these cases were often closed to the public, but in the late nineteenth and early twentieth centuries, public trials and newspaper coverage resulted in intense community scrutiny. Still, daughters and their familial allies testified against fathers or brothers and even registered their vocal objections to acquittals. When one 'respectable' man was acquitted in St Catharines, after strong pressure from the judge, a mother and daughter shouted out 'liar' as the father spoke in court.[60]

Simply telling someone else took fortitude and bravery, for family members might easily reject the story and thus, also, the daughter telling it. One mother conceded on the witness stand that she initially rejected her daughter's account of her father attacking her 'in the hay loft, in the barn and in the house' when the mother was away and only the younger siblings were at home. 'She told me five or six times' before [she] believed her, she admitted, finally accepting the daughter's story when it was substantiated by her brother, and also because she knew 'her daughter was not a bad girl.'[61] Other daughters, such as one hearing-disabled girl, were never believed, especially if they became problematic runaways afterwards.[62]

Indeed, most responses to incest never involved the courts. Often, agencies such as the CAS would warn the family or remove the daughter, placing her with a relative, in a foster home, or even in a training school. In many cases, girls responded by running away and using sex as a means of barter or a form of rebellion [. . .] Some, as we have seen, also escaped into marriage, though if they lived close to abusing fathers this did not necessarily stop the attacks. These instances of resistance to incest do not, admittedly, provide us with transparent, absolute understandings of its effects on its victims. Psychiatrists working with survivors in the OTSG could not even agree on possible treatment; some advocated repression of the past, others claimed the girls needed 'intensive psychotherapy', which the school could not provide.[63] Nor could they understand why some survivors could live through the pain and others seemed defeated by it. In two cases of very young victims, both noted above, one young woman managed, outwardly, to become an OTSG 'success' story, securing an education and a job and assuming her own family responsibilities. The other young victim, Priscilla, travelled in and out of foster homes for nine years. Even though she admitted that some foster parents offered her affection, she could not deal with her anger, resentment, and hatred of herself and others. The experts eventually designated her hopeless, with some blame attached to her 'weak' personality. Instead, they might have concluded that for some young women the ability to lead a 'normal' life had simply been crushed by the violence and domination at the heart of sexual abuse.[64]

The Triumph of Blaming the Mother

The damaged psyches of such young women would find little comprehension in the medical and psychiatric writing of the time. In the interwar period, and indeed into the 1950s, expert interpretations of incest stressed its abnormality and location in very peripheral social groups. Moreover, the legal preoccupation with accomplices was closely intertwined with medical suspicions of girls' complicity.

While few medical and social work journals broached the subject until the 1960s—a crucial silence—those that did, often focused on incest taboos in non-Western cultures[65] or on its eugenic outcomes. One famous psychiatrist writing in the 1930s, for example, examined the three offspring of a brother and sister, looking for mental defect, and expressed some surprise that two children were 'normal' in behaviour and scholastic ability.[66] Often basing their conclusions on one or a few cases, psychologists and psychiatrists also portrayed incest as the product of marginal, 'sexually lax' communities in 'slum areas'[67] and of families typified by 'poverty, alcoholism, and poor education'.[68]

By the 1940s, eugenic themes were increasingly replaced by psychoanalytic ones. Generalizing on the basis of five women who supposedly 'sought out substitutes in promiscuous sex' to replace earlier incestuous relations with their fathers, one study concluded that the emotional impact of incest on those in adolescence was more severe than for younger children. The former understood the incest taboo, they reasoned, while the latter often 'unconsciously desire the sexual activity and become a more or less willing partner.'[69] Indeed, the language in medical writing often betrayed a view that girls were complicit, referring to their 'indulgence', 'compliance', or 'attachment' to their fathers. We should not 'cloak all children in innocence', concluded one learned study, since some play a 'cooperative and initiating' role in sexual relations with adults.[70]

The Freudian thread of influence was starkly evident in one case study, published in the *Psychoanalytic Review*, which was then utilized by later experts as well. The doctor writing up the case first mused over whether he was dealing with anything other than incest 'fantasies'. After conceding the incest had happened, and even that it had severe emotional consequences for the woman he studied, he went on to offer his final conclusion concerning her 'neurotic' behaviour: it was explained by the fact that her 'early acquaintance with male anatomy led her to strongly envy the possession of a penis.'[71]

By the 1950s some Freudian interpretations had the benefit of including social fathers, such as step and foster fathers, as well as biological fathers in their analysis of sexual abuse. But incest was still located within the purview of the poor and, increasingly, the blame was placed squarely on inadequate mothers. In their first interviews, the mothers of incest victims appeared 'careless in dress, infantile, extremely dependent and intellectually dull',[72] wrote one team of experts. Moreover, scarred by 'controlling' maternal figures in their own families, these women often emotionally and sexually 'deserted' their husbands, then implicitly offered up their daughters as sexual surrogates for the father. Thus emotionally 'abandoned' by their mothers, girls 'in their loneliness and fear accepted the father's sexual advances as an expression of affection', though they would later compensate with 'repetitive [sexual] compulsion towards other men.'[73]

Such Freudian interpretations 'gave [experts] the opportunity to explain away incest'[74] rather than face its traumatic effects, a problem worsened, as Diana Russell argues, by the deliberate disregard, or rather, acceptance of adult/child incest by Kinsey researchers in the 1950s.[75] Well into the 1960s, criminologists writing on sexually delinquent girls repeated the idea that incest might be a fabricated response of girls to difficult relationships with mothers and fathers, or they reverted to the notion that it was an uncommon, aberrant, deviant behaviour of the 'lower classes'. A strong current of 'mother-blaming', with mothers portrayed as 'colluders, as helpless dependents, or as victims', permeated the expert literature until it was challenged by feminist analysis 20 years ago.[76]

It is hard to escape the conclusion that, as women's child-rearing roles were accorded more significance and were heavily scrutinized by professional experts after World War I, women were made responsible for preventing violence against children. A recent historical overview of sexual abuse in the United States has suggested that a number of interrelated factors produced a virtual silence on sexual abuse from the 1920s to the 1960s: the decline of feminism, blurred definitions of categories of violence and neglect, conflicting social work strategies for prevention and protection, the impact of psychoanalytic theory, and a focus on the difficult economic conditions in the 1930s.[77] These same factors shaped the Canadian silences about sexual abuse, as well as its representation as uncommon, emerging from poor, dysfunctional, possibly feeble-minded families.

In the years after World War I, the child-saving work of the Children's Aid Societies and Juvenile Courts focused on the ill treatment and desertion of children, as well as the immorality of parents (such as their adultery and drinking). Although violence against children was a concern for the CAS and the courts, family preservation often remained a central goal. In the interwar period, for instance, the Peterborough Children's Aid Society declared it aspired 'not to break up homes but make them better',[78] while simultaneously voicing its belief that only *mothers'* efforts would counter immorality against children.[79]

The logical end of these social and legal processes were vividly displayed in the parliamentary discussions concerning changes to the incest law (new section 142 of the Criminal Code) in 1954. Once again, the issue of corroboration reared its head. During an overhaul of the Criminal Code, parliamentarians discussed whether there should be consistency with regard to judicial warnings about the need for corroboration of rape, carnal knowledge, and incest charges.

Discussing the existing incest law, MP and lawyer Patrick Nowlan immediately invoked his personal experiences as evidence. He recently defended a case, he claimed, in which the girl was forced by her mother to testify against the father and thus send him to the penitentiary, as the mother wanted to 'take on' a new boyfriend. Defending his masculine lawyerly reputation, Nowlan added, 'I didn't have much trouble breaking [the girl] down on the witness stand.' He also claimed that he had recently seen three such incidents, noting that false accusations might be more prevalent in intra-family charges, though admittedly, this happened with a rather 'poor type' of family.[80] John Diefenbaker, known for his defence of civil liberties, agreed judges should be required to issue warnings to juries about convictions for incest where there was no corroboration. We need to 'protect the accused who is innocent from being convicted by those who by *design* invent a story . . . I do not believe parliament intends to take away that element of protection against the kind of unfounded charges frequently to be found in families when wives decide that they wish to disassociate themselves from their husbands.[81]

The matter was complicated further by their discussion of incest between adults, which, one MP reminded his fellows, 'implies consent upon the part of both parties . . . with the lady giving evidence, the accomplice'.[82] It was ultimately agreed that an incest conviction, like these other crimes, required 'corroboration in a material particular of evidence implicating the accused' as well as the testimony of 'one witness'.[83] This tightened protection for the accused, making it even more difficult to secure convictions. These deliberations were a stark contrast to those undertaken by MPs in 1890. There was no voice, like that of Edward Blake, speaking of the abuse of power involved in incest or worrying that girls would be wrongly convicted. Instead, the rights of the accused and a deep suspicion of women's abuse of their power to falsely accuse men predominates. Indeed, the 'designing' women that MPs feared would exploit the seduction charges in 1890 were replaced in 1954 by the 'designing' mothers who would pressure their daughters into making false accusations of incest. In the context of a weakened feminist movement little concerned with violence, with the triumph of Freudian thought shrouding incest, and with persisting class biases that denied violence existed across the social spectrum, the turn of events in the 1950s was entirely comprehensible. For incest victims, however, it was entirely tragic.

Conclusion

The irony of the incest law was that the late nineteenth-century discussions surrounding its creation incorporated a modicum of insight into the abuse of paternal power involved in familial sexual abuse, a view subsequently lost in the legal treatment and medical discussion of incest by the mid-twentieth century. Of course, we should not idealize the early legislative and legal attempts to deal with incest. The incest laws were also shaped initially by narrow reproductive and eugenic concerns, and conviction was also circumscribed by an intense concern for the rights of the accused, with little understanding of the situation of victims. For those girls and women who did attempt to use legal means to secure justice, the criminal justice system provided more barriers than encouragement. The court cases examined here, from the late nineteenth century to World War II, indicate that judges and juries were reluctant to convict without clear confessions, some corroboration, or the untouchable testimony of an ideal victim.

Incest trials, of course, were not undertaken in a vacuum; the legal process was intertwined with the dominant social, medical, and political ideologies of the time, as well as by the material realities of gender and class power structures. Social and economic conditions profoundly shaped the options of those who were abused and their ability to escape, resist, or confront abuse.[84] The possibility of pursuing incest through the courts was also restrained by a strong investment in familial privacy, an acceptance of paternal power, and disbelief that abuse occurred outside of very poor, immoral, and depraved families. The ideology of familial privacy always coexisted uneasily with intermittent calls, like the one articulated by Crown Attorney [George] Hatton, for public protection of disadvantaged children through the legal regulation of sex.

The medicalization of sexual offences and the increasing influence of psychoanalytic categories on legal processes, especially during the interwar period and after, meant that male perpetrators were seen as 'pathological'[85] individuals, and the very 'ordinariness' of sexual abuse was overlooked [. . .]. Moreover, medical discourse increasingly justified and accentuated the legal preoccupation with women's 'complicity', as mothers and daughters, not fathers, were held accountable for the abuse or perhaps were accused of fabricating it. Until a full-fledged critique of this medical model, of the sexual double standard, of familial privacy, and of the material, social, and emotional imbalances of power within male-dominated families emerged, efforts would be made to patch over, if not suppress, the fissures of sexual abuse within the family. [. . .]

[2001]

Notes

1. There were earlier nineteenth-century laws in some provinces such as Nova Scotia, Prince Edward Island, and New Brunswick, but no law in the larger provinces of Ontario and Quebec.
2. Canada, *Statutes of Canada*, Criminal Code, 176, 1890.
3. Ibid., 1927, ch. 36, s. 213.
4. Tamara Myers, 'Qui t'a Débauchée?: Sexual Histories of Female Adolescents in the Montreal Juvenile Delinquents Court in the Early Twentieth Century', paper presented at the Carleton Conference on the History of the Family, May 1997, 2. For example, in the cases before the Ontario Criminal Assize Courts, only one man was previously charged with contributing to juvenile delinquency for an 'indecent assault' on his daughter before the incest charge was laid. In a Quebec appeal, the higher courts ruled against using the Juvenile Delinquents Act to prosecute a father for incest (probably under the 'contributing' clause) because this offence could not be tried summarily, even on consent of the accused. *Leroux v. the King* (1928), D.L.R. 299. See also W.L. Scott, *The Juvenile*

Court in Law (Ottawa, 1941), 34–5. However, a case could be removed from the Juvenile Court to adult court, as described below.

5. MPs worried that 'designing women' might use seduction laws to 'blackmail them'. Canada, *House of Commons Debates*, 10 Apr. 1890, 3168, 3166. See Karen Dubinsky, '"Maidenly Girls" or "Designing Women"? The Crime of Seduction in Turn-of-the-Century Ontario', in Franca Iacovetta and Mariana Valverde, eds, *Gender Conflicts: New Essays in Women's History* (Toronto: University of Toronto Press, 1992), 27–66; Graham Parker, 'The Legal Regulation of Sexual Activity and the Protection of Females', *Osgoode Hall Law Journal* 21, 2 (1983): 187–244.

6. *House of Commons Debates*, 10 Apr. 1890, Sir John Thompson, 3162.

7. Ibid.

8. Ibid., Mr Casey, 3172.

9. Ibid., Mr Blake, 3172.

10. Ibid., Sir John Thompson, 3172.

11. This chapter is based primarily on incest charges, though some carnal knowledge cases involving close relations were taken into account. I do substitute the term 'sexual abuse' for incest, using it in its more modern sense as encompassing incest. For an excellent study of sexual assault in general, see Karen Dubinsky, *Improper Advances: Rape and Heterosexual Conflict in Ontario, 1880–1929* (Chicago: University of Chicago Press, 1993).

12. *Desellier v. R.*, 45 C.C.C. 246 (1925). As one appeal tried to argue, 'the purpose of the law is undoubtedly to prevent issue from such unnatural relations. Therefore the sexual relations must be such as may produce conception.' *R. v. Fournier*, 62 C.C.C. 397.

13. *R. v. Lindsay*, S.C.O. in 26 C.C.C. 163 and *R. v. Lindsay*, 3 Mar. 1916 in O.L.R. 171 (1916). See also AQ, RG 22-476-1-14, Judge Mulock's Benchbooks, 18 Feb. 1916.

14. This came up more than once; proof of consanguinity, other than testimony, was sometimes demanded, sometimes not. Quebec laws made written proof (other than testimony) essential. See *Rex v. Smith*, 13 C.C.C. 403 (1908) and *Queen v. Garneau*, 4 C.C.C. 69 (1899) on the first issue; on Quebec, *R. v. Garneau*, 4 C.C.C. 69 (1899).

15. *R. v. Bloodworth*, 9 C.A.R. 80 (1913).

16. Supposedly, incest was not named in the Criminal Code as one of the offences requiring corroboration of other witnesses. *Crankshaw's Criminal Code of Canada* (1935), 181. However, this is not always what happened in practice.

17. The word 'accomplice' is repeatedly used. See, for example, *R. v. Bloodworth*; *R. v. Gordon*, 19 C.A.R. 20. On the issue of sisters being automatically guilty, see *R. v. Draker*, 21 C.A.R. 47 (1919) and *R. v. Gordon*.

18. *Rex v. Elzear Pailleur*, O.W.R. 15, 3, 73. The court convicted him under s. 570 of the Criminal Code, which stated that everyone is guilty of an indictable offence who attempts an indictable offence.

19. *R. v. Bloodworth*, 9 C.A.R. 80 (1913).

20. *R. v. Proteau*, 33 B.C.L.R. 39 (1923).

21. Ibid.

22. For other historical studies on incest, see Linda Gordon, *Heroes of Their Own Lives: The Politics and History of Family Violence, Boston, 1880–1960* (New York: Viking, 1988), ch. 7; Elizabeth Pleck, *Domestic Tyranny: The Making of American Social Policy against Family Violence from Colonial Times to the Present* (New York: Oxford University Press, 1987), 95–7, 156–7. On child abuse more generally, see Carol-Ann Hooper, 'Child Sexual Abuse and the Regulation of Women: Variations on a Theme', in Carol Smart, ed., *Regulating Womanhood: Historical Essays on Marriage, Motherhood, and Sexuality* (London and

New York: Routledge, 1992), 53–77; Lela Costin, Howard Karger, and David Stoesz, *The Politics of Child Abuse in America* (New York: Oxford University Press, 1996).

23. For example, I found only one case of a male victim noted in the case law. Although it appears under incest cases, the charge was committing an act of gross indecency. An appeal was granted to the accused since he was convicted only on the testimony of the male 'accomplice' or victim. *R. v. Roynton* (1935), O.W.N. 11 (1934). Current research confirms the predominance of the sexual abuse of girls.

24. Fraad, 'At Home with Incest', 22.

25. This is based on 217 cases between 1858 and 1938. Marie-Aimée Cliche, 'Un secret bien gardé: L'inceste dans la société traditionnelle québécoise, 1858–1938', *Revue d'histoire amérique française* 50, 2 (automne 1996): 211.

26. Dorothy Chunn, 'Secrets and Lies: The Criminalization of Incest and the (Re)formation of the "Private" in British Columbia, Canada, 1890–1940', unpublished paper. My thanks to Dorothy for allowing me to read this work before publication.

27. *St Catharines Standard*, 6 Mar. 1923. The defendant was found not guilty.

28. AO, RG 4-392 (Attorney General: Criminal Assize Indictments), box 122, Perth County, 1929.

29. AO, RG 22-392, box 85, Lincoln County, 1895; box 85a, Lincoln County, 1902.

30. Ibid., box 167, Welland County, 1923; *St Catharines Standard*, 6 Mar. 1923.

31. AO, RG 22-392, box 167, Welland County, 1923. 'These people' would apply to the whole family, but clearly he was arguing for the father's respectability.

32. Moreover, the mother was quizzed on whether her daughter had a 'beau coming around', probably to cast doubt on the daughter's virginity. Ibid., box 26, Carleton County, 1927.

33. Ibid., box 56, Hastings County, 1909.

34. Karen Dubinsky gives one good example in *Improper Advances*, 60, for a carnal knowledge case involving a common-law stepfather. This did not come out in as many incest cases in this period, but it clearly was a subtext in other legal and medical commentary.

35. AO, RG 22-393, box 124, Peterborough County, 1913.

36. AO, RG 22-392, box 56, Hastings County, 1909. The lack of understanding by judges that incest may not leave 'visible' scars remains a problem in contemporary cases. See Judy Steed, *Our Little Secret: Confronting Child Sexual Abuse in Canada* (Toronto: Random House Canada, 1994), 201.

37. AO, RG 22-392, box 124, Peterborough County, 1923.

38. Ibid., box 258, York County, 1895. The father was found not guilty on charges against the older sister but guilty on the charge of rape against the younger one, presumably because the case was subsequently tried without a jury.

39. Ibid., box 143 and box 144, Stormont and Dundas Counties, 1890 and 1892; *Cornwall Freeholder*, 11 Mar. 1892.

40. This is also true of carnal knowledge cases. See AO, RG 22-392, box 5, Algoma.

41. Because Karen Dubinsky has covered this case in some detail, I have not. See Dubinsky, *Improper Advances*, 60–1.

42. AO, RG 22-5870, York County Court Judges Criminal Court (hereafter CCJCC), file 74–34 (1934).

43. *Bergeron v. the King*, 56 C.C.C. 62 (1930). The defence lawyers often called the girls 'accomplices', though the higher court rejected this language.

44. *Rex v. Pegelo*, 62 C.C.C. 78 (1934); *Rex v. Guilbault*, 72 C.C.C. 254 (1939). While these appeals failed, it is interesting that lawyers were still using these well-worn arguments. It is also possible that such arguments also swayed juries in lower courts.

45. AO, RG 22-5871, York County General Sessions (GS), file 34-39 (1939).

46. AO, RG 22-5870, CCJCC, 110-33 (1933). Since her statement was not in the file, we only have his interpretations for the court, which was designed to secure his acquittal.

47. AO, RG 22-5871, GS, file 35-31 (1931).
48. AO, Ontario Training School for Girls (OTSG) case file 275, 1930s.
49. AO, RG 22-5870, CCJCC, file 4-31 (1931).
50. AO, RG 22-5871, file 34-39 (1939). The father was also convicted of assault causing bodily harm.
51. AO, OTSG case file 75, 1930s.
52. AO, OTSG case file 275, 1930s.
53. AO, OTSG case file 1088, early 1940s.
54. AO, OTSG case file 250, 1930s.
55. Joan Sangster, 'Incarcerating "Bad Girls": The Regulation of Sexuality through the Female Refuges Act in Ontario, 1920–45', *Journal of the History of Sexuality* 7, 2 (Oct. 1996): 267–8.
56. AO, OTSG case files 1531 and 365, 1940s.
57. AO, OTSG case file 835, 1940s; emphasis added.
58. Ibid.
59. AO, RG 22-292, box 258, York County, 1892.
60. *St Catharines Standard*, 6 Mar. 1923.
61. AO, RG 22-392, box 143, 144, Stormont County, 1890, 1892.
62. AO, OTSG case file 853, 1940s.
63. The first two were articulated even within one file by different experts. See AO, OTSG case file 225, 1930s, and the latter, file 1651, 1950s.
64. AO, OTSG case files 835 and 225, 1940s, 1930s.
65. For example, see G. Devereux, 'Social and Cultural Implications of Incest Among the Mohave Indians', *Psychoanalytic Quarterly* 8 (Oct. 1939): 510–33.
66. L.S. Penrose, 'A Contribution to the Genetic Study of Mental Deficiency', *British Medical Journal* 1 (Jan. 1934): 10–11.
67. Eleanor Pavenstedt, 'Discussion' for Irving Kaufman, Alice Peck, and Consuelo Tagiuri, 'The Family Constellation and Overt Incestuous Relations between Father and Daughter', *American Journal of Orthopsychiatry* (Apr. 1954): 278.
68. Eva Karpinski and Paul Sloane, 'Incest: Effects on Participants', *American Journal of Orthopsychiatry* 12 (Oct. 1942): 666–73.
69. Ibid., 666.
70. L. Bender and A. Blau, 'The Reaction of Children to Sexual Relations with Adults', *Journal of American Orthopsychiatry* 7 (1937): 500–18.
71. It is important to note that this study was then drawn on by other researchers. J. Butler Tompkins, 'Penis Envy and Incest: A Case Report', *Psychoanalytic Review* (July 1940): 324.
72. Kaufman, Peck, and Tagiuri, 'The Family Constellation and Overt Incestuous Relations', 268.
73. Ibid., 271, 275.
74. Gordon, *Heroes of Their Own Lives*, 208.
75. Russell, *The Secret Trauma*, 5–8. See also Judith Herman, *Father-Daughter Incest* (Cambridge, Mass.: Harvard University Press, 1981).
76. Janet Liebman Jacobs, 'Reassessing Mother Blame in Incest', *Signs* 15, 3 (1990): 500–15. Jacobs explains the tendency for victims themselves to engage in mother-blaming.
77. Costin et al., *The Politics of Child Abuse*, 99. The authors noted other causes, such as disillusionment with Juvenile Courts, which would have been less important in Ontario, as widespread Juvenile Courts came somewhat later. See also Barbara Nelson, *Making an Issue of Child Abuse: Political Agenda Setting for Social Problems* (Chicago: University of Chicago Press, 1994), 129. For brief comment on Britain, see George Behlmer, *Child Abuse and Moral Reform in England, 1870–1920* (Stanford, Calif.: Stanford University Press, 1982), 225. On the negative influence of psychiatric thinking, see Pleck, *Domestic Tyranny*, 156–7.

78. Peterborough CAS Records, Minute Books, 9 Nov. 1926.
79. Ibid., Annual Report of the Superintendent, 27 Nov. 1928.
80. Canada, *Hansard*, 12 Feb. 1954, Mr Nowlan, 2037.
81. Ibid., Mr Diefenbaker, 2038.
82. Ibid., Mr Garson, 2038.
83. Canada, *Statutes of Canada*, 1954, Criminal Code, s. 131.
84. Recently, some have argued that the 'myth of classlessness' about abuse has been promoted to dissociate anti-abuse programs from more unpopular anti-poverty ones. As a result, material deprivation and the social causes of abuse are downplayed in favour of a 'medical' model of individual disease or deviance. See Nelson, *Child Abuse as Social Problem*, 13–14; Costin et al., *The Politics of Child Abuse*.
85. Bell, *Interrogating Incest*, 95.

Mother

Emily Carr

To show Mother I must picture Father, because Mother was Father's reflection—smooth, liquid reflecting of definite, steel-cold reality.

Our childhood was ruled by Father's unbendable iron will, the obeying of which would have been intolerable but for Mother's patient polishing of its dull metal so that it shone and reflected the beauty of orderliness that was in all Father's ways, a beauty you had to admire, for, in spite of Father's severity and his overbearing omnipotence, you had to admit the justice even in his dictatorial bluster. But somehow Mother's reflecting was stronger than Father's reality, for, after her death, it lived on in our memories and strengthened, while Father's tyrannical reality shrivelled up and was submerged under our own development.

Father looked taller than he really was because he was so straight. Mother was small-made and frail. Our oldest sister was like Father; she helped Mother raise us and finished our upbringing when Mother died.

I was twelve when Mother died—the raw, green Victoria age, twelve years old.

The routine of our childhood home ran with mechanical precision. Father was ultra-English, a straight, stern autocrat. No one ever dreamt of crossing his will. Mother loved him and obeyed because it was her loyal pleasure to do so. We children *had* to obey from both fear and reverence.

I heard a lady say to Mother, 'Isn't it difficult, Mrs Carr, to discipline our babies when their fathers spoil them so?'

My mother replied, 'My husband takes no notice of mine till they are old enough to run round after him. He then recognizes them as human beings and as his children, accepts their adoration. You know how little tots worship big, strong men!'

The other mother nodded and my mother continued, 'Each of my children in turn my husband makes his special favourite when they come to this man-adoring age. When this child shows signs of having a will of its own he returns it to the nursery and raises the next youngest to favour. This one,' she put her hand on me, 'has overdrawn her share of favouritism because there was no little sister to step into her shoes. Our small son is much younger and very delicate.'

[. . .]

Father insisted that I be at his heels every moment that he was at home. I helped him in the garden, popping the bulbs into holes that he dug, holding the strips of cloth and tacks while he trained Isabella. I walked nearly all the way to town with him every morning. He let me snuggle under his arm and sleep during the long Presbyterian sermons. I held his hand during the walk to and from church. This all seemed to me fine until I began to think for myself—then I saw that I was being used as a soother for Father's tantrums; like a bone to a dog, I was being flung to quiet Father's temper. When he was extra cranky I was taken into town by my big sister and left at Father's wholesale warehouse to walk home with him because my chatter soothed him. I resented this and began to question why Father should act as if he was God. Why should people dance after him and let him think he was? I decided disciplining would be good for Father and I made up my mind to cross his will sometimes. At first he laughed, trying to coax the waywardness out of me, but when he saw I was serious his fury rose against me. He turned and was harder on me than any of the others. His soul was so bitter that he was even sometimes cruel to me.

'Mother,' I begged, 'need I be sent to town any more to walk home with Father?'

Mother looked at me hard. 'Child,' she cried, 'what ails you? You have always loved to be with your father. He adores you. What is the matter?'

'He is cross, he thinks he is as important as God.'

Mother looked supremely shocked; she had brought her family up under the English tradition that the men of a woman's family were created to be worshipped. My insurrection pained her. She was as troubled as a hen that has hatched a duck. She wanted to question me but her loyalty to Father forbade. [. . .]

After Father and Mother died my big sister ruled; she was stern like Father. She was twenty years older than the youngest of us. Our family had a wide gap near the top where three brothers had died, so there was Mother's big family of two grown-up girls and her little family of three small girls and a boy. The second of the big sisters married. The biggest sister owned everything and us too when Father died.

Lizzie and Alice were easy children and good. Lizzie was very religious. Alice was patient and took the way of least resistance always. Dick too was good enough, but I was rebellious. Little Dick and I got the riding whip every day. It was a swishy whip and cut and curled around our black stockinged legs very hurtfully.

The most particular sin for which we were whipped was called insubordination. Most always it arose from the same cause—remittance men, or remittance men's wives. Canada was infested at that time by Old Country younger sons and ne'er-do-wells, people who had been shipped to Canada on a one-way ticket. These people lived on small remittances received from home. They were too lazy and too incompetent to work, stuck up, indolent, considering it beneath their dignity to earn but not beneath their dignity to take all a Canadian was willing to hand out.

My two elder sisters were born in England. The one who ruled us felt very much 'first born' in the English way, feeling herself better than the rest of us because she was oldest. She was proud of being top. She listened to all the hard-luck stories of the remittance people and said, 'I too was born in England.' She sympathized with their homesickness and filled our home with these people.

Dick and I hated the intruders. Lizzie and Alice resented them too, but quietly. My sister tried to compel my brother and me by means of the riding whip.

A couple called Piddington sat on us for six months. The wife was a hypochondriac and exploited ill-health. The man was an idle loafer and a cruel bully. Anger at his impertinence and sponging kept the riding whip actively busy on our young legs. Things came to a climax when we rented a seaside cottage in the holidays. The man took a party of boys and girls out in the boat. The sea was rough. I asked to be put ashore. Seeing my green face the man shipped his oars and cried delightedly, 'We'll make the kid seasick.' He rocked the boat back and forth till he succeeded. I was shamed before all the boys and girls. He knew, too, how it infuriated me to be called 'kid' by him.

'You are not a gentleman anyway!' I cried. 'You are a sponger and a bully!'

Purple with rage the man pulled ashore and rushed to his wife saying, 'The kid has insulted me!'

For insulting a guest in her house my sister thrashed me till I fainted; but I refused to apologize, and the bully and I went round glowering at each other. I said to my sister, 'I am almost sixteen now and the next time you thrash me I shall strike back.' That was my last whipping.

Dick went East to school. The whip dangled idle on the hall peg, except after school and on Saturdays when I took it out as an ornament and went galloping over the country on old Johnny.

Johnny had been a circus pony. He knew a lot. When he galloped me beyond the town and over the highway till all houses and fences were passed, he would saunter, stopping now and then to sniff the roadside bushes as if considering. Suddenly he would nose into the greenery finding a trail no one else could see, pressing forward so hard that the bushes parted, caressing him and me as we passed, and closing behind us shutting us from every 'towny' thing. Johnny pressed and pressed till we were hidden from seeing, noise and people. When we came to some mossy little clearing where soft shade-growing grass grew Johnny stopped with a satisfied sigh. I let down his bridle and we nibbled, he on the grass, I at the deep sacred beauty of Canada's still woods. Maybe after all I owe a 'thank you' to the remittance ones and to the riding whip for driving me out into the woods. Certainly I do to old Johnny for finding the deep lovely places that were the very foundation on which my work as a painter was to be built.

[1946]

Boys Will Be Men, Girls Will Be Mothers: The Legal Regulation of Childhood in Toronto and Vancouver

Dorothy E. Chunn

Introduction

During the past three decades, academics have produced a substantial body of research and writing about children premised on the view that childhood is an historical construct whose meaning and expression are worked out within the constraints of a particular structural-cultural context (Aries 1962; Donzelot 1980; Fitz 1981a, 1981b; Parr 1982; Rooke and Schnell 1982, 1983; Sutherland 1976). It is assumed, moreover, that conceptualizations of childhood are integrally tied to those of the family and sexuality (Foucault 1980; Weeks 1981, 1986). From this relativistic perspective, then, childhood is not a biological given, but rather the product of social interactions within a particular power structure. Consequently, the construction of childhood is the outcome of 'negotiation, struggle and human agency' (Weeks 1986, p. 25), and both reflects and sustains certain power relations between adults and children (Foucault 1980, pp. 94–8).

Since the eighteenth century, the conceptualization of childhood encapsulated in the middle-class or bourgeois family model, has become increasingly dominant across the entire population in Western nations. (Aries 1962; Barrett and McIntosh 1982; Donzelot 1980; Foucault 1980; Poster 1978; Thorne and Yalom 1982; Zaretsky 1976, 1982, 1986). More and more, children were defined as subordinate to and dependent upon adults. Thus while, on the one hand, they were subject to stringent monitoring and censure for engaging in adult pastimes, including sex, at the same time they were protected from the corrupting influence of predatory adults (Donzelot 1980; Fitz 1981a, 1981b; Foucault 1980; Muncie 1981). Similarly, men and women who embraced family forms and/or sexual practices outside the parameters of institutionalized respectability were considered deviant and sanctioned according to the perceived gravity of their behavioural perversity.

However, prevailing conceptions of childhood, family, and sexuality have not remained static throughout this period. On the contrary, there were substantial shifts in the precise content of these constructions during periods of crisis—moral, socio-economic, political, legal—when rapid social change threatened the status quo. These challenges to the existing order generated fierce debate and reformulation of dominant beliefs about the nature of childhood, marriage, and female sexuality, which markedly altered the relationships between adults and children, men and women, in both the public and private familial spheres.

One such period of social crisis and reorganization, extending roughly from the late nineteenth century to the early 1940s, marked the transition from laissez-faire to welfare state in Western countries, including Canada (Brown and Cook 1974; Cross and Kealey 1983; Garland 1985; Wiebe 1967). Against the backdrop of an emergent corporate capitalism, rapid urbanization and the implementation of mass democracy, middle-class fears about the disintegration of white civilization crystallized around issues related to marriage, family, and sexuality and fuelled moral/social reform movements aimed at inculcating the norms associated with the bourgeois family model among deviant populations (Bacchi 1983; Bland 1986; Epstein 1983; Kinsman 1987; Snell 1983; Walkowitz 1982). Although they emphasized educational strategies, reformers had no compunction about using legal coercion; the latter comprised a spate of legislation regulating the behaviour of adults and children both inside and outside the family, much of which was administered by the new, 'socialized' juvenile and family courts. As a result, by World War II there was virtually universal acceptance of, if not adherence to, middle-class standards of family life in all Western nations (Poster 1978; Zaretsky 1976, 1982, 1986).

This paper examines the growing hegemony of the bourgeois family pattern among Canadian working classes that accompanied the development of a welfare state and focuses on the legal institutionalization and regulation of childhood and sexuality in Ontario and British Columbia, particularly during the interwar years. The discussion centres on similarities and differences between the provinces with respect to two major issues: first, the enactment of criminal and quasicriminal legislation, ostensibly universal in application but directed primarily at poor children and the adults responsible for them, to force compliance with middle-class standards of morality and family life; and, second, the administration of many such statutes through the Toronto and Vancouver Juvenile Courts. I argue that legal coercion of those who flouted bourgeois norms of childhood and sexuality did effectively reproduce the desired social class and gender relations among a certain proportion of the recalcitrant.

Methodological Note

The common objective of historical researchers—reconstructing the past as systematically and accurately as possible—requires the location of as many disparate sources as possible to pre-empt any tendencies to generalize beyond the facts, force data to suppose preconceived theories, or simply reproduce the ideology of a particular individual or group. In researching the paper, my major sources of information were the detailed annual reports of the Toronto Family Court (TFC) supplemented by those I could locate of the Ontario Inspector of Legal Offices and the Vancouver Juvenile Court (VJC); newspaper articles; and other relevant archival materials. Although the primary data collected were arguably extensive and varied enough to be used with confidence, the numerous and well-documented pitfalls inherent in using historical materials must be underscored.

First of all, gaps are almost always a major problem and the largest one in my study stems from a lack of information reflecting the perspective of those who were the main targets of the reforms described; that is, a certain proportion of families among the working and dependent poor. Their voices are heard only obliquely, if at all. Other blanks in the research data on Ontario are the result of deliberate destruction of documents through weeding and the appropriation of files by provincial government officials when they left office.

A second weakness endemic to historical data is the unreliability and paucity of statistics. Although there is a complete set of Toronto Family Court Reports between 1920 and 1945, the emphasis on systematic record-keeping was only developing during the interwar years. Thus, the bases of statistical compilations in the reports, and changes therein, are unknown, making comparisons from year to year and/or with other jurisdictions difficult, if not impossible. Moreover, it cannot be assumed that statistical data on Toronto and Vancouver can be generalized, since neither city was representative of its province.

Notwithstanding these problems, my analysis of the available data revealed that the legal regulation of childhood in Ontario and British Columbia to 1945 followed the same general developmental trajectory as researchers in other jurisdictions have discovered. For this reason, it seemed reasonable to conclude that enough information was compiled from various sources to provide a reliable account of the Canadian experience.

Childhood, Sexuality, and the Law

To begin that account, it is necessary to briefly discuss the context wherein legislation was enacted in late nineteenth- and turn-of-the-century Canada that aimed to enforce the norms of childhood and sexuality associated with the bourgeois family model among those who did not voluntarily comply with them. As in other Western market societies, the social dislocation and upheaval during that period stemming from large-scale structural change—economic, political, demographic—had a technocratic resolution in the form of an emergent welfare state (Finkel 1977; Guest 1980; Moscovitch and Albert 1987). The general trajectory of development was an uneven one, however. While all provinces were moving in the same direction, there were marked regional differences related to the history of settlement and racial/ethnic composition of the population; the relative political strength of women and the working class, of maternal feminism and socialism; and the rate and character of economic expansion.

Thus, although both Ontario (Palmer 1983; Schull 1978) and British Columbia (McDonald 1981, 1986) became increasingly industrial and urban prior to World War II, with Toronto and Vancouver emerging as major centres, these processes were shaped by factors unique to each province.[1] The former had a long history of settlement; a strong Tory tradition extending through the 1920s and early 1930s; and, a pattern of all-white immigration (Oliver 1977). In contrast, British Columbia was sparsely populated until the railroad link was completed in 1885; had a relatively influential feminist and socialist presence in political life during the inter-war years; and had an entrenched policy of overt racism directed at the physically distinct Asian population (Roy 1981; Ward 1981). These regional disparities generated similar yet somewhat different responses when concern about the future of society erupted during the 1880s in Ontario and after 1900 in British Columbia.

Like their counterparts in other jurisdictions, urban, middle-class English-Canadians attributed the seemingly imminent disintegration of social order to a crisis of the family, reflected in rising rates of divorce, separation and desertion, juvenile crime, and rampant immorality (Houston 1982; Morrison 1976; Snell 1983; Sutherland 1976). Pathological behaviour was considered to be the inevitable outcome when one or more members of a family deviated from the norms governing their biologically prescribed roles within the domestic unit. With respect to adult family members, this meant that men and women were not fulfilling their 'natural' obligations as breadwinners and full-time homemakers respectively and/or that they were engaging in, condoning or contributing to acts, such as adultery and drunkenness, that flouted acceptable moral standards. So far as children were concerned, any independent, adult-like behaviour was viewed as a violation of their natural status as dependents, which would preclude the careful preparation they required for their future roles as husbands/fathers and wives/mothers.

Of course, the belief that the true state of childhood was one of dependency requiring moral and physical care within a biological or surrogate nuclear family unit had informed middle-class child-rearing practices and reform initiatives from the eighteenth century onward (Fitz 1981b, pp. 37, 39; see also Donzelot 1980; Foucault 1980; Rooke and Schnell 1983). Reformers spearheaded campaigns to prevent children from working (e.g., factory legislation); to implement systematic sex-specific schooling for boys and girls; to regulate the leisure activities of youth; and to separate children from adults in the legal sphere (ibid, pp. 31, 35; see also Donzelot 1980; Foucault 1980; Gillis 1975; Muncie 1981).

Nonetheless, by the late nineteenth century, although many middle-class children experienced childhood as a stage of dependency, most of their working-class counterparts did not. Despite factory acts, many children continued to labour in the unregulated areas of agriculture, domestic service, mining, retail shops, and street trading. Schooling remained under parental control and was thus generally spasmodic and dependent upon the exigencies of the family economy. The leisure time of working-class youth was largely free from adult supervision and frequently centred on street activities (Gillis 1975; Muncie 1981). The progressive differentiation between children and adults as legal subjects in relation to property rights, for example, had little importance for those with no assets. The establishment of separate court hearings for children and the creation of distinct segregative institutions (e.g., reform and industrial schools) within the criminal justice system still left children subject to adult procedures and sanctions (Fitz 1981a, 1981b).

Thus, the participants in the social/moral reform movement that marked the beginning of the transition from laissez-faire to welfare state did not invent the conceptions of childhood and sexuality associated with the bourgeois family model.

Rather, they reformulated and popularized them among the working classes. During the late nineteenth century, under the influence of romantics like Froebel, childhood acquired a dualistic character. It was a period of innocence, 'easily corrupted'; of 'incipient waywardness' requiring control; of dependence, which made the young more malleable but also protected them from the 'brutalities of the adult world'; and, of subordination owed by youth to 'its natural superiors' (Fitz 1981b, p. 39; see also Muncie 1981; Rothman 1980; Sutherland 1976). All children were now perceived to be simultaneously innocent and evil; in danger but also dangerous (Fitz 1981b, pp. 37, 38; see also Donzelot 1980, pp. 82, 96; May 1973; Platt 1969).

After the turn of the century, particularly during the interwar years, these beliefs were reshaped again by knowledge produced and disseminated by a burgeoning cadre of experts in the social and mental sciences. By the 1940s, 'normal' childhood, sexuality, and family life were the ones created by numerous child psychologists and psychiatrists like G. Stanley Hall, William Healey, John Watson, and Sigmund Freud (Donzelot 1980; Miller 1982; Muncie 1981, p. 20; Rothman 1980, pp. 207–8, 211–12; Strong-Boag 1982); sexologists such as Havelock Ellis (Weeks 1981, 1986); and sociologists (Lasch 1979). Consequently, good mothering, parenthood, marital sex were not simply a matter of following biological instinct: they were activities requiring the most specialized knowledge and training (ibid.).

Once childhood had been defined as a period of institutionalized dependency consisting of distinct and complex psycho-sexual stages (e. g., adolescence) and integrally linked to a particular type of family, English-Canadian child-savers, like their counterparts in other market societies, confronted the challenge of developing strategies to prevent young people from engaging in behaviours that were the prerogative of adults. Allowing immature young people freedom from control could only have disastrous consequences in the form of increased crime and sexual immorality. As elsewhere, reformers in Ontario and British Columbia preferred educational policies and programs for inculcating middle-class norms. At the same time, they also believed in coercion to virtue when necessary and pushed successfully for the enactment of laws regulating the activities of children and their relations with adults, both inside and outside the family. Because of the multitiered nature of the Canadian state, however, Ottawa, the provinces and local governments were all empowered to pass such legislation. While federal statutes had national scope, provincial laws, and municipal by-laws were restricted in jurisdiction and lacking in uniformity.

Nonetheless, between 1880 and 1930, reform initiatives contributed to the legal codification of childhood as a period of institutionalized dependency and, especially in relation to girls, pre-sexuality. The 1892 Criminal Code established the basis of an extremely comprehensive and wide-ranging category of offences aimed at protecting young women from male sexual predators (Snell 1983, p. 118). Anxiety about prostitution was reflected in clauses prohibiting the procuring of underage females and the operation of brothels, which were considerably expanded in 1913 at the height of the 'white slavery' panic (McLaren J.P.S. 1986; Nilsen 1980; Rotenberg 1974). Seduction and abduction clauses in the Code which applied both to pimps and to employers (although significantly not to those who hired women domestics) were strengthened in 1900, when the minimum legal age for carnal knowledge of a young woman was raised from sixteen to eighteen (Leslie 1974; Snell 1983, p. 121). Legislation directed primarily at the control of young women's sexual behaviour outside the family included statutes governing venereal disease, adopted by Ontario (Dymond 1923), British Columbia (MacGill 1939, p. 39), and other provinces, as well as the 1924 revision of the Juvenile Delinquents Act which added 'sexual immorality' to the definition of juvenile delinquent (Théoret 1987).

Although not directly concerned with sexuality, the spate of laws that institutionalized childhood as a period of forced dependency were clearly premised on the assumption that boys and girls are pre-sexual. From the late nineteenth century, provincial statutes and municipal by-laws were enacted and extended to prohibit child labour altogether in factories, mines, shops, and street trades and to closely regulate and protect working youth, especially women, who would ultimately marry and give up paid employment (Houston 1982; MacGill 1939; Strong-Boag 1982; Ursel 1986). Although the children excluded from the paid labour force did not necessarily show up at school, compulsory attendance laws reduced parental powers by forcing them to surrender their children to a systematic regime of full-time education to a set age and sanctioning them and/or their truant offspring if they did not comply (Dunn 1980; Sutherland 1976).

Leisure activities of children and youth, particularly among the working classes, were also subject to legal regulation. The behaviour of the years when not at school or work was circumscribed by provincial and municipal curfews, by vagrancy and loitering laws and by-laws restricting the time that young people could legitimately be on the streets; by censorship of films and reading materials; by policing of public places of entertainment such as pool and dance halls; and by prohibitions on gambling, drinking, and smoking (Jones and Rutman 1981; Sutherland 1976). Moreover, because the definition of delinquency in the federal Juvenile Delinquents Act (JDA) covered both status and criminal offences, the statute could be, and was, used to sanction children for engaging in many of the same activities.

Intra-familial relations were also regulated. Reformers from the 1880s onward were concerned about what they perceived to be a growing threat to marriage evidenced by rising divorce rates, and mobilized to defend the sanctity of marriage. Stringent Criminal Code provisions aimed at restricting sexual relations to heterosexual, monogamous marriage, and to procreation. Thus, bigamy, polygamy, some forms of extra-legal cohabitation and incest were banned, although the latter was not explicitly prohibited between step-parents and step-children (Snell 1983, pp. 118–20). Abortion and birth control were also criminalized in the late nineteenth century (McLaren 1978; McLaren and McLaren 1986). Thirty years later, concern about illegitimacy in the aftermath of war stimulated the enactment of legislation governing unmarried parenthood in Ontario (1921), British Columbia (1922), and other provinces as well as the 'sexual immorality' clause of the JDA mentioned above. Although many reformers linked illegitimate babies to mentally unfit mothers, only in BC (1933) and Alberta (1928) were they successful in obtaining laws allowing the sterilization of the mentally defective. Ironically, maternal feminists like Helen Gregory MacGill, a Vancouver Juvenile Court judge between 1917 and 1945, were amongst the strongest proponents of such statutes (MacGill 1939; McLaren A. 1986).

Reform initiatives centred on enforcing the obligation of the parents to raise children in accordance with middle-class norms. Provincial desertion, child protection, and illegitimacy statutes, as well as various Criminal Code sections, were designed to make parents, primarily fathers, maintain their dependants, both physically, and morally. In addition, under the JDA parents were liable to prosecution if they contributed to the delinquency or truancy of their off-spring through indifference or moral turpitude. Ultimately, mothers and fathers who failed to mend their ways could lose their children. At the same time, provincial legislation governing 'incorrigibility' allowed parents to place 'uncontrollable' children in Training and Industrial Schools (MacGill 1939).

Viewed as a whole, the legislation governing relations between adults and children in public and private sites not only institutionalized childhood as a 'natural' period of dependency but also made it an increasingly lengthy stage in the life cycle. The trend from the late nineteenth century onward was to raise the minimum age at which young people could leave school and enter the workforce, engage in sexual relations, exercise citizenship rights, and be held criminally responsible. Moreover, these minimums were not uniform; they often differed by type of activity, gender, and locale. For example, by 1940, youths in both Ontario and British Columbia were required to attend school to age fifteen, at which point they could legally take up paid employment and live away from home. Yet they could not vote and were still juveniles under the criminal law. Indeed, following a 1923 amendment to the JDA that gave the provinces some flexibility in setting the age limit for juveniles, Ontario retained the cut-off point at sixteen while British Columbia raised it to eighteen (MacGill, 1939). Thus, a youth might have been self-supporting for one to three years but still be categorized and treated as a juvenile. This had an enormous effect on how the norms of childhood and sexuality were enforced in different provinces.

Childhood, Sexuality, and Socialized Courts

In Canada, as in other jurisdictions, demands for implementation and refinement of legislation aimed at upholding the norms of childhood and heterosexual marriage were accompanied by demands for new enforcement mechanisms. The traditional police courts, reformers argued, were totally inappropriate vehicles for resolving domestic problems because they were criminal courts premised on an adversarial model of justice with open hearings and adherence to due process and were administered either by lawyer-judges or by personnel with some legal training. What was required were socialized tribunals that would hold private hearings, employ inquisitorial procedures, and use primarily 'expert' workers—social workers, probation officers—who could diagnose, treat, and rehabilitate deficient families.

Partly as a result of reform pressure, juvenile courts were established in several provinces prior to World War I, and family courts in Ontario during the interwar years. The new tribunals blurred the boundaries between the social and legal, civil, and criminal spheres. Between 1920 and 1945, the personnel and operations of socialized courts in many urban centres were increasingly separated from the regular legal system and professionalized, most extensively in Toronto and less so in

Vancouver, where the Juvenile Court remained a part-time enterprise. Nonetheless, by World War II the foundations were in place of a private, technocratic justice system for adjudicating domestic cases (Chunn, 1988).

The way juvenile and family court workers carried out their work clearly reflected adherence to prevailing assumptions about childhood, sexuality, and family. The long-term goal was to prepare delinquent and/or neglected boys and girls to assume their places as working-class husbands/fathers and wives/mothers in legal marriage relationships, who would adhere to middle-class standards of child-rearing and family life. In processing delinquency cases, their immediate objective was to stop the offenders from behaving in an unchild-like manner; with neglect cases, to protect children at risk of becoming delinquent. It was therefore necessary to repair both the individual and environmental deficiencies which brought youthful deviants, or potential deviants, before the court. Thus, children appeared in juvenile court for two major reasons: either they had directly threatened middle-class property and morality by committing thefts, engaging in premarital sex, and other unchild-like behavior; or they were potentially threatening because adults, particularly parents, were not adhering to appropriate child-rearing practices.

Over time, however, this distinction between neglected and delinquent youth became more and more nebulous. Moreover, because court workers subscribed to the belief that men and women have inherently different characters, they explained and treated delinquency and neglect differentially along gender lines. For example, boys were clearly considered more directly menacing to society than girls. They were eight or nine times more likely to be charged with delinquency than young women during the interwar years in Toronto; a ratio which prevailed generally in Ontario's juvenile courts during that period (Ontario Inspector of Legal Offices (ILO), 1931–37) and continues to the present day. In contrast, statistics for neglect cases under the Children's Protection Act show near parity in the numbers of boys and girls brought to court.

The differences between boys and girls charged with delinquency become even more striking when the offences that led to formal court hearings are analyzed. With the former, property violations constituted the major reason for a court appearance while the latter were much more likely to find themselves before the judge for status/morality infractions; in Toronto, at least 50 per cent of delinquency charges against boys involved property violations and 40 per cent of charges against girls involved status/morality infractions, in each year between 1920 and 1940. However, if status offences are analyzed separately and broken down into specific types, truancy stands out as the noncriminal behaviour by both boys and girls of most concern to court workers. What the statistics do not reveal is the extent to which gender considerations influenced charging decisions. Contemporary studies of juvenile justice, for example, have revealed that when young women and men commit both criminal and status violations, the women are much more likely to be charged with sexual offences (Chesney-Lind 1986; Smart 1985; Smart and Smart 1978). It may therefore be reasonable to assume that some of the girls brought before the early juvenile courts for sexual promiscuity had also committed property violations that were ignored by the authorities.

Indeed, the work of court personnel was clearly influenced by an assumption of natural differences between men and women. Boys were considered to be the aggressive, sexually explosive, and rational members of the species and girls the peaceful, sexually passive, and emotional ones. These stereotypical conceptions were reflected in sex-specific explanations of deviance which, in turn, led court workers to gender-based conclusions about what types of delinquency were most threatening. Although during the war years and early 1920s a large number of delinquents were diagnosed in terms of individual pathology—usually mental defectiveness (Sutherland 1976)—as time went on, wayward boys were viewed more and more as victims of social pathology—poor parenting, bad neighbourhood, an inappropriate peer group—and low intelligence was the explanation reserved for recidivists (TFC 1944, p. 29). Moreover, even in 1912, 75 per cent of the boys on probation to the Toronto Juvenile Court were considered 'little different from other average and mischievous boys' except for the fact that they were caught (TFC 1912, p. 12).

In contrast, girl delinquents, like their adult counterparts, have always been explained primarily in terms of psychogenetic theories, a tradition that continues today (Campbell 1981; Chesney-Lind 1986; Gavigan, 1987; Smart, 1976). Thus, women are considered to be predisposed toward deviance, and a 'bad' environment liberates this 'natural' impulse, which most often takes the form of sexual immorality:

> In the case of girl delinquents, almost without exception, it is inherited tendencies that are responsible for the girl's first mis-step. After the appetite has been created, it requires patient and careful handling to divert their thoughts and energy into other channels (TFC 1922, p. 18).

The same view of deviant women was expressed during World War II in Vancouver when there was widespread concern about the increase in unwed mothers. Poor home training, it was asserted, left girls with 'weaker inhibitions' and a desire for attention which led them to 'submit to early immoral sex relationships—one step away from professional prostitution' (*Sun* 13 Dec. 1945).

Despite their adherence to sex-specific explanations of deviance, juvenile court personnel considered immoral behaviour, exemplified by pre-marital sex, drinking, and gambling, to be a very serious matter regardless of who was involved, but for different reasons. On the one hand, immorality in boys prevented them from acquiring the discipline and good habits—thrift, deferred gratification—that they needed for their future role as family breadwinners. On the other hand, girls who ran around, stayed out late, and flouted sexual norms jeopardized their chances of pursuing the only appropriate career for women—marriage and motherhood. Thus, the general concern about truancy, noted earlier, was most likely tied to a perception of schools as major socializing agents; places where even children from deficient homes could receive the necessary education and skills to prepare them for adulthood.

Indeed, once young people left school and entered the workforce, they needed a sound moral grounding if they were to resist temptations. During the war years, Vancouver Juvenile Court workers were gravely concerned about the number of employed youth who succumbed to the lure of easy pleasures. They lamented the fact that juveniles, many of whom were transients or from families that had only recently moved to the city, were earning more than their parents had during the Depression, yet they had 'never been taught to save and [did] not know how to adjust themselves with overflowing pockets' (VJC 1943, p. 9). Inevitably, the lax control over these young men and women led to increased drinking, a 'sinister' rise in 'sexual immorality and promiscuity', evidenced by 'the pregnancy of very young girls', and the spread of venereal disease (see also VJC 1940, 1942).

How did socialized courts actually process delinquency cases? They seemed to prefer informal, out-of-court settlements, known as 'occurrences', which were effected by the Probation Department. During the interwar years, Toronto Family Court 'occurrences' increasingly outnumbered formal hearings before the judge. In 1920, for example, there were 3,400 'occurrence' interviews and 2,206 hearings of cases involving adults and children, a ratio of approximately 3 to 2. In 1945 the respective numbers were 20,283 and 3,669, a ratio of more than 6 to 1 (TFC 1920, 1945). Although the Vancouver data are scanty, they indicate that the city's Juvenile Court also settled 'many minor juvenile offences such as . . . stealing fruit . . . breaking windows, staying out late at night contrary to the Curfew Bylaw' out-of-court (VJC 1940, p. 11).

However, whether they proceeded formally or informally, court personnel had the same range of dispositions at their disposal. The most frequent outcome of juvenile delinquency hearings in Toronto was that the cases were dropped for whatever reason; especially from the mid-1920s to the early 1930s, when at least 70 per cent of formal court cases ended with the judicial hearing (see also Ontario ILO, 1931–37). This pattern was markedly different to that in Vancouver, where the Juvenile Court was seemingly more reluctant to dispose of formal delinquency cases without assessing a penalty, dropping no more than 21 per cent of delinquency cases each year in the early 1940s (VJC 1940, 1942, 1943).

The most popular sentence in Vancouver and the second most popular in Toronto was probation, which placed not only the delinquent child but also his/her entire family under surveillance. Not that court personnel considered their monitoring activities as in any way oppressive for the families involved. On the contrary, they viewed this aspect of probation as positive and in the best interests of their clients. As one court worker put it:

> . . . it is interesting to note that by regular supervision of the home by one of the Court Officers a house divided against itself has been united and conditions made safe under which the child could live (TFC 1922, p. 16).

Essentially, probation required parents to mend their ways if, as in many cases, they were viewed as major contributors to their children's delinquency. As for the delinquents, they were expected to embrace the norms of childhood exemplified by regular school and church attendance and participation in wholesome leisure activities such as Boy Scouts or Girl Guides. From the Court's perspective, the success of a probationer could be measured in terms of conformity to middle-class standards of hygiene, education, and morality, as the following comment illustrates.

His improved home condition was reflected in his personal appearance. Nowadays his clothes are always neat and tidy, and he is always clean. The boy looks forward to reporting every week and takes the greatest pride in having an excellent report from his teacher and relatives, who have given so much assistance in making a real boy of him (TFC 1924).

Perhaps because of the higher juvenile age in British Columbia, Vancouver probation officers monitored sites outside the family as well as the homes of probationers. There were regular visits to boarding homes where young workers lived and to places of public entertainment. While this aspect of the Court's work clearly predated the war, it was pursued more vigorously in the early 1940s:

Our Probation Officers patrol bowling alleys, poolrooms, beer-parlours, dance-halls, theatres, etc., and give advice and help when needed (VJC 1943; see also 1942, p. 9).

Considering that the Court had a probation staff of only four people during this period, the amount of supervision carried out was quite remarkable.

Ultimately, if a delinquent did not respond to community treatment and continued to steal, run away, or go joy-riding, the juvenile courts would commit him/her to institutional care, often using the 'incorrigibility' legislation. Only a very small proportion of juveniles were sent away. Nonetheless, institutional sentences were indeterminate and, in Vancouver at least, when industrial school superintendents wanted to release an inmate, they could not do so without the signatures of both the provincial superintendent of child welfare and the juvenile court judge. Moreover, the latter could return 'unsatisfactory probationers to the school for further training' (VJC 1943). Again, this does not reflect any malevolence on the part of personnel working in socialized courts. On the contrary, industrial schools, and the newer training schools established in Ontario during the interwar years, were viewed as excellent homes for rehabilitating the most hard-core delinquents; not, in any sense, like prisons (TFC 1934, p. 21).

So far as the disposition of neglected children was concerned, juvenile courts tended to drop relatively few such cases. Seemingly, there was an assumption that child welfare agents would not apprehend a child without good reason. Hence, the most frequent outcome of these court hearings was that the child or children would be removed from their biological parents and placed in wardship. Until 1927 in Ontario this meant that natural parents were permanently stripped of all rights to their offspring. Thereafter, some children were made temporary wards and their parents were given a chance to redeem themselves by creating a healthy home environment. However, if they failed to do so within a certain time period, the temporary wardship would become permanent. Thus, most neglected children who came before the courts spent at least a few months in a foster home. The alternative to permanent wardship was adoption, which was not all that infrequent. Between 1920 and 1928, the Toronto Juvenile Court processed 1,542 adoption cases (TFC 1920–28).[2]

When Court dispositions of delinquent and neglected children are broken down and analyzed in terms of gender, marked differences between boys and girls become apparent. The more sociological explanations of male deviance that guided the work of probation officers and other experts were reflected in treatment plans aimed at eliminating the social pathologies in the immediate environment of male offenders. Thus, a change of neighbourhoods, friends, and schools often figured prominently in rehabilitating boy probationers. Central to the reclamation process was the inculcation of the discipline which was presumably lacking in the young man's life.

Most often, the Court felt that a boy could learn discipline while remaining with his own family if the other members were co-operative. When the home was not deemed suitable, boys were frequently sent to work on farms, where it was presumed they could acquire good work habits. Older youth were encouraged to join the armed services. For example, the 1940 Vancouver Juvenile Court Report (1940, p. 9) commented on the success of former 'black sheep' delinquents, especially those with low intelligence, who had 'found the emotional outlet [they] sought, though happily with the steadying effect of discipline' in the services. Occasionally, at least in Ontario, physical punishment was used as a disciplinary measure. During the 1930s, a small proportion of delinquent boys outside Toronto, never more than 1 per cent, were subjected to corporal punishment (Ontario ILO 1931–37).

Although girls were not spanked, those brought to Court on formal delinquency charges were seemingly penalized more stringently than their male counterparts, all things being equal. This finding is consistent with contemporary studies of juvenile justice, which have shown that young women appear in court largely for committing status offences yet they are treated as harshly as boys who have perpetrated more serious property violations (Campbell 1981; Chesney-Lind 1986; Smart and Smart 1978). Why? Because no matter what the specific charge, girls usually find themselves in court for sexual promiscuity, behaviour that contradicts their 'true' nature and has infinitely more negative consequences for their future than it does for men.

Thus, while the early juvenile courts were apparently reluctant to bring girls to court on formal delinquency charges, those who found themselves before a judge were considered more deviant than boys in the same situation. In Toronto and throughout Ontario generally, this attitude was reflected in terms of dispositions; girls were more likely to be placed under some sort of supervision (Ontario ILO 1931–37). For example, the courts dropped fewer cases involving girls than boys. Moreover, if young women were placed on probation, in some jurisdictions at least, they were subject to more frequent visits from their probation officers and remained on probation for longer than young men. In a survey conducted during the late 1930s, the Hamilton-Wentworth Family Court reported that the average period of probation for boys was eight months as opposed to two years for girls; boys received monthly home visits while girls received weekly visits, at least 'in the early stages'.[3]

With regard to institutionalization, a larger proportion of young women than men found delinquent by the courts were sentenced to industrial and training schools. Moreover, virtually none of the girls were incarcerated for perpetrating actual crimes. One study of admissions to the BC Industrial School for Girls between 1914 and 1936 showed that 84.5 per cent of the approximately six hundred committals directly involved incorrigibility and moral offences but all of the young women sentenced to the institution were sexually experienced (Matters 1984, pp. 269–70). During World War II, there was so much concern about unmarried mothers and venereal disease in Vancouver that the Juvenile Court actually incarcerated more girls than boys: 24 of 84 and 21 of 117 delinquent girls as opposed to 21 of 474 and 17 of 496 delinquent boys were sentenced to industrial schools in 1942 and 1943 respectively (VJC 1942, 1943).

Provincial sterilization legislation was also applied more frequently to women than to men. Under the BC Act, inmates of any institution diagnosed as being mentally deficient or ill, including boys and girls committed to industrial schools, could be subjected to the procedure. Although the number of juveniles who were sterilized is unknown, an analysis of 64 sterilization cases at Essondale Mental Hospital between 1933 and 1945 revealed that the typical case involved a young, unmarried mother who had been classified as mentally retarded (McLaren, 1986, p. 146). Forty-six of the 57 women sterilized were in this category; only 1 of the 7 men was unmarried. Moreover, 6 of the men were 25 or older while 33 of the women were under 25 and 3 were under 15 (ibid.).

Notwithstanding the above, the juvenile courts were more protective of girls than of boys because the former were considered much less able to avoid falling into the abyss of immorality when controls were absent. Thus, although adults who contributed to the delinquency of any minor were subject to prosecution, men who seduced young women were pursued with special vigour, particularly in wartime:

> No effort is spared by the [Probation] Department to control this type of delinquency and we are greatly assisted by the Morality Squad of the City Police Department who relentlessly track down and bring before the Police Department the men involved in such cases (VJC 1943, p. 4).

Protectionism towards young women by juvenile court workers was also reflected in the treatment of those who were considered potentially threatening. As was discussed previously, in Toronto and Ontario during the interwar years almost as many girls as boys were brought to court under the child protection legislation. When the disposition of neglected child cases is considered, the same pattern can be discerned; girls were made permanent or temporary wards proportionately as often as boys. Moreover, an analysis of Toronto Family Court adoption cases between 1921 and 1928 reveals that girls actually outnumbered boys by a ratio of three to two; 977 of the former were adopted as opposed to 615 of the latter during that period (TFC 1921–28). Overall, then, delinquent girls who appeared at juvenile court hearings seemingly received harsher dispositions from judges for less serious offences than delinquent boys. At the same time, when all girls and all boys who came to the attention of the socialized courts are compared, the former were more subject to informal and/or protectionist treatment than the latter.

Conclusions

As research on other jurisdictions has shown (Donzelot 1980; Rothman 1980; Zaretsky 1982), one of the most striking characteristics of the transition from laissez-faire to welfare state in Western market societies was the increasing hegemony of the bourgeois family pattern within all social strata. Canada was no exception to this trend. By 1945, adherence to middle-class norms of childhood, sexuality, and domestic life by the working masses was well advanced. A majority of Canadian children experienced a prolonged state of dependency during which they were excluded from the paid labour force, were closely supervised in their leisure pursuits, and attended school regularly. Most boys and girls completed elementary and at least some secondary schooling before assuming their respective, 'natural' roles as breadwinners and homemakers in legal marriage relationships.

While compliance with bourgeois standards of child-rearing and family life by nonmiddle-class populations seems to have been primarily voluntary, this paper has focused on another question; namely, the extent to which law and its enforcement through juvenile and family courts induced conformity among the non-compliant. Recidivism can be considered as a partial measurement of court success: the available statistics for the Toronto Family Court from 1920 to the early 1930s reveal that the number of repeaters each year was usually well below 25 per cent (TFC 1920–34). However, recidivism rates do not reveal how many children continued to deviate without coming to the notice of the authorities nor do they indicate shifts in law enforcement strategies.

Nonetheless, it seems safe to assume that most children processed by the juvenile and family courts did not continue the sanctioned behaviour, although the efforts of court workers may have had less to do with this than they believed. First of all, recent studies have demonstrated conclusively that age is the best cure for delinquency. While the reasons are not entirely clear, most youthful offenders do not become adult criminals (West 1981). A second important consideration is that perhaps the courts were successful in rehabilitating children from families where one or both of the parents already subscribed to the requisite middle-class standards of hygiene, education, and morality and wanted their offspring to do likewise. There is clear evidence that many fathers and mothers approached the Toronto and Vancouver Courts for assistance, particularly with uncontrollable sons and daughters. Indeed, until the late 1920s, the provincial incorrigibility legislation stipulated that only parents might initiate the proceedings that sometimes led to the institutionalization of their children; court personnel could not do so (MacGill 1939, p. 22).

And, finally, even when 'bad' parents were viewed as the cause of deviant children, massive bombardment of all family members with middle-class ideas and practices undoubtedly produced 'successful' outcomes in a certain proportion of these cases; that is to say, the reproduction of the desired social class and gender relations. The story of Bill, who was brought to the Toronto Family Court because of his membership in 'a gang of youthful bandits', illustrates how this ideological indoctrination was typically carried out. To wrest Bill away from his delinquent friends, the probation officer persuaded the family to move, enlisted the help of the church, and enrolled the boy in a technical school, with the result that:

> Bill began to weaken. The combination of Home, Sunday School, Vocational School and Probation Officer were too much for him ... [He] is discharged now and if he continues, he is going to be a mighty useful citizen. He has learned the lesson that everyone will gladly help the boy [and girl] who plays the game. ... (TFC 1927, pp. 17–18).

Is the discovery that most deviant children processed by the Toronto and Vancouver Juvenile Courts were not recidivists a significant one? In closing, I want to briefly consider the implications of my research with reference to similar studies on the state-family relationship during the late nineteenth and early twentieth centuries in Western market societies. Some of the most influential modern analyses of this period are premised on a repressive, social control perspective (Lasch 1979; Platt 1969; Strong-Boag 1982). Both the legislation aimed at upholding the norms of childhood and sexuality associated with the middle-class family and enforcement mechanisms like juvenile courts, it is argued, were components of a new, urban policing strategy, orchestrated by the powerful and implemented by their designated agents, which intensified and extended state control over the poor. Marginal families are thus perceived as the victims of arbitrary decisions imposed upon them.

In this view, then, the relatively low recidivism rates among children adjudicated by the Toronto and Vancouver Juvenile Courts were the result of direct or implicit intimidation and coercion on the part of probation officers and other personnel. Parents who did not want to forfeit their progeny to the state embraced middle-class norms of child-rearing and family life. Delinquent boys and girls who did not want to be sent away from their homes accepted their status as forced dependents. Apparently plausible as this scenario is, however, it is not entirely accurate. While evidence can be found of how parents and children were sometimes manipulated by court workers, it is also evident that would-be clients, particularly single mothers (TFC 1920, p. 19), frequently approached the Court. As one Vancouver probation officer put it:

> Parents come to court for help because their children make undesirable friends, leave school or run away from home in defiance of parental wishes. Even girls run away, 'hitch-hike' or travel around the country on freight cars (VJC 1940, p. 11; see also VJC 1942, p. 5; TFC 1923, p. 17).

The voluntary nature of many interactions between parents and the juvenile courts is illustrated most dramatically by the statistics on committals of children to industrial and training schools. Although the incorrigibility legislation was eventually amended to allow probation officers to initiate proceedings for the incarceration of uncontrollable boys and girls, parents, for both benign and malevolent reasons, continued to request the institutionalization of their sons and daughters. Thus, between 1929 and 1933, more than a quarter of admissions—438 of 1,623—to Ontario training and industrial schools were the result of voluntary application by mothers and fathers (Ontario, 1935, pp. 3–4).

My research also points to the importance of including gender in any analysis of law and its enforcement. None of the most influential historical studies on the legal regulation of childhood and sexuality during the transition to welfare states in Western nations have done so in a systematic way (Donzelot 1980; Platt 1969; Rothman 1980; Sutherland 1976). Analyses lumping boys and girls together as children can sometimes be relevant, since personnel in the pioneer juvenile courts clearly assumed that institutionalized dependency was the natural state of all youth. However, the same workers also operated on the assumption that boys and girls had inherently different characters, which not only created different motivations for their deviance but also necessitated different diagnosis and treatment. Thus, using only aggregate statistics may produce a very misleading picture of how the courts operated.

To summarize my main points, then, I have argued that the norms of childhood and sexuality linked to the bourgeois family model were entrenched across the population during the emergence of the Canadian welfare state. Although not the primary means of achieving this end, legislation regulating adult-child relations, both inside and outside the family, and its enforcement through the juvenile and family courts played an important role in 'rehabilitating' deviant children and/or their parents. Analysis of the Toronto and Vancouver Juvenile Courts to 1945 contradicted some aspects of the current social control explanation of these tribunals and revealed the importance of considering gender—as well as social class and race/ethnicity—in such studies.

[1990]

Acknowledgements

I thank Bob Menzies for his invaluable assistance and support. This research was supported by a Postdoctoral Research Fellowship from the Social Sciences and Humanities Research Council of Canada (1987/88).

Notes

1. The population of metropolitan Toronto rose from 96,000 and 5 per cent of the provincial population in 1881 to 1,264,000 and 26.5 per cent in 1941. The population of metropolitan Vancouver rose from 13,709 and 14.0 per cent of the provincial population in 1891 to 394,000 and 48.2 per cent of the provincial population in 1941. See: D. Kubat and D. Thornton, *A Statistical Profile of Canadian Society*, p. 21, Table P-6. Toronto: McGraw-Hill Ryerson, 1974; F.H. Leacy (ed.), *Historical Statistics of Canada*, 2nd ed., Series A2-14. Ottawa: Statistics Canada, 1983.
2. The Vancouver Juvenile Court did not have jurisdiction over the provincial adoption legislation and the annual reports of the court do not give the precise dispositions of neglected child cases.
3. Public Archives of Canada, CCSD Papers, MG28 110, v. 85, Juvenile Courts—Returns from Ontario 1938–41.

References

Aries, P. 1962. *Centuries of Childhood: A Social History of Family Life*. New York: Vintage Press.

Bacchi, C. 1983. *Liberation Deferred?* Toronto: University of Toronto Press.

Barrett, M. and M. McIntosh. 1982. *The Anti-Social Family*. London: Verso Editions/NLB.

Bland, L. 1986. 'Marriage Laid Bare: Middle-class Women and Marital Sex c. 1880–1914'. In *Labour and Love*, edited by J. Lewis, pp. 123–46. Oxford: Basil Blackwell.

Brown, R.C. and R. Cook. 1974. *Canada 1896–1921: A Nation Transformed*. Toronto: McClelland and Stewart.

Campbell, A. 1981. *Girl Delinquents*. Oxford: Basil Blackwell.

Chesney-Lind, M. 1986. 'Women and Crime: The Female Offender'. *Signs* 12:78–96.

Chunn, D.E. 1988. 'Rehabilitating Deviant Families through Family Courts: The Birth of Socialized Justice in Ontario, 1920–1940'. *International Journal of the Sociology of Law* 16, 2:137–58.

Cross, M. and G. Kealey (eds). 1983. *The Consolidation of Capitalism, 1896–1929*. Toronto: McClelland and Stewart.

Donzelot, J. 1980. *The Policing of Families*. New York: Pantheon.

Dunn, T.A. 1980. 'The Rise of Mass Public Schooling in British Columbia 1900–1929'. Pp. 23–51 in *Schooling and Society in the Twentieth Century*, edited by J.D. Wilson and D.C. Jones. Calgary: Detselig.

Dymond, A.M. 1923. *The Laws of Ontario Relating to Women and Children*. Toronto: Clarkson W. James.

Epstein, B. 1983. 'Family, Sexual Morality, and Popular Movements in Turn-of-the-Century America'. Pp. 117–30 in *Powers of Desire*, edited by A. Snitow et al. New York: Monthly Review Press.

Finkel, A. 1977. 'Origins of the Welfare State in Canada'. Pp. 344–70 in *The Canadian State* edited by L. Panitch. Toronto: University of Toronto Press.

Fitz, J. 1981a. 'The Child as a Legal Subject'. In *Education and the State, 2. Politics, Patriarchy and Practice*. Milton Keynes: Open University Press.

——— 1981b. 'Welfare, the Family and the Child'. In *Education, Welfare and Social Order*. Block 5. Milton Keynes: Open University Press.

Foucault, M. 1980. *The History of Sexuality*, 1. New York: Vintage Books.

Garland, D. 1985. *Punishment and Welfare*. Brookfield, VT: Gower.

Gavigan, S. 1987. 'Women's Crime: New Perspectives and Old Theories'. Pp. 47–66 in *Two Few To Count*, edited by E. Adelberg and C. Currie. Vancouver, BC: Press Gang.

Gillis, J.R. 1975. 'The Evolution of Juvenile Delinquency in England, 1890–1914'. *Past and Present* 67 (May): 96–126.

Guest, D. 1980. *The Emergence of Social Security in Canada*. Vancouver: University of British Columbia Press.

Houston, S.E. 1982. 'The "Waifs and Strays" of a Late Victorian City: Juvenile Delinquents in Toronto'. Pp. 129–142 in *Childhood and the Family in Canadian History*, edited by J. Parr. Toronto: McClelland and Stewart.

Jones, A.E. and L. Rutman. 1981. *In the Children's Aid: J.J. Kelso and Child Welfare in Ontario*. Toronto: University of Toronto Press.

Kinsman, G. 1987. *The Regulation of Desire*. Montreal: Black Rose.

Lasch, C. 1979. *Haven in a Heartless World*. New York: Basic Books.

Leslie, G. 1974. 'Domestic Service in Canada, 1880–1920'. Pp. 71–125 in *Women at Work*, edited by J. Acton et al. Toronto: Women's Educational Press.

McDonald, R.A.J. 1981. 'Victoria, Vancouver and the Economic Development of British Columbia, 1886–1914'. Pp. 369–75 in *British Columbia: Historical Readings*, edited by W.P. Ward and R.A. J. McDonald. Vancouver, BC: Douglas and McIntyre.

———1986. 'Working Class Vancouver, 1886–1914: Urbanism and class in British Columbia'. *B.C. Studies* 69–70: 33–69.

MacGill, H.G. 1939. *Laws For Women and Children in British Columbia*. Vancouver, BC.

McLaren, A. 1978. 'Birth Control and Abortion in Canada, 1870–1920'. *Canadian Historical Review* 59: 319–40.

———1986. 'The Creation of a Haven for "Human Thoroughbreds": the Sterilization of the Feeble-minded and the Mentally Ill in British Columbia'. *Canadian Historical Review* 67, 2:127–50.

McLaren, A. and A.T. McLaren. 1986. *The Bedroom and the State*. Toronto: McClelland and Stewart.

McLaren, J.P.S. 1986. 'Chasing the Social Evil: Moral Fervour and the Evolution of Canada's Prostitution Laws, 1867–1917'. *Canadian Journal of Law and Society* 1: 125–65.

Matters, I. 1984. 'Sinners or Sinned Against? Historical Aspects of Female Juvenile Delinquency in British Columbia'. Pp. 265–77 in *Not Just Pin Money*, edited by B.K. Latham and R.J. Pazdro. Victoria, BC: Camosun College.

May, M. 1973. 'Innocence and Experience: The Evolution of the Concept of Delinquency in the Mid-19th Century'. *Victorian Studies* 18, 1:7–29.

Miller, P.J. 1982. Psychology and the Child: Homer Lane and J.B. Watson. Pp. 57–80 in *Studies in Childhood History*, edited by P.T. Rooke and R.L. Schnell. Calgary: Detselig.

Morrison, T.R. 1976a,b. '"Their Proper Sphere": Feminism, the Family, and Child-centred Social Reform in Ontario, 1875–1900'. *Ontario History* 68, 1: 45–64 and 68, 2: 65–74.

Moscovitch, A. and J. Albert (eds). 1987. *The Benevolent State*. Toronto: Garamond Press.

Muncie, J. 1981. 'Youth and the Reforming Zeal'. In *Law and Disorder: Histories of Crime and Criminal Justice*. Block 4. Milton Keynes: Open University Press.

Nilsen, D. 1980. 'The "Social Evil": Prostitution in Vancouver', 1900–1920. Pp. 205–28 in *Not Just Pin Money*, edited by B.K. Latham and R.J. Pazdro. Victoria, BC: Camosun College.

Oliver, P.N. 1977. *G. Howard Ferguson: Ontario Tory*. Toronto: University of Toronto Press.

Ontario. Inspector of Legal Offices. 1931–1937 Annual Report. Toronto. (Sessional Paper No. 5).

Ontario. Dept. of Public Welfare. 1935. Report of the Committee to Investigate the Present Reformatory School System of Ontario. Chairman: H.S. Mott. Toronto.

Palmer, B.D. 1983. *Working-Class Experience: The Rise and Reconstitution of Canadian Labour, 1800–1980*. Toronto: Butterworths.

Parr, J. (ed.). 1982. *Childhood and Family in Canadian History*. Toronto: McClelland and Stewart.

Platt, A. 1969. *The Child Savers: The Invention of Delinquency*. Chicago: University of Chicago Press.

Poster, N. 1978. *Critical Theory of the Family*. New York: The Seabury Press.

Rooke, P.T. and R.L. Schnell (eds). 1982. *Studies in Childhood History*. Calgary: Detselig.

———— 1983. *Discarding the Asylum*. Lanham, MD: University Press of America.

Rotenberg, L. 1974. 'The Wayward Worker: Toronto's prostitute at the turn of the century'. Pp. 33–69 in *Women At Work*, edited by J. Acton. Toronto: Women's Educational Press.

Rothman, D.J. 1980. *Conscience and Convenience*. Boston: Little, Brown.

Roy, P.E. 1981. 'British Columbia's Fear of Asians'. Pp. 657–70 in *British Columbia: Historical Readings*, edited by W.P. Ward and R.A.J. McDonald. Vancouver: Douglas & McIntyre.

Schull, J. 1978. *Ontario Since 1867*. Toronto: McClelland and Stewart.

Smart, C. 1976. *Women, Crime and Criminology*. London: Routledge and Kegan Paul.

———— 1985. 'Legal Subjects and Sexual Objects: Ideology, Law and Female Sexuality'. Pp. 50–70 in *Women In Law*, edited by J. Brophy and C. Smart. London: Routledge and Kegan Paul.

Smart, B. and Smart, C. (eds). 1978. *Women, Sexuality and Social Control*. London: Routledge and Kegan Paul.

Snell, J. 1983. 'The White Life for Two': The Defence of Marriage and Sexual Morality in Canada, 1800–1914. *Histoire Sociale* 16, 31: 111–28.

Strong-Boag, V. 1982. 'Intruders in the Nursery: Childcare Professionals Reshape the Years One to Five, 1920–1940'. Pp. 160–78 in *Childhood and Family in Canadian History*, edited by J. Parr. Toronto: McClelland and Stewart.

Sutherland, N. 1976. *Children in English-Canadian Society: Framing the Twentieth Century Consensus*. Toronto: University of Toronto Press.

Théoret, B. 1987. *La Loi et les Filles au Canada: Les détours du contrôle social et du contrôle de la sexualité*. Montreal: Département de sociologie, Université du Québec.

Thorne, B. and M. Yalom (eds). 1982. *Rethinking the Family*. New York: Longman.

Toronto Family Court. 1912. 1920–52. *Annual Report*. Toronto.

Ursel, J. 1986. 'The State and the Maintenance of Patriarchy: A Case Study of Family, Labour and Welfare Legislation in Canada'. Pp. 150–91 in *Family, Economy, and State*. Toronto: Garamond Press.

Vancouver Juvenile Court. 1940; 1942–3. *Annual Report of the Juvenile Court and Detention Home*. Vancouver, BC.

Walkowitz, J. 1982. 'Male-vice and Feminist Virtue: Feminism and the Politics of Prostitution in Nineteenth-century Britain'. *History Workshop Journal* 13: 79–93.

Ward, W.P. 1981. 'Class and Race in the Social Structure of British Columbia, 1870–1939'. Pp. 581–99 in British Columbia: *Historical Readings*, edited by W.P. Ward and R.A.J. McDonald. Vancouver, BC: Douglas and McIntyre.

Weeks, J. 1981. *Sex, Politics and Society*. New York: Longman.

——— 1986. *Sexuality*. London: Tavistock.

West, W.G. 1981. *Young Offenders and the State*. Toronto: Butterworths.

Wiebe, R. 1967. *The Search For Order, 1877–1920*. New York: Hill and Wang.

Zaretsky, E. 1976. *Capitalism, the Family and Personal Life*. New York: Harper and Row.

——— 1982. 'The Place of the Family in the Origins of the Welfare State'. Pp. 188–224 in *Rethinking the Family*, edited by B. Thorne. New York: Longman.

——— 1986. 'Rethinking the Welfare State: Dependence, Economic Individualism and the Family'. Pp. 85–109 in *Family, Economy and State*, edited by J. Dickinson and B. Russell. Toronto: Garamond Press.

Problems of Modern Life and Young Offenders

Roderick Haig-Brown

I suppose more nonsense has been talked and written about 'juvenile delinquency' in the years since the war than about any other subject except Russia. Everyone has had a try at it—PTAs and service clubs, parsons and psychiatrists, members of parliament and members of the public. Almost inevitably, some good sense has come out of it all. But there has been a disproportionate amount of wild talk, based on misinformation, misunderstanding, and plain panic. Newspapers love this sort of thing and usually make the most of it; so the average citizen is likely to believe in a muddled sort of way that the situation is little short of critical and that most teenagers can only be saved from the mobs by burning comic books, banning strides, and reintroducing the birch rod.

I cannot qualify as an expert in these matters. I am juvenile judge in a fast-growing small town and a large rural area; I was a child once myself, not so long ago that I have forgotten all about it; I have known a lot of other children and a lot of men and women who grew out of being children. As nearly as I can make out from this and from the assorted reading I have done about other times than my own, children are much the same as they always were. Some of the circumstances they have to face are different, and some of their fads and fashions may look a little different; but they themselves are good, bad, and just ordinary children in much the same proportions as always, with only this difference: that the general level of intelligence, humanity, and moral responsibility is probably higher than in any previous generation of children.

To understand this it is necessary to think a little, instead of just glancing at statistics, nursing the standard prejudices of age against youth, and howling with the pack. Statistics, in this matter of youthful offenders against laws, mean nothing at all. Controlling circumstances have changed enormously in the past ten or twenty years and are still changing year by year. Canada is growing up for one thing. Her population is increasing and it is becoming increasingly urban. Offenses that were once handled informally in rural communities where 'everyone knew everyone' are now likely to be dealt with formally and so become matters of record. We are far more aware of this thing vaguely called 'juvenile delinquency' than we used to be, and we have far better machinery for dragging it out into the open—better welfare services, better schools, better and bigger police forces. We also have a faster and more demanding civilization, with much more money, far more automobiles and far more liquor than was the case a few years ago. All these things add to the likelihood of offenses against law of some sort by young people.

The euphemism 'juvenile delinquent' has become in popular use a term of genuine abuse—if it were one word instead of two it would be a dirty word. On the whole, it is far more offensive, both in meaning and as jargon, than the 'young criminal' or 'young offender' it replaces. This is the inevitable fate of all euphemistic jargon and I often wonder why the social reformers still bother with it. Things are what they are, not what some abuser of the language calls them; the most elegant front parlor delicacies soon take on all the implications of their rough predecessors, and usually an extra roughness or two because of their own vagueness. This has happened to the elegant evasion that created 'juvenile delinquent'; yet legally the words can mean anything from a child who has committed murder to one who has accidentally broken some minor traffic law.

The Juvenile Delinquents Act, under which all juvenile courts must function, is in most respects an excellent act. It permits simple and easy procedure, and is extremely flexible; it provides plainly that 'the child's own good' shall be considered before everything else, and generally offers means for doing just this. Perhaps its flexibility gives too much power to the presiding judge, especially as appeal is difficult and seldom taken; certainly section 33, which covers 'contributing to juvenile delinquency', is a lazy prosecutor's refuge and can be extremely dangerous in the hands of a careless or ignorant judge; but these defects in no way limit the usefulness of the act or interfere with its purpose. It is good machinery for dealing with young children who are in trouble.

Yet in practice very few children who fit the public conception of 'juvenile delinquents' are dealt with in juvenile court. The public thinks in terms of gangs of children, vicious and to some extent organized, planning and carrying out violent crimes; the public thinks of riots and thefts, of hold-ups and armed robberies, of spring knives and street attacks. Nearly all these offenses are rated indictable under the Criminal Code, which means that any child over fourteen who has committed one of them may be transferred to adult court; and in most instances the children involved in such affairs are well past fourteen—usually they are between sixteen and twenty, which places them outside the scope of juvenile court in most provinces. Where it does not—one or two provinces have set the juvenile age limit at eighteen instead of sixteen—transfer of serious offenders to adult court is almost inevitable because juvenile court can only sentence to the industrial schools, which are in no way suitable for such children.

The children one deals with in juvenile court bear little or no resemblance to the popular conception of juvenile delinquents. They rarely belong to criminal gangs and are seldom charged with violent or vicious crimes. They have, perhaps, committed small thefts, broken into stores or garages, or taken part in a teen-age drinking party. Most of them have been tripped by some circumstance of adolescence—a confused home life, a muddled moral standard, a temporary sense of failure—and their offense is a one and only affair, easily straightened out by the shock of detection and a short spell of probation. A few repeat and need more attention; a very few are real problems and perhaps have to be sent away.

In British Columbia, children are classed as juveniles until they are eighteen. This is both a good and a bad thing. It gives the court plenty of discretion in dealing with the difficult ones who commit many minor offenses while they are sorting themselves out. But it also means that a lot of children, especially boys, are brought into juvenile court for trivial offenses against provincial statutes, such as the Motor Vehicles Act and the Liquor Act. Boys, and girls too, quite nice boys and girls, are going to be caught sometimes with liquor they are not supposed to have, and they are going to be caught driving cars a little faster or a little more carelessly than they should.

It doesn't help at all to bring them into court and solemnly read out to them that they did on such and such a day drive faster than thirty miles an hour on the main street of the village, thereby becoming juvenile delinquents. According to the act, there is no doubt they did. According to the ideas of their parents and the general public and their contemporaries, as well as themselves, juvenile delinquents are characters who do much more desperate things than breaking traffic laws. Minor traffic offenders, whether they are adults or juveniles, should never be made to feel that they are criminals or even delinquents. Traffic offenses and other trivial offenses of an essentially civil nature do not belong in juvenile court.

Some few children do begin to show definite signs of criminal tendencies in the early teens, but they are rare enough for a wise man to be both cautious and reluctant in identifying one. Nearly all the juvenile delinquency that the public imagination plays upon so excitedly is the work of older children, sixteen- and seventeen-year-olds perhaps, but more commonly eighteen- and twenty-year-olds, some of whom are already confirmed criminals.

The problem of the courts is not so much to detect these last—they discover themselves quickly enough and a little mistaken leniency never does any harm. The important thing is to recognize and deal wisely with the temporary troublemakers, the ones who will leave it all behind if they are given the right kind of help.

By far the most useful tool in the hands of any court dealing with young offenders is probation. The child is simply released under certain conditions, among them a promise to report regularly to the probation officer and to be available to him whenever called upon. Quite often that is all there is to it. The child simply settles down and behaves and the one lapse, even thought it may have been a fairly serious one, is soon completely forgotten. Almost as frequently, the term of probation, which may be a year or two years, is a long succession of alarms and excitements. At seventeen or eighteen some boys, and occasionally girls too, seem to be in a disturbed phase that makes for an endless series of relatively minor offenses.

The problem then is to carry them patiently through the time it takes to sort things out, scolding, imposing fines, tightening or relaxing the terms of probation, constantly maintaining the illusion that one more offense will bring serious consequences. Sometimes one carries a boy through ten or a dozen infractions of probation during the course of a couple of years; then suddenly the disturbed phase is over and there are no more infractions. This pattern has been common enough in my own judicial experience to seem highly significant, and I am pretty sure I can recall teen-age moods of my own which would have produced much the same effect.

Sometimes, when a young nuisance is working in a good job, a heavy fine can be more effective than either probation or a jail sentence. Occasionally two or three heavy fines are needed before the lesson is learned, but to put in a month of eight-hour days in the woods or the mine or the mill and then have to endorse the paycheque over to the magistrate is a sobering punishment.

Finally there are times when neither fines, nor probation, nor patience can help any longer. Fortunately, even this is no longer the utter defeat it used to seem. In British Columbia we have the single phase Borstal institution at New Haven and the Young Offenders' Unit in the provincial jail, both of which are ably and intelligently run along thoroughly constructive lines. There is every reason to expect that a boy or a young man will come out of either of these institutions a good deal better than he went in, unless he is an acute psychiatric rather than a moral problem.

There is little doubt that we shall always have young criminals who cannot be straightened out, and we shall always have gangs of youthful toughs and hoodlums. These are not new things or things in any way peculiar to our time. Society, any society, produces a certain number of anti-social individuals and invariably has to do something about them. Our system is far from perfect—we could use dozens more probation officers in every province, for instance, and we could probably use a federal Borstal system. But it has probably reached the stage where it is straightening out young criminals instead of creating them.

The courts will never be able to do much more than this, because the real remedy is back with family. So perhaps it is right that the PTAs and similar organizations should be concerned about juvenile delinquency; I once heard a wise school principal tell a large group of parents: 'The people in this town need to punish their children more—and love them more'. Even that might not solve everything but it would cut the work of the juvenile courts to very little.

[From *Saturday Night*, 28 May 1955]

Suggestions for Further Reading

Chunn, Dorothy E., *From Punishment to Doing Good: Family Courts and Socialized Justice in Ontario, 1880–1940*. Toronto: University of Toronto Press, 1992.

Keshen, Jeffrey, 'Wartime Jitters over Juveniles: Canada's Delinquency Scare and its Consequences, 1939–1945,' in Jeffrey Keshen, ed., *Age of Contention: Readings in Canadian Social History, 1900–1945*. Toronto: Harcourt Brace, Canada, 1997.

Maynard, Stephen, '"Horrible Temptations": Sex, Men, and Working Class Male Youth in Urban Ontario, 1890–1935,' *Canadian Historical Association* 78 (June 1997): 191–235.

Meyers, Tamara, '"Qui t'a débouchée?" Family Adolescent Sexuality and the Juvenile Delinquents Court in Early-Twentieth Century Montreal' in Edgar-André Montigny and Lori Chambers, eds, *Family Matters: Papers in Post-Confederation Canadian Family History*. Toronto: Canadian Scholars' Press, 1998: 377–394.

Sangster, Joan, *Girl Trouble: Female Delinquency in English Canada*. Toronto: Between the Lines, 2002.

Valverde, Mariana, 'Families, Private Property and the State: The Dionnes and the Toronto Stork Derby,' *Journal of Canadian Studies* 29, 4 (Winter 1994-5): 15–35.

PART 6

Narratives of Childhood: The Instance and Legacy of Residential Schools, 1938–1949

While the state was not legally sanctioned to interfere with private family life until the late nineteenth century, such intervention has a longer history in First Nations families. The following articles discuss the instance and legacy of residential schools on Aboriginal children and in First Nations communities. Within the diversity of cultural practices, social organization, and forms of governance, indigenous societies based education on looking, learning, and listening. Oral histories by First Nations elders and memoirs of childhood presented in fictional works show that elders and traditionalists have preserved these educational practices in ceremony and daily life. Their successful retention of cultural customs and traditions defied the central purpose of residential schools: assimilation. Initially, indigenous leaders hoped a European education would complement traditional teachings, giving their children the skills to compete in a changing world and to defend indigenous treaty rights. The earliest industrial schools were located near indigenous settlements, where, colonial officials argued, parents still had too much influence over their children. The residential-school model replaced the day-school model to remove children from traditional education. Jean Barman demonstrates that the legacy of residential schools on educational policy for Aboriginal children in British Columbia was to further marginalize them from mainstream Canadian society.

Former residential students' disclosure of deprivation and physical and sexual abuse have generated public interest in the impact of residential schools on individuals and on First Nations families and communities. The recollections of Inez Deiter and Ben Stonechild show that students had different school experiences. Dian Million argues that historians must analyze these narratives in the context of contested conceptualizations of nation. These narratives gave meaning and power to individual experiences as they transformed personal disclosures to political issues.

Nancy Janovicek

Schooled for Inequality: The Education of British Columbia Aboriginal Children

Jean Barman[1]

The residential school has become a metaphor for the history of Aboriginal education in British Columbia, as in Canada more generally. Any discussion of the broader topic must begin with, and centre on, the residential school, for its existence both curtailed and set the agenda for other educational options. Recent critics of residential schools have very persuasively drawn attention to a range of unacceptable practices from prohibitions on speaking Aboriginal languages to incidents of physical and sexual abuse, and to their consequences for the quality of Aboriginal life in Canada into the late twentieth century.[2] 'Subjugation has taken its toll on our cultures. Indigenous peoples have the highest rates of impoverishment, incarceration, suicide, and alcoholism in Canada. Much of this can be traced back to the abuse received at the residential schools.'[3]

Residential schools' stark legacy assumes an element of tragedy when set in context. The schools' origins in the late nineteenth century lay in a federal policy premised on Aboriginal peoples' assimilation into mainstream Canadian society. 'The Indian problem exists owing to the fact that the Indian is untrained to take his place in the world. Once teach him to do this, and the solution is had.'[4] By taking children away from the old ways and 'civilizing' them into European ways, so the argument ran, 'the Indian problem' would have been solved in a single generation.[5] The initial goal of the residential school—and of its less favoured counterpart, the federal day school—was the absolute opposite of what occurred. Instead of becoming agents of assimilation, they served, so students' recollections attest, as vehicles for marginalizing generations of young men and women both from the Canadian mainstream and from home environments.[6]

The purpose of this essay is not to assess the rightness or wrongness of the federal goal of assimilation, but rather to examine why that policy's principal vehicle, the residential school, became such a dismal failure with far-reaching consequences for the history of Aboriginal education. The reasons for the failure had to do less with the actions of individual teachers or administrators than with a federal policy that legitimized and even compelled children to be schooled, not for assimilation but for inequality. While teachers and administrators of good will were able to ameliorate the worst aspects of the system for their pupils, all of the individual good will in the world could not have rescued a system that was fundamentally flawed.

The inequality inherent in federal schools for Aboriginal children rests in four complementary attributes of the system as devised and overseen by the federal Department of Indian Affairs. The first was an assumption of the sameness of Aboriginal peoples across Canada. Differences existing between tribes, bands, and individuals played no role in a federal policy which viewed Aboriginal peoples solely as a singular 'object' to be acted upon. In British Columbia some Aboriginal families were already sending their children to public school when federal policy intervened in the late nineteenth century to declare the residential school, and its lesser complement the day school, their sole educational options. Secondly, despite a parallel curriculum between federal schools and the provincial schools that educated other Canadian children, Aboriginal children were allotted less time in the classroom than were their non-Aboriginal counterparts. The difference was particularly marked in the residential schools that formed the system's showplaces. Thirdly, through the mid-twentieth century the instruction of Aboriginal children occurred within the much older Western tradition of voluntarism as opposed to the growing professionalism of public-school teachers across Canada. Aboriginal schooling was carried on with few exceptions by Christian missionaries primarily concerned with saving souls, only secondarily with literacy education. Fourth, federal funding of schools for Aboriginal children quickly fell below provincial funding levels for public schools. However fine a school's intentions, they became unrealizable. For these four reasons, as well as others, generations of British Columbia Aboriginal children were, effectively if not always deliberately, schooled for inequality.

Assumption of Aboriginal Peoples' Sameness

When British Columbia joined Confederation, it became subject to the provisions of the British North America Act which made Aboriginal peoples 'wards' of the federal government, eligible for federally sponsored schooling, health care, and other services on their agreeing to treaties that surrendered traditional lands for much smaller reserves. The policy combined economics with racism. At the time the Canadian Confederation was created in 1867, Aboriginal peoples still occupied much of the land on which newcomers hoped to settle. The rhetoric of the day, premised in biological determinism, assumed that persons who were non-White were inferior by virtue of their race alone and so incapable of using the land to best advantage or otherwise determining their own destiny.[7] The British North America Act was consistent with this thinking. It made no attempt to distinguish Aboriginal peoples in all of their diversity and individuality, but simply reduced them to a single dependent status.

Schooling was initially viewed as something of a panacea by the new Department of Indian Affairs (DIA) encharged with overseeing all aspects of federal policy. Using reasoning very similar to that gaining force in the United States, policy makers looked to Aboriginal peoples' civilization 'so as to cause them to reside in towns, or, in the case of farmers, in settlements of white people, and thus become amalgamated with the general community.'[8] The residential school became viewed as the best means to achieve that goal, by separating the young from their families and thereby from the old ways.

> The Indian youth, to enable him to cope successfully with his brother of white origin, must be dissociated from the prejudicial influences by which he is surrounded on the reserve of his band. And the necessity for the establishment more generally of institutions, whereat Indian children, besides being instructed in the usual branches of education, will be lodged, fed, clothed, kept separate from home influences, taught trades and instructed in agriculture, is becoming every year more apparent.[9]

Two types of residential schools came into being in Canada, boarding schools for younger children and industrial schools for their older siblings. Not only did the latter put greater emphasis on occupational training, but they tended to be larger and located further away from pupils' home reserves.[10] Over time the distinction broke down between the two types of schools, and they all became known as residential schools. Day schools were perceived as less acceptable than either boarding or industrial schools, to be established only where circumstances did not permit their preferred counterparts.

For Aboriginal peoples in British Columbia, the consequences of federal policy favouring residential schools were particularly poignant, for it removed an educational option already in place that might have given the children rough equality with their contemporaries across the young province. For more than a decade British Columbia Aboriginal children had been finding their way into provincial public schools alongside their neighbours and, to some extent, gaining acceptance there. Another narrative might well be constructed today about British Columbia Aboriginal peoples had not federal policy intervened.

Part of the explanation for this situation lies in demographics and part in Aboriginal peoples' circumstances of everyday life. At the time British Columbia entered Confederation in 1871, Aboriginal peoples still formed the overwhelming proportion of the population. They totalled some 25,000 or more as compared to about 1,500 Chinese, almost all of them adult males, some 500 Blacks, and approximately 8,500 Europeans.[11] In many outlying settlements Aboriginal children were necessary to secure the minimum enrolment necessary for a public school's establishment and survival.

British Columbia Aboriginal peoples were among the world's most distinctive. Linguistic divisions were complex, economies self-sufficient, and cultures more developed, in many respects, than in any other part of the continent north of Mexico.[12] Generational continuity was assured through ongoing, lifelong education premised on the young modelling their behaviour upon their elders. There was, moreover, a long tradition of economic and social interaction with Europeans, initially in the fur trade and then during the gold rush beginning in 1858. The continued availability of such traditional staples as salmon, cedar, and game animals meant that British Columbia Aboriginal peoples never experienced the wrenching despair and utter dependency that befell their prairie counterparts. As the Department of Indian Affairs phrased it with particular reference to British Columbia, 'The Indians have been from the earliest times self-supporting, and the advent of white population, which in the west caused the complete disappearance of the buffalo, did not occasion any serious change in their source of food-supply.'[13] Long after British Columbia entered Confederation in 1871, contemporaries continued to distinguish the province's Aboriginal population from those elsewhere in North America. A guide to prospective settlers asserted: 'The intending settler may depend on finding the Indians peaceable, intelligent, eager to learn and industrious to a degree unknown elsewhere among the aborigines of America.'[14] More than one settler was struck by how 'the Indians differ *toto caelo* from the North West plains Indians. They are very well off.'[15]

The published annual reports of the Department of Indian Affairs repeatedly lauded British Columbia's Aboriginal peoples. 1874: 'The intelligence of the Indians of that province gives encouragement to the expectation that with liberal encouragement the Indians, who form so large a proportion of the population may, as they are not deficient in enterprise, be transformed into valuable members of the community.'[16] 1880: 'The Indians of British Columbia exhibit more enterprise than those of any other Province in the Dominion.'[17] 1890: 'The Indians of this Province, with but few exceptions, pursued their wanted course of manly independence, intelligent enterprise, and unflagging industry during the past year.'[18] 1902: 'Taking them altogether, the British Columbia Indians are remarkably industrious, enterprising, self-reliance, honest, sober and law-abiding. They are good neighbours, and friendly with the whites and with each other.'[19]

Perhaps then, it is not surprising that as public schools became established across the far-flung province in the 1870s and 1880s, Aboriginal children were often among the first pupils to enrol alongside their settler neighbours. The Superintendent of Education received numerous letters from teachers and others enquiring about provincial policy toward 'Indian children of school age in the immediate vicinity whose parents express a willingness to send to School'.[20] 'There are a few bright-looking native children here. Would it be all right if I get them to attend the school?'[21] 'There are numbers of Indian children that for whom no provision in the way of education has hitherto been made.'[22] 'There are three Indian children that wish to attend the school when it is established.'[23]

The Superintendent of Education was consistently supportive. 'You are doing perfectly right in admitting Indian children so long as they are not taken [by force] & conduct themselves properly. . . . If they are troublesome or dirty the trustees must prohibit their attendance—Personally I am glad to hear of their attendance wherever circumstances will admit of it.'[24] The Superintendent responded in 1886 to a query by some 'parents of white children' about Indian children's attendance: 'There is no authority given in the School Act to refuse them admittance. Since the inception of the present School system they have been admitted on an equality with other pupils.'[25]

Aboriginal children's attendance was for the most part accepted without question, as a matter of course, perhaps because they were often not that different in actions and even appearance from their non-Aboriginal contemporaries. Some teachers encouraged Aboriginal children into their schools. One young woman wrote the

Superintendent about a young Aboriginal boy who 'sent another boy to me to get a book as he wanted to learn to read. . . . I told him if he was so anxious to learn he could come to school as long as he behaved properly. He has come ever since and is acquitting himself creditably both to himself and me.'[26] This teacher may have started a trend. 'Since then another Indian boy has come to me wanting to come. I permitted him to do so on the same conditions.'[27] Another teacher wrote with particular reference to the Aboriginal children in her classroom: 'I love the children, black and white, are the same to me. I am an impartial Teacher. Act conscientiously and as long as I am able to impart instruction to them they shall all have it in equality.'[28]

Aboriginal families in British Columbia demonstrated a resourcefulness that would have served them well had not a federal education policy assuming their sameness across Canada intervened. Although only a handful of treaties were ever made in British Columbia, similar federal services were gradually provided there as well. And despite the repeated statements in the annual reports of the Department of Indian Affairs lauding the distinctiveness of British Columbia Aboriginal people, they were treated no differently than their counterparts across Canada.

As the number of federal schools grew, it became increasingly difficult for Aboriginal children to attend their local school. The shift began in about 1888. A teacher noted concerning an 'application to admit an Indian as a pupil' that the Trustees 'are of the opinion that the Dominion Government undertakes to provide for the educational interests of the Indians', to which the Superintendent responded:

> Although Indian children are considered to be wards of the Dominion Government, yet it has not been the custom to refuse them admittance to Public Schools whose attendance is not over large. Of course they are required to comply with the Rules and Regulations as to cleanliness, supplying themselves with books etc. In all cases refer such matters to the Board of Trustees.[29]

The Superintendent was less sanguine a year later, considering that 'Indian children are wards of the Dominion Government, and are not presumed to be entitled to attend the Public Schools of the Province.'[30]

Yet so many Aboriginal children continued to attend British Columbia public schools that in the fall of 1891 the Superintendent of Education somewhat relented, stating in a circular that 'the matter of attendance of Indian children is left entirely in the hands of the [local] Board of Trustees.'[31] Responses from individual teachers and boards of trustees almost all supported Aboriginal children's continued presence. A teacher wrote that they were 'quiet, tidy and much more devoted to study than the average child',[32] another that 'the rate-payers seem to be of the opinion that it is of advantage to the community if the young Indians who reside here was [sic] educated.'[33] The secretary of a school board reported that 'the present Trustees all think the privilege of getting a better education should not be denied them especially as their parents seem grateful for it.'[34] Two years later, in the fall of 1893, the Superintendent ruled that, 'if a single parent objects to the attendance of Indian pupils, they cannot be permitted to attend',[35] to which one trustee responded indignantly that 'it is desirable that in every locality the relations between Indians & settlers should be friendly but this ruling is not likely to secure it.'[36]

While some Aboriginal children continued to attend individual public schools up to the time of the First World War and a few thereafter, they were the exceptions rather than the rule. Growing numbers of settlers meant that Aboriginal pupils were no longer essential to most schools' survival, schools received no funding for Aboriginal pupils, and federal policy discouraged their attendance. The moment of opportunity had passed. By 1900 British Columbia possessed 14 residential and 28 day schools, enrolling 675 and 893 pupils respectively.[37] Two decades later totals had risen to 1,115 children in 17 residential schools and 1,197 in 46 day schools, by 1940 to 2,035 children in 15 residential schools and 2,025 in 65 day schools.

Into the mid-twentieth century federal policy toward Aboriginal peoples, adults as well as children, refused to acknowledge their distinctiveness within geographical areas or as individuals. They were treated as a single category to be dealt with as expeditiously and economically as possible. The initiative demonstrated by British Columbia Aboriginal peoples, in political and economic matters as well as schooling, only served to label them as nuisances for refusing to conform into dependency.[38]

Time in the Classroom

Logically, the shift of British Columbia Aboriginal children from provincial to federal schools should not have made any difference to them academically, for in 1895 the newly established School Branch of the Department of Indian Affairs laid down a uniform curriculum little different in form from its provincial counterparts. Aboriginal pupils were to move between six 'standards' or grades centred around readers similar to those being used in provincial systems.[39] Instruction was to be offered in writing, arithmetic, English, geography, ethics, history, vocal music, callisthenics, and religion. It was anticipated that 'the work done and results obtained [would] equal those of the common-schools of the rural districts.'[40]

The new curriculum would have boded well for the proclaimed federal goal of Aboriginal peoples' assimilation had not children been expected somehow to get through it in less time each day than was allotted their counterparts in provincial schools. While some flexibility existed in day schools which were never that closely monitored by federal authorities, in residential schools only half of each day was usually spent in the classroom. Sometimes this occurred in segments. At one school, the hours of instruction ran 9–11:30 and 2–3 p.m.[41] Regardless of format, the total was two to four hours per day compared with the five hours or longer that other Canadian children spent on the prescribed curriculum.

The reports on individual schools included in the annual reports of the Department of Indian Affairs often implied longer hours of instruction, but accounts from individual schools almost always reveal a shorter time period. Personal testimonies are damning. 'We went to school in the mornings about ten o'clock. I would stay there till dinner time. Twelve o'clock.'[42] 'We spent very little time in the classroom. We were in the classroom from nine o'clock in the morning until noon. Another shift [of children] came into the classroom at one o'clock in the afternoon and stayed until three.'[43] At a third, 'We knew we had to do our chores, such as sweeping the dormitory, cleaning the washrooms, in the morning, and go to school half a day. We had our chores to do in the afternoon.'[44] This pupil's daily round grew more onerous as he got older: 'Our job was getting tougher. We went to school for half a day. One month you worked in the mornings and the next month you worked in the afternoons. We never went to school full-time until the last year, in grade eight.'[45] In his discussion of the academic subjects taught in British Columbia Catholic residential schools, oblate historian Thomas Lascelles concluded:

> Usually they occupied the students several hours a day, the remainder being devoted to training in practical skills such as farming, shoemaking and housekeeping, an arrangement which was not abandoned until the 1940s or 1950s when pupils began to spend full time on academic subjects, and to follow Provincial curricula more closely.[46]

Shorter time periods for classroom instruction existed despite many children's being forced to study in a second language. As part of their becoming 'civilized', federal policy asserted that Aboriginal children be 'taught in the English language exclusively'.[47] The languages that most boys and girls brought with them to school were almost always prohibited, even for private conversations between pupils. 'Native languages were forbidden. English was the only allowable language.'[48] 'What I could never understand, we weren't allowed to speak our language. If we were heard speaking Shuswap, we were punished. We were made to write on the board one hundred times, "I will not speak Indian any more."'[49] 'In my first meeting with the brother, he showed me a long black leather strap and told me, through my interpreter, "If you are ever caught speaking Indian this is what you will get across your hands."'[50]

The logic behind the limited time allotted to the formal curriculum was obvious to policy makers. While it was important that Aboriginal children be made literate in English, it was even more critical that they acquire the practical skills permitting their entry into mainstream society, but only at its very lowest rungs. Although assimilation was a desirable goal, its achievement should not challenge the status quo. During the second half of each school day boys learned how to do farm chores or some low-status trade such as shoemaking, girls to perform household tasks ranging from potato peeling to dusting to needlework. As a pamphlet widely distributed by the Methodist church put the case in 1906:

> The girl who has learned only the rudiments of reading, writing and ciphering, and knows also how to make and mend her clothing, wash and iron, make a good loaf of bread, cook a good dinner, keep her house neat and clean, will be worth vastly more as mistress of a log cabin than one who had given years of study to the ornamental branches alone. . . . The Indian must be educated along industrial lines. It should be along the line of the physical rather than the mental.[51]

However much federal rhetoric might have maintained the illusion of assimilation, the Department of Indian Affairs was assuring failure in terms of Aboriginal pupils competing socially or intellectually with their White neighbours. Whereas most pupils in provincial schools reached the upper elementary grades by the end of the First World War, the overwhelming majority of Aboriginal children never got beyond grades 1 or 2. Up to 1920 four out of every five Aboriginal boys and girls attending a federal school across Canada were only enrolled in grades 1, 2, or 3. This did not mean that they had been in the school so short a time period, but more likely that they were simply kept in the lower grades year after year for convenience's sake or because the level of instruction was so poor. 'We only had two hours of classes when I went to residential school. We worked . . . you had to get out as soon as you're sixteen. I didn't get much education, very little education.'[52]

Aboriginal pupils were in any case long prohibited by law from going beyond the elementary grades. 'There was a rule at that time that Indians could not go past Grade 8. I do not recall many boys staying around long enough to protest the education that was being denied us.'[53] 'We had to stay in school until we were eighteen years of age to go as high as grade eight. And then no high school after.'[54] Through the middle of the twentieth century the proportion of Aboriginal children in school across Canada who were in grades 1–3 stagnated at two-thirds or more. In sharp contrast the percentage of their counterparts in provincial schools who were enrolled in grades 1–3 fell by mid-century to just over a third, indicating that almost all non-Aboriginal children were by then completing the elementary grades. Similarly, whereas the proportion of children of the dominant society reaching grade 7 or higher grew from less than one fifth in 1920 to about one third by 1950, the percentage of Aboriginal children to reach grade 7 moved up from none in 1920 to 3 per cent a decade later and then to just 10 per cent by mid-century.[55] Father Lascelles summed up the situation in his observation that, 'The half-day academic program in effect until the middle of this century ensured that the children did not receive an education on a par with that given in the public schools.'[56] Even then, a boy at school during the mid-1950s recalled that 'Classes were from nine in the morning until three in the afternoon, but many times we were taken from class to work outside.'[57]

Teachers and Teaching

The third attribute of federal policy ensuring that Aboriginal children were schooled for inequality grew out of the remarkable symbiosis in purpose that developed between the federal government and the various religious denominations across Canada. Unlike the American education policy where missionaries were subordinated to the federal government, in Canada they were left in charge. The major churches had already carved Canada up into spheres of influence for the purposes of Aboriginal conversion and they eagerly accepted the new challenge, subsidized by a federal per-pupil grant to existing schools and sometimes also by funding to build needed new ones. The Department of Indian Affairs restricted itself to general oversight which included annual reporting by each school and periodic visits by local officials, known as Indian agents.

While the Canadian policy was justified as suitable acknowledging a school system already underway, it was also an economy move alleviating the federal government from having to create and maintain its own institutions. 'The department has fully recognized its inability to conduct such institutions as economically as can be done by denominations, and consequently it has endeavoured to have their management placed in the hands of the respective churches.'[58] A student has recalled, 'One day Sister Catherine told us in the classroom, "We work so hard for you, we don't get any pay at all for looking after you Indians."[59]

By leaving schools' ongoing operation to missionary groups, the federal government relieved itself of direct responsibility for the provision, payment, or supervision of teaching staffs. In residential schools teachers were most often missionaries principally motivated by commitment to Aboriginal peoples' conversion. 'We had prayers ten, twenty times a day and when we weren't praying, we were changing clothes for prayers. We prayed when we got up, we prayed before breakfast and after breakfast, and we prayed when we got to the classroom and when we were in the classroom, I lost count of how many times a day we prayed.'[60] One pupil shrewdly observed: 'Mr Hall wasn't paid to teach us, I don't think. I think he was just paid as a minister.'[61] At their best teachers possessed, as one federal official phrased it, 'infinite patience and tact, although without scholarly attainments.'[62]

The situation was comparable between residential and day schools.[63] Although individual teachers were sometimes sympathetic to pupils' plight and so remembered by them, they were with rare exceptions untrained. A group of local parents informed the Department of Indian Affairs in 1936 that 'The Indians of our Band are quite willing and anxious to do their part in educating their children, but we are asking the Department to give us a capable Instructor who will take a deeper interest in the progress of our children.'[64] Having considered the request, DIA concluded, 'While he is not a trained teacher, and the children do not make the same progress as they might with a modern highly trained instructor, he is rendering good service to the Department in a variety of ways.'[65]

The contemporary literature is replete with observations attesting to the poor quality of teaching. A pupil of the 1920s has mused, 'it is said by many that the teachers are not really teachers at all. They are not trained as the teachers are in the [local public] school.'[66] Conversely, a sister teaching at the same school recalled being informed by the federal inspector of Indian schools that, 'There is no training for your situation anyway, just for public schools.'[67] An anonymous comment in DIA's internal files dated 1932 acknowledged that teaching positions are sometimes 'merely posts provided for persons for whom billets had to be found.'[68] The next decade the refrain was the same, that teachers 'were often unqualified to teach. They used to just send old missionaries to the village to try and do the best they could.'[69] The situation continued largely unchanged into the mid-twentieth century in sharp contrast to the growing professionalism distinguishing teachers and teaching in the dominant society.

Where individuals' religious commitment conflicted with their role as a teacher, the former usually triumphed. A local Indian agent observed in 1912 that 'there is a disposition to devote too much time to imparting religious instruction to the children as compared with the imparting of secular knowledge, which is perhaps not unnatural when the teachers are employed and selected by the various churches.'[70] The pupil-teacher relationship outside of the classroom was often determined more by religious than by didactic considerations. 'If you passed them [the nuns] in the hall or anywhere, you're to stop and bow your head. They were really up on the pedestal. . . They sure put themselves somewhere where you couldn't touch them. You couldn't teach them and you had to bow to them . . . it made me to a certain extent very bitter by the time I left school.'[71] Language sometimes compounded difficulties. Whereas Aboriginal children were expected, once in school, totally to abandon their Aboriginal tongue in favour of English, their teachers did not necessarily know the English language sufficiently well to speak it, much less teach it to others. 'But them French teachers you know they don't really pronounce their sounds right. There was only Sister Patricia who was Irish.'[72] The Department of Indian Affairs acknowledged a possible conflict in its observation that 'the dual system of control between the department on the one hand and the church on the other, each with their different ideals, the one requiring a secular education, and the other looking more to the spiritual instruction of the children, is almost somewhat anomalous.'

Underfunding

The fourth and perhaps most fundamental reason why Aboriginal children were schooled for inequality lay in schools' low levels of federal financial support. Even taking into account the largely volunteer labour available as a consequence of schools' missionary ties, they were underfunded when compared with provincial institutions or even with the bare basics of survival. The per-pupil subsidy provided by the federal government assumed that much of the teaching would be volunteer, but even then it was inadequate to provide a minimum standard of everyday life, much less material conditions conducive to learning. The men and women who ran the schools were expected to scramble for donations simply to survive. Father Lascelles has made an important link: 'Crucial to the determined efforts [of Catholic residential schools to secure better qualified teachers], however, were dollars; dollars which were few and far between.'[74]

The published reports of the Department of Indian Affairs were very open in acknowledging the inadequacy of funding of residential schools, as in 1896: 'The denominations interested in the last-named, owing to the smallness of the annual per capita grant, are forced to meet any shortage of the Government grant by contributions from outside sources.'[75] A decade later the annual report stated bluntly that residential schools across the country were 'all largely supplemented by the missionary societies'.[76] Father Lascelles concluded that between 1915 and about 1950, 'funding for the education of Indian children by the Department [of Indian Affairs] remained at a relative standstill.'[77]

The half-day program adopted in most residential schools became little more than pupils' undertaking of the manual labour necessary for institutions' survival. From the early years, federal officials aspired to schools 'becoming self-supporting' through pupils raising crops, making clothes, and generally doing 'outside work.'[78]

> The longer half of our day was spent in what the brothers called 'industrial training'. Industrial training consisted of doing all the kinds of manual labour that are commonly done around a farm, except that we did not have the use of the equipment that even an Indian farmer of those days would have been using.[79]

The need for manual labour cut across the sexes, and many 'an Indian girl washed, cooked, cleaned, and mended her way through residential school.' 'We had to patch.

We had to patch the boys' clothes. We had to wash and iron on Mondays and Tuesdays. We had to patch and keep on patching till Saturday.' 'We made all of the dresses and uniforms worn in the school, and socks, drawers, chemises, and aprons.' The situation was, in this woman's view, even more detrimental for her male counterparts:

> The bigger ones spent almost no time in class. Instead, they were cutting down trees and pulling up stumps, or else they were up before daylight feeding the horses and milking the cows. Long after he left Lejac [residential school] one boy said, 'I'm just a human bulldozer!'[82]

'I was up at five-thirty every morning either to serve as an alter boy for Mass or to work on the farm, milking cows, working in the garden, and so forth.'[83]

From the perspective of some pupils, poor or too little food caused most distress. 'Hunger is both the first and last thing I can remember about that school. I was hungry from the day I went into the school until they took me to the hospital two and a half years later. Not just me. Every Indian pupil smelled of hunger.'[84] Particularly difficult for pupils was their being expected to eat the barest of fare day after day while subjected to the smells and even the sight of schools' staffs dining far more sumptuously:

> After Mass we put our smocks over our uniforms and line up for breakfast in the hall outside the dining room. We can talk then because Sister goes for breakfast in the Sisters' dining room. They get bacon or ham, eggs, toast and juice. We can see when they open the door and go in for breakfast. We get gooey mush with powder milk and brown suger.[85]

'The food given to us daily was not of the best. I am saying the food for the staff was of better quality and more palatably prepared.'[86]

> At school it was porridge, porridge, porridge, and if it wasn't that, it was boiled barley or beans, and thick slices of bread spread with lard. Weeks went by without a taste of meat or fish. . . . A few times I would catch the smell of roasting meat coming from the nuns' dining room, and I couldn't help myself—I would follow that smell to the very door. Apart from the summers, I believe I was hungry for all seven of the years I was at school . . . we were on rations more suited to a concentration camp![87]

The comparison was not inapt: according to the wife of the commander of a First World War camp for German prisoners of war, they were provided only with 'cheap' food, the allocation for food being limited to 'approximately seventeen cents per person per day', or just over $50 a year.[88]

The actual situation on the ground was that many Aboriginal children fared less well than did prisoners of war. Up to 1910 boarding schools received from the federal government a grant of $60 a year per qualifying pupil, which was intended to cover all costs, not just food. Industrial schools received double that amount or even a bit more, but the consequence for all residential schools was what one administrator termed 'frugal maintenance'.[89] Moreover, because most schools, as part of their religious commitment to service, accepted additional children to the total allotted them by the Department of Indian Affairs, federal funds were usually stretched over a larger pupil body than intended. Federal day schools in British Columbia received an annual federal grant of $12 per pupil. The paucity of the amount becomes evident on comparison to neighbouring British Columbia public schools, whose budgets rose from an average of $15 per pupil at the turn of the century to double the amount by 1908.[90]

From 1900 to 1908 some industrial and boarding schools' statements of income and expenditure were published in DIA's annual reports. They make clear the extent to which schools struggled to make ends meet. Including donations, the annual income per pupil at the three British Columbia boarding schools whose financial statements were published for 1900 averaged $94. Of this total, $41 comprised the government subsidy, which in theory was $60 per pupil but in practice much less due to the schools' greater enrolments than allotted by DIA. The remaining $53 of income per pupil consisted of donations, contributed primarily to further the schools' religious purposes. Housekeeping expenses alone, principally food, exceeded total federal funding at $44 per child. Physical upkeep of facilities added another $16 per pupil. Salaries for the minority of staff who received wages totalled $28 per pupil, and miscellaneous expenses ranging from school books to clothing $9 per pupil.[91] Financial statements were published for 1908 for seven British Columbia boarding schools. Their average income per pupil was $87, of which $46 comprised the federal subsidy and $41 donations. Out of necessity, housekeeping expenses including food had fallen to an average of $38 per pupil. Physical upkeep was $13, salaries $21 and miscellaneous expenses $13.[92]

The parsimony of federal funding is particularly evident when comparison is made to private schools for children of the dominant society. At the only British Columbia boarding school enrolling both Aboriginal and White female boarders, the latter's families were charged $160 a year in 1900.[93] At the turn of the century even a relatively modest private day school had fees of $50 a year, roughly the amount on which the federal government expected Aboriginal boarders to survive.[94]

Federal subsidies for Aboriginal pupils were revised upward in 1910, but not to adequate levels. Moreover, 'increased financial assistance' came at the cost of 'greater demands' in the standard of buildings, care, and administration. For instance, the per pupil subsidy for boarding schools was doubled from $60 to $125, but only after schools met rigorous new requirements demanding more space per pupil, better physical facilities, and far higher health and sanitation standards, no easy matter given that capital costs for upgrading were not integral to the revised policy.[95] By comparison, in 1912 an elite private school for White boys charged $470 a year for boarders, $150 for day pupils.[96]

Day school grants were raised in 1910 to $17 per child, but by then the comparable allocation per pupil in the British Columbia provincial system had reached $34.[97] As the reports of Indian agents repeatedly emphasized, teachers' salaries were a central issue for day schools often compelled to hire from outside of religious orders. 'Complaint is continually made of the small amount allowed for a teacher. The teachers of the public schools receive at least $80 per month, with a long summer vacation, and have fewer scholars than the teachers of Indian day schools.'[98] Another Indian agent noted that 'the churches do not pay an adequate salary and trained teachers prefer to go to white schools, where social surroundings are always preferable to the isolated location among the Indians.'[99]

Within a few short years, federal schools in British Columbia, and across Canada, were in even worse financial straits. A school inspector on the prairies reported in 1915 concerning residential schools:

> Although the per capita grant given by the department was increased about four years ago, the religious bodies, under whose auspices these schools are operated, find the grant to be inadequate to meet the advanced cost of foodstuffs daily in use in these schools. Moreover, contribution toward the support of such institutions are said to have been diminished, owing chiefly to the financial stringency caused by the war in Europe.[100]

Contributing to a deteriorating situation was some missionaries' growing interest in conversion of Asians, viewed as more tractable and perhaps more glamorous than Aboriginal peoples.[101] To some extent Aboriginal schools ended up with the leftovers, missionaries lacking the zeal and determination to put themselves in the front line of Christianity's advance.

Federal stinginess was not lost on contemporaries. The respected anthropologist Diamond Jenness undertook considerable personal observation across Canada during the 1920s prior to writing his landmark description of the country's Aboriginal peoples. While damning the quality of teaching in many schools as 'exceedingly poor', he was very concerned that missionaries not be blamed since 'they lacked the resources and the staffs to provide a proper education. . . . It was not the missions that shirked their responsibility, but the federal government, and behind that government the people of Canada.'[102] Yet, as late as 1947, even as a Joint Parliamentary Committee was finally being established to probe Aboriginal affairs, the federal government was spending $45 a year per Aboriginal pupil in a federal day school compared with about $200 that the British Columbia government allocated per pupil in a public school.[103] As Father Lascelles insightfully concluded, 'Financial problems were one of the major handicaps the schools laboured under for more than half a century.'[104]

The Aboriginal Response and Changing Times

Perhaps the most fundamental critique of federal policy was its deluding of Aboriginal peoples. Certainly, not all parents sought formal schooling for their offspring. Concerning 'a large no. of children of the pure Siwash [Chinook word for Indian] persuasion between the ages of 5 and 16 in the district', an early British Columbia public teacher reported that 'it will be a difficult matter to get them to attend school as their respected progenitors believe them to be as well off without book learning as with it.'[105] Many an Indian agent reported that 'parents see in education the downfall of all their most cherished customs.'[106]

Yet many more families accepted at face value what they were given every reason to believe was, despite its obvious tradeoffs, a genuine opportunity for their children. Aboriginal parents in British Columbia sent their children, first to public schools and then to federal schools, as one former pupil put it, 'to learn White people's ways'.[107] A woman born in 1931 remembered her mother's words: "'You're going to have to learn to read and write because when you grow up you're going to have to get a job.'"[108] Other times it was fathers who made their children aware of changing times. "'It's going to get crowded in the valley in a few years", he said, ". . . you kids want to get yourselves an education. Get a job. That way you'll be okay.'"[109] The deception wrought on Aboriginal parents was deliberate. Pupils were repeatedly admonished against giving their families details of what went on in school and in some cases prohibited from doing so. As late as the 1950s, letters were routinely censored. 'Sister Theo checks our letters home. We're not allowed to say anything about the school. I might get the strap, or worse.'[110]

British Columbia families became frustrated as they realized that their children were being treated unfairly. The refrain was the same regardless of geographical area or particular circumstances. 'Children are not taught enough.'[111] 'They just get nicely started—they just get their eyes opened the same as young birds and then they are turned out to fly. They don't get enough education for a livelihood nor are they taught a trade of any kind.'[112] 'The boys are not learning how to hunt and trap and set a net for fish. . . . They are supposed to go to Lejac to be educated, but they are not in the classrooms. They are in the fields or the barns, and the girls are too much in the sewing room or the kitchen.'[113] 'We all apply to have school at our own place. . . . Please look into matter as soon as possible. We feed our children at home then.'[114]

Not only were such voices unheard by federal policy makers, but individual parents faced tremendous obstacles when they sought to intervene in their children's best interests. Two examples from Vancouver Island are indicative. 'I wanted my boys to go to high school, so I went to see the Indian agent, M.S. Todd, and told him so. He said to me, "Nothing doing!" I asked him, "Isn't it for everybody?" and he answered me, "Not for you people."'[115] A second father was forced to desperate measures so that his children 'would be able to go to school a full term'.

> The school at Village Island was run by the Indian Department and we used to have that schoolteacher for three months a year. . . . I went over to the Indian Office at Alert Bay and pleaded with the Indian agent to keep her on for another couple months. He told me that he had no authority to pay her for another month and that they had spent all that was allowed. So I went to the school teacher and asked if she would accept $50 to stay for another month. . . . So the next month Simon Beans paid her $50 to stay for another month. That's how hard it was.[116]

Parents who resisted federal schools altogether in favour of the local public school rarely succeeded. One exception was a North Vancouver parent who, having spent a decade in residential school, was determined that his children would not do so. Given that this was at the beginning of the Second World War, it may be that the system was beginning to crack, alternatively that this father was particularly determined:

> We didn't want to send them to no boarding school because I was working and we wanted them at home. We had quite a time to have them accepted into the public school. We finally got them admitted. Priscilla and Barbara were the first Indian chil-

dren to be accepted into the public school. . . . I had to struggle with Indian Affairs, the North Vancouver School Board, the West Vancouver School Board to get my children in school. I had to pay their tuition myself for two years to have my children go to the public school. I paid five dollars a month per child.[117]

It was not just adults but also children who became actors. In some cases pupils through their own efforts mitigated the schools' worst characteristics not just for themselves but for their fellow pupils. As one of them recalled about his time at residential school:

> Sometimes we used to help the ones who needed it. I always had that in my mind because I was brought up by my people, the teaching I got was to always try to help the other person. . . . I used to take the lower class out who were having problems, go for a walk. . . . I taught them about nature, making a bow and arrow, little canoes, to get their minds off problems.[118]

More often, pupils simply refused to cooperate as they realized that residential school was not what it purported to be. 'The boys often rebelled and I didn't blame them. They were supposed to be in Lejac to get educated, but instead they were unpaid labourers, living on poor food and no more freedom than if they were prisoners in a jail.'[119] Pupils protested treatment deemed unfair and discriminatory and, in cases of desperation, they ran away. 'I ran away from the bus that was going to take me back to school and I hid in the bush until the priests and the police officers stopped looking for me.'[120] 'Some were successful and managed to reach their parents' traplines, but more often, they were caught by the Mounties, brought back and whipped.'[121] Sociologist Celia Haig-Brown has argued that resistance was integral to everyday life in residential school.[122]

Over time Aboriginal peoples did effect change, but extraordinarily slowly. Unlike the United States where federal policy began to encourage children into public schools during the interwar years, in Canada the symbiosis between state and church was too comfortable to be altered until it became absolutely impossible to ignore changing times.[123] Only after the Second World War did increased awareness of Aboriginal peoples lead to the creation of a Select Joint Committee of the Senate and House of Commons, which in 1951 called for Aboriginal peoples' integration into the Canadian mainstream. Although Aboriginal education was still under federal jurisdiction, Aboriginal children were encouraged to attend provincial schools or a private school run by one of the religious denominations that had previously operated federal residential and day schools. Funding still came from the federal government, through tuition agreements negotiated with provincial governments or religious denominations. Early integration during the 1950s was often top down, Aboriginal children attending a local public school for grades beyond those available in an existing federal school. 'Dorothy goes to classes at St Mark's now, the Catholic high school in town. All the pupils in grade ten, eleven and twelve do. Father Pitt drives them in a yellow school bus every day.'[124] Integration sometimes led to new forms of discrimination. 'We still had to wear the residential school clothes and this made an obvious distinction between us and the other students who would taunt us.'[125] For individual Aboriginal children integration sometimes existed more in theory than in practice. 'It was difficult going to [public] school, a lot of ideas and attitudes haven't changed much. Segregation is happening, not visibly but in the classes.' At this school Aboriginal children were seated separately in the classroom, and it remained very much a 'white man's school'.[126] Other children continued to attend federal schools not that much changed from previous decades. 'We had a school that taught Grades One to Seven, with teachers hired by the Department of Indian Affairs. Some of them were good, but others were young and didn't give a hell. The villagers, the chief, and the councillors had no say in the qualifications or lack of them in the teachers who were hired—we just took what we could get.'[127] By 1970 three quarters of the 13,000 Aboriginal pupils of British Columbia were attending integrated institutions.

About the same time, in 1969, Prime Minister Pierre Elliott Trudeau issued a white paper, or policy document, calling for total Aboriginal integration into his 'just society'. He proposed to repeal the Indian Act and abolish Aboriginal peoples' special status in Canada. The Aboriginal response was overwhelmingly negative, a decade and more of growing awareness having awoken pride in heritage and culture. The white paper was withdrawn in favour of Aboriginal self-determination looking toward Aboriginal control over their own affairs. Band-operated schools, whose numbers have steadily increased across Canada, were intended to encourage pride in Aboriginal languages and cultures alongside the necessary skills to participate in mainstream society.

The official shift in Aboriginal education policy did not effect change immediately. As one band leader recalled about the 1970s: 'We had to fight for every dollar and every bit of independence we could get for the education of our children. A policy of delay, delay, delay, was practised and is still practised.'[128] The schooling of Aboriginal children remains a federal responsibility overseen by the Department of Indian Affairs, but tuition agreements with provinces, churches, and bands means that children in British Columbia, like their counterparts across Canada, no longer have a single educational option. Aboriginal children living on a reserve often attend a school operated by the local band, especially at the lower grade levels. Older children usually go by bus to the nearest public or Catholic parochial high school. Other families living on a reserve may have chosen to send their children from kindergarten on to a nearby public or parochial school. Most Aboriginal children living in urban settings now attend school alongside their non-Aboriginal contemporaries almost as a matter of course. Children in some urban areas also have alternative Aboriginal-oriented facilities available to them. These shifts, as important as they are, only go part way. A paucity of Aboriginal teachers, inadequate support for teaching Aboriginal languages, and lack of appropriate Aboriginal content in textbooks and in the classroom are only some of the difficulties yet to be resolved for the education of British Columbia Aboriginal children to become truly equal to that of all other British Columbia children.[129]

The Legacy

Although the residential school has disappeared from the Canadian educational landscape, its legacy endures. Federal policy resulted in practices whose consequences are still being lived across British Columbia and in the rest of Canada:

> If I had to pick one area where the federal government, through the Department of Indian Affairs, inflicted the most harm on my people, it would have to be in the field of education. . . . At the beginning of the white man's rule, Aboriginal people were confined to reserves, most of them far away from schools. When the government was finally forced to do something about the lack of educational facilities, the solution was a partnership between church and state to set up residential schools. Children were removed from their communities and placed in an alien environment that almost destroyed their culture and their language; we call it cultural genocide.[130]

The personal accounts used to ground this essay have ranged through time and across British Columbia, but they have all told a similar story.

Half or fewer British Columbia Aboriginal children of past generations actually attended residential school, but numbers were sufficient for family life to deteriorate. A pupil has recalled her 'inability to show love to my mom, brothers, and sisters.'[131] Students of different sexes were almost always separated in residential school, and siblings in the same school often could not even speak to each other for months and years on end. 'I never did get to know my brothers. We were kept away from each other for too long. To this day I don't know much about my brothers. I just know that they are my brothers.'[132] 'After a year spent learning to see and hear only what the priests and brothers wanted you to see and hear, even the people we loved came to look ugly.'[133] 'Some of the most damaging things that resulted from my experiences at residential school was lack of nurturing as well as being denied learning parenting skills.'[134] The next generation reaped the consequences:

> Although my older brother and I didn't attend residential school, we didn't really escape it either as it visited us every day of our childhood through the replaying over and over of our parents' childhood trauma and grief which they never had the opportunity to resolve in their lifetimes . . . I grieve for the gentle man in my father who was never allowed to grow, and I grieve for my mother who never had the loving relationships she deserved, nor the opportunity to be the mother I knew she could have been.[135]

Languages became a casualty. A father who spoke six languages in his job as a court interpreter deliberately refrained from teaching his children.

> He speaks lots of Indian languages, but he won't teach us. Mom won't either. She says the nuns and priests will strap us. . . . The nuns strapped her all the time for speaking Indian, because she couldn't speak English. She said just when the welts on her hands and arms healed, she got it again. That's why she didn't want us to learn Indian.[136]

The practice was widespread. 'Because my parents also attended residential school they didn't see the value in teaching us our language. The Indian Agent told them not to speak to their children in Haida because it would not help them in school.'[137]

'It didn't matter that Carrier was the only language we knew—we were told not to use it and, if we did, wham! right now. I think now that it was the worst thing that happened to us.'[138]

The self-fulfilling prophecy inherent in racism came to fruition as Aboriginal peoples deemed to be inferior were schooled for inequality and thereby largely did end up at the bottom ranks of Canadian society. 'The residential school (not just the one I went to—they were the common form of Indian education all across Canada) was the perfect system for instilling a strong sense of inferiority.'[139] The reasons are not difficult to fathom:

> For many of us our most vulnerable and impressionable years, our childhood years, were spent at the residential school where we had always been treated like dirt and made to believe that we weren't as good as other people. . . . I find it hard to believe that these schools claim to have groomed children for success when we were not allowed to be normal children . . . the constant message [was] that because you are Native you are part of a weak, defective race, unworthy of a distinguished place in society. That is the reason you have to be looked after. . . . That to me is not training for success, it is training for self-destruction.[140]

'I was frustrated about how we were treated, humiliated, and degraded, so I drank and took drugs to numb the frustrations of how my life had turned out.'[140] And,

> A lot of us left residential school as mixed-up human beings, not able to cope with family or life. Many of us came out with a huge inferiority complex realizing something was missing, but not knowing what it was. Many searched for love and support in the wrong way. Girls became promiscuous, thinking this was the only way they could feel close to another person. Never having learned to cope with the outside world, many turned to drinking and became alcoholics.[142]

For almost a century the federal government in Canada sought to control the lives and souls of Aboriginal peoples. Outwardly espousing assimilation through education, the federal government neither took the leadership nor provided the financial resources to achieve any other goal than the self-affirming prophecy inherent in racist rhetoric. Religious denominations may have acted from the highest of motives, in their view, but lives were destroyed nonetheless. The logic behind the concept of the residential school was muddled at its best, duplicitous at its worst. The system's attributes made possible no other goal than Aboriginal peoples' absolute marginalization from Canadian life—a goal that schools achieved with remarkable success.

Unable to consider Aboriginal peoples as different between time and place or capable of exercising control over their daily lives, federal policy deliberately bypassed the opportunity to integrate Aboriginal peoples into the larger society at their own pace, a process which had begun at least in a small way in late nineteenth-century British Columbia. The Department of Indian Affairs may have saved a few dollars in the short run, but the cost was generations of diminished and even wasted lives. The past cannot be undone, but it can be better understood. Only then can the cycle of the residential school, and its dominance of Aboriginal educational

history, be broken. 'The silent suffering has to end. It is time for the healing to start and the only way that will happen is if we acknowledge the past, face it, understand it, deal with it, and make sure that nothing like that ever happens again.'[143]
[1995]

Notes

1. Funding was provided by the Social Sciences and Humanities Research Council of Canada made possible research on which this essay draws. I am grateful to SSHRCC and to Donna Penney, Clint Evans, Dana Whyte, Valerie Giles, and Roger Wiebe for their research assistance. Selections of this essay draw on Jean Barman, Yvonne Hébert, and Don McCaskill, ed., *Indian Education in Canada*, vol. 1: *The Legacy* (Vancouver: UBC Press, 1986); and Jean Barman, *The West Beyond the West: A History of British Columbia* (Toronto: University of Toronto Press, 1991).
2. See, for example, *Breaking the Silence: An Interpretive Study of Residential School Impact and Healing as Illustrated by the Stories of First Nations Individuals* (Ottawa: Assembly of First Nations, 1994); Linda Jaine, ed., *Residential Schools: The Stolen Years* (Saskatoon: Extension University Press, University of Saskatchewan, 1993); Maddie Harper, '*Mushhole': Memories of a Residential School* (Toronto: Sister Vision Press, 1993); Jo-ann Archibald, 'Resistance to an unremitting process: Racism, curriculum and education in Western Canada', in J.A. Mangan, ed., *The Imperial Curriculum: Racial images and education in the British Colonial experience* (London: Routledge, 1993), 93–107 and 223–7; Isabelle Knockwood with Gillian Thomas, *Out of the Depths: The Experience of Mi'kmaw Children at the Indian Residential School at Shubenacadie, Nova Scotia* (Lockeport, NS: Roseway, 1992); Marilyn Millward, 'Clean Behind the Ears? Micmac Parents, Micmac Children, and the Shubenacadie Residential School', *New Maritimes* (March/April 1992): 6–15; Shirley Sterling, *My Name is Seepeetza* (Vancouver: Douglas & McIntyre, 1992); Linda R. Bull, 'Indian Residential Schooling: The Native Perspective', *Canadian Journal of Native Education* 18 (supplement 1991): 1–64; N. Rosalyn Ing, 'The Effects of Residential Schools on Native Child-Rearing Practices', *Canadian Journal of Native Education* 18 (Supplement 1991): 65–118; Jo-Anne Fiske, 'Gender and the Paradox of Residential Education in Carrier Society', in Jane Gaskell and Arlene McLaren, ed., *Women and Education*, 2nd ed. (Calgary: Detselig, 1991), 131–46; Basil H. Johnston, *Indian School Days* (Toronto: Key Porter, 1988); and Celia Haig-Brown, *Resistance and Renewal: Surviving the Indian Residential School* (Vancouver: Tillicum Library, 1988). For a generally positive perspective, see Thomas A. Lascelles, *Roman Catholic Residential Schools in British Columbia* (Vancouver: Order of OMI in BC, 1990).
3. Jaine, ed., *Residential Schools*, x.
4. Department of Indian Affairs [DIA], *Annual Report* [AR], 1895, xxi.
5. DIA, *AR*, 1895, xxi.
6. Personal testimony is used not to set apart individuals or schools but rather to demonstrate how federal policy constructed Aboriginal pupils' experience of education regardless of individual or institution. At the same time, it is important to note that the recollections of residential school used here, all of which are in the public domain, do refer to a variety of schools: All Hallows (Clara Clare), Christie (Francis Charlie), Kamloops (George Manuel, Shirley Sterling), Lejac (Lizette Hall, Mary John), Port Alberni (Vera Manuel, Charlie Thompson), St Eugene's at Cranbrook (Troy Hunter), St George's at Lytton (Simon Baker), St Joseph's at Williams Lake (Bev Sellars, Augusta

Tappage), St Mary's Mission (Mary Englund), St Michael's at Alert Bay (Mabel James, Clayton Mack), St Paul's at North Vancouver (Lois Guss), and Edmonton (Rosa Bell, Art Collison, sent from Haida Gwaii/Queen Charlotte Islands). Testimonies not otherwise footnoted are in Jaine, ed., *Residential Schools*.

7. For elaboration, see for Canada, Daniel Francis, *The Imaginary Indian: The Image of the Indian in Canadian Culture* (Vancouver: Arsenal Pulp Press, 1992); and Robin Fisher, chapter entitled 'The Image of the Indian' in his *Contact and Conflict: Indian-European Relations in British Columbia, 1774–1890* (Vancouver: UBC Press, 1977 and 1992); and for the United States, Robert F. Berkhofer Jr., 'White Conceptions of Indians', in Wilcomb E. Washburn, ed., *History of Indian-White Relations*, vol. 4 of *Handbook of North American Indians* (Washington: Smithsonian Institution, 1988), 522–47, which summarizes Berkhofer, *The White Man's Indian: Images of the American Indian from Columbus to the Present* (New York: Knopf, 1978).

8. DIA, *AR*, 1887, lxxx.

9. DIA, *AR*, 1880, 8.

10. On the industrial school, see E. Brian Titley, 'Indian Industrial Schools in Western Canada', in Nancy M. Sheehan, J. Donald Wilson, and David C. Jones, ed., *Schools in the West: Essays in Canadian Educational History* (Calgary: Detselig, 1986), 133–53.

11. See Table 5 in Barman, *West beyond the West*, 363.

12. For detail, see Barman, *West beyond the West*, 13–17.

13. DIA, *AR*,1910, 327.

14. *The West Shore*, September 1884, 275, cited in Patricia E. Roy, '*The West Shore's* View of British Columbia, 1884', *Journal of the West* 22:4 (October 1984): 28.

15. Charles Mair to George Denison, Okanagan Mission, 5 December 1892, Mair Correspondence in possession of Duane Thomson and used with his permission. Emphasis in original.

16. DIA, *AR*, 1874, 37.

17. DIA, *AR*, 1880, 3.

18. DIA, *AR*,1890, xxx.

19. DIA, *AR*, 1902, 283.

20. Alex Deans to John Jessop, Superintendent of Education, Langley, 26 June 1876, in British Columbia Superintendent of Education [hereafter BCSE], Inward Correspondence [IC], British Columbia Archives and Records Service [BCARS], GR 1445.

21. Walter Hunter, teacher at Lillooet, to S.D. Pope, Superintendent of Education, Lillooet, 7 August 1886, in BCSE, IC.

22. Petition from a group of parents at Port Essington to S.D. Pope, Port Essington, 27 August 1888, in BCSE, IC.

23. O.N. Hughett, Secretary of Genoa Trustees Board, to S.D. Pope, Genoa, 21 September 1891, in BCSE, IC.

24. John Jessop to J[ane] E. Trenaman, Victoria, 30 October 1876, in BCSE, Outward Correspondence [OC], BCARS, GR 450.

25. James Malpass, Secretary of North Cedar Trustee Board, to S.D. Pope, North Cedar, 17 May 1886, BCSE, IC; and S.D. Pope to James Malpass, Victoria, 20 May 1886, in BCSE, OC.

26. J[ane] E. Trenaman, teacher at Hope, to John Jessop, Hope, 25 October 1876, in BCSE, IC.

27. Trenaman to Jessop, 25 October 1876.

28. Mrs [Catherine] Cordiner, teacher at Granville, to John Jessop, Granville, 16 September 1875, in BCSE, IC.

29. S. Shepherd, teacher at Yale, to S.D. Pope, Yale, 12 December 1888, in BCSE, IC; and S.D. Pope to S. Shepherd, Victoria, 15 December 1888, in BCSE, OC.

30. S.D. Pope to George Hopkins, Victoria, 29 July 1889, in BCSE, OC.
31. S.D. Pope to Samuel Cutler, Victoria, 1 August 1893, in BCSE, OC. The circular's date is inferred from M.E. Sheirs, teacher at Port Kells, to S.D. Pope, Port Kells, 13 October 1891, in BCSE, IC.
32. M.E. Sheirs, teacher at Port Kells, to S.D. Pope, Port Kells, 13 October 1891, in BCSE, IC.
33. William McAdam, teacher at Port Hammond, to S.D. Pope, Port Hammond, 2 November 1891, in BCSE, IC.
34. Samuel Cutler, Secretary of Sooke Trustees, to S.D. Pope, Sooke, 31 October 1892, in BCSE, IC.
35. S.D. Pope to H[arriet] Young, teacher at Pavillion, Victoria, 27 March, 1894, in BCSE, OC.
36. Samuel Cutler, Secretary of Sooke Trustees, to S.D. Pope, Sooke, 8 November 1893, in BCSE, IC.
37. For historical statistics on BC, see Lascelles, *Roman Catholic Residential Schools*, 95–8.
38. This argument grounds Paul Tennant, *Aboriginal Peoples and Politics: The Indian Land Question in British Columbia, 1849–1989* (Vancouver: UBC Press, 1990).
39. Reproduced in DIA, AR, 1895, 348–51; also DIA, AR, 1894, xxi.
40. DIA, AR, 1896, xxxvii.
41. Jacqueline Gresko, 'Creating Little Dominions Within the Dominion: Early Catholic Indian Schools in Saskatchewan and British Columbia', in Barman, Hébert, and McCaskill, *Indian Education*, v. 1, 96.
42. Jean E. Speare, ed., *The Days of Augusta* (Vancouver: J.J. Douglas, 1973), 18.
43. George Manuel and Michael Posluns, *The Fourth World: An Indian Reality* (Toronto: Collier Macmillan Canada, 1974), 64. According to Celia Haig-Brown's portrait of the same school, 'no child attended school for longer than two hours a day.' Haig-Brown, *Resistance and Renewal*, 61.
44. Verna J. Kirkness, ed., *Khot-La-Cha: The Autobiography of Chief Simon Baker* (Vancouver: Douglas & McIntyre, 1994), 30–1.
45. Kirkness, ed., *Khot-La-Cha*, 29.
46. Lascelles, *Roman Catholic Residential Schools*, 30.
47. DIA, AR, 1895, *xxiii*.
48. Lizette Hall, *The Carrier, My People* (Fort St James: n.p., 1992), 81.
49. Speare, *Days of Augusta*, 7.
50. Manuel and Posluns, *Fourth World*, 64.
51. Thompson Ferrier, *Indian Education in the Northwest* (Toronto: Department of Missionary Literature of the Methodist Church, Canada, c1906), 17 and 25. The Methodist Church was parroting federal rhetoric; see, for instance, DIA, AR, 1888, x, and 1897, 60.
52. Francis Charlie, quoted in Lascelles, *Roman Catholic Residential Schools*, 44.
53. Manuel and Posluns, *Fourth World*, 66.
54. Hall, *Carrier*, 81.
55. Data on Indian pupils taken from 'School Statements' in DIA, *Annual Reports*; on pupils in provincial schools from *Annual Survey of Education* (Ottawa: Dominion Bureau of Statistics), renamed *Elementary and Secondary Education in Canada*.
56. Lascelles, *Roman Catholic Residential Schools*, 83.
57. Bridget Moran, *Justa: A First Nations Leader* (Vancouver: Arsenal Pulp Press, 1994), 51.
58. DIA, AR, 1896, xxxviii.
59. Hall, *Carrier*, 81.
60. Moran, *Justa*, 57.
61. Clellan S. Ford, *Smoke from their Fires: The Life of a Kwakiutl Chief* (New Haven: Yale University Press, 1941), 100.

62. Correspondence concerning Lejac School, 1910, cited in Jo-Anne Fiske, 'Life at Lejac', in Thomas Thorner, ed., *Sa Ts'e: Historical Perspectives on Northern British Columbia* (Prince George: College of New Caledonia Press, 1989), 243.
63. The yearly reports submitted by individual day schools and extracted in DIA's *Annual Reports* often include information on teachers. See, for example, 1910, 328–41.
64. Letter from Chehalis band following meeting of 5 March 1936, cited in Archibald, 'Resistance', 101.
65. Inspector's response to letter from Chehalis band following meeting of 5 March 1936, cited in Archibald, 'Resistance', 101.
66. Bridget Moran, *Stoney Creek Woman: The Story of Mary John* (Vancouver: Tillicum, 1988), 53–4.
67. Quoted in Fiske, 'Life at Lejac', 244.
68. Notation dated 1932, cited in Norma Sluman and Jean Goodwill, *John Tootoosis: A Biography of a Cree Leader* (Ottawa: Golden Dog Press, 1982), 157.
69. James P. Spradley, *Guests Never Leave Hungry: The Autobiography of James Sewid, a Kwakiutl Indian* (New Haven: Yale University Press, 1969), 191.
70. DIA, AR, 1912, 399.
71. Mary Englund, quoted in Margaret Whitehead, *Now You Are My Brother: Missionaries in British Columbia, Sound Heritage series* no. 34 (Victoria: Provincial Archives of British Columbia, 1981), 64.
72. David Johnson, quoted in Whitehead, *Now You Are My Brother*, 50.
73. DIA, AR, 1911, 374.
74. Lascelles, *Roman Catholic Residential Schools*, 42.
75. DIA, AR,1896, xxxvii.
76. DIA, AR,1906, 251.
77. Lascelles, *Roman Catholic Residential Schools*, 42.
78. DIA, AR, 1891, xiii.
79. Manuel and Poslums, *Fourth World*, 64.
80. Marjorie Mitchell and Anna Franklin, 'When You Don't Know the Language, Listen to the Silence: An Historical Overview of Native Indian Women in BC', in Barbara K. Latham and Roberta J. Pazdro, eds., *Not Just Pin Money: Selected Essays On The History Of Women's Work In British Columbia* (Victoria: Camosun College, 1984), 24.
81. Speare, *Days of Augusta*, 18.
82. Moran, *Stoney Creek Woman*, 44–5.
83. Moran, *Justa*, 51.
84. Manuel and Posluns, *Fourth World*, 65.
85. Sterling, *My Name is Seepeetza*, 24.
86. Hall, *Carrier*, 83.
87. Moran, *Stoney Creek Woman*, 39.
88. Gwen Cash, *Off the Record: The Personal Reminiscences of Canada's First Woman Reporter* (Langley: Stagecoach, 1977), 23.
89. *All Hallows in the West* [school magazine of All Hallows School], Yale, British Columbia, 6, no. 8 (Ascension 1906): 538.
90. Comparisons were made for the school years 1899/1900 and 1907/08. The two years compare Aboriginal and rural public schools operating in close geographical proximity, in the case of 1899–1900 Alberni, Alert Bay, Comox, Quamichan, Saanich, and Somenos, in 1907/08 Alert Bay, Bella Coola, Clayoquot, Hazelton, Lytton, Telegraph Creek, and Ucluelet. Comparative data extracted from British Columbia, Department of Education, *Annual Report*, Tables A and D, and DIA, AR, 'School Statement'.

91. DIA, *AR*,1899/1900, pt. 2, 14–15, financial statements for All Hallows, Port Simpson and St Mary's boarding schools.
92. DIA, *AR*, 1907/08, pt. 2, 21–4, financial statements for Ahousat, Alberni, All Hallows, Port Simpson, St Mary's, Sechelt, and Squamish boarding schools.
93. Calculated from financial statements in *All Hallows in the West*.
94. Advertisement in *News-Advertiser* (Vancouver), 10 August 1902.
95. DIA, *AR*, 1911, xxvi and 294–5.
96. University School, *Prospectus*, 1912, in St Michaels-University School Archives, Victoria.
97. Because no breakdown of financial support for individual Indian day schools is included following the 1910 revision, mean support per pupil across British Columbia is compared with mean cost in rural public schools operating in geographical proximity to an Indian day school, being in this case Alert Bay, Bella Coola, Clayoquot, Hazelton, Lytton, Masset, Similkameen, Telegraph Creek, and Ucluelet. Comparable data is extracted from British Columbia, Department of Education, *Annual Report*, Tables A and D.
98. DIA, *AR*, 1912, 408. For another example, see DIA, *AR*, 1911, 378.
99. DIA, *AR*, 1912, 399.
100. DIA, *AR*, 1915, 238.
101. This point is made in John Webster Grant, *Moon of Wintertime: Missionaries and the Indians of Canada in Encounter since 1534* (Toronto: University of Toronto Press, 1984), 191.
102. Diamond Jenness, 'Canada's Indians Yesterday. What of Today?', *Canadian Journal of Economic and Political Science* 20, no. 1 (February 1954), reprinted in A.L. Getty and Antoine S. Lussier, eds, *As Long as the Sun Shines and Water Flows: A Reader in Canadian Native Studies* (Vancouver: UBC Press, 1983), 162.
103. Data comes from DIA, *Annual Reports*.
104. Lascelles, *Roman Catholic Residential Schools*, 83.
105. Thomas Leduc, teacher at Lillooet, to John Jessop, Lillooet, 8 January 1876, in BCSE, IC.
106. DIA, *AR*, 1888, 104.
107. Clare Clare, cited in Jean Barman, 'Separate and Unequal: Indian and White Girls at All Hallows School, 1884–1920', in Barman, Hébert, and McCaskill, *Indian Education*, v. 1, 112.
108. Ruth Cook, quoted in Dorothy Haegert, *Children of the First People* (Vancouver: Tillicum, 1983), 21.
109. Sterling, *My Name is Seepeetza*, 125.
110. Ibid., 12.
111. DIA, *AR*, 1911, 381.
112. William Sepass, Sto:lo Chief, testifying before Royal Commission on Indian Affairs reporting in 1916, cited in Archibald, 'Resistance', 100.
113. Moran, *Stoney Creek Woman*, 53.
114. Stoney Creek Council to DIA, 1917, cited in Fiske, 'Life at Lejac', 240.
115. Harry Assu with Joy Inglis, *Assu of Cape Mudge: Recollections of a Coastal Indian Chief* (Vancouver: UBC Press, 1989), 95–6.
116. Spradley, *Guests Never Leave Hungry*, 125–6.
117. Kirkness, ed., *Khot-La-Cha*, 73.
118. Ibid., 31.
119. Moran, *Stoney Creek Woman*, 44.
120. Moran, *Justa*, 10.
121. Moran, *Stoney Creek Woman*, 44.
122. Haig-Brown, *Resistance and Renewal*.

123. See Margaret Connell Szasz and Carmelia Ryan, 'American Indian Education', in Wilcomb E. Washburn, ed., *History of Indian-White Relations*, vol. 4 of *Handbook of North American Indians* (Washington: Smithsonian Institution, 1988), 284–301; Irving G. Hendrick, 'The Federal Campaign for the Admission of Indian Children into Public Schools, 1890–1934', *American Indian Culture and Research Journal* 5 (1981): 13–32; Margaret Connell Szasz, *Education and the American Indian: The Road to Self-Determination Since 1928* (Albuquerque: University of New Mexico Press, 1977); and Guy B. Senese, *Self-Determination and the Social Education of Native Americans* (New York: Praeger, 1991).

124. Sterling, *My Name is Seepeetza*, 41.

125. Art Collison, 'Healing Myself Through Our Haida Traditional Customs', in Jaine, ed., *Residential Schools*, 38.

126. Sharon McIvor Grismer, quoted in Niehaus, Valerie, 'Mrs Sharon McIvor Grismer', *Nicola Valley Historical Quarterly* 1: 4 (October 1978): 7.

127. Moran, *Justa*, 103, referring to 1971.

128. Moran, *Justa*, 156.

129. This assessment is necessarily simplistic; on the complexities see Archibald, 'Resistance', 93–107 and 223–7; and the essays in Marie Battiste and Jean Barman, eds, *First Nation Education in Canada: The Circle Unfolds* (Vancouver: UBC Press, 1995).

130. Moran, *Justa*, 155–6.

131. Rosa Bell, 'Journeys', in Jaine, ed., *Residential Schools*, 13.

132. Bell, 'Journeys', 10.

133. Manuel and Posluns, *Fourth World*, 67.

134. Charlie Thompson, 'The First Day', in Jaine, ed., *Residential Schools*, 129.

135. Vera Manuel, 'The Abyss', in Jaine, ed., *Residential Schools*, 115.

136. Sterling, *My Name is Seepeetza*, 36, 67, and 89.

137. Bell, 'Journeys', 10.

138. Moran, *Justa*, 55.

139. Manuel and Posluns, *Fourth World*, 67.

140. Bev Sellers, 'Against All Odds', in Jaine, ed., *Residential Schools*, 131.

141. Collison, 'Healing Myself', 39.

142. Lois Guss, 'Residential School Survivor', in Jaine, ed., *Residential Schools*, 92.

143. Sellers, 'Against All Odds', 129.

From Our Mothers' Arms

Constance Deiter

Inez Deiter

Inez Deiter is from the Peepeekisis Indian reserve in Southern Saskatchewan, but she was born and raised at the Red Pheasant reserve in the North Battleford region. She attended the Onion Lake Indian Residential School and the Prince Albert Indian Residential School as a child from 1938 to 1946. Her memories are typical of the experiences of children attending the school. She is in her early sixties. I interviewed her; she is also my mother.

I was born on the Red Pheasant reserve in a little log cabin in 1931 or 1932. I was raised on the reserve until my mother separated from father and took me to a Métis settlement in Alberta called Fishing Lake.

Tell me a little about your education, did you attend primary school? Day school?

Inez: Nothing, in those days there was not anything like that. There wasn't a day school, that was in the thirties. Everyone was poor, the Métis people were really poor. The people I used to stay with didn't have floors. I remember Joe Pareanteau, they were very, very good to me. My mother died when I was four years old. I lived with the Métis until I was eight years old. My stepfather took me to an orphanage-convent in Edmonton.

Then the people in Red Pheasant were looking for me, but my mother changed my name to Letendre. A relative in Edmonton spotted me, Jesse Latta, told my people in Red Pheasant. My people made arrangements for me. I don't remember too much about the orphanage. There were white girls there. Then one day a nun called me in and told me that I was an Indian and not a Letendre. That I had relatives and I had a father in Red Pheasant reserve. Your people want you, so they put me on the train and someone met me at Lloydminster. A Sam Decouteau met me, then took me to the Onion Lake School. They took me straight to the school.

My first contact was with my relatives, Freda, Gladys, Florence, and my cousin Willie, and my brother Maurius. I remember my cousin Florence spent all night trying to tell me my name was Inez Wuttunee. She was teaching me how to spell the name Wuttunee. I said no, I was not Inez. I was stubborn because I thought I was a real Roman Catholic and my name was Mary. They told me there was already another Mary Wuttunee and you have to stick with Inez. That was my first contact with my relatives. They were happy to meet me.

I got there [my first day at school] at night. I was ashamed to undress in front of my cousins. They were so fed up with me, so my cousin Gladys threw me in clothes and all. They gave me some charcoal to brush my teeth. I had a tooth brush and a towel. I remember the supervisor gave me a number; it was 142. It was the number I would use all through boarding school. It was more or less adjusting from the convent to learn my relatives.

The next day they told me I had a brother. I went upstairs. They called it a parlour where people would go and visit. I remember seeing Maurius for the first time since I was a little girl. I saw this man Maurius, he was fifteen then. He had big tears in his eyes when he saw me. He told me, 'Gee, you ugly.' That's the first thing he told me cause we looked exactly alike. He was teasing me about my freckles. He was happy to see me. He told me about my Dad. He found out I couldn't speak Cree, and he knew that was going to be a problem. The first word he taught me was *mistick*, and that was for a stick. And then I knew that my Dad didn't speak Cree and my relatives all spoke Cree, so I knew I had to try and grasp some of this Cree. I heard the girls speaking Cree and I would copy them. The Cree was forbidden to be spoken at the school, so they would teach me on the *kimooch* (sly) at night. We would sit up and the girls would teach me Cree. I noticed that everything was secretive, and that's what I found out when I went there. Everything was secretive.

I soon learned the ropes. We didn't have enough to eat. We were given jobs. At nine years old I didn't have as many jobs. I was kind of daring. They always made me—I'd be the one to go into the pantry. The big girls would go work in the staff dining room. They would come up with butter. They would steal butter. And we used to be hungry at night. I remember going to the bakery and I stole a loaf of bread. We used to wear bloomers and I stuck the loaf and raced up the stairs. I was kinda a hero after that 'cause we all shared this bread and butter and whatever we could get. It was really hard. We learned to be on the sly, secretive, because I noticed that they would all keep quiet when the supervisors would come in. I didn't have any problems like a lot of girls had with cultural experiences, where they had to have their braids cut off and all these stories about them wearing moccasins and having to fit into white man's shoes. I didn't have those problems because I knew these things from the convent. We were treated okay.

The Cree was what I was really interested in. I learned how to speak Cree at residential school. I made a lot of friends there. I was very friendly. I don't remember getting beaten up, I was kinda a ham, kinda leader.

A month after I started at the school, we were going back to our reserves. All the girls were excited, they got their little treasures, little suitcases, little gym bags, but I didn't have anything. My supervisor felt sorry for me, so she gave me a nice box to go home with. There was nothing in there except chocolate wrappers, and that is what I took home with me, and maybe a few clothes that were given to me. We went on a truck, we were all put in the back. The truck was covered, and there were benches. I remember sitting with my brother and he was busy trying to teach me

Cree. He was trying to prepare me for home. My cousins were all excited about what they were going to do for the summer.

When we got to Red Pheasant my dad was there and a lot of people were there to welcome me because they hadn't seen me for years. And the Cree was a problem. They were talking to me in Cree and Maurius was talking to me. He was my interpreter. My Dad said I looked like my mother and that I had freckles. They did not know what to do with me because I only spoke English. So they put me with Eli, my oldest brother. He was established with a wife and two kids, and lived in a log house. I remember meeting with my brother. I remember he was so happy to see me. I know he loved me and my other brothers came, Sam and Harry. It was a homecoming and it was nice. I learned to pick up a few words in Cree by the end of the summer.

Then it was time to go back to school. Maurius was not going to go back this time. Auntie Gladys and Eli put some clothes together for me. They took me back to school, and I started adjusting. When you were little you don't see all those things, but then as time went I heard, my ears were always open for Cree. They would talk about their summers. I spent time with Auntie Nancy's mother, she was a medicine woman. When I would go and visit she would say in Cree, 'a gift'. Like my presence was a great gift to her. That's the way those old people used to be. They were so very nice.

Then it dawned on me that things were not the way they should be. I was becoming sneaky too, lying, in order to survive, we had to do these things. We used to lie and I think all those ten commandments that we were taught when we were in church all the time. We learned to be soldiers. That was nice. I used to like the band. But the roughness I didn't like, the supervisor was rough. The principal was rough, Mr Ellis. He used to strap the girls. I remember I ran away one time. He told us to undress and put our nightgowns on and take this great big web strap. He would give us strappings; we would see the foam on his mouth. He used to get so mad, maybe close to a heart attack. He used to do the strappings. I remember I was kinda like a leader then. I noticed the little girls being abused. I remember I spoke out in line. We used to have to line up in a great big dining room. I remember we used to have a great big dining room. We fought for survival from the other girls. They would beat us up if we did not watch our p's and q's. So we had to resort to our relatives. I would have to look to our kinship to look after me. After Freda and Gladys left, there was Florence. We were kinda close, and we would look after each other. After Florence left, I had to be kinda tough for survival. I would help the younger girls who would be getting beat up by the other students. Of course we were all put together.

There was the junior, intermediate, and senior girls. By the time I was a senior girl, I was getting to be hard, and taking up for the junior girls and in order to survive we had to resort to a lot of things that were not normal. Then after a while you become bitter and you blame things. One instance, I would get mad when I went out with the little girls and we would go out on the playground. Most of my trouble was my big mouth. I would get mad when I would see the little girls outside in the winter time with wet pants. They wouldn't let them in to go to the washroom during the times we were to be outside. Not enough clothes, warm clothes. It was to become that way. I guess that is why Indians today look after one another because they had to survive. I became a big sister to a lot of those young girls. I remember one time talking out of line and the supervisor came and slapped me really hard on the face in front of everybody.

And another time Miss Hover, she was great for hitting kids on the ears, cuffing them. At that time, I had a running ear, neglect. No one bothered to take me to the hospital to get it looked after. She used to cuff me on the ear and say, 'You silly little hussy.' She used to call us down. These supervisors, this was during the war. They were not qualified, they were just there for the money. Consequently I got into a lot of trouble because I used to speak out. And today now, I can't hear. I'm deaf. Both my eardrums are damaged, and I have to wear a hearing aid. I always think that was from neglect. The girls used to have toothaches and they would suffer.

I think that the generation that Auntie Eleanor went through was terrible, the days before us. When we went it wasn't too bad, except for being hungry and not having enough clothes to wear in the winter. It was survival, but we used to have to learn to steal and lie, and be sneaky. I remember we used to tease each other, we used to have boyfriends, etc.

But the girls used to have girlfriends, boyfriends, passing notes in school. I remember one case while I was there at school. I think it was Georgina Vandel and Bertha Sanqui. They ran off, Bertha Sanqui's boyfriend was Tommy Bird, she eventually married him. And Georgina Vandel with Noel Wuttunee, my cousin. They ran off together. They were about fourteen and fifteen. After they were apprehended, they were brought back, and their heads were shaved, all their hair was gone. This was close to summer holidays and we were all so shocked.

I don't know who brought them back. I think the night watchman. We used to go in the truck, there was a lot of staff working there. Maybe someone reported them. I ran away too, in Prince Albert. It was dangerous, there was a ledge running outside the building; it was three stories high. We left through a window and outside on the ledge until we got to the fire escape. But I know lots of people who ran away, even this man Victor McNab. He ran away three times. He used sheets to get out. There were reasons that people ran away. Maybe if you don't get your way I guess. We all had to conform. A lot of it was the abuse others were suffering. Morale was very low. It was depressing. People would complain about the food. The food wasn't very good, watery porridge, and applesauce, mutton, and we didn't care for those. While I was in Onion Lake somebody burned the school down. It was in January and in the night. We were all put on trucks and sent to the Roman Catholic school at Onion Lake. I told them, I always used my wits. I said I was a Roman Catholic, then I was treated a little better. We were then sent back to the reserve.

I guess I could say the bitterness was brushed off on us. It was dull, it wasn't a happy place. Now, I think of little zombies. Us you know little zombies, like little puppets, not like today. Kids can do whatever they want. Over there you had to do it. One thing that came out is that today I find myself very rigid, doing things making sure they are done quick. I find myself jumping. I learned to become very anxious. That was part of our training from the boarding schools, and always finding a way to cope, even if it meant lying. We had to resort to devious methods for survival. I remember going home when I was fifteen. I remember I was always smart and good in school.

After the school burned in Onion Lake they found another school for us in Prince Albert, St Alvins. It was right across from the high school. I remember getting into a fight there. They were two sisters. That is what we had to do was to fight, take up for one another. We learned our culture from each other. We knew lots about different things. One time a girl said she was going to make it rain. She showed me how to do it, but when I went home and showed my relatives, they laughed at me. They taught me about the Round Dance, and the northern lights. One time in Prince Albert we were all sitting in the dorm. One girl said if you whistle, the northern lights they will come to you. Someone whistled and suddenly you heard a 'whoosh' and everybody crawled under their bed.

We weren't taught to be kind and gentle, we were taught to be rough except when we went back to the reserve. It was nice to go home to the reserve. One time I went to a Sundance, not to participate but just for the joy of seeing other students from the school. Already we were like brothers and sisters, forming a kinship because we were together ten months out of the year. This would be the time we would talk about our experiences at residential school. This would be the time we would tell our secrets from the school. Like it was the time for holidays, and this person had about four boxes of stuff to take home. So the supervisor asked her to open the boxes in front of all of us, and discovered that she was taking home sheets from the school. And she really embarrassed the girls. We were taught by public humiliation. Like the students that ran away, they had to go to school like that. They had to sit in the front of the class as if to say this is what will happen to you if you run away.

Bertha and Tommy did eventually get married and this was a real experience to them. I found out from that experience we were not really honest. We were taught to be deceitful, never honest. That beauty was taken from us, that innocence that caused us to be hard. We knew we were different from the white people, so consequently, when it came time to assimilate with them I couldn't stand them. I just couldn't even when I had my children, and there were PTA meetings. I would stay away, not realizing I was hurting my children. But just for the fear, because we were treated as if we were not accepted. I remember when we went to Prince Albert school. Freda knew how to act with white people, this was a stumbling block for us. Pretty well all of us were that way. We never had any love, or nurturing, mothering. My father was kinda cold. My friends were those in boarding school. I went to visit a friend a few years ago. The one I ran away with, she remembered how we walked all night to Duck Lake from Prince Albert. There was timber wolves and everything. When we got back we got a strapping.

I liked the kinship of the schools, but to prepare us for life, for our own families, we didn't know nothing, we didn't know any parenting skills. Those who didn't go to residential school had it much better. So some people say the residential school was all right. It was okay if you had enough relatives to keep an eye on you to take care of you. But those that didn't they had it pretty rough. They were being abused. There was no one there to take up for them. And if they had a strong family back home they would be looked after, the supervisor would look after them, treat them better. But not if they had nobody and didn't know anything, didn't know how to speak English, and no relatives. One little boy was there when he was four years old.

His parents died, he had nowhere to go. He never got any loving, he needed a mother, and he was with the boys. He turned out to be a severe alcoholic. We always asked about him, and still ask about him because we remember when he was just a little kid and having nobody.

What about this sign language, you learned at residential school?

Inez: What we used to do was sign language. I learned that quick, it was the British form of signing. It was a common thing for everybody, when they wanted to get [information]. We weren't allowed to speak in class, in the dining room, and in church. We used to have to use this sign language to communicate. So we learned another language.

How many hours a day would you not be talking?

Inez: Oh I don't know, church, sometimes early in the morning, make our beds, go to church, then for breakfast, then go and do our chores, washing, scrubbing floors, working in the laundry, working in the bakery. The supervisor would make our work orders. We all wanted to work in the bakery and the dining room because that meant food. We weren't allowed to speak in boarding school, in church, in the dining room. If we were caught we were slapped, strapped, or humiliated in some way, so consequently we learned this sign language. It came in handy.

I don't know who taught me, I just picked it up. But, anyway years later, I was going to university, and I thought of quitting the second year. Then I went to visit my friend Rosenna, we attended residential school together. There used to be special treatment given to those students who went to high school; we were allowed to sit in the dining room, etc. There weren't very many of us, maybe five. The other students from the school did not attend high school, and they were stuck doing the hard work. Rosenna was one of those, she worked as a janitor. She reminded me of that. She said she was not ashamed of it, but the staff used to make a fuss over the high school girls. So, after that I went back to university to finish because I felt I owed it to them.

Ben Stonechild

Ben Stonechild attended the File Hills school on the Okanese reserve. The band that lives on this reserve, northeast of Balcarres, is one of the bands that make up the File Hills agency. The school was operated by the Presbyterian Church, then by The United Church of Canada. Ben Stonechild was attending the school when it closed in 1949. He is interviewed by Constance Deiter.

That residential school was something that I cannot say anything bad about. The only thing bad I could say about it was that we felt we never got enough to eat. As kids we were always on the move. Always seem to be looking for something extra to eat, and if the cook left bread out to cool, boy we would get it. For breakfast we would eat porridge mostly. We ate a lot of raw vegetables, like carrots. We may have got a little meat, now and then. It's been such a long time since I've been there.

We always done something to get something extra to eat. It was nothing for the boys to go behind the chicken house and shoot a chicken. Take off in the bush, we had pails out there, different places. Go and cook our chicken up. We had salt to cook. We were lucky. Saturdays and Sundays we went hunting rabbits with our sling shots.

I think if we ever shared with the girls they cooked the rabbit. It was quite the thing, there would be a lot of boys. When we used to go out Sundays hunting rabbits. Someone would say 'a rabbit, a rabbit, surround him, surround him.' Away we would go, that rabbit never stood a chance. We were about nine or ten years old. We would shoot it with a sling-shot. We get a bunch and trade it for bannock on the weekend, trade it with the older people who would come to visit on the weekend. They always brought lots of bannock because they knew we always had rabbits. [It was] a treat you know. Sometimes the boys who lived near the school would run home on weekends. Sometimes boys would be lucky enough to run home with them. They would get bannock there.

When I think back about it, they were the best years of my life, even at the time we thought they were tough, but we weren't molested in any way at the schools. It wasn't like the stories you hear at other places. I say we were treated good, it's kind of surprising to have to say that. When you hear of all the injustices at other boarding schools. I would say we were fortunate in that we didn't have to go through what other schools, other children had to go through.

How old were you when you started?

Ben: I was raised in Drumheller, Alberta, East Coulee. My father was a coal miner, there. In 1944 or 1943, they brought me to boarding school, they lived down there [East Coulee]. I might have went home on holidays to my uncle Harry Stonechild. Most of the time I spent at the boarding school. I can't recall, I think my dad moved back in 1945. When he moved back, we had to work hard, even in the boarding school we had to work hard. We all had jobs, chores to do, wood to cut. We burnt wood all winter. One of the things, it kind of got cold in there, wintertime, but we survived. I guess it was healthy for us.

We had one death in there when I went to school. There was some kind of strange sickness that they couldn't do nothing about. A young boy, he was quarantined and all the windows and doors were kicked shut.

You were the last to attend the File Hills residential school?

Ben: All of us guys like me and Keith [Dieter], Grant [Dieter] and Joey Ironquill. We were the last, they built a school down in our district [Peepeekisis], they closed the boarding school. I wish they would have kept it open, at least we could have had a landmark, some history, etc. We had some boys in there that rebelled and burnt down part of it. I guess [the] late Jimmy [name not supplied] had something to do with the burning. It was rebuilt, you could not tell where the fire was. I guess it was a routine thing, it wasn't a change thing.

I know one time a boy supervisor went out hunting with the boys with a twenty-two. He made a mistake, well I wouldn't say he made a mistake. He wouldn't let the boys take a turn at the twenty-two. So they got him and tied him up, then they got the twenty-two and used it. That happened with the senior boys, it was kind of the talk around there at that time. My uncle Chappie was one of them, they were quite the rag-a-tag bunch in those times. But one of the things in the end times there, we had some bullies, eh. They kind of bullied us. We would gang up on them, so that it kind of stopped the bullying.

But I would say my best years were there. After I got out of the boarding school, I started to live at home. There were tougher years there. For myself, boarding schools were enjoyable to me.

[From *From Our Mothers' Arms: The Intergenerational Impact of Residential Schools in Saskatchewan*, by Constance Deiter (Toronto: United Church Publishing House, 1999]

Suggestions for Further Reading

Barman, Jean, "Aboriginal Education at the Crossroads: The Legacy of Residential Schools and the Way Ahead," in David Long, et al., *Visions of the Heart: Canadian Aboriginal Issues* Toronto: Harcourt Brace, 1996: 271–303.

Fournier, Suzanne and Ernie Crey, *Stolen from our embrace: the abduction of First Nations children and the restoration of aboriginal communities*. Vancouver: Douglas & McIntyre, 1997.

Haig-Brown, Celia, *Resistance and Renewal: Surviving the Indian Residential School.* Vancouver: Tillacum Library, 1988.

Highway, Tomson, *Kiss of the fur queen.* Toronto: Doubleday Canada, 1998.

Miller, J. R., *Shingwauk's Vision: A History of Native Residential Schooling.* Toronto: University of Toronto Press, 1996.

Million, Dian, 'Telling Secrets: Sex, Power, and Narrative in Indian Residential School Histories', *Canadian Women Studies/les cahiers de la femme* 20, 2 (Summer 2000): 92–107.

PART 7

Children's Rights: The Influence of War on Peace, 1940–1960

Today, youth activists argue that the legal sanction of corporal punishment is an affront to children's rights. In the early twentieth century, these arguments were unthinkable because children did not have rights. The concept of children's rights first appeared in 1924 when the League of Nations endorsed the Geneva Declaration of the Rights of the Child. The Geneva Declaration was the first affirmation of the concept that children had rights. Conceptualizing children's basic needs as rights was an attempt to guarantee that all children would have access to food, clothing, and shelter.

World War II changed how people conceived rights. The Holocaust and the extermination of the European Jews raised questions about whether nation-states could protect minority groups. After the war, thousands of Jewish children were displaced orphans. Robbie Waisman's encounters with international aid organizations, adult survivors, and foster parents in Europe and Canada demonstrate the massive effort it took to find homes for young survivors. There was also an urgent desire to make amends for the wrongs of the past, and to develop international mechanisms that would prevent them from happening again. Diplomats began to talk about what international mechanisms were needed to defend *human rights*. Dominique Marshall explores international reconstruction politics that underpinned the 1959 Declaration of the Rights of the Child, and their impact on domestic policy. National obligations to protect children's rights obliged parents to adhere to standards established outside the family, standards that were difficult for poor families to reach.

Nancy Janovicek

Holocaust War Orphans— A Scrap Book Set

Robbie Waisman (Romek Wajsman)

Pre-War Life

I was born in 1931 in Skarszysko, Poland, a very tight-knit community. I was the youngest of six children, with four older brothers and one sister. My parents were religious. I remember the Sabbath as a very special time when my father would tell us stories of the great Rabbis and the stories of Sholom Aleichem. I was very pampered and felt that everything revolved around me. My early memories are full of warmth and love.

My only regret is that I do not have any photographs of my family. I am always envious of people who have a picture of their parents.

After Hitler's rise to power, I remember my parents' discussions. They were frightened and could not believe the situation that was developing around us. My father believed that Germany was the epitome of civilization and was not capable of atrocities.

Experiences During the Holocaust

I was eight years old in 1939 when my city was bombed and occupied by the Nazis. I thought that it was a game until I saw a man shot to death. I matured forty years in that instant.

In 1940, the ghetto was formed. At this time my parents sent me to stay with a non-Jewish family. After three weeks I ran away and returned to my family in the ghetto. In 1941, my eldest brother, Chaim heard that the ghetto was going to be liquidated. That night he smuggled me out of the ghetto. The next day, everyone in the ghetto was sent to Treblinka and gassed. My mother was among them.

Even though I was too young, I managed to work alongside my brothers in the munitions factories until I came down with typhoid fever. I was unconscious for about 10 days and covered up and hidden so as to go unnoticed. My brother, Abraham, also contracted the disease but was discovered and shot.

Robbie Waisman, just after liberation in
Paris, 1946.

I was separated from my father and brothers. I befriended Abe Chapnick, a boy
one year older than me. We remained together for the rest of the war. In 1944, when
I was 13, Abraham and I were sent to Buchenwald Concentration Camp and placed
in a barrack with Polish, French, and German political prisoners. These prisoners
helped protect us.

Postwar

When I was liberated in the concentration camp of Buchenwald on April 11, 1945
at the age of fourteen, my immediate concern was to be reunited with my family. At
that time I was not yet aware of the enormity of the Holocaust or of the extent of
our losses. The human mind doesn't accept some of these things. I knew that my
brother, Abraham, had died and I suspected my father was also dead but I still hoped
to find the rest of the family. I had no idea that my mother had died in Treblinka.
My sister, Leah, is the only one that survived in my immediate family.

Among the camp inmates there were leaders who gathered up all the children
and began to take charge of us. I had no idea that there were 430 children scattered through Buchenwald. I had thought my friend and I were the only children
there. We were marched out from the inner camp to the SS barracks to give us a
better environment. We each had a bed and clean sheets. I remember being examined by many doctors and nurses and the Red Cross taking down our stories.
Strangely enough, being together we all caught those childhood diseases we had
never had before.

Robbie Waisman's provisional identification card.

Displaced Persons Camp

We all wanted to go home but we remained in Buchenwald for about three months because there was no where else to go. The authorities had a hard time convincing us that we could not go home and that our homes were no longer there. In my case, they explained how dangerous it would be to go to Poland, where there had been pogroms against returning Jews. I could not understand why people, other than the Nazis, wanted to kill us. It took us a long time to understand our circumstances.

During the war, many of us had promised our elders that should we survive, we would tell the world about what had happened. But when we were liberated, the memories were too terrible to deal with. It was too soon to speak. Besides, no one was interested.

A very powerful bond developed amongst the children. All we had was one another. Looking back I realize what a blessing it was that we were together. They were my family.

It took us a while to realize that we could go outside the gates of Buchenwald. At first we didn't dare to leave the camp but then we started to go on little excursions around Buchenwald. We really savoured this new-found freedom.

Once the euphoria of surviving subsided, we had the need to search for surviving relatives. We registered our history and pictures with the Red Cross for distribution.

I remember a journalist from Paris who visited us and then wrote an article titled 'J'Accuse', accusing the world of indifference towards the 430 youngsters who had returned from hell and yet were still in a concentration camp. As result of public

This picture was taken 2 or 3 weeks after liberation in Buchenwald, outside the camp. Our clothes were made from Hitler Youth uniforms, cut down to fit us children.

pressure, the government of France agreed to receive the children of Buchenwald, even offering us citizenship. And so we left for Ecouis, a town in northern France. I can still remember the relief of leaving that God-forsaken country, as we crossed the border into France.

'Where are our parents?'

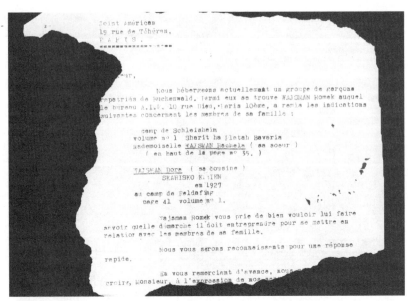

This letter helped me to find out my sister Leah was still alive. In translation it reads: 'Amongst the group of boys fom Buchenwald, we have one Romek Wajsman of whom the A.I.P. has the following information concerning his family: Schleisheim camp . . . Mlle Wajsman, Rachela (his sister); Wajsman, Dora (his cousin), Feldafing Camp. Romek would like to know what process he must undergo to get in touch with his family members. A quick response would be appreciated.'

Orphanage

We were taken to a huge old mansion with dormitories, run by the OSE (Oeuvre de Secours aux Enfants). There some of the children, including Elie Wiesel, demanded prayer books, services, and Kosher food. Although most of us had come from Orthodox homes before the war, many of us were reluctant to return to these practices. I had started to question God. Had he been on a leave of absence during the Holocaust? I was part of the group that broke away from religious observance, so we became divided.

As a group we were headstrong, angry, and unmanageable. They called us 'les enfants terribles'. We resisted going to classes and disrupted cultural events organized for us. Later on I had a chance to read some of the reports written about us at that time which concluded that we had seen and suffered too much and could not be rehabilitated. They said that we were without redeeming value and likely to end up in jail as criminals. Obviously experts had no understanding of our trauma. As it turned out none of us ended up in jail. Many of us became professionals, doctors, lawyers, and many of them in the helping professions. My friend Jezyk became a well known physicist. Another member of our group, Elie Wiesel, won the Nobel prize for literature.

One day an expert was brought in to talk to us. When he came in, he took off his jacket and very deliberately began to roll up his sleeves. When we saw his Auschwitz number, there was a complete hush. I think our silence shocked him a little. He

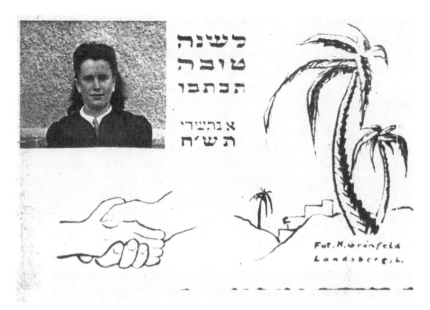

לשנה
טובה
תכתבו

א נתצירי
ת ש'ח

Fot. H. Grinfeld
Landsberg. L.

First New Year's card sent by my sister Leah after the war, it was sent from Tel Aviv on Aug. 29, 1947. She found out I was alive through the Red Cross.

seemed taken aback and it took awhile before he could begin. He looked at us and finally he said 'mein tiere kinder', (my dear children) and started to cry. That was the first time we openly shed a tear. I cried for the first time in five years. It is still very emotional to me.

After that things changed, even though I am not sure I realized it at the time. From then on I suddenly understood that this was my life and I had to make something of it. My toughened attitude was broken.

Eventually a group of about eighty of us was taken to Vesinet, a town outside of Paris, where we attended a regular school. I think they had decided that the sooner we were integrated the better our chances to resume normal lives. I remained there for about three years. I worked very hard at school, I had so much catching up to do. I graduated high school.

During this period a prominent Jewish couple, Jean and Jane Meyer, came to our school and offered to adopt me. They introduced me to the opera and the theatre. But I felt very strongly about not giving up my name and I think that I had already decided to turn my back on Europe. The memories were too strong. They were devastated when I applied to Canada for a visa. We remained close until they died and I am still in close contact with their children.

Family

I had become friends with a French boy, Jacques Mydlarski. Just before I was to leave for Canada, he invited me home to meet his family. We got along very well and they invited me back. On the second visit, a Polish relative of his mother's was also there.

She overheard me mentioning the name of my home town and came in from the kitchen, wiping a dish. When I told her my father's name she dropped her dish, ran to me, hugged me, and began speaking to me in Yiddish. She was my father's sister, my aunt. I had found a whole family I had not known about.

Expectations

I had some regrets about leaving France, my godparents, and my newly discovered aunt and cousins with whom I had become very close. I thought of Canada as a young country full of wheat fields. It seemed to be a place where I would never run out of bread. Canada represented a new life and a new beginning. Although I was anxious about the unknown, I remember feeling a tremendous amount of anticipation and excitement.

Immigration to Canada

I remember being told that no country in the world, with the exception of Palestine, wanted us. Nearly all of the orphans put their names on the list for Palestine but getting into Palestine was made nearly impossible by the British blockade at the time.

I came very close to emigrating to Palestine. I was actually on a boat in Marseilles destined for Palestine, when I was ordered off with all my belongings. Later I discovered that Madame Rachel Minz had me removed. She was a member of the Jewish group, the Bund, that believed in a strong Diaspora, and who had worked with us in the orphanage. I was absolutely furious, of course.

The two other options open to us were Canada or Australia. Australia was attractive to many of us because of its distance from Europe. In those days it took 3 or 4 months to get to Australia by boat and we figured that if there was ever another war, it would be the safest place to be.

Getting into Canada was tough. The process was a very lengthy one and you had to be absolutely healthy. Wearing glasses was enough to disqualify you. I had trouble getting approval because of my very low blood pressure. I had repeated blood tests and had all but given up hope when I finally got a letter accepting me into Canada.

The Voyage

The voyage took about a week, which seemed quite long to me. I have fond memories of the trip and remember reading Margaret Mitchell's *Gone with the Wind* in French.

Arrival

I was seventeen when we landed in Halifax on 3 December 1948. I was disappointed to learn that I was not going to either Montreal or Toronto. As I spoke French and not English I hoping to go to Montreal. My second choice had been Toronto because I had some contacts there. I wasn't told that I was going to Calgary until I was already on the train.

On the trip west, I couldn't get over the immensity of the huge spaces and the sparse settlements along the way. You could see forever. As I crossed Canada by train, it occurred to me that so many people could have been saved in this vast country. So much land and yet no room for Jewish refugees during the war.

We were accompanied by Roweena Pearlman, a Congress volunteer who was just a wonderful lady with a heart of gold. I think she used psychology on me by telling me how wonderful the Jewish community was in Calgary and suggesting that I stop over in Calgary for just a few days to meet her family. To please her, I stopped over for two days and stayed nine years.

Calgary seemed so new and so friendly. I was astounded to learn that I did not need a passport or ID card on a day-to-day basis and that I could travel to other provinces without a visa. I remember asking how I could go to another province, thinking I needed a visa, and was told to go to an office with a dollar. At the office, I got my first Canadian driver's license.

Foster Family/Adjustments

The availability of food stuffs was amazing to me. Everything was a discovery. Although I appreciated the material things, the most important thing for me was just living and experiencing. I could not get enough of the life around me.

The first night in Calgary I stayed with Roweena Pearlman's brother-in-law. I was so anxious to earn a living, that the very next day I went to work at Smithbuilt Hats. That evening I went to live with Harry and Rachel Goresht and their children Ida and Sam. To this day, they remain my family.

I was getting paid eighteen dollars a week, five of which went to pay for my room and board. When I had learned enough English I travelled around the country for Smithbuilt.

I remember the Jewish community really opening their hearts to us. The orphans always had a standing invitation to all the simchas, the weddings, and bar mitzvahs, particularly to the receptions.

School/Career Path

I had always wanted to be an electrical engineer. My mechanical and electrical aptitude had helped save me during the Holocaust. As a forced labourer in an ammunitions factory, it had been my job to monitor ten machines and repair them when they broke down.

Instead, I went to night school and got a diploma in accountancy because it was a quick way to get a job and I desperately wanted to be on my own and independent. Later, I brought my sister, her husband, and son over from Israel. By then it seemed too late to go back to school to study electrical engineering.

I worked for Sam and Lina Hanen in their store. I liked meeting the public. After I got my accountancy diploma I worked more in the office. They were good years and I learned a lot, especially from Lina.

I left Calgary in 1959 when I married Gloria Lyons and moved to Saskatoon. I started a children's wear store, which eventually became three stores. I have always been involved in the Jewish community. I was president of the Jewish community in Saskatoon and president of B'nai Brith. In 1978, after eighteen years, we moved to Vancouver so that my son, Howard, and my daughter, Arlaina, could be part of a larger Jewish community. In Vancouver I have been in the hospitality industry (hotel business).

Response to themes of community, anti-racism, refugees, immigration, message to young people

I think this is the greatest country in the world. I have had nothing but wonderful experiences since coming to Canada. The only time I have heard insulting remarks towards Jewish people was recently from Doug Collins' supporters at the Human Rights Inquiry.

I would ask young people to keep an open mind when they see and meet new-comers to this country. Do not stop by looking at the surface of people. Experience the adventure of getting to know other kinds of people. Each one of us possesses unique, wonderful qualities, regardless of colour or religion.

[From *Holocaust War Orphans—A Scrapbook Set*. Vancouver: Holocaust Education Centre, 1999.]

Reconstruction Politics, the Canadian Welfare State, and the Ambiguity of Children's Rights, 1940–1950

Dominique Marshall

The Second World War reintroduced human rights into western political and social discourse. The right to economic and social security was now added to the older list of civil, political, and democratic rights proclaimed in the American Declaration of Independence, the United States Constitution, and the French Declaration of Rights of Man. In Canada, the international movement towards these new economic rights emphasized the universal rights of children to welfare and education. At the same time, some of the ideas about individual rights which were evolving in Canada were incorporated into the United Nations' conventions on human rights, which became a regular feature of postwar international relations. This paper on reconstruction politics underlines the relationship between international developments and social policy-making in Canada. Drawing upon government archives associated with the enactment and implementation of early universal welfare programs, it focuses on the external and internal aspects of 'state formation' to show how advances in the rhetoric of universal rights were linked to a deeper transformation in Canada's political culture.[1]

From the Atlantic Charter to a Children's Charter

The Covenant of the League of Nations linked universal peace and social justice, but included nothing about the protection of individual human rights. Rather, it sought to protect citizens by protecting their states.[2] The Second World War demonstrated how inadequate that protection was, and by the early 1940s: 'a war that [had begun] as an old-style struggle over territory in Europe . . . began to be seen as a crusade for basic rights and freedoms . . . as it escalated, as the scale of Nazi atrocities became apparent and as American arms and manpower were drawn increasingly into the conflict.'[3]

On 14 August 1941, at the conclusion of their meeting off the coast of Newfoundland, British Prime Minister Winston Churchill and American President Franklin Roosevelt issued an eight-point statement of 'peace aims'. Devised largely to counter the claims of American isolationists that the North Atlantic meeting committed the United States to entering the global conflict, the declaration promised a postwar world marked by liberalized trade and non-aggression. In effect, this Atlantic Charter (as it came to be called) constituted an 'internationalization of the New Deal'.[4] Indeed, the prime minister and the president announced that they:

> desire[d] to bring about the fullest collaboration between all nations in the economic field with the object of securing, for all, improved labor standards, economic advancement and social security; [and], after the final destruction of the Nazi tyranny, they hope[d] to see established a peace which [would] afford all nations the means of dwelling in safety within their own boundaries, and which [would] afford assurance that all the men in all lands may live out their lives in freedom from fear and want.[5]

Canada had played no part in writing the Atlantic Charter. Prime Minister William Lyon Mackenzie King had been excluded from the secret meeting.[6] The language of the document was clearly Roosevelt's, whose annual state of the union address in January 1941 had promised Americans the 'Four Freedoms: freedom of speech, expression, and worship and freedom from want and fear'. Coming just a few months after his lend-lease policy had set the domestic war effort in motion, the joint statement with Churchill was clearly part of Roosevelt's effort to 'stir popular imagination . . . to stamp [the Four Freedoms] in American hearts and identify them with the policy of assisting Great Britain'.[7] In January 1942, after the Americans had entered the conflict, twenty-six allied nations signed the Atlantic Charter, to which they added the assertion that 'complete victory over their enemies is essential to decent life, liberty, independence, and religious freedom, and to preserve human rights and justice, in their own land as well as in other lands'.[8]

Although the Atlantic Charter galvanized popular support for human rights and placed them firmly on the international agenda, advancing these rights was rarely easy. When they met with the Soviet Union and China to define the nature of the postwar world, Roosevelt and Churchill watered down their commitment to the Four Freedoms. At Dumbarton Oaks, in the fall of 1944, the leaders of the four great powers agreed to a set of proposals on postwar organization, which 'reflected their current absorption with military security [and] contained only a general reference to human rights'.[9]

In Canada, the successive international commitments to universal social and economic rights bolstered the plans for comprehensive schemes for social security already under way in the name of reconstruction. 'The very need to . . . mobilize [the] support [of the population] seems to have been a crucial component in wartime social policy'.[10] As early as October 1942, Mackenzie King had adopted Roosevelt's language as his own. In an address to the American Federation of Labor convention in Toronto, the Canadian prime minister assured workers that their wartime efforts would not go unrewarded:

> the work of repairing and restoring the ravages of war will not be enough. . . . Until these fears [of unemployment and insufficiency] have been eliminated . . . the war for

freedom will not be won. The era of freedom will be achieved only as social security and human welfare become the main concern of men and nations.[11]

Leonard Marsh, the McGill sociology professor who had, in early 1943, written the principal plan for postwar social policy in Canada for the federal Advisory Committee on Reconstruction, later commented that the Atlantic Charter gave his proposal impetus by signifying to his Canadian contemporaries that social and economic rights were 'not only an avowed national aim but an international idea'.[12]

This international development was not lost on the prime minister. In January 1943, as he contemplated the next general election, Mackenzie King wrote in his diary that 'a postwar program of reform was to be "the main subject of appeal"'.[13] At the end of that month, the speech from the throne presented this reform program and wrapped it in the rhetoric of rights. The government promised that a 'comprehensive national scheme of social insurance should be worked out at once which will constitute a charter of social security for the whole of Canada'.[14] By 1944, as a senior civil servant later recalled, the government had come to believe that the population considered universal measures of social welfare their right:

> We soon found an increasing resistance on the part of the public to the idea that any person, social worker or not, should presume to decide who is a deserving case and who isn't a deserving case. We got to the stage where people began to demand that legislation be written down in specific terms to provide as a matter of right certain benefits to people under clearly defined conditions that were prescribed in the law rather than left to the judgment of some individual.[15]

In reaching this conclusion, King and his colleagues were also helped by the threatening popularity of the Cooperative Commonwealth Federation (CCF) on their left and, on their right, by the exceptional readiness of entrepreneurial organizations to accept a measure of state economic regulation. More generally, Mackenzie King's government was compelled by the possibility of creating a national ideology that celebrated social policies to replace the anglo-centric patriotism that divided French and English Canada.[16]

There was another way reconstruction politics helped in the birth of Canada's postwar social security programs. The Second World War had seen a dramatic increase in state activity. Large new social programs could suddenly be envisaged and created by simply converting the financial resources and human energies mobilized on the domestic front for the war effort into peacetime activities. Such transfers were numerous. For instance, hundreds of women who volunteered for wartime activities on behalf of the federal government were later asked to help put together the huge machinery for mailing the millions of family allowance payments. The accompanying leaflets, designed to educate parents about the new program, were created by many of the same experts who operated the formidable propaganda machine on the domestic front during the conflict.[17]

In his government's 1944 speech from the throne, Mackenzie King promised social security 'from the cradle to the grave'. Rather than adopting Roosevelt's 'Four Freedoms', the prime minister now chose the words of the British advocate of comprehensive welfare, Lord Beveridge, who proposed a stronger commitment from the state towards social and economic rights.[18] Mackenzie King enacted a 'Charter for Veteran's Rights', an array of programs aimed at demobilized soldiers, which was more generous than the measures established after the First World War and involved the state in a larger capacity. However, at the end of the war, the promises of universal social and economic rights were translated largely into programs directed at the next generation.[19]

Indeed, of all the ideas for new universal social and economic programs advocated by politicians, reformers, experts, and welfare organizations, the prime minister chose to introduce only one—family allowances, the first universal social program in Canadian history.[20] Significantly, this selection reflected the bureaucracy's view, borrowed from Keynes, that family allowances were the best way 'to pay for the war'.[21] In the province of Quebec, the most important social reform of Adélard Godbout's liberal government, and the only significant universal public measure for many years to come, was the enactment of compulsory schooling in 1943. These two laws were more closely linked than one might assume: federal allowances would not be paid to children who did not obey provincial education regulations. Provincial and federal politicians alike invoked the rights of youngsters to a 'minimum welfare' and to a 'minimum of education' in the various elections held during the final years of the war. Thus, they sought to distract voters from immediate social and economic issues, and to focus their attention on their children. The leaflet introducing family allowances, published not long before the June 1945 federal election, was pointedly entitled 'A Children's Charter'.[22] This successful electoral tactic was also used to sell Canada's new postwar social programs. The illustrators of the literature which accompanied the first family allowance cheques used many devices to convince parents to think of the country's younger citizens rather than the future of the country. For instance, one pamphlet showed a child with a key in his hands, walking through a keyhole towards a bright map of Canada.[23]

The Ideological Role of Children's Rights in Domestic Social Policy Making[24]

Thus, a peculiar version of human rights informed postwar social policy-making in Canada. The focus on children had an impact on the material and ideological worlds of young Canadians of the postwar years, and on the formation of the Canadian state in ways that marked the political culture of the country. Furthermore, the expedient role that children's rights played in reconstruction politics created problems that later coloured the making of social policies for children, both domestically and internationally.

In Canada and in Quebec, the promotion of the rights of children aided governments by providing an ideological detour around the harsh debates about the welfare of adults.[25] To Quebec leaders, children's rights served as a justification for opposing the Catholic high clergy's view of the Church as the necessary guarantor of 'parents' rights'. Federal authorities also used the idea of children's rights to answer trade unions' demands for the 'economic rights' of their members without having to raise the wage ceilings fixed by Ottawa's wartime legislation.[26] In these ways, children's rights were used to isolate adults from old solidarities.

In addition to weakening religious and professional solidarity, children's rights were used by the state to develop and promote a specific image of individual and universal parents. To fulfil the state's expectations that parents were best suited to oversee the social and economic rights of their offspring, fathers and mothers had to be 'normal'. Although those who failed to raise their children for reasons which the state decided were not valid remained a minority, officials now had the authority to question parents about their traditional prerogatives.

Political leaders and professional associations increased their potential for domination over individuals in still another fashion. Through the isolation, in early childhood, of a 'core of consciousness and of will' in young Canadians, family allowances and compulsory schooling became part of a larger process involving the penetration of individualist notions into families; a world that had long been impervious to them.[27] By conferring onto children a 'particularity', or a dose of independence, they undermined the idea that children should submit to their parents.

It would be wrong, however, to think that the rights enjoyed by children after the Second World War necessarily empowered them. As children obtained their political rights progressively during their youth, and as they rarely participated in associations through which they could convey their demands to public powers, it was easy for politicians and interested members of the public to pretend that children had consented to these developments. Moreover, children were not included in the elaboration of their rights and they could not monitor their application.[28] Children's lack of power in this new context could have important consequences, by giving them profound reasons to doubt the legitimacy of public institutions when they became adult citizens.[29]

The legislation on children's rights to minimum levels of welfare and education had other negative consequences for young people. Governments and social agencies often attached the realization of these rights to the purchase of consumer goods. This equation could reduce children's independence. For instance, the new models of consumerism encouraged by the state's educational literature on how to spend family allowances might incite a child to leave school early in order to earn money. More generally, by helping the individualist values linked to mass consumption enter households, the welfare state could diminish the significance that family members attached to their interdependency.

These ideological manoeuvres were facilitated by the fact that the poorer classes rarely participated in ethical discussions about the possibility of universal human rights to both enhance and weaken family autonomy. For the time being, the tradition of defending the integrity of families still belonged primarily to conservative elites.[30]

Children's Rights and Democratic Traditions in Canada

Mackenzie King and Adélard Godbout could count on a certain automatic legitimacy when dealing with children's rights. The idea belonged to an older democratic tradition that shaped discussion in Canada and in international welfare organizations. In the interwar period, Canadian social workers, lawyers, reformers, and diplomats had crafted particular concepts of children's rights. Their work was inspired by internationalist and egalitarian movements, and by their ambitious desire to enhance their professional status and legitimacy.[31] Canadian reformers also played a significant role in drafting the League of Nations' first international agreements on child welfare.[32] Montreal Senator Raoul Dandurand, who pioneered the first federal juvenile delinquency legislation just after the turn of the century, served as president of the Assembly of the League of Nations in 1926. Similarly, Charlotte Whitton, the head of the Canadian Council on Child Welfare from 1920 to 1941, participated in that international organization's social projects.[33] From 1926 until its collapse in 1939, she was the Canadian assessor, and subsequently Canada's delegate, to the League's Child Welfare Committee.

This exposure to international developments had a profound impact on the evolution of domestic support for children's rights in Canada. In 1924, for example, after lobbying by such voluntary groups as the London-based Save the Children Fund, which raised funds for war orphans, and the Scottish chapter of the Council of Women, the League of Nations adopted 'The Geneva Declaration of the Rights of the Child'. Obligations to procure for children the material means to develop and the opportunity to work according to their potential and talents were among the five principles of the declaration. The Canadian Council of Child Welfare promptly published the declaration and distributed it across the country.[34]

Children's rights evolved significantly over the course of the next two decades. In the aftermath of the Second World War, promises which were once directed only toward 'abandoned', 'juvenile', or 'neglected' children were now made to all 'normal' young citizens. The rights of youngsters were tied to the idea of universality, not simply because of these international developments, but because this evolution in the notion of children's rights was encouraged by developments elsewhere. For instance, as psychologists and psychiatrists debated the nature of childhood in Canada and in other countries during this period, they broadened their focus to include all children.[35]

Many social groups and citizens also linked their war efforts to entitlements for their children. The government-funded program of Soldiers' Dependent Allowances, for instance, provided Canadian soldiers with supplementary payments for their children and established a precedent that demobilized soldiers and civilians would later invoke.[36] For trade unions, the link between enlistment and children's social citizenship was an important principle for political action. In 1943, for instance, the editors of Le Monde ouvrier, a weekly newspaper published by the American-based international unions operating in French Canada, tied the war effort to their support for compulsory schooling. 'Pourquoi, à la lumière des graves événements où son sort se joue, vouloir persister à rogner sur ce qui revient au peuple en fait de progrès et de sécurité?'[37] In his annual report for 1945–1946, the school inspector for the Chaudière district in Quebec invoked the same notion of exchange:

> Serait-il présomptueux de croire que nous pouvons aider à donner le coup de barre,
> pour qu'enfin nous puissions avoir l'école humaine non seulement pour une élite,

mais aussi pour tout les Canadiens français? . . . C'est le voeu implicite de tous ceux qui sont morts ou ont combattu pour la défense de nos institutions démocratiques.[38]

In 1944, Josaphat Lapierre, the truant officer for La Sarre, complained to the superintendent of public instruction about his reluctance to enforce compulsory education among families who did not possess sufficient resources to keep their children in school until they were fourteen years old. After the sacrifices these families had already endured for the country's defence, this additional burden did not seem fair:

> Quand pendant près de 10 années, on a tenu un peuple dans la misère dans un pays d'abondance, et qu'ensuite on vient lui ravir ses fils à la fleur de l'âge, leur réclamant l'impôt du sang et que de part et d'autre il se voit imposer toutes sortes de restrictions et d'obligations lui enlevant presqu'entièrement la liberté d'agir conformément à ses goûts et à ses aspirations, rien de surprenant qu'il se produise des réactions fâcheuses au sein de la population.[39]

The idea of delaying promises of equality until the next generation had been the basis of many reform movements since the nineteenth century. The declaration issued by the fifty social organizations from the province of Quebec, meeting in February 1944 under the auspices of the *Ligue de la jeunesse féminine*, shows how widespread this attitude was:

> Les problèmes créés par la guerre et les transformations d'un mode de vie, particulièrement dans les grands centres, sont devenus de plus en plus difficiles. L'enfance n'y échappe pas et c'est vers elle que se tournent les personnes et les groupes qui s'intéressent aux oeuvres sociales.[40]

In the same way, the report of the subcommittee on women of the federal government's Advisory Committee on Reconstruction listed help to children as its third priority, after full employment and an end to the scarcity of resources. Indeed, the authors translated the economic and social commitments of the Atlantic Charter directly into measures for the protection of children:

> The reconstruction policies of the government must adequately protect from want those individuals who are unable to obtain gainful employment through no fault of their own and, as an integral measure of social security in the broadest sense, the children of Canada should be protected from malnutrition and inadequate educational opportunities. . . . To strive for more would unduly complicate the problem: to content ourselves with less would belie the professions of faith embodied in the Atlantic charter and all the pronouncements that have followed it.[41]

The decision of governments in Canada to adopt these new rights for children shifted the discussion of rights onto new, and often unintended, ground. For instance, when parents wrote to the provincial or the federal administration to ask to be exempted from the regulations governing compulsory schooling, they underlined the contradiction between the new universal children's rights and the older principle of parental responsibility. In the Montmorency district of Quebec, for instance, one farmer, whose children could not attend school because they did not have shoes, informed the superintendent of public instruction that: '[l]a loi doit prévoir des exceptions. J'espère que les parents peuvent encore avoir soin des enfants. Nous ne sommes pas en Allemagne n'est-ce pas?'[42]

Once programs for compulsory education and family allowances were implemented, the rhetoric of universal rights advanced through government propaganda channels, which charged parents with the responsibility for securing the new rights of their children, may eventually have helped strengthen these egalitarian convictions among poor adults. A father in Roberval with four sons in college and three daughters in the convent was forced to pay $9.50 a month in tuition fees in addition to the money he spent for books and clothing. In a letter to the provincial minister of education, he adopted the government's own rhetoric to protest against its demands on him and declared 'je trouve cela bien drôle monsieur le Ministre, et même un peu écoeurant quand j'ouvre un journal et que l'on nous parle de famille, famille et famille, démocratie et liberté.'[43] In the view of many parents in these circumstances, provincial authorities were not guaranteeing the right to education as they had promised. As one of them wrote: 'Puisque nous sommes sous le contrôle d'une loi obligatoire, il me semble qu'on devrait avoir le droit d'exiger les avantages de la suivre fidèlement.'[44]

In the case of native parents, whose spending was monitored by public agents, family allowances and the promises attached to them provided new grounds on which to attack old practices. The Cooperative Commonwealth Federation (CCF) member of parliament for Selkirk denounced the government's paternalism in the House of Commons:

> Si ces hommes se battent pour nous, ils devraient pouvoir toucher cet argent au bureau de poste ou là où on le paiera sans qu'il leur soit nécessaire de passer par l'agent des Indiens. . . . L'Indien est un Canadien dans le sens même du mot. C'est lui le Canadien véritable. On ne viendra certainement pas demander de verser l'allocation à quelqu'un d'autre pour son compte, s'il assez bon pour aller combattre.[45]

Finally, the notion of children's rights pointed towards an increase in children's individual sovereignty. In particular, the government encouraged parents to allow their children to assume more responsibility for their own spending. The relative financial ease provided by family allowances brought with it the chance for freedom and opportunity, and could also produce a pride that poverty had denied. This new sense of worth may have helped lessen the feeling among poorer children that there was some urgency for them to leave school and earn their own income. In other instances, the new financial possibilities coming from 'economic rights' helped young people honour what they perceived as their family obligations. Moreover, the language of universal rights and the images associated with the implementation of universal programs encouraged, with some success, the homogenization of the experiences of boys and girls, rural and urban children, at a time when the large majority of instances of child labour were to be found among poor daughters and farmers' sons.[46]

Thus, the rhetoric of children's rights introduced in Canada through reconstruction politics had become as ambiguous and diverse as the many elements in Canadian society by which it had been adopted. Like the human rights of Churchill and Roosevelt, the children's rights of King and Godbout had a life of their own. This was broader than Canada's federal and provincial leaders intended. However reduced, and however cynically used by public administrations of the day, children's rights led to some measure of autonomy for parents and children. Reborn abroad in the face of a fight against fascism, and used at home to answer the many hopes of a democracy expanded by the massive commitment of its citizens to the defence of their nation, universal economic and social rights infused state programs with the possibility of material and political freedom. They contributed to the arrival of new forms of childhood; to a certain equalization of the experiences of girls and boys, both urban and rural; to a larger autonomy of children within their family. More generally, they played an active part in the creation of a political environment where questions of fairness and individual material gains became central.

An Ambiguous Legacy For the Postwar World

With the end of the Second World War, compulsory education and welfare receded from the political agenda. Most historians attribute this withdrawal to the collapse of the wartime consensus and, beyond this phenomenon, to a disengagement of the population from social welfare. The diagnosis proposed by Dennis Guest in his history of Canadian social security is commonplace:

> In the rush to plan a collectively oriented postwar society, had there been any time to build a supporting political constituency? Apparently not, if we are able to judge by the ease with which the glittering prize of comprehensive health, housing, and social security was withdrawn from public gaze.[47]

In a way, the programs themselves contributed to this decline of popular interest: with the general enrichment of households during and after the war, the proportion of families susceptible to an economic crisis that would render them dependent on the state was diminishing. The nature of suburban life and the insecurity brought by the Cold War enhanced this defensive individualism.[48] Support for the left-leaning CCF declined steadily until the early 1960s. Reassured by postwar prosperity, many economic elites, professionals, and trade union leaders were abandoning their wartime commitment to a stronger measure of industrial democracy. Often, the same reformers who sought improvements in the social security system were also pressing for tax reductions.[49] To these factors, we can add that the politically expedient features of the original programs had weakened their universalist nature, from the moment of their inception.

A comparable retreat was underway in the international sphere. The diplomatic movement towards human rights was shaken by the very authors of the Atlantic Charter. Cold War tensions, national jealousies, and the fear among western governments of the national liberation movements that were emerging in many European colonies, threatened the bill of universal rights planned by the new United Nations in 1945. Within some quarters of the UN's secretariat itself, 'there was a tendency ... to play down the human rights program as an exotic in an international organization'. In 1948, when the General Assembly's third committee examined the declaration closely, Canada surprised observers by abstaining from the vote. Canadian policy-makers in Ottawa later cited many factors to excuse their 'bad grace' including their unwillingness to infringe on provincial jurisdictions and the imprecise nature of the declaration. Ottawa's general indifference towards human rights questions at the UN is hardly surprising against the background of its use of children's rights as an expedient political tool during the reconstruction years, and considering the lack of interest that characterized large segments of the Canadian population.[50]

However, as Fiorello H. La Guardia, the major of New York, optimistically stated at the end of the war, 'the Atlantic Charter could not be reduced . . . its authors could not evade what had gone into its making and what now flowed from it.'[51] Allied tribunals used human rights to 'override the defense that those arraigned had been acting in accordance with the laws of the regime they served'.[52] In June 1945, at the San Francisco Conference, 'some forty-two private organizations representing various aspects of American life—the churches, trade unions, ethnic groups, peace movements, etc.—[invited by the United States government to act] as consultants to its delegation . . . aided by the delegations of some smaller countries . . . conducted a lobby in favor of human rights for which there is no parallel in the history of international relations, and which was largely responsible for the human rights provisions of the Charter.'[53] The agreement 'reaffirm[ed] faith in fundamental human rights, in the dignity and worth of the human person, in the equal rights of men and women of nations large and small.' At the same time, the UN Economic and Social Council (ECOSOC) 'was instructed to create a commission on human rights; and it was generally understood that this commission would draw up an international bill of rights.'[54] John Humphrey, a Canadian law professor at McGill University, was asked to head the UN secretariat's Division of Human Rights when it was created in 1946. In 1948, the Universal Declaration of Human Rights which he drafted was adopted by the General Assembly with the support of 58 member states. Canada, embarrassed by its presence in the group of repressive countries which had abstained in the third committee's vote, endorsed it.

Behind the work of the American non-governmental organizations (NGOs), and in the performance of Canadians like Humphrey, one can sense the profound transformation of the political culture that led to—and was consolidated by—the formation of universal welfare programs at home. The social and economic work of the United Nations seemed to be supported with enthusiasm by Canadians. By the mid-1940s, according to international historians, after 'the horror aroused by the discovery of the Nazi extermination camps', it was the 'weight of public opinion [that] compelled governments . . . to draft an international Bill of Rights.'[55]

Similarly, the specific history of children's rights was to be marked by their ambiguous role in reconstruction politics at the international level. Initially, the significant wartime enhancements to the concept of universal rights quickly made their way into international discussions about children. As early as 1946, the same groups that had compelled the League of Nations to act after the First World War asked the United Nations to update the Geneva Declaration of 1924. In particular, they wanted the world organization to include provisions covering the new duties of the state in protecting children, integrating wartime advances in social security, and in the promotion of the family environment. This pressure met with some success. In 1946, the United Nations' temporary social commission recommended that the organization add a clause on 'respect of the family as an entity' to the 1924 Geneva Declaration on the Rights of the Child. The commission, influenced by the atrocities of the Second World War, also proposed adding a provision to extend these rights regardless of 'race, nationality, or creed'.[56]

However, the process that started in 1946 quickly slowed down. Only in 1959 did the UN's human rights commission succeed in having its 'Declaration on the Rights of the Child' adopted by the General Assembly. According to Philip Veerman, the principal historian of the international movement for children's rights, the delay came from the fact that the declaration was not 'politically urgent' for the member states. Moreover, there were repeated questions from member states about the binding nature of the principles on states and individuals.[57] Again, Canada was a reluctant participant: when ECOSOC's social commission first discussed the principle of a declaration on children's rights in July 1950, '[t]he Canadian delegate . . . did not favor a separate Declaration concerning certain age groups. He pleaded for a thorough review of the course taken by the Social Commission'.[58]

The uncooperative position adopted by Canada in 1950 was hardly surprising. Indeed, the entire history of the evolution of children's universal rights in Canada between 1940 and 1950 was characterized by a contradictory tendency both to promote these rights and to subordinate them to more immediate political and social objectives. The expedient nature of reconstruction politics channelled popular hopes for increased economic and political democracy after the war, and elite aspirations for an enhanced state role in Canada and abroad, into a peculiar notion of universal children's rights. This involved supplying children with minimum levels of welfare and education. The ambiguity inherent in this conception of human rights and the history of its evolving position on the international agenda are intricately articulated to the social and political history of Canadian families.

[1996]

Acknowledgements

I would like to thank Bruce Curtis, Greg Donaghy, Robert Goheen, Jim Kenny, and Norman Hillmer for their comments and suggestions on earlier versions of these ideas. This work has been supported at various stages by grants from the Social Science and Humanities Research Council of Canada.

Notes

1.   On the meaning and the use of the concept of 'state formation', see Philip Abrams, 'Notes on the Difficulty of Studying the State', *Journal of Historical Sociology*, 1, 1, March 1988, pp. 58–89.

2. Richard Wild, 'Human Rights: In Retrospect', in K.J. Keith, ed., *Essays on Human Rights* (Wellington: Sweet and Maxwell, 1968), pp. 4–5.
3. Jeremy Waldron, ed., *Nonsense upon Stilts: Bentham, Burke and Marx on the Rights of Man* (London: Methuen, 1987), p. 154.
4. Theodore A. Wilson, 'The First Summit', in Douglas Brinkley and David R. Facey-Crowther, eds, *The Atlantic Charter* (New York: St Martin's Press, 1994), pp. 1–31; Warren F. Kimball, 'The Atlantic Charter: "With All Deliberate Speed"', in ibid., pp. 89–90.
5. 'The Atlantic Charter', in Douglas Brinkley and David R. Facey-Crowther, eds, *The Atlantic Charter*, p. xvii. See also John Humphrey, 'The Magna Carta of the World', in Clyde Sanger (ed.), *Canadians and the United Nations* (Ottawa: Department of External Affairs, 1988), p. 19.
6. J.L. Granatstein, 'The Man Who Wasn't There: Mackenzie King, Canada, and the Atlantic Charter', in Brinkley and Facey-Crowther, eds, *The Atlantic Charter*, p. 123.
7. Theodore A. Wilson, *The First Summit: Roosevelt and Churchill at Placentia Bay, 1941* (Lawrence: University Press of Kansas, 1991), pp. 3–4, 154.
8. Cited in Waldron, p. 154; see also Richard Wild, 'Human Rights: In Retrospect', *Essays on Human Rights*, p. 4.
9. Humphrey, p. 18. See also Escott Reid, 'Hopes That Vanished at San Francisco', in Sanger, ed., *Canadians and the United Nations*, pp. 7–9.
10. Rob Watts, 'Family allowances in Canada and Australia 1940–1945: A comparative critical case study', *Journal of Social Policy*, 16, 1 (1987), pp. 1–48.
11. Cited in Raymond Blake, 'Mackenzie King and the Genesis of Family Allowances in Canada, 1939–1944', in Raymond Blake and Jeff Keshen, eds, *Social and Welfare Policy in Canada: Historical Readings* (Toronto: Copp Clark, 1995), p. 245.
12. J.L. Granatstein, 'The Man Who Wasn't There', p. 128, citing the preface to the 1975 edition of *Marsh's Report on Social Security for Canada* (Toronto, 1975). Marsh himself was to work for the United Nations Relief and Rehabilitation Administration. For details, see David J. Bercuson and J.L. Granatstein, *The Collins Dictionary of Canadian History: 1867 to the Present* (Toronto: Collins Publishers, 1988), p. 133. See also the report by W.E.C. Harrison on the discussions of the 9th annual study conference of the Canadian Institute of International Affairs [CIIA], held at the University of Toronto on 23–4 May 1942 entitled 'The United Nations in War, Victory and Peace'. This is in *Canada and the United Nations: Report of a Conference of the Canadian Institute of International Affairs* (Toronto, 1942), p. 31. Conference participants included Dorothy Stepler, who was later associated with the movement for family allowances. The participants were aware that the problem of 'fear from want' was linked to the attitudes of the 'Great Powers'. This may explain why they launched their own booklet to promote family allowances. See Dorothy Stepler, 'Family Allowances for Canada', *Behind the Headlines*, Vol. 3, No. 2, published jointly by the CIIA and the Canadian Association for Adult Education.
13. J.L. Granatstein, *Canada's War: The Politics of the Mackenzie King Government, 1939–1945* (Toronto: Oxford University Press, 1975), p. 3, citing Mackenzie King's diary.
14. Cited in Raymond Blake, 'Mackenzie King and the Genesis of Family Allowances', p. 248.
15. George Davidson, 'Maintenance as an Eligibility Factor. Dr Davidson's Remark at Supervisors' Conference with Introductory Discussion', Ottawa, March 1948, National Archives of Canada [NAC], Department of National Health and Welfare [DNHW], RG 29, vol. 1934, R233/100-6/25. Davidson was a former director of the Canadian Welfare Council and the deputy minister of the department of national health and welfare.
16. Peter Baldwin, 'The Welfare State for Historians: A Review Article', *Comparative Studies in Society and History*, 1992, p. 706. Philip Resnick, *The Mask of Proteus: Canadian*

Reflections on the State (Montreal and Kingston, 1990), pp. 208–11. I have explored these ideas further in 'Nationalisme et politiques sociales au Québec depuis 1867. Un siècle de rendez-vous manqués entre l'État, l'Église et les familles', *British Journal of Canadian Studies*, Vol. 9, No. 2, (November 1994), pp. 301–47.

17. Canada, Ministère de la Santé nationale et du Bien-être social, *Économisez les vivres*, 1946, NAC, RG 29, Education and Nutrition-Cooperation with F.A. re Inserts, 109, 180-26-15. F.W. Rowse to Harvey W. Adams, 21 June 1954, NAC, DNHW, RG 29, 111-181-1-15, 'Information Service Division'. Fournier to Lafrance, 1 August 1949, Archives du Bureau régional des allocations familiales à Québec, 8-0, vol. 1. *Rapport annuel du ministère de la Santé nationale et du Bien-être social, 1951–1952*, p. 120. *Rapport annuel du Bureau régional des allocations familiales à Québec, 1952–1953*, p. 10.

18. For British reactions to the conservatism of the Atlantic Charter in comparison with Beveridge's proposals, see Kimball, p. 91.

19. For a more detailed analysis of the immediate political circumstances of the enactment of these laws, see my essays 'Family Allowances and Family Autonomy: Quebec 1945–1955', in Bettina Bradbury, ed., *Canadian Family History: Selected Readings* (Toronto: Copp, Clark, Pitman, 1992), pp. 401–37. 'The Decline of Child Labour in Quebec, 1940–1960: Conflict Between Poor Families and the State', in Tina Loo and Lorna McLean, eds, *Historical Perspectives on Law and Society in Canada* (Toronto: Copp, Clark, Longman, 1994), pp. 254–88. For a discussion of the meaning and limits of the Veterans Charter, see Peter Neary and Shaun Brown, 'The Veterans Charter and Canadian Women Veterans of World War Two', in J.L. Granatstein and Peter Neary, eds, *The Good Fight: Canadians and World War Two* (Toronto: Copp Clark, 1995), pp. 387–415.

20. The first payments were announced in the summer of 1945, a few weeks after King's re-election.

21. Mark E. Palmer, 'The Origins and Implementation of Family Allowances in Canada', unpublished MA Thesis (History), Queen's University, 1976, p. 101.

22. Canada, Department of National Health and Welfare, *Allocations familiales. Charte de l'enfance* (Ottawa, 1945–56). Drawings by the National Film Board of Canada, Government Printed Documents, NAC.

23. *Santé et Bien-être social au Canada*, Vol. 3, no. 10, July 1948, Supplement on family allowances, p. 1.

24. I have developed the ideas in the two following sections further in 'The Language of Children's Rights, the Formation of the Welfare State, and the Democractic Experience of Poor Families in Quebec, 1940–55,' *Canadian Historical Review* 78, 3 (September 1997): 409–41.

25. The general argument, by which the initially substantial promises for a better life that were made in the name of international reconstruction were later narrowed down considerably, is summarized in Michiel Horn, 'Leonard Marsh and the Coming of the Welfare State in Canada: A Review Article', *Histoire sociale/Social History*, 9, (1976), pp. 197–204.

26. For those interested in the relationship between diplomacy and welfare, it is worth noting that Norman Robertson, the under-secretary of state for external affairs, was the first senior civil servant to suggest that family allowances might help calm the labour unrest which the National War Labour Board faced. More than his colleagues in the departments of finance, pensions and health or labour, he adopted the language of 'social justice', although he applied it not to children, but to labour. Specifically, he wrote of 'the rights and status of workers and their organization' and of a 'national labour charter'. Cited in Palmer, 'The Origins and Implementation of Family Allowances', pp. 133–8.

27. Marcel Gauchet and Gloria Swain, *La pratique de l'esprit humain. L'institution asilaire et la revolution démocratique* (Paris: Gallimard, 1980), p. 18.

28. 'Home thoughts: Germaine Greer on the folly of "children's rights"', *The Independent Magazine*, 20 January 1990, p. 16. Gill Jones and Claire Wallace, *Youth, Family and Citizenship* (Buckingham, 1992), chapters 1 and 7.

29. Paul Thompson, 'The War With Adults', *Oral History*, 3, 2 (Fall 1975), p. 37; See also Stephen Humphries, *Hooligans or Rebels: An Oral History of Working-Class Childhood and Youth 1889–1939* (Oxford: Basil Blackwell, 1981), pp. 21–3.

30. See, for instance, Charlotte Whitton, *The Dawn of an Ampler Life* (Toronto: MacMillan, 1943), pp. 14–15. See also Carole Pateman, 'Feminist Critiques of the Public/Private Dichotomy', in *The Disorder of Women* (Cambridge: Polity, 1989), pp. 118–40; Raymond Boudon and F. Bourricaud, 'Égalitarisme', *Dictionnaire critique de la sociologie* (Paris: Presses universitaires de France, 1986), p. 217; Norton Grubb and Marvin Lazerson, *Broken Promises: How Americans Fail Their Children* (New York: Basic Books, 1982).

31. The main work on the history of child reform in Canada during this period is Neil Sutherland's *Children in English-Canadian Society: Framing the Twentieth Century Consensus* (Toronto: University of Toronto Press, 1976).

32. Robert Bothwell and Norman Hillmer, *La politique extérieure du Canada, 1919–1939* (Ottawa, Museum of Man and the National Film Board of Canada). Collection of slides from 'Histoire du Canada en Images', Vol. 27, p. 11.

33. On this point see P.T. Rooke and R.L. Schnell, *No Bleeding Heart: Charlotte Whitton: A Feminist on the Right* (Vancouver: UBC Press, 1987). See also Mack Eastman, *Canada at Geneva*, (Toronto: Ryerson Press, 1946), pp. 37–9 and Marcel Hamelin, ed., *Les mémoires du Sénateur Raoul Dandurand (1861–1942)* (Quebec: Presses de l'université Laval, 1967). In the early 1900s, the senator's wife was closely associated with the international and domestic work of the Council of Women that adopted its own charter in 1922 (p. 115) and that was to be central to the elaboration of the Children's Charter in 1924. It is also interesting to note that the Montreal industrialist and city reformer, Herbert Brown Ames, was the financial director of the Secretariat of the League of Nations, between 1919 and 1926. For additional details, see Richard Veatch, 'League of Nations', *Canadian Encyclopedia* (Edmonton: Hurtig, 1988) and P.W.F. Rutherford, ed., 'Introduction', *The City Below the Hill* (Toronto: University of Toronto Press, 1972), first published by Ames in 1897, pp. xi and xviii.

It is also worth noting that the International Labour Office (ILO) of the League of Nations had promoted family allowances since the 1930s. It had amassed considerable expertise in this area, and when, in the spring of 1941, the federal government's advisory committee on reconstruction began its work, it consulted with the ILO. Subsequently, an ILO technical advisor, Maurice Stack, helped write the Marsh Report. See Palmer, 'The Origins and Implementation of Family Allowances in Canada', pp. 28, 118 and 121. See also The League of Nations, Child Welfare Committee, *Report by the ILO on Family Allowances* (Geneva, 1928) C.P.E. 150.

34. Philip E. Veerman, *The Rights of the Child and the Changing Image of Childhood* (London: Martinus, Mijhoff Publishers, 1991), pp. 155–9. Coll. International Studies in Human Rights. Tamara Hareven, 'An Ambiguous Alliance: Some Aspects of American Influences on Canadian Social Welfare', *Histoire sociale/Social History*, 3, (April 1969), p. 93. In Canada, the Montreal suffragist and professor at McGill University, Idola Saint-Jean, after working in a similar manner with Canadian children affected by the war, was proposed as a representative of Canadian welfare agencies at the League of Nations. For details, see Andrée Lévesque, *Résistance et transgression. Études en histoire des femmes au Québec* (Montreal: Remue-ménage, 1995), p. 45, citing *The Montreal Herald*, 2 November 1929.

35. Cynthia R. Comacchio, 'Nations Are Built of Babies': Saving Ontario Mothers and Children 1900–1940 (Montreal & Kingston: McGill-Queen's University Press, 1993). On international changes in the status of children, see Lawrence J. Le Blanc, The Convention on the Rights of the Child: United Nations lawmaking on human rights (Lincoln, Nebraska: Nebraska University Press, 1995), p. xvi.

36. 'Canadian Provisions for Aid for Dependents of Members of the Army and Air Force', Social Security Bulletin, November 1941, pp. 19–24.

37. 'Fréquentation scolaire obligatoire?', Le Monde ouvrier, 20 March 1943, p. 1.

38. M.J.-H. Bessette in Québec, Rapport annuel du Surintendant de l'Instruction publique, 1945–1946, p. 108.

39. Rapport annuel 1943–1944, 4 July 1944, Centre de documents semi-actifs [CDSA] of the Archives nationales du Québec à Québec [ANQQ], 1946-789, 112 398. Lapierre said that he was conveying parents' opinions. Letter to Victor Doré, 4 July 1944, CDSA, 1946-789, 112 398. See also the opinion of one of his anonymous colleagues in the same file, 12 July 1944.

40. 'La protection de l'enfance', Le Soleil, 23 February 1944.

41. Canada, Advisory Committee on Reconstruction, VI, Post-War Problems of Women: Final Report of the Subcommittee, 30 November 1943, (Ottawa, 1944), pp. 10–11.

42. CDSA 1943-1200, box 112 317, case n. 71.

43. Gagnon Boulanger, Roberval County, to Hector Perrier, Secrétaire provincial, 21 September 1943, ANQQ, E-13, C. r., 1942-199, 2223.

44. CDSA 1943-1200, box 112 317, case n. 124; 6–43.

45. Canada, Chambre des communes, Débats, 1944, p. 5690.

46. See my article, 'Le recuil du travails des enfants au Québec entre 1940 et 1960: une explicatrice des conflicts entre les familles pauvres et l'Etat-providence', Labour/Le Travail, No. 24 (automne 1989), pp. 91–129.

47. Dennis Guest, The Emergence of Social Security in Canada (Vancouver: UBC Press, 1985), pp. 217–18.

48. See Arlene Skolnick, Embattled Paradise: The American Family in an Age of Uncertainty (New York, 1991), p. 68.

49. Alvin Finkel, 'Paradise Postponed: A Re-examination of the Green Book Proposals of 1945', Journal of the Canadian Historical Association/Revue de la Société historique du Canada, 1993, pp. 120–42. See also Peter McInnis, 'Planning Prosperity: Canadians Debate Postwar Reconstruction'.

50. Humphrey, 'The Magna Carta of the World', pp. 23, 19. F.R. Scott warned against such constitutional impediments to the spirit of the Atlantic Charter in 'The Constitution and the post-War World', in Alexander Brandy and F.R. Scott, eds, Canada After the War (Toronto: MacMillan, 1944), pp. 60–87. He urged the parties to 'put forward . . . specific themes . . . offering advantages to the great mass of the people.' The contribution by F.H. Soward and Charlotte Whitton to this collection also refer actively to the Atlantic Charter.

51. La Guardia cited in Lloyd C. Gardner, 'The Atlantic Charter: Idea and Reality, 1942–1945', in Brinkley and Crowther, The Atlantic Charter, p. 50.

52. Wild, 'Human Rights in Retrospect', p. 5.

53. Humphrey, 'The Magna Carta of the World', p. 18. A last minute opening and the commitment of the United States' Secretary of State gave them a chance to get their propositions enshrined.

54. Charter of the United Nations, cited in Wild, 'Human Rights in Retrospect', p. 5. See also Humphrey, 'The Magna Carta of the World', p. 18. Accordingly, the Charter 'did not define or even list' the rights.

55. Wild, 'Human Rights in Retrospect', p. 5. See also Bothwell and Hillmer, La politique extérieure du Canada.

56. Veerman, *The Rights of the Child*, pp. 159–62. The Canadian family allowance program included similar concerns: For the first time, natives were included in a welfare program designed for the general population, even if a significant minority of them were to receive the allowance only in kind and through the office of the local Indian agent. The payment of allowances was also associated with the promotion of child placement agencies in order to favour foster families and discourage orphanages.

57. Ibid., chapter 10. On the role of Canadian NGOs in the international development of children's rights between 1946 and 1967, it is worth noting Adelaide Sinclair's important contributions made to the United Nations' International Children's Emergency Fund (UNICEF). On this point, see Desmond Morton, *The United Nations: Its History and the Canadians who Shaped It* (Toronto: Kids Can Press, 1995).

58. Veerman, *The Rights of the Child*, p. 219, notes 42 and 43.

The Geneva Declaration of The Rights of the Child (1924)

By the present Declaration of the Rights of the Child, commonly known as the Declaration of Geneva, men and women of all nations, recognizing that mankind owes to the child the best that it has to give, declare and accept as their duty that, beyond and above all considerations race, nationality or creed:

I. The child must be given the means requisite for its normal development, both materially and spiritually.

II. The child that is hungry must be fed; the child that is sick must be nursed; the child that is backward must be helped; the delinquent child must be reclaimed; and the orphan and the waif must be sheltered and succored.

III. The child must be the first to receive relief in times of distress.

IV. The child must be put in a position to earn a livelihood and must be protected against every form of exploitation.

V. The child must be brought up in the consciousness that its talents must be devoted to the service of its fellowmen.

The Declaration of the Rights of the Child (1959)

Preamble

Whereas the peoples of the United Nations have, in the Charter, reaffirmed their faith in fundamental human rights and in the dignity and worth of the human person, and have determined to promote social progress and better standards of life in larger freedom,

Whereas the United Nations has, in the Universal Declaration of Human Rights, proclaimed that everyone is entitled to all the rights and freedoms set forth therein, without distinction of any kind, such as race, colour, sex, language, religion, political or other opinion, national or social origin, property, birth or other status,

Whereas the child, by reason of his physical and mental immaturity, needs special safeguards and care, including appropriate legal protection, before as well as after birth,

Whereas the need for such special safeguards has been stated in the Geneva Declaration of the Rights of the Child of 1924, and recognized in the Universal Declaration of Human Rights and in the statutes of specialized agencies and international organizations concerned with the welfare of children,

Whereas mankind owes to the child the best it has to give,

Now therefore,

The General Assembly

Proclaims this Declaration of the Rights of the Child to the end that he may have a happy childhood and enjoy for his own good and for the good of society the rights and freedoms herein set forth, and calls upon parents, upon men and women as individuals, and upon voluntary organizations, local authorities and national Governments to recognize these rights and strive for their observance by legislative and other measures progressively taken in accordance with the following principles:

Principle I
The child shall enjoy all the rights set forth in this Declaration. Every child, without any exception whatsoever, shall be entitled to these rights, without distinction or discrimination on account of race, colour, sex, language, religion, political or

other opinion, national or social origin, property, birth or other status, whether of himself or of his family.

Principle 2
The child shall enjoy special protection, and shall be given opportunities and facilities, by law and by other means, to enable him to develop physically, mentally, morally, spiritually and socially in a healthy and normal manner and in conditions of freedom and dignity. In the enactment of laws for this purpose, the best interests of the child shall be the paramount consideration.

Principle 3
The child shall be entitled from his birth to a name and a nationality.

Principle 4
The child shall enjoy the benefits of social security. He shall be entitled to grow and develop in health; to this end, special care and protection shall be provided both to him and to his mother, including adequate pre-natal and post-natal care. The child shall have the right to adequate nutrition, housing, recreation and medical services.

Principle 5
The child who is physically, mentally or socially handicapped shall be given the special treatment, education and care required by his particular condition.

Principle 6
The child, for the full and harmonious development of his personality, needs love and understanding. He shall, wherever possible, grow up in the care and under the responsibility of his parents, and, in any case, in an atmosphere of affection and of moral and material security; a child of tender years shall not, save in exceptional circumstances, be separated from his mother. Society and the public authorities shall have the duty to extend particular care to children without a family and to those without adequate means of support. Payment of State and other assistance towards the maintenance of children of large families is desirable.

Principle 7
The child is entitled to receive education, which shall be free and compulsory, at least in the elementary stages. He shall be given an education which will promote his general culture and enable him, on a basis of equal opportunity, to develop his abilities, his individual judgement, and his sense of moral and social responsibility, and to become a useful member of society.

The best interests of the child shall be the guiding principle of those responsible for his education and guidance; that responsibility lies in the first place with his parents.

The child shall have full opportunity for play and recreation, which should be directed to the same purposes as education; society and the public authorities shall endeavour to promote the enjoyment of this right.

Principle 8
The child shall in all circumstances be among the first to receive protection and relief.

Principle 9
The child shall be protected against all forms of neglect, cruelty and exploitation. He shall not be the subject of traffic, in any form.

The child shall not be admitted to employment before an appropriate minimum age; he shall in no case be caused or permitted to engage in any occupation or employment which would prejudice his health or education, or interfere with his physical, mental or moral development.

Principle 10
The child shall be protected from practices which may foster racial, religious and any other form of discrimination. He shall be brought up in a spirit of understanding, tolerance, friendship among peoples, peace and universal brotherhood, and in full consciousness that his energy and talents should be devoted to the service of his fellow men.

Suggestions for Further Reading

Covell, Katherine and R. Brian Howe, *The Challenge of Children's Rights for Canada.* Waterloo: Wilfrid Laurier University Press, 2001.

Johnston, Charles M., 'The Children's War: the mobilisation of Ontario youth during the Second World War' in Roger Hall, William Westfall, and Laurel Sefton MacDowell, eds, *Patterns of the Past: Interpreting Ontario's History.* Toronto: Dundurn Press, 1988: 356–380.

Kogawa, Joy, *Obasan.* Markham, ON: Penguin Books, 1981.

LeBlanc, Laurence J., *The Convention on the Rights of the Child: United Nations Lawmaking on Human Rights.* Lincoln: University of Nebraska Press, 1995.

Marshall, Dominique, 'The Language of Children's Rights, the Formation of the Welfare State, and the Democratic Experience of Poor Families in Post War Canada, 1945–1960,' *Canadian Historical Review* 78, 3 (September 1997): 409–41.

Montgomery, Emilie L., '"The war was a very vivid part of my life": The Second World War and the Lives of British Columbia Children,' in Jean Barman, Neil Sutherland, and J. Donald Wilson, eds, *Children, Teachers and Schools in the History of British Columbia.* Calgary: Detselig, 1995: 161–74.

PART 8

Being an Immigrant Child in Late Twentieth-Century Canada, 1970–1985

In the last half of twentieth century, a series of amendments to the Canadian Immigration Act removed explicit discrimination from immigration legislation. The Immigration Act of 1953 no longer targeted specific groups, but still restricted immigration on the basis of ethnicity, class, or country of origin. Only a 1967 order-in-council eliminated regulations that discriminated on the basis of race and nationality and introduced a universally applicable point system that allowed 'skilled' immigrants into the country. The 1976 Immigration Act guaranteed that immigrants would not be discriminated against on the grounds of race, national or ethnic origin, colour, religion, or sex. However, in practice the skills discourse and point system that have been at the core of Canadian immigration policy produces differential results depending on class, race, ethnicity, and gender. The children's memories presented below illustrate how these policies influenced immigrant and refugee children's experiences in a multicultural Canada and how they adapted to life in their new home.

Although the objective of immigration policy in 'multicultural Canada' has been to preserve the nation's character, Canada was a much more diverse nation by the end of the twentieth century than it had been at the beginning. Before 1961, more than 55 per cent of immigrants came from the United States or Great Britain; by 1991 only 10 per cent of immigrants came from these countries. In the same period, the proportion of immigrants from Asian countries increased from 2.4 to 42 per cent; from Central and South America from 0.5 to 9.1 per cent; and from the Caribbean from 0.7 to 5.4 per cent. Between 1984 and 1989, 160,000 of these immigrants and refugees were children.

What was it like to be an immigrant or refugee child? For many immigrant and refugee children, language was a considerable barrier. In 1986, the mother tongue of 40 per cent of immigrant children was a language other than English or French. In 1985, one-third of immigrant children lived in poverty, compared to 19 per cent of Canadian children overall. In addition, the educational and socio-economic backgrounds of their parents varied. Once in Canada, many doctors, engineers, nurses, teachers, and lawyers could not find employment in their profession because their education and training were not recognized in Canada. Changes in socio-economic status and the anxieties associated with resettlement made home life stressful, and this stress sometimes manifested itself in violence. The children's discussions of family life in *Rivers Have Sources, Trees Have Roots* demonstrate that family was also source of strength for many children from racialized minorities.

The immigrant and refugee children's pictures reproduced from *Come with Us* illustrate poignantly the pain of separation from family, the joy of reunion, and the injury caused by classmates' teasing. Immigrant children from Europe had faced ridicule from their peers in previous decades. But over time these children could integrate themselves into teenage culture, or at least conform to the 'national character' in adulthood. Racialized children could discard their 'fresh off the boat' image in dress and demeanour, but they remained vulnerable to hateful racist taunts because they could not change the colour of their skin. Many Canadian-born children who are not 'white' encountered the racist taunt to 'go back to where they came from'.

Multicultural education was designed to change these attitudes. Rather than treating diversity as a problem to be fixed, policy following the 1971 Multicultural Act has promoted and celebrated cultural diversity within a bilingual framework. School boards designed English as a Second Language programs to help immigrant and refugee children integrate into the school system. These programs are concentrated in urban areas and children living in smaller centres and rural communities often do not have access to language training. Heritage Language programs promote children's pride in their heritage, and street festivals and multicultural celebrations expose Canadians to different foods, music, and traditions. However, Dionne Brand and Krisantha Sri Bhaggiyadatta explain that the development of these programs was extremely political. The interviews with children from racialized minorities demonstrate that the celebration of difference does not address the systemic groundings of racism and discrimination.

Nancy Janovicek

Rivers Have Sources, Trees Have Roots

Dionne Brand and Krisantha Sri Bhaggiyadatta

Childhood

Children of colour grow up quickly; they have to, because the adult figures of authority they encounter all too often do not see their youth, their childhood, they see only their colour. The children's play, horsing around on a bus or in the subway, is seen by the bus driver, the white passengers, the white society, not for what it is—play—but as behaviour characteristic of the children's race.

Children get these messages at daycare centres, in playgrounds, walking along the street. They learn very quickly how they are expected to behave with each other. As early as the pre-school years, white children learn that they can, more often than not, get away with name-calling, teasing, and putting-down those children whose difference in colour marks them as somehow strange, not normal. Eventually this play hardens into a racism that they, as white children, understand works to their benefit.

Children of colour learn that they cannot win this cruel game. They come to know themselves by their racist ascriptions, as a 'nigger', 'Paki', or 'Chink'. At first, they may understand racism only as a source of discomfort, but soon they learn it is more than that. They learn that white society is not as caring or kind toward them. They spend more and more time thinking of what they will say or do, how they will act to avoid these humiliations. They wonder if they should ignore or fight the jeering and hurtful behaviour of their white peers. They enter gyms, cafeterias, and playgrounds cautiously. There they are accepted provisionally. A Black child is always 'the nigger who plays hockey' not 'the kid who plays hockey'.

Their teachers, their schools, let them down. There is no place Black children can take their hurt except to their families. The family is the one safe place among many unsafe, where you learn who you are, what to do, what to expect, and what is right. It is the place where perceptions of the world are reinforced or negated; where the outside is filtered through the family's choices, opinions, and decisions.

But how do you teach kids what to be if what they see differs from what they are? Panic strikes the moment the child realizes that, outside their family, authority and power are in the hands of whites. Children have to learn to cope with the loneliness and the isolation that comes from never seeing their reflection on TV, in the news, from being constantly on guard for racist indications. They try all means at hand to fit in. They change the way they speak. They try to change the way they look. They try to distance themselves from their neighbours, their background. Some drown.

Often it is too hard for children to tell their parents what is happening to them. Many of their parents immigrated to Canada as adults, and are not intimate with the culture of childhood in which their children live. Children, understanding this, try to keep the burden of this knowledge from their parents.

Parents do know. Many have been through it before and don't want their children to get the same treatment as they did. But parents' strategies differ. Some parents want to mete out the reality in small doses and too often wait until the child is already in pain before alerting him or her to the presence of racism. Some say, 'Try harder. You have to mix,' believing that goodwill alone can counter racism. They do not want to believe that society negates their children. Sometimes they cannot deal with racism themselves. They cannot live without hope, but they cannot change the culture to protect their child. They cannot ask their children to forget the daily humiliations and isolation, and they cannot themselves forget.

Some parents say, 'Fight back. Don't take any shit.' They believe that in order to make the right decisions, to know when to fight back, their children must have the right information. One parent told us she wants her child to belong here. Another told her child, 'Canadian doesn't mean white, Canadian means being here.' Parents want their children to be left alone: to be children.

[. . .]

Most children are aware of where their parents or ancestors came from. Contemporary Canadian culture forces them either to comply with or reject the negative images associated with those countries. Encounters with the racist attitudes of other children and adults as early as in the sandbox, teaches them the tools of avoidance and confrontation. In confronting racism, children go through a learning experience that matures their critical abilities. In fighting racism they reach for concepts of morality and logic. They are forced to develop an analysis of the world.

[. . .]

I can remember a time in grade six, when I was the only Black person on the hockey team. After the game, they'd come up to me and say, 'Hey you're pretty good for a nigger.' I'd walk by and they would whisper 'That's the nigger that plays hockey.' They'd use 'nigger' like it was my name. That really got me mad. It was like Black people aren't supposed to be good at anything!

Their parents don't teach them that other people have names too. It makes you feel really low, that it was bad to be Black, as if I should have been white.

[. . .]

Every year in the summer, on the first holidays, we would like to take family outings to the zoo, to Centre Island, or to the Exhibition. We have a large family, six kids, and I guess we stand out in a crowd. Every now and then we heard comments, your basic name-calling. It would make you feel uncomfortable and hurt, but you didn't really understand what was going on.

One incident I remember very clearly from about sixteen years ago. I couldn't have been more than nine or ten years old. My sister and I had joined this swimming class, and we ran into these two white girls, in the dressing room, and they started verbally abusing us. I couldn't understand why. I don't know if the Chinese are basically very passive or whatever, but we didn't say much. But after a while it started bothering me so I told them to mind their own business. One of the girls came up to me and she kicked me. I was ten at the time, and when you come from a sheltered background you don't really know how to handle this. These two girls, they started saying, 'Why don't you go back where you came from? We won the war anyway.' And I was thinking, what war are you talking about? I didn't even know there was a war. My younger sisters were frightened. Until this day, I could never really understand what the hell war they were talking about. Until it finally occurred to me that maybe they thought they were talking about the Japanese and Pearl Harbour.

[. . .]

In high school a lot of people asked me if I was on a sport or athletic team and it bothered me. They'd ask 'Are you on the football team?' or 'You look like a football player.' I thought, I'm not overly anything, why do they assume that? They wouldn't go to a big white person and say that, but that was how they approached me as a way of making friends. I'd say, 'No! I'm not. I just came from the West Indies and I'm in grade twelve.' Later on I started dealing with that stereotype of me, of having to be a basketball player or a sports fan.

When it got around that I was doing well, people kept coming up to me and saying, 'Oh wow. You really do well in school. Is it really easier here than back home in Jamaica? Why do you do so well?' It was unbelievable!

The very first time I ever cried in high school, we were taking social studies and the teacher was showing a film on Asian religions. He happened to be showing one on Chinese religious and the film pictured the Chinese as very ignorant, very primitive people. I became very upset and started crying beyond my control, and the girl next to me said to me, 'Why are you so upset? It's nothing personal.' But it was personal. She said, 'You'll forget about it by the end of the week.' I didn't forget. I was very, very upset.

[. . .]

I came to Canada from the Punjab in 1970 when I was eight years old. I went to Regal Road Junior Public School. I was put into a Special English class because I couldn't speak English. I didn't experience much racism when I was a little kid. It started in grades seven and eight, in Senior Public School at Winona Road. Name-calling, and things like that.

When there were fights, the Jamaican and Trinidadian kids would help us. When you're young it's not that important. Sure, there was the name-calling and people not sitting beside you, but that was mostly the English-Canadians. Most of the time I ignored it. When I couldn't, I would fight back, sometimes physically. My parents never found out. I wouldn't keep these things in my mind, I'd forget it.

I started feeling it more in high school. There teachers talked to their own kind, they wouldn't help us out. They greeted other kids in the halls, but they ignored us. There are a fair number of immigrant and non-white kids in the school. The South Asians stuck together, ate lunch together, and played soccer together.

The guidance counsellors were the worst. Once I had to make a change in the timetable, and the counsellor refused to change it. He said, 'It's our rules.' I knew a white kid, a friend, who'd just got his changed. We went to the office together. I was mad and upset. I said, 'How come you make changes for him and you don't make changes for me?' He made the change! The guidance counsellors don't guide us into the educational levels. You don't know the difference at first, but you need grade thirteen to get into university. They don't tell students this. They don't want us to advance.

If you have a turban and a beard you are always prepared to deal with name-calling and people not wanting to sit next to you. I don't avoid things. I deal with them, sometimes physically. The name-callers are only making a fool of themselves. As for the teachers: deep inside they don't want you to advance, but if you get good marks there is nothing they can do about it. Most of the South Asian and Chinese kids get through to university.

[...]

Racism is very stressful. When I do something I feel that my peers, or somebody behind me, is going to be judged because of what I've done. If I happen to make a mistake of some kind, somebody is going to get it. You're supposed to be an ambassador for the entire race. You feel like you have to go out and you have to prove yourself to everybody. You have to prove yourself to your parents, to your teacher, to everybody. It's really monotonous.

There's pressure from parents. They say because you're a Black person it's hard and you have to strive more. They're not judging you as an individual, either. They say you have to get better marks, because it's going to be tougher for you to get into university and to get into the work-force. Part of what they are saying is true, it is harder. Still, you've got to be the best person you can be for yourself.

Once I chaired a Black History Week assembly. Afterwards, someone came and congratulated us, saying it was very good and how well I chaired. He said, 'I didn't know you could do that!'

I told this to someone just to hear what they would say and they said, 'Well, it sounds like you've been put down again'. It's as if the person who congratulated me was saying, 'Because you're a Black student, you're not supposed to be able to do that sort of thing.' I know the person is really nice and I'm not really sure if he was conscious of what he said. When I was younger in grade nine or ten, if something like that happened, I would automatically think this is happening because I'm Black. Now I think that I'm more willing to find out more of what's going on. Only then, if I feel the person is being racist because of my colour, would I say something.

[...]

Family

I talk to them about racism, but it is a word that is hard to grasp at their age, although Christiana who is eleven is beginning to grasp it. She asserts herself. She associates with a mixture of races. Her best friends are Chinese and people of colour, I guess she identifies with them more. I talk to them about where mommy and daddy came from; about the country we lived in. I told them to be careful about living here and not to be surprised if one day they were called a 'Chink' or some other racist term. We bring them up to be tough, to fight back. We told them that if they were attacked by a racist, simply to assert the fact that they are as Canadian as anybody else. We told them that Canadian doesn't mean being white, Canadian means being here—that's all it means—and that the first Canadians were Indians. We talk about who is in power, who calls the shots, and that if they are white they will definitely keep you from being part of the good things, from partaking of the good things in this society, not that there is much of it.

My mother always urged me, 'You've got to make friends; you've got to integrate; you've got to mix to make it in this country.' She said, 'You've got to get to know, to get involved.' And I said, 'I don't feel comfortable.'

[. . .]

Education

It's significant that non-whites have made a major organizing effort around issues of education. They have made this effort because they recognize it as one of the most important places where the culture of the society is perpetuated. For non-white people, it is a setting where concessions such as heritage languages are gained and lost on a recurrent basis. The heritage language program was introduced into the Toronto Board of Education schools in 1978. In the mid-1970s, children whose first language was not English, or whose parents were immigrants from non-English-speaking countries, made up fifty per cent of the school population in the city. Many groups lobbied for the program, initially an after-school program. Teaching the cultures of the children's homelands and such languages as Greek, Italian, Portuguese, Cantonese, Hindi, and Urdu to children from these backgrounds was a tip to the new multicultural make-up of the schools. The program arrived on the heels of a debate around bilingualism and francophone education in Ontario.

The Black Heritage Program began some eighteen months later than the other programs. It appealed to the idea of culturalism more strongly than other programs. The community felt that Black children should learn about the history of Blacks in Canada and that those who were of Caribbean parents should not lose their cultural heritage. Behind this focus on heritage culture was a strategy to fight the endemic racism of the educational system.

For non-whites, the fight for a fair and equal education became the fight for anti-racist education. Liaison committees of parents and teachers were set up in schools and at the Board to oversee the programs. Many community activists, who had fought outside of the school system for years for equal education for non-Anglo and non-white children, joined these committees.

The Toronto Board of Education took the leadership in integrating community concerns into education planning. This was true of the board of elected trustees; the bureaucracy was another matter. The School Community Relations Department, established by the board some years earlier, now mediated the integration of the Heritage Languages Program. But the department walked a fine line between the bureaucracy and the community. Made up of workers from many different racial and cultural backgrounds, it played (depending on the community involved) a cagey advocacy role in implementing the program.

In predominantly Anglo areas, the program was resented. Even non-Anglo and non-white parents were sometimes wary of the program fearing that their children would be further 'pointed out' for their difference. But, more overwhelmingly, these groups felt that the educational system was obliged to acknowledge the presence of non-Anglo and non-white children in the schools.

The integration of these programs into the regular school day a few years later brought the seething resentment against the program to a head. The Toronto Teachers' Federation, claiming that it made the workday longer, threatened to strike against the integration of the program. They launched a work-to-rule action that lasted for two years. Parent liaison committees accused the Federation of racism. The situation prompted a Black teacher, Clem Marshall, to challenge the president in the Federation's elections of that year.

Racism was certainly present in the educational system. For years, Black community groups had lobbied against the streaming of their children into lower-level and vocational schools. Children of West Indian parents, for example, were often kept back both because of their accents and because of the assumption that they were slow learners. Community agencies have promoted after-schools programs and parent advocacy to fight the racism inherent in these assumptions.

But racism continues to be a problem. Statistics released in 1983 show that Black and Native children are most likely to be found in vocational and basic level courses that give no hope of a university of even a college education.[1] This is happening despite studies and depositions and despite the Toronto Board of Education's million-dollar race relations report of 1979. This report acknowledged that there was disadvantage in education, but was vague on identifying where the disadvantage stemmed from. The Board's Race Relations Department, much applauded when it was first established in 1979, offers little more than anti-racism camps for students, intervention in racist incidents in schools, and voluntary sensitivity workshops for teachers.

The voluntary nature of post-secondary education places universities and colleges somewhat beyond the effect of community protest or action. But their curricula and structures are no less racist. Here, students fight racism on an individual basis or through Black student unions. The most notable concession won by non-whites in a post-secondary institution is the Transitional Year Program at the University of Toronto, established in 1972. This program, won through the efforts of the Black Student Union, is designed to help entry into the university for students disadvantaged by race or class.

We asked people to comment on their perceptions and experiences of primary, secondary, and post-secondary education. As our respondents point out, the concessions gained in the fight for fair and equal education for non-white children are minimal, flexible, and are continually undercut as the basic structures—the bureaucracy, rules, personnel, and curriculum—remain the same. An anti-racist education for all children remains a distant prospect.

[. . .]

I went to Laurier Collegiate in Scarborough. My first day there was really interesting. My stepfather took me down to see a guidance counsellor, and there was some hassle. I had just finished grade eleven but they said the equivalent of the West Indian school system was one grade lower. My stepfather got really upset. He said he had expected this but that he and my mother thought I should go into grade twelve and they wouldn't settle for anything less. She kept saying she knew how he felt, but if kids were put one year back they do better. They find that's where their levels are really at. Eventually she gave in and said, 'OK. Try him in grade twelve, but if he doesn't do very well, we're going to have to put him back. That's all there is to it.'

My first term in history class I ended up having the highest mark. It was odd, the way the teacher treated it. He came over to me quite quietly and said, 'Where did you go to school before?' I said I was from Jamaica. 'Did you go to a special kind of school for exceptionally bright kids, gifted children?' I said, 'No, it was just a high school. There were kids who did much better than me. It's no big deal.' He said, 'But you ended up with the highest mark in the class for the term.' He was very surprised, and I felt a bit flattered. But my mother was very upset. She said, 'How dare he? What is he trying to say? That a Black child from Jamaica could not possibly do that? It's such an unusual thing?' She was saying it was an example of how Blacks were treated in this country—as if they were not expected to achieve, and if they did, it was treated as some kind of oddity. That's not fair.

[. . .]

I think that underlying this is a fear, a growing fear in the Anglo community, of losing what they so far have had firmly in hand. On the one hand, I don't think that minority parents have gained a lot. They've got the Heritage Language Program, but it's only one part of the school program, it's peripheral. The Heritage Language Program is a smoke screen to make minority parents think that they've got equal access and rights in education, but it's not true yet. Not to mention the fact that they haven't got much out of the program. The ministry and the school board are not wholeheartedly committed to the Heritage Language Program.

On the other hand the Anglo community does not seem to realize that minority parents have got very little so far, and that they have a long way to go in order to threaten Anglo power. Yet, the Anglos are already shaken and the nervousness, the insecurity, that they've expressed is out of proportion to what they have actually lost. I don't think they have lost anything yet.

[. . .]

The boards of education believe so much in multiculturalism; the Ontario Government believes so much in multiculturalism; the Federal Government believes so much in multiculturalism; but when it comes to the practice of multiculturalism, they do not hire the right people. For example, they do not hire non-white teachers in our schools. That suggests that the culture of non-white children is not important. Check the schools and find out. In Toronto, Etobicoke, Scarborough, the schools are crowded with people from different cultures, non-white people, non-white children. The proportion of non-white teachers representing those students is ridiculously low. A teacher always teaches within a cultural context and they hire people that can train children to become nice WASP Canadians. They expect that to be perpetuated in the schools.

[...]

At Woodfield Road school, the Chinese students make up about one quarter of the school. But the number of Chinese students on the honour roll is much higher than one quarter. So at the graduation ceremony, Chinese names kept being called, and Anglo parents whispered to their neighbours, 'Another Chinese'.

[...]

[1986]

Note

1. E.N. Wright and G.K. Tsuji, *The Grade Nine Student Survey: Fall 1982*, Research Dept., Toronto Board of Education, Oct. 1983, Research Report no. 173.

From *Come with Us: Children Speak for Themselves*

Judy McClard and Naomi Wall

I Wish I Could Go to Portugal Again

When my father came to Canada, my mother didn't want to come. So my father came and told my aunt to come, and my aunt told my grandfather to come, and my grandfather told my grandmother to come. And now my mother wanted to come, but she couldn't because my other grandmother was almost dying. My mother has to look after her.

My father felt sad and so did I because I can't see her. And in the summer I went and saw my mom. And the saddest part was when I had to come to Canada. I wish I could go to Portugal again. My mother has to look after my grandmother.

I Remember Too

September the 11th, 1973. In Chile soldiers killed the President. They burned the house where the President lived. The windows were broken. It had a flag on top and the flag was burning like it was just paper.

Every day my mother had to go to the embassy and she said, "Please I want to see my husband. Please could you sign this for me, please?"

Every day the man said **"No."**

We saw the soldiers putting cannons and machine guns and rifles and guns and all those things in the ground of the beach.

And after all those things we went to Honduras and now we are here. We like Canada. We have friends, we learn English and we are happy here. But I like better there. I'm sad because we cannot be in Chile. I miss my friends, my grandmother, and I hope we could go back in a little while when the soldiers are gone.

Suggestions for Further Reading

Kelly, Jennifer, *Under the Gaze: Learning to be Black in White Society.* Halifax: Fernwood Publishing, 1998.

McAndrew, Marie, 'Ethnicity, Multiculturalism, and Multicultural Education in Canada' in Ratna Ghosh et al., *Social Change and Education in Canada* 2nd edn. 1991: 130–41.

McDiarmid, Garnet and David Pratt, *Teaching Prejudice.* Toronto: OISE Press, 1971.

Moodley, Koogila A., 'Multicultural Education in Canada: Historical Development and Current Status' in James A. Banks and Cherry A. McGee Banks, eds, *A Handbook of Research on Multicultural Education.* New York: Simon & Schuster MacMillan, 1995.

Wideen, Marvin and Kathleen A. Barnard, *Impacts of Immigration on Education in British Columbia: An Analysis of Efforts to Implement Policies of Multiculturalism in Schools.* Vancouver: Research on Immigration and Integration in the Metropolis: January 1999. Available at: http://riim.metropolis.net/

PART 9

'Let's Talk about Sex': Learning about Sexuality, 1950–1984

One constant feature of the history of sexuality is the tension between the pervasive public chatter about sex and the notion that sexuality is a private matter best discussed within the family. The social reformers of the early twentieth century, influenced by eugenics and panics about the 'degeneracy' of the white race, believed that the strength of the nation rested on the morality of its citizens. Adults expected both boys and girls to be moral, nonsexual beings. However, they excused boys' misdeeds because they 'naturally' had more energy. The onus was on girls to defend their chastity and judges and social workers cast their sexual explorations as inherent character flaws. Girls learned that their value lay in their future as a wife and mother and that only 'good' girls could grow up to be 'moral' mothers. In the postwar years, national stability was equated with the nuclear family. Advice literature that targeted adolescents was designed to ensure that teenagers grew up to be 'normal' heterosexual adults. The underlying assumption of the literature was that normal teenagers were not sexually active.

The predominance of heterosexuality in teenage culture made exploring other sexualities difficult. Homophobia made it dangerous to be openly gay. The gay and lesbian movement, inspired by the 1969 Stonewall Riots in New York City, encouraged gays and lesbians to come out of the closet in order to confront homophobia and end the fear that dominated the lives of lesbians and gay men. The pamphlets reproduced from the Canadian Lesbian and Gay Archives map the evolution in anti-homophobia education. It is difficult to gauge the impact they had on young people in the 1970s and 1980s because, to date, there are few memoirs, novels, and histories that document the lives of adolescent lesbians and gay men. One result of the movement, however, was that there were more places where young people could seek advice about coming out, and find alternative support systems if friends and family shunned them because of their sexual identity.

Salt 'N Pepa's 1989 dance hit, 'Let's Talk about Sex', encouraged young people to 'talk about all the good things and the bad things that can be.' Historically, parents have been uncomfortable with public discussions about youthful sexuality, especially those that conflicted with their own values. Mary Louise Adams examines the heated debates between parents and the Toronto School Board about introducing sex education into postwar classrooms. In the 1980s, HIV/AIDS changed attitudes about sex education. Young people who did not use prophylactics had always risked contracting sexually transmitted diseases, but AIDS effectively equated sexual activity with mortality. Sexual knowledge became a matter of life or death. As a collective of young women explained in their guide to healthy sexuality, 'AIDS is something we all have to learn about and it's something we need to really think about before we have sex. Yes, it's a drag but so is DYING' (Quigley, et al., 2000, p. 133; see Suggestions for Further Reading). The acknowledgement that straight and gay youth are at risk is a recent development. When AIDS emerged as a social issue, it was considered a 'gay disease'. The gay community shouldered the responsibility of raising awareness about safe sex. Sex education had to move beyond the classroom and into the streets to reach street-involved youth who were engaged in the sex trade, many of whom were IV-drug users. More recently, First Nations community groups have developed HIV/AIDS awareness programs because a disproportionate number of street-involved youth are of Aboriginal ancestry, and because there is a rapidly increasing rate of HIV/AIDS in First Nations communities.

Nancy Janovicek

Sex at the Board, or Keeping Children from Sexual Knowledge

Mary Louise Adams

These days, when we think of sex education we're as likely to think of controversies over condom machines in school washrooms as we are to think of the mechanics of reproduction or the functioning of our ductless glands. It's been half a century since the subject was first debated by the Toronto Board of Education, but changes and additions to the sex ed curriculum remain as controversial in the 1990s as the original proposals were toward the end of World War II. Over the past few years, debate has flourished over issues like appropriate safer sex education, policies on heterosexism and homophobia, and approaches to sexual violence. And while these issues seem a long way from the more modest aims of the earlier proposals, the fears they generate in people who are opposed to them are similar.

Sex education, like other forums for discussion about sexuality, is profoundly influenced by notions of morality. Even today sexuality and morality are conflated. There exists no morally neutral zone where we may discuss the 'facts' of sexual reproduction, sexual attitudes, or sexual behaviours. Whether we consider ourselves to be progressive or conservative, our own moral outlook shades our understanding of even the most scientific information. Sex, for all we are surrounded by it, is still seen by many people to be a private realm, one best left within the confines of the nuclear family. In part, this is because of the undue weight sexuality carries in our notions of what it means to be a person. Sexuality has become central to the ways we define our development as individuals; it has become central to our identities. Thus, teaching about sexuality is thought to be of a different order than the teaching of basic algebra or geography. Sex education is perceived to have, indeed it is intended to have, an effect on the shaping of students as they grow up. The topic gets controversial when people—parents, teachers, 'concerned citizens'—have different ideas about what that shape might be.

But sex ed is not solely, nor primarily, aimed at the personal development and adjustment of students. Instead, sex ed curriculums respond to concerns about social issues. The topics discussed in sex ed classes are widely perceived to have tremendous social significance with consequences that stretch far beyond both the individual and sexual realms. For instance, issues like teen pregnancy and sexually transmitted diseases, while they may mark difficulties in individual lives, are also assumed by some people to lead to poverty and social decay. They are seen to represent tears in the fabric of an otherwise orderly society. Sex ed, in this sense, is an effort to restore order and to effect social control.

At present the regulatory aspect of sex education can be difficult to see because debates about its place in the general curriculum and the scope of its teaching are so heated and polarized. When sex education programs are threatened by conservative opposition to them, it can seem like their very existence is a sign of a progressive approach to education. But this isn't necessarily the case as the history of state-sponsored sex education in Toronto schools makes clear.

Wartime and the Loosening of Morals

> The last war [World War I] ushered in jazz, women smokers, disregard for authority . . . popular profanity and general looseness of behaviour . . . If we are about to experience a similar decline from our modern standards, I shudder to think of the results. Let us be cool-headed in these trying times and carry on, war or no war, behaving sanely as we ought. For why should we carelessly cast aside the very ideals for which our soldiers are spilling their life blood.[1]

While the writer of this 1940 appeal for moral restraint was a high-school journalist, his fears weren't adolescent ones. During World War II, the disruptions of social and familial networks made changes in sexual and moral behaviour possible, even if not entirely acceptable. The intensity of wartime emotions, the availability of higher incomes for young men and women, and freedom from parental control all forced teenagers to grow up quickly. Some commentators claimed all this 'opportunity' led young people to be more concerned with themselves than with their society.

In an article in the Ontario public health nurses' *Bulletin*, John Stokes wrote that 'the prevailing hedonism of the day' and individualistic attitudes had led to a 'character problem in sex and self control'.[2] One of the social manifestations of this 'problem' he said, could be found in rising statistics for venereal diseases. According to the *Toronto Star*, there was a seven per cent increase in the number of fifteen- to nineteen-year-olds attending venereal disease clinics between 1939 and 1944.[3] Some commentators thought it was time for the schools to intervene.

In 1944, Trustee E.L. Roxborough, a member of the Toronto Board of Education and a vice-president of the Big Brother Movement, proposed to the Board that social hygiene be placed on the secondary-school curriculum. 'Social hygiene' is a term for sex education that had roots in the eugenics movements of the earlier part of the century. Eugenicists, who believed in the science of racial betterment, promoted social hygiene as a means of preventing VD. But Dr Gordon Bates, a leading Canadian expert in venereal disease control during the first world war, claimed that social hygiene involved much more than VD prevention: 'I would suggest that "social hygiene" simply means social health or the establishment of normal relations between all individuals in society. . . .'[4] While this meaning of social hygiene might have been simple—consensus on the definition of 'normal' notwithstanding—any program to put it into action would have had to be far-reaching in its consequences. An editorial in the *Star* made this point by referring to Roxborough's proposal not as sex ed but as 'character education'. The editorial deemed social hygiene important not only because of the urgency needed 'to combat the spread of social disease', but also as an antidote to the more general 'weakening of morals'.[5] Nevertheless, Roxborough's motion was treated with caution by the Board of Education. 'We should go slow', said Trustee Dr J.P.F. Williams. 'If we go at all', added Trustee Chambers.[6]

In March 1944, a month after Roxborough's motion, Dr Charles Goldring, Superintendent of Schools, presented a report on social hygiene to the Board's Management Committee.[7] He told the trustees that the provincial Department of Education had no provisions for the teaching of social hygiene. In fact, he could find only two Canadian examples of social hygiene teaching. A program for secondary school girls had been in existence in London, Ontario, since 1942. A similar boys' program had been in place, but it was postponed when the male doctor who taught it went away on active service. In British Columbia, lectures on venereal disease were presented in secondary schools. In Ontario, Goldring hoped that leadership on the matter would be extended by the Department of Health, which would lead to development of a formal curriculum by the Department of Education. He suggested that the social hygiene material be taught, during regular health periods, to boys and girls in separate classes. The Department of Health, he said, should be responsible for organizing training talks on social hygiene to be given to physical education instructors.

Members of Management Committee decided to endorse the proposal to teach social hygiene on the condition it be approved by the Department of Education. But even after the endorsement was official, it wasn't clear what types of material were to be included in social hygiene classes; Goldring wanted the province, particularly the Department of Health, to make those decisions.

Certainly concerns about venereal disease motivated much of the public support for sex education in the schools. The Anglican Church, for instance, endorsed a resolution supporting sex education (and that's the term they chose to use—perhaps as a way to de-emphasize the 'scientific' sound of social hygiene in favour of morals) in homes, churches, and schools 'in order to stop the spread of venereal disease'. The Diocesan Council 'attributed the spread of venereal diseases to a breakdown of moral standards, a general decay of faith, and economic causes and widespread dislocation of society'. But still, sex ed was only to be taught in schools if a 'Christian point of view' could be safeguarded.[8]

At the annual convention of the Ontario Educational Association in April 1944, a resolution to make sex ed a part of the provincial school curriculum passed by a vote of ten to one. Arguments in favour of the resolution claimed that sex education would help to check both juvenile delinquency and social disease. 'It is a disgrace to Ontario and Canada that there should be so much venereal disease', said Dr P.B. Proudfoot of Russell.[9] Those not in favour of the resolution argued that 'parents or preachers were the people to give sex counsel and that [the issue] was a moral [as opposed to a social] question'.[10] But, of course, moral questions frequently have social implications.

A June 1944 Gallup pole garnered almost the same results as the OEA resolution, claiming that ninety-three per cent of Canadians wanted high school students to be exposed to lectures on the prevention of venereal disease.[11] In a 1943 poll, seventy-six per cent of those asked had said they wanted sex education in the schools.[12] Whether the difference between these two figures was due to the progression of the war and resulting social problems or whether it was because of the more specific focus of education about venereal disease versus education about sex, it is impossible to say. But clearly, there was a social consensus on the issue despite both-sides-of-the-story newspaper accounts which might suggest otherwise. However, to agree that students should learn about VD is not to agree on how they should learn it.

Five months after Roxborough's proposal, venereal disease was approved as part of the Ontario curriculum for grades ten and twelve, though students would not encounter the material until almost two years later. Curriculum guidelines stipulated that VD would be covered in regular (segregated) phys ed health classes where it would be part of general study about communicable diseases. Before any mention of VD was made in the classroom, parents would receive informational letters from the Department of Education and teachers would be provided with special manuals. Students, who would be requested not to make their own notes on VD (which might extend the bounds of decency), would receive provincially produced booklets on the subject when their lessons were over. But even with all these preparatory and precautionary measures, the teaching of venereal disease would not be mandatory.

Some commentators had hoped that concerns about venereal disease would have been able to justify the place of a more broadly defined sex education on the curriculum. The 'menace' of syphilis and gonorrhea was a hook for arguments that education about sexuality was socially relevant and therefore within the jurisdiction of the school. An editorial in the *Star*, for instance, began with discussions of VD, before outlining a model of education, which the writer said

> depends largely on the education of persons in the responsibilities of social living. It requires that boys and girls should receive scientific education about the origin of life and their responsibility for life. It requires that young men and women should be inspired with a wholesome attitude toward one another.[13]

The *Star*'s definition clearly had implications that stretched beyond the needs of VD prevention. The newspaper's proposal was similar to one suggested by Miriam Chapin in an article which appeared in *Saturday Night* magazine. Advocating for not just venereal disease education but for sex education more broadly defined, Chapin claimed such a program needed to consist of two things: 1) 'instruction in the physiology of sex', and 2) 'guidance to young people working out a code of conduct which is socially approved'.[14] She also said that the instruction of this material was outside the capabilities of not only the average parent but also the average teacher.

Arguments both for and against formal sex instruction revolved around parents, both their rights and obligations and their capabilities. In early 1945, the Toronto Teachers' Council endorsed a report that advocated sex education in elementary and secondary schools as well as courses for adults in night schools. The report addressed concerns that

> Venereal diseases have reached an alarming level and menace the present and future welfare of Toronto and Ontario generally. . . . Many parents neither know the facts of sex nor the proper technique of imparting them to their children. Among adults and parents there is widespread ignorance. Organizations fighting venereal disease need the support of an educational program designed to assist in removing its causes.[15]

In suggesting classes for parents, the Teachers' Council was lending support to popular middle-class sentiments that 'bad', usually working-class parents, and not the prevailing wartime social conditions, were responsible for youth problems, especially VD and juvenile delinquency. Just a few weeks before the Council's endorsement of the report, the Management Committee of Board of Education had discussed the possibility of setting up mandatory 'parenting' classes for the parents of delinquent children.[16]

But the discussion of parental inadequacies in terms of sex education weren't limited to working-class parents. While many assumed that working-class children were exposed to too much sex, middle-class children were thought to be too protected. Their parents were accused of being prudes and too easily embarrassed by frank discussion. Psychiatrist W.E. Blatz (of the Toronto Juvenile and Family Court and the Institute for Child Study) wrote in *Maclean's*:

> Many parents side-step their responsibilities in the education of their youngsters in sex matters. . . .
>   Parent shortcomings in this respect are further complicated during wartime because so many fathers, so many elder brothers, are included in the 730,000 Canadian men who are in the armed forces and away from their homes.[17]

Still, Blatz was not in favour of passing on the responsibility for sex education to either school or church. Parents, he thought, just needed more direction on how to do the job. A *Globe* editorial writer came to the same conclusion from a different angle: the state is 'a useful instrument of the public will, but there are aspects of life which it cannot enter with impunity.'[18] Apparently sexuality was one of them.

One way that parents were thought to contribute to sex education, whether it was actually a part of the school curriculum or not, was by providing an example of the 'serene and happy companionship between husband and wife [which would] have a definite influence on the emotional attitude of the child'.[19] Parents were to model socially desirable forms of heterosexual relationships. The suggestion that they do so was one of the ways that sex education was not simply a means of moulding children. As Blatz said, 'we aim not only that individuals conform to our social standards, but that they enjoy marriage and its sexual aspects to the full in legitimate circumstances.'[20] If, by chance, there were parents who didn't fit the mainstream image of a successful couple, here was a way of bringing that point home both to them and to their children. In magazines and newspapers (except the *Globe*), sex education was discussed as a far-reaching and necessary project which could form exemplary citizens. Nevertheless, the Department of Education and the

Toronto Board of Education persistently treated the matter as one of delicacy and potential danger.

In November 1945, the Department of Education put out its guide for teachers on venereal disease. But some teachers felt the booklet played it too safely by emphasizing only the scientific aspects of the topic at the expense of the spiritual and social which were, to be sure, more controversial. A committee of male teachers from the Toronto Board stressed that there was a need for some sort of basic sex education to precede any information about venereal disease. 'In this way', their report said, 'first impressions will be positive and stress the normal. . . . The need for a high standard of moral conduct, the normal girl and boy relationships, the significance of marriage and the conditions upon which happy family life is built will all be emphasized in a normal and objective way.'[21] Furthermore, the male teachers wanted to stress the hopeful aspects of the VD problem instead of the morbid ones. They emphasized the need to avoid compromising the 'higher aims' of sex education and its focus on 'healthful living', and they warned against using VD to frighten young people into changing their sexual behaviour. The men also suggested that 'the most normal place' on the curriculum to insert sex education would be in grade ten, following the study of the ductless glands and the secondary sex characteristics. In 1945, the secondary sex characteristics were as far as teachers were permitted to go in the discussion of sexuality. There was still no place on the curriculum where they could deal with human reproduction.

A committee of women teachers also met to discuss the provincial teachers' guide. They also advocated an educational framework which would enable students to understand venereal disease in the 'proper perspective':

> Although we recognize the importance of instruction in Venereal Disease, we consider that of even greater importance is the development of a healthy, sane, and moral attitude toward sex matters in general.[22]

The women teachers wanted to see discussion of menstruation but not of sexual relations. The teacher, they said, had to be concerned with the development of 'proper attitudes to all matters pertaining to sex'. As part of this program, 'convincing reasons against the practice of promiscuity should be presented to [the students] and the discussion guided in such a way that it will be of real value to them in establishing a standard of conduct which will ensure rather than jeopardize their future happiness.' Like the men, the women thought it best to introduce sex ed in grade ten. In the 1940s, many students left school after grade ten; if sex ed were taught in grade ten teenagers who quit school to work would be assured of exposure to the material.

Despite their efforts, these two committees did not achieve an expansion of the VD curriculum. Instead, the Board offered a series of five lectures on the topic of Family Life to be attended separately by male and female physical education teachers. Subsequently members of the Board and some vocational school principles screened sex education films and authorized them for showing in the vocational schools.[23] Why these films were not authorized for the collegiates is unclear. One can speculate that: the topic may have been deemed too sensitive for the predominantly middle-class students who were enrolled in the heavier academic programs; or middle-class students were thought not to need the films as badly as the predominantly working-class kids at vocational schools; or middle-class parents were thought more likely to complain that such films represented the encroachment of the school into family life.

Despite these Toronto initiatives, it wasn't until the fall of 1946 that the venereal disease education program, very narrowly defined, was actually taught to high-school students in Ontario. And while individual schools and individual teachers may have taken a more expansive approach to the subject, the Toronto Board didn't mention sex ed again until the spring of 1948.

Preventing Sex Crime

While fears about the spread of VD had been the catalyst for wartime discussions of sex ed, a different social menace had taken its place by the late 1940s. Sex crime and sexual perversion (the terms were often used interchangeably) were the social threats that put sex ed back on the school board's agenda. At a time when ideologies about the nuclear family and the benefits of domesticity were gaining strength, sexual 'abnormalities' were a serious threat to social stability. In the postwar period the trend to social conformity reflected a general need for security. In the aftermath of global conflict and in the face of the Cold War, middle-class North Americans took refuge in the safety and comfort of sameness.[24] Part of this homogenization required the sublimation of what were perceived to be 'potent' sexual energies. Social conventions limited sexual expression to the bounds of heterosexual marriage; anything else might prove socially dangerous. In this context, so-called sexual perverts, a category which included groups as different as homosexuals and rapists, were a threat not simply because of any potential harm they might cause to individuals, but because they showed up the impossibility of ever achieving complete social accord.

On 21 April 1948, the Canadian Penal Association presented the findings of a study on ways to curb sexual offenses. Sponsored by the Kiwanas Club, the report was widely quoted in the daily press. While the *Star* was restrained in its reporting, the *Globe*'s coverage twisted the focus of the study from sex offenses, or criminal sexual behaviour, to sex perversion, a much broader and more loosely defined category.

One of the general conclusions of the Kiwanis study was that most sex offenders in Canadian prisons had 'begun their abnormal habits in boyhood—between 9 and 14'.[25] Consequently the Penal Association recommended the teaching of sex education in elementary and secondary schools as one means of curbing sex crime. Sex ed, according to Dr Kenneth Rogers of the Canadian Welfare Council, 'can prevent the normal boy or girl from becoming a sex offender or from being influenced by an aggressive sex offender'.[26] Rogers also recommended both education for parenthood and the education of parents:

> Many parents are ignorant. By our attitudes we have produced all our abnormalities. We must stop being prudes. Sound information is the factor for protection. Children who know the truth are far less inclined to experiment with it and less inclined to drift into one of the abnormalities.[27]

On the day after the Penal Association released their report, school board trustees passed a motion requesting Goldring to prepare a report on

(a) what is now being done and (b) what might be done by the schools of the Board to impart instruction calculated to implement the suggestions made by the committee reporting to the Toronto Kiwanis Club as reported in the daily press on April 22nd.[28]

While the wording of the motion was exceedingly vague, it did get sex ed back on the Board's agenda. The motion was sent to the Management Committee where it was adopted five days later. Goldring took less than two weeks to prepare his report. In it he quoted liberally from the Penal Association Report. He also detailed the sequence of events around the earlier implementation of the units on venereal disease. He concluded that:

It would appear ... that many of the objections outlined in Dr Rogers' speech [on behalf of the Canadian Penal Association] are now being employed in our schools. It should be remembered that the scope of the instruction in this or any other subject of the curriculum is determined by the Department of Education. ... [I]nstruction in this phase of helpful living is probably as extensive as is permitted under existing regulations.[29]

Goldring also suggested that the interest generated by the Kiwanis project might prompt the province to make some changes to the curriculum. But he offered no suggestions as to what direction those changes might take.

At the end of May, the Management Committee appointed a special committee to consider sex ed. Committee chair, Charles Edwards, told the *Telegram* that sex ed in the schools might keep children from picking up misinformation on the street. And an enthusiastic superintendent of secondary schools, C.W. Robb, claimed that 'No more important subject exists today . . .', marking a shift in the Board's public discussion of what was still perceived by many to be a sensitive topic.[30]

Before the special committee met for the first time, Edwards wrote to an American authority on sex education, Dr Adolf Weinzirl of the University of Oregon, asking for information about the teaching of sex education in public schools. In his lengthy reply, Weinzirl outlined the same kind of 'character building' program that had been proposed by critics of Ontario's VD education program. According to Weinzirl, sex ed programs, best referred to as programs for 'family living', had to respond to the needs of parents to have their children educated in 'morals' and to the needs of students to learn about sex and 'family living'.

Broadly speaking, parents do not have a clear idea as to how 'morals' are 'taught'. From our standpoint, we can understand that what is meant here is the transmission of our cultural attitudes with respect to the exercise of reproduction in connection with monogamous marriage to the oncoming generation. It really means the establishment in children of feelings and emotions that will compel attitudes and behaviour leading to a minimum of promiscuity and to restricting sex to monogamous marriage with the expectation of having and raising children.[31]

Mothers and fathers had an important role to play in all this, teaching by example that marriage 'is the ideal relationship'. Weinzirl suggested that family living—

scientific information; materials confirming the family 'as the basic unit of society'; discussions on family relations—be integrated into the curriculum as a whole, for instance into biology, social science, and home economics classes. With such an approach, opposition from conservative members of the public could be minimized, although surveys in Oregon had calculated the rate of opposition to be no more than two to three per cent.

The 'family living' approach to sex education marked a transition from the earlier social hygiene efforts. Where social hygiene, as promoted by the Toronto Board of Education, was reactive—it was a response to a particular problem at a particular time—family living was both reactive and proactive. Intended to address problems like VD and juvenile delinquency, family living was also meant to shape a new kind of youth, young women and men well-versed in and committed to the moral values of their communities.

At its first meeting, the Board's special committee on family living asked Charles Goldring to prepare a report on a possible program of sex education suitable for students in grades seven and eight. Goldring passed the task on to a committee of teachers under the leadership of N.R. Speirs, Director of Physical Training. This eight-member Committee was joined on occasion by three consultants, all participants on the Canadian Penal Association's study of sex crime: Dr J.D.M. Griffen, psychiatrist and member of the Canadian Council on Mental Hygiene; Dr Kenneth H. Rogers, psychologist at the University of Toronto and staff member of The Big Brother Movement; and, J. Alex Edmison, KC.

The teachers' report on Family Living Education took its cues from Weinzirl and other prominent American sex educators and was a far step from the Ontario teaching guidelines on venereal disease. Indeed the whole 'family life' approach precluded 'morbid discussions' of venereal disease. The report suggested that venereal disease not even be mentioned by the teacher.

The aims of the grade seven and eight programs were:

1. To enable pupils to appreciate and value the normal, natural husband-wife-child relationship in the home and recognize in that the sustaining of successful happy family life.
2. To give pupils standards of values that will enable them to distinguish what is good in sexual life from what is sordid, selfish or perverted.[32]

Classes would be co-ed in grade seven and segregated in grade eight when reproduction would be discussed.

The guiding principles for teachers of this innovative course were to be found in the provincial curriculum on health education. Of particular importance was the directive that 'the establishment of habits, attitudes and ideals of life, is more important than mere psychological information'. Thus, in family living education, the biology of reproduction was overshadowed by social considerations around the topic of sex. In particular, children were to be instructed in the mores and conventions of their society, with an emphasis on the control and direction of sexuality into the one sanctioned form of expression—heterosexual monogamy. Children would learn that there are good and justifiable reasons behind the conventions governing sexual behaviour and that they protect the home and particularly women and children.[33]

They would not learn about alternatives to marriage nor about the difficulties and problems of family life. Material about sex delinquency was also deemed unfit for children. Instead pupils 'should be made to feel the excellence of sex and its immense potentialities'.[34]

One of the ways of showing 'the excellence of sex' was by demonstrating the superiority of the human being over other life forms. The definition of superiority here is firmly tied to the human ability to form families. So in a discussion of amoebas, for instance, the teacher would emphasize 'there is no infancy, no dependence, no care and no family'. The same thing with fish:

> two parents required—some family life—mother lays eggs father fertilizes. There is some slight protection of the eggs until they are hatched and, in some cases, even a protection of the young fish, but there is little indication of any family life—no affection—sometimes young are eaten by parents.[35]

And so we go until we get to human beings:

> The child is born into a family unit with a mother and father who were married and agreed to love and cherish each other and care for their children. Human mating is not merely seasonal or purely instinctive. It can be affected by intelligent choice and governed by long-term considerations. It takes two parents living together to provide a happy, healthy person. That is why down through the ages we have had the institution of marriage and the family as a setting for babies.[36]

This picture of family life was offered right after the war, with the increase in single parent families caused by divorce, desertion, and widowhood.

The teachers' report received a strong endorsement from the Board's special committee on sex education. The Board's Management Committee was less enthusiastic and wouldn't approve the proposal until the province gave its go-ahead. But provincial approval was conditional: family life would be offered only on an experimental basis and only on the grounds that a) those teaching the materials be given special training and b) Department of Education officials be permitted to observe classes.

Public reaction to the family life program was equally prudent. If one of the goals of sex education, by whatever name, was to forestall the development of sexual perversions, to assist children in achieving 'normalcy', then it was crucial that instructors be sanctioned representatives of the norm. As a *Globe* editorial writer put it: 'It is not just a question of knowing facts and being able to recite them to a class, but a teacher of sex must have the manner, moral attitude and psychological balance which are absolutely essential [to this topic].'[37] While teachers of math or spelling were not required to embody their subject matter, teachers of family life were. Students, too, were thought to be either suited or not suited to sex ed teaching. Trustee Isabel Ross (who also sat on the moral issues committee of the local Council of Women) asked, 'What about the boy or girl who is not ready for sex education in grade 7 or 8? . . . I would hesitate to give the information to some children. It would be necessary to pick and choose, and carry some over into later grades, before they are taught the subject.'[38] What 'not ready' actually means here is not clear. Presumably it runs the gamut from immature to already 'oversexed'.

Part of the general feeling of caution around the program might be attributable to the fact that, as a new departure, the sex ed curriculum was assumed to be powerful. It had been designed to shape children into morally correct citizens. If indeed it was capable of achieving that end when taught well, what might be the outcome if it was presented badly? Critics of the program feared unintended and undesirable effects.

In March, N.R. Speirs presented the first in what was planned to be a series of five instructional lectures for family life teachers. During the afternoon meeting the family life curriculum was outlined and teachers were given an opportunity to view a number of films being considered for the course. The lectures were designed to reassure the teachers of the importance of the family living course and to allay any doubts about the suitability of the material for young students. In this vein, Speirs began by citing the results of '[unnamed] studies made in Toronto' which showed that only thirteen per cent of students received any sex instruction from their parents. Clearly the school needed to intervene. He then went on to address concerns that parents might be expected to raise, all the while stressing the high calibre of the teachers themselves, and the quality of the program. In particular, he put distance between these chosen instructors and the 'emotional quacks' who had been behind earlier, old-fashioned, and embarrassing efforts at sex ed and social hygiene. Family life, he said, had developed in contrast to those dated, turn-of-the-century pedagogical failures. Family life was a modern program rooted in modern teaching principles, based on positive values, not on fear or shame. 'Instead of appealing to adolescent altruism and idealism, the [earlier] approach was apt to be either cynical or sentimental. Most of these historic misadventures are now hoary with age and deserve to be forgotten.'[39]

In spite of the 'excellence' of family life, Speirs made frequent reference to the need for caution and tact in its implementation. 'Nothing should be done', he said, 'to suggest that family life education is "risky" or "questionable" in the opinion of teachers or authorities' although 'questionable' is the word that some trustees and some members of the public would have applied to the whole experiment. It may have been fear of the public's wary appraisals that prompted Speirs to declare that 'nothing is to be given to the pupil that could be taken home—no notes—no examination—no pamphlets or books and, of course, no advertising matter [for the program itself]'.[40] Further he wanted no mention of sex delinquency: 'We do not want to lay ourselves open to the rumour which circulated in Forest Hill that they were using the Kinsey Report as a text book.'[41] His final advice to teachers was to operate along conservative lines, 'When in doubt—don't.'

His fears were well-founded. Two weeks after the introductory lecture for teachers, Goldring was called to report to the Board on the 'nature and suitability' of the films that had been screened. On April 7, the Board met behind closed doors to discuss the entire project. Apparently one of the teachers at Speirs's lecture had objected to the nature of the material presented, saying it had 'no morals'.[42] Some trustees agreed with the complaint, saying that children in grades seven and eight were too young to be exposed to the course. In the end, the proposed course was postponed and referred to Management Committee for yet more discussion. The *Globe*, not surprisingly, applauded the decision to hold off:

> To oblige teachers paid by the State to take over this intimate function of parenthood . . . is an unjustified intrusion into the privileges of the home. . . . Now that the Board has come to see the problems [of the family living course] more clearly it might be a good time to drop the business.[43]

But the trustees didn't drop it. They discussed it again in another closed-door meeting—much to the chagrin of the dailies—after which they re-screened three movies that had been shown to the teachers. The result of all the hush-hush meetings and discussion was that Goldring was asked to prepare yet another modified report on the family life program. He was to keep 'in mind that the instruction to be given be chiefly that which is outlined in the course for Grade 7. . . .'[44] That meant, of course, that the grade eight curriculum was to be scrapped. That meant the end of anything sensitive enough to demand boys and girls separated. 'Sensitive' in this case meant anything to do with the actual human bodies that lived in the families which were under discussion. The grade eight program had included topics like: 'the hygiene of adolescence, including menstruation and nocturnal emissions'; sexual vocabulary; social behaviour, including 'sex-releasing activities' and, most importantly, 'the meaning of "growing up"' which was all about reproduction and bodily functions. The grade seven curriculum, which was suitable for co-ed classes, was focused on the family (including fish and amoeba families) and on 'getting along with others'. Some of the critical topics suggested for discussion were: 'hogging the phone', cheating, tattletales, 'turning down a date gracefully', 'taking sister to the party', and chores. A short section on boy-girl relationships stressed that 'interest in the opposite sex was normal', and that 'rough play [was] undesirable'. A much longer section on community life discussed 'loyalty to family ideals', 'conventions and customs', and 'development of a scale of values'. In some schools 'where girls mature earlier', menstruation would be discussed (by girls only) in grade seven.

In stripping the grade eight portion of the program, the Board took the sex out of the sex education course. Family living ceased to be a euphemism for sex ed and came to mark the limitations of the course. In the cleaned-up version, family living was about being a teenager under the authority of parents and community, whereas in the original version, it was about growing up and anticipating adult roles. In the family living course, students would receive little guidance on puberty and they would certainly learn nothing about their own sexual capabilities and what they might mean as they began to date. Instead, students would become well-versed in the ideology of the Canadian version of the nuclear family. They would learn the importance of rules and standards of conduct and they would come to understand the significance and the face of normality. Even in this watered down form, the package as a whole remained an offence to the sensibilities of some trustees. The Board passed the course with a vote of ten to eight.[45]

Over the next decade there is not a single reference made to sex education in the Board's records. According to the *Telegram*, the family life program was dropped from the curriculum, without comment, in the fall term of 1952. It wasn't until the mid-1960s that the whole debate began anew. Finally, in 1966, a comprehensive program on Family Life was introduced to students in grades seven to twelve

Conclusion

One of the things we learn from this story is that the invocation of sex in the public realm is not always a progressive event. While we might deplore a social climate that prohibited open discussion of the basic physiology of sex in schools, we might find equally offensive explicit attempts to mould children via their legitimate desire for sexual knowledge. At the risk of stating the obvious, both the family living and social hygiene approaches to sex ed tried by the Board started from the social needs of particular adults. In the both curricula, young people were being employed to assuage the fears of the postwar middle class. Boys and girls were never present in these discussions as individuals who might have their own sexual concerns, who might already be engaging in sexual behaviour. When young people were inserted into these debates, they were the raw material for the development and reproduction of normative heterosexual standards.

This history of sex ed in Toronto schools leaves me with contradictory feelings. On the one hand I blanch to think that trustees prevented children from acquiring accurate knowledge about their bodies. On the other hand, the heavy moral agenda of the proposed sex education course left me thinking that maybe those children were better off without it. This ambivalence, oddly enough, puts me in the same camp as the *Globe and Mail* who figured that the outcome of sex education done wrong might be monstrous.

[1994]

Notes

1. *Toronto Star*, 17 February 1940. Quoting from an article by Walter Swayze in the student newspaper, *Hermes*, from Humberside Collegiate.
2. Stokes, John H. 'Some general considerations affecting present-day sex and sex education problems', in the *Bulletin*, Public Health Nurses of Ontario. Ontario, Department of Health, Division of Public Health Nursing, December 1944, p. 4. [Archives of Ontario, RG 10-30-A-I, 4.1]
3. 'A sound proposal', *Toronto Star*, 10 February 1944 [editorial].
4. Dr Gordon Bates cited by Mariana Valverde, *The Age of Light, Soap and Water: Moral Reform in English Canada, 1885–1925* (Toronto, McClelland and Stewart, 1991), p. 47.
5. 'A sound proposal', *Toronto Star*, 10 February 1944 [editorial].
6. 'Goldring to report on social hygiene', *Toronto Star*, 12 February 1944.
7. C.C. Goldring, Report to the Management Committee of the Board of Education. Toronto, 6 March 1944. Toronto Board of Education, Social Hygiene File.
8. 'Church group would study sex education', *Globe and Mail*, 9 March 1944.
9. 'Trustees approve teaching sex subjects in schools', *Toronto Star*, 11 April 1944.
10. 'Teach young how to live is obligation, Drew says', *Telegram*, 11 April 1944.
11. 'A challenge to the schools', *Toronto Star*, 29 November 1944 [editorial].
12. Miriam Chapin, 'Sex instruction in the school curriculum', *Saturday Night*, 15 April 1944.
13. 'A challenge to the Schools', *Toronto Star*, 29 November 1944 [editorial].
14. Chapin.

15. 'Sex education scheme approved by teachers', *Globe and Mail*, 23 January 1945.
16. Toronto Board of Education, Reports by Board Officials, 'Parenting School', 8 January 1945.
17. Blatz, W.E. 'Your child—sex', *Maclean's*, 1 January 1945, p. 7.
18. 'Problems of sex instruction', *Globe and Mail*, 22 March 1946.
19. Winnifred Ashplant, secondary health counsellor from London, Ontario quoted in 'Sex education classes said vital to school health', *Globe and Mail*, 4 May 1945.
20. Blatz, p. 38.
21. 'Guiding principles in the presentation of the subject of venereal diseases', p. 1. Appended to C.C. Goldring's report to the Management Committee of the Board of Education, Toronto, 13 May 1948. Toronto Board of Education Archives, Sex Education File.
22. Guiding principles in the subject of venereal diseases, p. 3.
23. C.C. Goldring, Report to the Management Committee of the Board of Education, Toronto, 13 May 1948, p. 3. Toronto Board of Education Archives, Sex Education file.
24. For a discussion of the need for security in the American context, see Elaine Tyler May, *Homeward Bound: American Families in the Cold War Era* (New York, Basic Books, 1988).
25. 'Study of sex perverts in prisons', *Globe and Mail*, 22 April 1948.
26. 'Psychiatric treatment said best for sex offenders', *Toronto Star*, 22 April 1948.
27. 'Study of sex perverts in prisons', *Globe and Mail*, 22 April 1948.
28. Toronto Board of Education, *Minutes*. 22 April 1948.
29. C.C. Goldring, Report to the Management Committee of the Board of Education. Toronto, 13 May 1948. Toronto Board of Education Archives, Sex Education file.
30. 'Sex education to be studied by committee', *Telegram*, 25 May 1948.
31. Letter to Charles Edwards from Adolf Weinzirl, 24 July 1948. Toronto Board of Education, *Minutes* of Special Committee appointed to consider and report on the matter of Sex Education in Schools, 2 September 1948, Appendix A. Toronto Board of Education Archives.
32. Report of Teachers' Committee on Sex Education for Grades VII & VIII, p. 1. *Minutes* of Special Committee appointed to consider and report on the matter of Sex Education in Schools, 22 November 1948, Appendix A. Toronto Board of Education Archives.
33. Report of teachers' committee on sex education, p. 1.
34. Report of teachers' committee on sex education, p. 4.
35. Report of teachers' committee on sex education, p. 6.
36. Report of teachers' committee on sex education, p. 7.
37. 'No need for haste', *Globe and Mail*, 26 January 1944 [editorial].
38. 'Sex education in public schools report is tabled', *Globe and Mail*, 8 December 1948. 39. N.R. Speirs, 'Family Life Education—Introductory Lecture', 23 March 1949. Appended to C.C. Goldring, Report to Management Committee of the Board of Education, Toronto, 6 April 1949.
39. N.R. Speirs, 'Family Life Education—Introductory Lecture', 23 March 1949. Appended to C.C. Goldring, Report to Management Committee of the Board of Education, Toronto, 6 April 1949.
40. N.R. Speirs, 'Family Life Education—Introductory Lecture', p. 8.
41. N.R. Speirs, 'Family Life Education—Introductory Lecture', p. 8.
42. 'School board bans sex behind closed doors', *Globe and Mail*, 8 April 1949.
43. 'A lesson in sex education', *Globe and Mail*, 11 April 1949.
44. Board of Education, Management Report, No. 9, Part II, 26 April 1949. Toronto Board of Education Archives.
45. 'Board approves sex in very modified form', *Globe and Mail*, 5 May 1949.

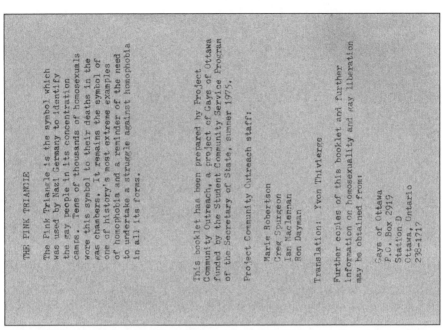

THE PINK TRIANGLE

The Pink Triangle is the symbol which was used by Nazi Germany to identify the gay people in its concentration camps. Tens of thousands of homosexuals wore this symbol to their deaths in the gas chambers. It remains the symbol of one of history's most extreme examples of homophobia and a reminder of the need to undertake a struggle against homophobia in all its forms.

This booklet has been prepared by Project Community Outreach, a project of Gays of Ottawa funded by the Student Community Service Program of the Secretary of State, summer 1975.

Project Community Outreach staff:

Marie Robertson
Greg Spurgeon
Ian Maclennan
Ron Dayman

Translation: Yvon Thivierge

Further copies of this booklet and further information on homosexuality and gay liberation may be obtained from:

Gays of Ottawa
P.O. Box 2919
Station D
Ottawa, Ontario
238-1717

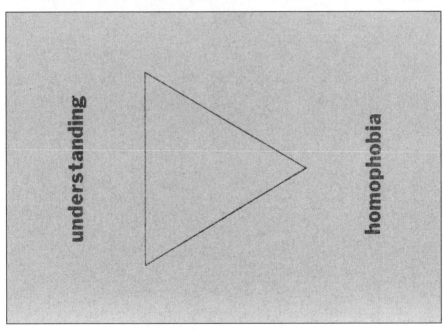

understanding

homophobia

[1975, Canadian Lesbian & Gay Archives]

"THE RELEVANT QUESTION IS NOT WHAT MAKES HOMO-SEXUALS, OR WHAT TO DO WITH THEM, BUT RATHER, WHAT MAKES SOCIETY PERSECUTE THEM." 1

What is homophobia?

For too long homosexuality itself has been thought of as the central problem of gay men and women. In fact, the real issue for gay people is not homosexuality, but homophobia, society's fear and persecution of us:

"Homophobia is a pervasive, irrational fear of homosexuality. Homophobia includes the fear heterosexuals have of any homosexual feelings within themselves, any overt mannerisms or actions that would suggest homo-sexuality, and the resulting desire to suppress or stamp out homosexuality. And it also includes the self-hatred and self-denial of homosexuals who know what they are but have been taught all their lives by a hetero-sexual society that people like them-selves are sick, sinful and criminal." 2

Up until now gay people have been too apologetic in trying to establish the legitimacy of our sexuality, legitimacy on other peoples' terms. In fact homosexuality is as valid a lifestyle as any other. We see no reason to apologize for ourselves and reject the condescending pathological approach implicit in the usual

1 Seidenberg, R. "The Accursed Race". In Ruitenbeek, H., ed. Going Crazy, p.270.
2 Weinberg, G. Society and the Healthy Homosexual, p.5.

questions asked about homosexuality, questions like:

What are the causes of homosexuality?
How can you tell if you are a homosexual?
Can homosexuality be cured?

The questions that really need to be asked are:

What are the causes of homophobia?
How can you tell if you are a homophobe?
Can homophobia be cured?

What are the causes of homophobia?

Homosexuality has been practised in all societies throughout history and has been openly accepted in many cultures. The taboo on homosexuality in Western civilization has largely been the result of the wide-spread acceptance of the Judeo-Christian ethic with its general repression of any form of sexuality unrelated to childbearing.

Today the repression of gay sexuality is enforced through the life patterns and institutions that make up our society: family, educational system, church, government, business, media, legal, medical and psychiatric professions, all effect-ively combine to enforce the heterosexual model with its rigid role structures. Male supremacy, sexism, and homophobia are society's reactions to those women and men whose lifestyles challenge its confining aggressive male/passive female sex roles. Gay women challenge male supremacy in our society: by choosing to love and devote most of their energy to other women, lesbians are refusing to feed into a system where power and prestige are based on gender, and where a woman takes her status from the man she is attached to. Similarly gay men, through their disdain for the usual requirements of manhood and through their integration of attributes like warmth and emo-tionality that have traditionally been considered 'female characteristics', belie the importance of the 'masculine identity' others struggle so hard to achieve.

How can you tell if you are a homophobe?

Homophobia like other kinds of prejudice - racism, sexism - manifests itself in many ways. Historically the routing out and murder of homo-sexuals during the Inquisition and in Nazi Germany have been among the most extreme forms of anti-homosexual oppression. Today there is a whole gamut of homophobic reactions - outright queer-bashing, psychiatry's attempts to 'cure' the homosexual, discriminatory laws and employment practices, inability on the part of social service agencies to deal with the homosexual, the media's demeaning and stereotypical images of the homo-sexual, pseudo-liberalism's tolerance of the homosexual so long as she or he remains invisible - all reactions from a combination of ignorance and fear.

In the face of these pervasive homophobic pres-sures, a gay person experiences a split between his or her natural sexual preference and what is socially acceptable. And all too often, homo-sexuals themselves, conditioned to think of them-selves as inferior, have internalized this homo-phobia to the point where even self-acceptance is difficult. They accept the stigma attached by others to them without realizing they are oppressed and often see society as justified in keeping them down. This is borne out by the great numbers of gays who carefully conceal their identity and by many others who actively seek psychiatric help to be 'cured' of their homosex-uality. In turn psychiatrists largely reinforce this self-oppression by treating each homosexual as a neurotic rather than as a victim of an impossible social structure.

Can homophobia be cured?

"Homosexuality is not the disease to be studied, homophobia is, because it vict-imizes, twists and distorts the mental health of homosexuals and heterosexuals alike." 3

As gays we are naturally concerned with combat-ting homophobia both amongst ourselves and in the world at large. Within our own community many gays are working with each other to overcome our own homophobic history by fostering a positive self-image and by living openly as gays.

Beyond ourselves we are also trying to educate and encourage people in the community at large to recognize their own homophobia and to take some responsibility for combatting the anti-gay bias that runs through our culture and institutions. In particular social workers, psychologists and doctors, lawyers, teachers, and the clergy must examine their own conceptions of homosexuality in order to be effective in dealing with the gay people they are all in a position to come into contact with. Self-education on the part of these individuals through reading and discussion with gays, as well as improved co-operation between their services and gay organizations in matters of counselling and referral, are essential to com-batting homophobia in these services. A healthy community requires an end to the conspiracy of

3 Shoemaker, E. "The homosexual in the new therapies", in Myth of Madness, a special issue of Long Time Coming, Jan./75, p.40.

silence about homosexuality through open discussion and confrontation of homophobia wherever it appears by gays and straights alike.

As gays our goal cannot be tolerance from straight society, tolerance as inferiors. It is a question, not of the homosexual adjusting to society's hostility, but of society learning to accept the homosexual as an equal.

****

BIBLIOGRAPHY ON HOMOPHOBIA

The following books treat the topic of homophobia and were used as the inspiration for this booklet:

ABBOTT, Sidney, & LOVE, Barbara. Sappho Was a Right On Woman: a liberated view of lesbianism. Stein and Day, 1973. Especially the chapter on "Curing Society".

CHURCHILL, Wainright. Homosexual Behaviour among Males: a cross-cultural and cross-species investigation. Prentice-Hall, 1967.

GAY INFORMATION. Psychiatry and the Homosexual: a brief analysis of oppression. Gay Liberation pamphlet no.1. Gay Information, 1973.

HODGES, Andrew, & HUTTER, David. With Downcast Gays: aspects of homosexual self-oppression. Pomegranate Press, 1974. Written chiefly for gays.

LAURITZEN, John. The Religious Roots of the Taboo on Homosexuality. New York, 1974.

MYTH OF MADNESS: a special issue of Long Time Coming, Jan./75. Especially the article "The Homosexual in the New Therapies".

SZASZ, Thomas. The Manufacture of Madness. Harper and Row, 1970.

WEINBERG, George. Society and the Healthy Homosexual. Anchor Books, 1973.

Those seeking a more traditional approach to the question of homosexuality are encouraged to read the Operations Socrates Handbook, published in 1973 under an Opportunities for Youth Project Grant. The booklet is available from Waterloo University Gay Liberation Movement, c/o Federation of Students, U. of Waterloo, Waterloo, Ontario, at 35 cents a copy.

A more complete bibliography on homosexuality and gay liberation can be obtained from Gays of Ottawa. A complete catalogue and most of the above books can be ordered from Androgyny Books, 1217 Crescent St., Montreal or from Glad Day Books, 139 Seaton St., Toronto.

****

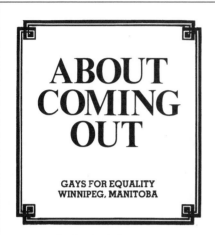

ABOUT COMING OUT

GAYS FOR EQUALITY
WINNIPEG, MANITOBA

For Further Information

Coming Out (TV Program), 6 p.m., Saturdays, Cable TV channel 13. Box 27 UMSU, University of Manitoba, Winnipeg, Manitoba R3T 2N2.

Council on Homosexuality and Religion, Box 1912, Winnipeg, Manitoba R3C 3R2. Telephone 269-8678 (weekday evenings).

Dignity/Winnipeg/Dignité, Box 1912, Winnipeg, Manitoba R3C 3R2.

Families of Gays, Box 1912, Winnipeg, Manitoba R3C 3R2. Telephone 783-4549.

Gay Friends of Brandon, Box 492, Brandon, Manitoba R7A 5Z4. Telephone 727-4046.

Gays for Equality, Box 27 UMSU, University of Manitoba, Winnipeg, Manitoba R3T 2N2. Telephone 269-8678 (weekday evenings). Lesbian counsellors Tuesday evenings .

New Freedom Group: Gay AA. Telephone 774-1234.

Pamphlet adapted from:
"Coming Out". R. Adam De Baugh, Metropolitan Community Church.
"About Coming Out". National Gay Task Force.

Introduction For too long we have been told that we must hide our homosexuality. We have been asked to live a lie. We have been forced to lead double lives. We have been told by our homophobic society to deny who we really are and whom we really love. We have lived with enormous fear — fear for our rights; fear for our jobs; fear of the loss of those whom we care about; and, at times, fear for our lives. Coming out is a step towards greater integration in our lives. It is a testing of our fears and paranoias about personal rejection. It leads us towards fuller and more honest and satisfying relationships with those around us. Coming out will not solve all of our problems; indeed it can create new ones. But coming out offers to many of us a greater sense of reality about the loves, fears, and relationships in our lives.

Those who have come out, in whatever ways and to whatever degree, have generally experienced a great sense of relief and increased self-esteem through sharing the "secret" of their sexual orientation. This fact is documented in a growing number of personal accounts written by lesbians and gay men and in studies carried out by professional researchers.

The Process of Coming Out *Coming out of the closet* is an on-going issue in the life of virtually every gay person. There are many stages in the process, and most of us embark on that process time and again. It is not simply telling one's parents, joining a gay organization, having a lesbian or gay love affair, or moving to the gay "ghetto" in a large city. Coming out has to do with how we perceive ourselves, with how we deal with our sexuality, with how we structure our lives, and with how we present ourselves and our loved ones to our families, to our friends, or to the world. It is a life-long process, in which we constantly deal with the acceptance and integration of our gayness within a partially repressive and hostile society.

For some lesbians and gay men the process of coming out is a relatively easy one — there never is any great difficulty in recognizing or accepting homosexual feelings. For many others of us, the process in its initial stages is often far more painful. We may struggle with great difficulty for a long time before we are able to affirm ourselves as gay people, to say nothing of sharing that fact with those whom we love.

We live in a society in which we have been consistently indoctrinated with the worst myths, fears,

[1983, Canadian Lesbian & Gay Archives]

and stereotypes about homosexuality. We were consistently told as young people that it is not good to be gay. Indeed, our society is structured in a way which often assumes that everyone both is, and ought to be, heterosexual. Within such a context it is not surprising that many people — be they young or old — have experienced the gravest difficulty in accepting their homosexual feelings or orientation. The guilt has been unwarranted. The pain cannot be justified. The occasional suicides represent a tragic fact. The homophobia which so affects the feelings and behavior of non-gays towards us still has a very damaging effect upon the ways in which we may perceive ourselves.

The process of recognizing and accepting one's gayness can be a very lonely experience. But it is becoming increasingly easy for us to accept our feelings and our gay or lesbian identities. We can see our sexuality as a positive and joyful part of our lives. We can see the injustice of the discrimination, fear, and oppression which are a part of our day-to-day experience. We can see the immorality in failing to tell young people the truth and the facts about homosexuality. If we have problems in our lives, we can, like many people who are heterosexual, seek professional help to deal with those problems rather than be told that we need to change our sexual orientation.

The Stages of Coming Out There are a number of stages in the coming-out process. The first step is *acceptance*, which presupposes the *recognition* of being homosexual. You say to yourself, as one lesbian put it, "I always knew I was different, and this was it!"

Coming to have positive feelings about one's homosexuality is an essential part of the coming out process. Until one feels good about being gay, it makes little sense to share the fact of one's sexual orientation with others (unless they are very clearly friends or helping professionals who are prepared to assist you towards greater self-acceptance). The person who says to a parent, friend, or employer, "I have something horrible I need to tell you about myself," is not "coming out". She or he is seeking pity or revealing self-hatred.

Celebration comes next, as you begin to co-ordinate your feelings and desires with your place in society and to feel good about yourself. Celebration is when you are happy about being you. Celebration is saying, "This is who I am, and I am going to enjoy it!" Celebration is taking the God-given gift of your sexual orientation and embracing it with joy and pride.

The next stage in the coming out process is *sharing* the fact of your sexual orientation with others. This goes hand-in-hand with the integration of your sexuality with the rest of your life and consciousness. Most individuals consider their sex life, including their sexual orientation, to be a very personal matter which they do not want to discuss with all and sundry. But among heterosexuals, by social convention, while details of sex practices are kept private, relationships are openly acknowledged and celebrated: wedding bands are worn, expressions of affection are exchanged, shared activities are described, joint invitations are given and received. This kind of public acknowledgement gives support and pleasure to the couple. And it is this kind of public acknowledgement which gay couples, also, need and want.

The steps are not always taken in this order. The process is not always a smooth and easy one. As one gay man said, "I seem to take two steps forward and one step back, sometimes. I get scared, occasionally."

The final step in coming out — after other gay people, friends and family are told — is the general feeling that "I don't care who knows. I'll come out to the world." Sometimes this is done by wearing buttons or T-shirts with gay slogans, sometimes by exaggerated, overtly "gay" behavior. But, most often, secure and confident gay women and men let the world know by just living their normal lives and not lying any more.

An Educational Rationale for Coming Out *Coming out* is undoubtedly the most effective educational tool available to gay people as we try to change people's attitudes about homosexuality and lesbianism. In recent years excellent books, improved media coverage, visible lesbian and gay individuals — including celebrities — and more supportive attitudes from most mental health professionals and many religious leaders have led to greater acceptance of gay people within Canadian society. But homophobic myths, fears, and stereotypes continue to receive widespread expression in our homes and workplaces, on our streets, in our municipal councils and provincial legislatures, in the courts, and at the polls. The powerful threat of homophobia has not yet gone away. The educational task which lies ahead for us is a massive one.

Several recent polls have indicated that support

for gay rights is far more likely to come from those non-gay people who have identified their gay friends than from those who have not. As gay people we are aware that we are indeed everywhere. But our relative invisibility continues to allow countless Canadians to overlook us; to tell cruel jokes about us; to assume that no ordinary person is gay; and to believe that they do not know or love any lesbians or gay men. Each time even one gay person comes out to such non-gay persons, their world view is challenged, their fears about homosexuality are confronted, and their level of understanding is raised. The awareness that a loved or respected friend is gay often has a profound impact on non-gay persons' willingness to re-examine their ideas, attitudes, and feelings about our lives and our rights.

This is not, however, an invitation to every gay person to come out to everyone under any circumstances. At the present time that is an unrealistic goal. Ill-timed or unplanned revelations about one's sexual orientation can result in unemployment, disinheritance, or personal rejection. Nevertheless, thousands of lesbians and gay men can testify that in most instances the experience of coming out to selected relatives, friends, and co-workers has been a positive one.

Some Suggestions for Coming Out to Parents, Relatives, and Straight Friends When you do begin to come out to non-gay people, your experiences will probably vary. Sometimes it will go well. Occasionally a relationship will be terminated abruptly or will fade away unexpectedly. From the experiences of many lesbians and gay men, their parents, and friends, we offer a number of suggestions about coming out to non-gay people. You need to evaluate these suggestions in the light of your own personal situation and needs.

1. Be clear about your own feelings about being gay. If you are still dealing with a lot of guilt or depression, seek help in getting over that before coming out to parents or other non-gay people. If you are comfortable with your gayness, those to whom you come out will often sense that fact and be aided in their own renewed acceptance of you.

2. Timing can be very important in coming out. Be aware of the health, mood, priorities, and problems of those with whom you would like to share your sexuality. The mid-life crises of parents, the relationship problems of friends, the business concerns of employers, and countless other factors over

which you have no control can affect another's receptivity to your information.

3. Never come out during an argument. Never use coming out as a weapon. Never encourage parents to feel guilty for having "caused" your sexual orientation — they didn't.

4. When coming out to parents or family, try to affirm mutual caring and love before launching into your announcement about your gayness.

5. Be prepared that your revelation may surprise, anger, or upset other people at first. Try not to react angrily or defensively. Try to let other people be honest about their initial feelings even if they are negative. Remember that the initial reaction will not likely be the long-term one. Ultimately the individuals who have really faced and dealt with their homophobia may be far more supportive than those who give an immediate but superficial expression of support.

6. Emphasize that you are still the same person. You were gay yesterday and will be tomorrow. If you were loving and responsible yesterday, likewise you will be loving and responsible tomorrow.

7. Keep lines of communication open with people after you come out to them — even if their response is negative. Respond to their questions and remember that they are probably in the process of reexamining the myths and stereotypes about gay people which we all have received from our culture.

8. Be sure that you are well informed about homosexuality. Read some good books about the subject (see *Suggestions for Further Reading*) and share them with individuals to whom you have come out.

9. Encourage your parents or others to whom you come out to meet some of your lesbian and gay friends.

10. Remember that it took many of us gay men and lesbians a very long time to come to terms with our own sexuality and even longer to decide to share the fact with others. When you come out to non-gay people, be prepared to give them time to adjust and to comprehend the new information about you. Don't expect immediate acceptance. Look for ongoing, caring dialogue.

11. If you are rejected by someone to whom you have come out, do not lose sight of your own self-worth. Remember that your coming out was a gift of sharing an important part of yourself which that person has chosen to reject. If rejection does come, consider whether the relationship was really worthwhile. Is any relationship so important that it must

LESBIANISM
breaking the silence...

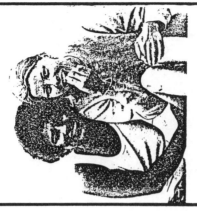

Do you think of a strange looking woman driving a truck and smoking a cigar? Or a poor, pitiful, tortured creature who couldn't get a man and so turned to women as second best? Does thinking about lesbians make you uncomfortable? Scared? Angry?

Most people's ideas about lesbians come from jokes and rumours. Most people would say that they don't know any lesbians... but they would say that lesbians are man-hating, aggressive, promiscuous, and molest young girls.

These are old ideas based on ignorance and fear.

LOCAL RESOURCES FOR LESBIANS

GAYS FOR EQUALITY PHONELINE: 786-3976 Tuesdays, 7:30 - 10:00pm. Staffed by lesbian peer counsellors. Counsellors will listen to peer concerns on the phone; you can also arrange to talk with them in person. You can obtain information about any of the other things listed below by calling the GFE phoneline.

WOMEN'S COMING OUT SUPPORT GROUP: Meets every second Thursday 7:30-10:00pm. at 277 Sherbrook.

FAMILIES OF GAYS: is a group which provides information and mutual support to the parents, children, husband, wife, and other family members of gay/lesbian persons. Contact BEV SCOTT by phoning 783-4549, or writing Box 27, UMSU, University of Manitoba, R3T 2M2.

LESBIAN MOTHERS: Call the GFE Phoneline for more information.

COMING OUT: a lesbian/gay cable TV program produced by the Winnipeg Gay Media Collective and financed through donations by Gay Groups. Tuesdays at 6:00pm. on channel 13. Call CHRIS VOGEL at 772-8215 or 783-8922 if you would like to help.

GAY ALCOHOLIC ANONYMOUS: Meetings at the Unitarian Church, 790 Banning St. Meetings Wednesdays at 8:00pm. For more information call the Manitoba Central AA Office at 233-3508.

LIBERATION BOOKS: 160 Spence. Call 774-0637 for more information and hours of operation. Stocks feminist and lesbian books.

RELIGIOUS WORSHIP SERVICE: The Council on Homosexuality and Religion offers a non-denominational service every second and fourth Sunday of the month. Counselling re: integrating homosexuality and religious beliefs is also available. Contact the GFE phoneline for more information.

WINNIPEG GAY YOUTH: Co-ordination of programs by and for teenaged and young adult gay people. Enquiries through GFE phoneline 786-3976, Wednesday evenings. Postal Address: Box 27, UMSU, University of Manitoba, Winnipeg, R3T 2N2.

ALCOHOL AND DRUG FREE SOCIALS: Various times. For more information contact the GFE phoneline at 786-3976.

GIOVANNI'S ROOM: Licensed Restaurant and Clubroom for members and guests of the Oscar Wilde Memorial Society. Located within the Winnipeg Gay Community Centre, 277 Sherbrook St., Open evenings, Monday to Saturday, Telephone: 786-1236.

HAPPENINGS SOCIAL CLUB: Licensed Dance Bar and Beverage Room for members and guests of the Mutual Friendship Society Inc., Located in the Sun Quod Sum Building at 272 Sherbrook St., Winnipeg, MB., Open evenings Monday to Saturday, Telephone: 774-3576.

MS. PURDY'S SOCIAL CLUB: 226 Main Street: 942-8212. Open Tuesday to Saturday from 4:00pm to 1:00am. Women's membership club. Men allowed Wednesdays only when accompanied by a member. All women are welcome.

LESBIANISM

WHAT IS THE TRUTH ABOUT LESBIANISM?

A lesbian is a woman who loves other women. She prefers to create her intimate and loving relationships with other women. Other than that lesbians are as unique and diverse as all women.

Lesbians come from a variety of backgrounds, work in every conceivable occupation, have different political affiliations, religious beliefs, and lifestyles. Lesbians are mothers, sisters, daughters, wives, neighbours, co-workers, cousins, aunts, grandmothers . . .

Lesbians are found everywhere. We form a significant percentage of the population. We live full, rich, rewarding, productive lives.

ISN'T LESBIANISM UNNATURAL?

No. Studies of human development show that people are not just naturally heterosexual. We are naturally loving, and naturally sexual. We are, in fact, taught to be heterosexual.

SO WHY DON'T I KNOW ANY LESBIANS?

Partly because you really can't tell by looking who is a lesbian. And partly because, until very recently, almost all lesbians were very careful to hide the fact that they loved women. Lesbians have been rejected by families and friends, fired from their jobs, locked up in mental hospitals, lost their children, been beaten up — when someone else 'found out'. With that kind of punishment waiting, most lesbians lived their lives pretending to be heterosexual.

BUT DON'T LESBIANS MOLEST YOUNG GIRLS?

No. Statistics show that 95% of all cases of sexual abuse of children involve heterosexual men and girls.

WHY ARE WE TALKING ABOUT THIS?

Lesbians are no longer willing to lie and hide and live in fear. Lesbians are working together to educate people about lesbianism to dispel the ignorance and lies. We have set up drop-ins and support groups. We are producing positive material that celebrates loving women. We are active in the Women's Movement as part of our struggle for respect and value for all women. We are active in trade unions, gay rights groups, community groups . . . everywhere . . .

But there's such a long way to go.

There is still so much fear and prejudice. There are still many women who worry that there's 'something wrong' with loving another woman. There are lesbians living in isolation and loneliness. Lesbian mothers are still being denied custody of their children. Lesbians are still being fired from jobs, and being harassed on the street.

It has to stop . . .

WHAT CAN I DO?

- Educate yourself. Get your local library or bookstore to order some good factual books on lesbianism. Read them, and then pass them on.
- Talk with your friends, your co-workers and children about lesbianism. Ask that groups you belong to invite speakers from lesbian organizations.
- Speak out when someone tells a 'queer' joke. They're not funny.

BOOKS/PAMPHLETS YOU MAY FIND HELPFUL TO READ:

Baetz, Ruth. LESBIAN CROSSROADS-PERSONAL STORIES OF LESBIAN STRUGGLES AND TRIUMPHS. William Morrow and Company Inc, 1980.

Califia, Pat. SAPPHISTRY: THE BOOK OF LESBIAN SEX. Naiad Press Inc, 1983.

Covina, Gina and Galana, Laurel, eds. THE LESBIAN READER. Amazon press, 1975.

Grier, Barbara. LESBIANA. Naiad Press Inc, 1976.

Harris, Bertha and Sisley, Emily. THE JOY OF LESBIAN SEX. Simon and Schuster, 1977.

Lynch, Lee. OLD DYKE TALES. Naiad Press Inc, 1984.

Martin, Del and Lyon, Phyllis. LESBIAN/WOMAN. Glide, 1972.

Stanely, Julia and Wolfe, Susan, eds. THE COMING OUT STORIES. Persephone Press, 1980.

Vida, Ginny, ed. OUR RIGHT TO LOVE: A LESBIAN RESOURCE BOOK. Prentice-Hall Inc, 1978.

LESBIAN CONNECTION. Nationwide lesbian forum. c/oAmbitious Amazons, Box 811. East Lansing, MI 48823. (Periodical)

Produced by: Gays For Equality,
Box 27, University Centre,
University of Manitoba,
Winnipeg, MB.,
R3T 2N2

Suggestions for Further Reading

Frank, Blye, 'Queer Selves/Queer in Schools: Young Men and Sexualities' in Susan Prentice, ed., *Sex in Schools: Canadian Education & Sexual Regulation*. Montreal: Our Schools/Ourselves, 1994: 44–59.

Gleason, Mona, 'Growing up to be "Normal": Psychology Constructs Proper Gender Roles in Post World War II Canada, 1945–1960' in Edgar-André Montigny and Lori Chambers, eds, *Family Matters: Papers in Post-Confederation Canadian Family History*. Toronto: Canadian Scholars' Press, 1998: 39–56.

Larkin, June, *Sexual Harassment: High School Girls Speak Out*. Toronto: Second Story Press, 1994.

Maynard, Steven, 'The Maple Leaf (Gardens) Forever: Sex, Canadian Historians and National History,' *Journal of Canadian Studies* 36, 2 (Summer 2001): 70–105.

Petrie, Anne, *Gone to Aunt's: Remembering Canada's Homes for Unwed Mothers*. Toronto: McClelland and Stewart, 1998.

Quigley, Hillary, Suvi Siu, Chauntae Walls, Emma Brown, Kristina Pellitier, Annie Grainger, Chi Nguyen, and Rebecca Hodgson, *The Little Black Book, a healthy sexuality guide written by grrls for grrls*. Toronto: St Stephens Community House, 2000.

Sethna, Christabelle, 'The Cold War and the Sexual Chill: Freezing Girls Out of Sex Education,' *Canadian Women Studies/las cahiers de la femme* (Winter 1997): 57–61.

Permission Credits